for intro

√180 in nmis + RR

√181 cite for scttism in intro

hist - but
subsant - hot
union, skeleton
scaffred of
events, etc (effect),
even but
richness of lived
lives - textures of
experience +
materiality -
connectiveness
in context - ?

not cause activities
that are not only of
here - +
assumptions exist?
vs elite? ___ Cal H
X - uses f both ___
139 + X (X) nmis
(142), 144 146 √
148

√ bib

overland monthly 25
[June 1895]
675 √
"CA + the RR"

---

for ch 2

— in crit of stanford

√ in to overland monthly ?

√17 + for in RR - hikes to newspapers, etc

√ 41   RR crisis

— 45 two accts stanford in opposing the masses — y/c R alB

√61-2 the huntington - corton letters

√65-6 + R alB's people + the state ... take the law
into their own hands

√125 (S) e RR post 1865

— 130 in SP machiavellian — RR strategies

~ 138 S as "anti-monopoly tract" - ? +
give context — other anti RR novels e close
of the century

✓ for ch 5/Cather

√3

- 153 Jews in LA politics — largely ignored by historians
- 158 Leng's cig?
  - 253 → Szymd to read mayer Lissner papers?
                        Dept of Special Collections + Archives

✓ for epilogue - ?

✓ 10, 11-12 RR is impt ncln - ntim: section
    + connect y mena + mexican workers emigrity to
    us @ turn y the century + during Pryfiriato?
    ii, RR is mfabricile?

Railroad Crossing

Railroad Crossing

Californians and the Railroad, 1850–1910

WILLIAM DEVERELL

University of California Press

BERKELEY   LOS ANGELES   LONDON

University of California Press
Berkeley and Los Angeles, California

University of California Press, Ltd.
London, England

Library of Congress Cataloging-in-Publication Data
Deverell, William Francis.
    Railroad crossing : Californians and the railroad, 1850–1910 /
William Deverell.
        p.   cm.
    Includes bibliographical references and index.
    ISBN 0-520-08214-1 (alk. paper)
    1. Railroads—California—History.   I. Title.
TF24.C3D48   1993
385'.09794—dc20   92-40128

Printed in the United States of America
9 8 7 6 5 4 3 2 1

For my parents, Bill and Marne, and my sister, Debbie

RAILROAD, n.   The chief of many mechanical devices enabling us to get away from where we are to where we are no better off. For this purpose the railroad is held in highest favor by the optimist, for it permits him to make the transit with great expedition.

—Ambrose Bierce, *The Devil's Dictionary*

Contents

Acknowledgments

When I started this project as a graduate student, I hardly knew where to begin. And when I finished the dissertation on which this book is based, I found myself in a similar predicament. Now the same dilemma confronts me, several years further down the professional road. Dozens of individuals and many institutions have helped me along the way, and this brief acknowledgment is but a small indication of my heartfelt gratitude.

One of my most profound debts is to the remarkable collection of scholars and teachers I have been associated with since entering college. During my undergraduate years, Don Fehrenbacher, Jay Fliegelman, and Albert Camarillo—each in his own way—inspired me and gave me something to shoot for as I decided on an academic career. I owe a monumental thank-you to the entire Camarillo family. As an undeniable role model—in and out of the academic halls—Al Camarillo has shaped my life for the better; and Susan, Jeffrey, Gregory, and Lauren have provided support and unceasing encouragement. As a teaching assistant in an American history course I took at Stanford, David Gutierrez offered me a glimpse into the often strange world of professional history. He continues to do the same as my best friend and my colleague at the University of California, San Diego. I am deeply grateful to him for his abiding friendship and always thoughtful, probing criticisms of my work.

As a graduate student, I had the good fortune to work closely with such historians as John Murrin, Arthur Link, Stanley Katz, Richard Challener, and Gary Gerstle. I owe a special thanks to Stan Katz for taking me on as assistant master of Rockefeller College when I sorely needed the position's personal as well as financial rewards. Daniel Rodgers has helped me perhaps more than he realizes. I am grateful to him for his incisive readings of my work. My deepest scholarly debt is to James McPherson, my thesis adviser and good friend. Jim was for me the ideal supervisor. His advice, friendship, and support have made this journey much more pleasant than it otherwise might have been.

Other friends also have contributed to my intellectual and personal development. My two closest friends in graduate school, Jim Goodman and Dan Ernst, helped make my time at Princeton all the more enjoyable and enlightening. Alfred Bush, curator of Princeton's Western Americana Collection, has been a constant source of encouragement and support.

Portions of this work were completed while I was a Haynes Fellow and a Robert Middlekauff Fellow at the Huntington Library, and I gratefully acknowledge that generous support here. But the Huntington's influence on me has been largely personal rather than institutional. Martin Ridge has unselfishly and generously given of his time and advice. I am very grateful for his interest in this project and in my development as an American historian. Robert Middlekauff, former director of the Huntington, kindly gave of his time when I am certain he had little to spare. I also appreciate the support of former director James Thorpe and the current director, Robert Skotheim. The staff and Readers' Services librarians at the Huntington were forever helpful to me. Brita Mack, Bob Schlosser, Alan Jutzi, and Jenny Watts deserve special thanks for their help and friendship. I also thank the staffs at the Bancroft Library and the Department of Special Collections and Archives at Stanford, especially Irene Moran of the Bancroft and Michael Ryan, Maggie Kimball, Mark Dimunation, and Sara Timby across the Bay.

Anne Hyde not only showed me the ropes at the Bancroft Library years ago but also introduced me to the graduate history community at Berkeley and made me feel at home. I will always be grateful to her for that, as well as for our wonderful friendship. As a member of the history dissertation group at Berkeley several years ago, I received advice and encouragement from many fellow historians, and I thank them all.

My colleagues in the political history group at the California Institute of Technology during the years 1988–1990—Morgan Kousser, Leonard Moore, Laird Boswell, and Doug Flamming—helped me strengthen the analytical content of this work, and I especially thank Morgan Kousser for giving this manuscript his usual deep reading. I am grateful for the encouragement of Dan and Bettyann Kevles as I moved along in the process from research to dissertation to book.

I am also grateful to my colleagues at the University of California, San Diego. I would like especially to thank my friends in our small reading group—David Gutierrez, Robert Friedman, Pamela Radcliff, and Mark Kleinman—for helping me sharpen the arguments in several of the chapters. Richard Attiyeh, dean of graduate studies at UCSD, generously provided me with subvention funds, which I used to gather the photographs in the book.

Richard Orsi of California State University, Hayward, has helped me at several critical junctures along the way. I am also grateful to him—and to *California History*, which he edits—for granting permission to reprint in chapter 4 parts of the article I wrote for the journal in its spring 1991 issue. My friends and fellow California historians Tom Sitton, David Karnes, and Sherry Katz have added refreshing perspective to my work. Marion Ingersoll knows more than she cares to about the railroad's troubling familiarity: I thank her for her forbearance. I am further grateful to the two outside readers for the University of California Press: one anonymous; the other, Professor R. Hal Williams of Southern Methodist University. Both helped to make this a better book by insightful comments; thanks particularly to Hal Williams for his two patient readings of the manuscript. Needless to say, any errors that remain after his suggestions—and those of many other friends—remain entirely my responsibility.

Stanley Holwitz and Lynne Withey of the University of California Press deserve thanks for showing an early interest in this project and for helping me see it through. It has been a distinct pleasure to work with both of them. Thanks, too, to project editor Laura Driussi and copyeditor Dorothy Conway, both of whom were immensely helpful in getting this book into shape.

Bill, Marne, and Debbie Deverell—my father, mother, and sister—stood patiently by me in the long years that it took to finish graduate school and this book. Their interest in my work and their constant good cheer are gratefully acknowledged here. This book is dedicated to them.

Introduction:
The Varieties of
Railroad Antagonism

We live, as it were, in the dawn and blush of the era of
railroads; and it may take centuries to round out the full
interpretation of them to the slow intelligence of man.
—Reverend Israel Dwinnell
. . . *A Highway for Our God*, 1869

Think about the iron horse: that marvelous technological triumph that
forever changed the American landscape, that "prodigy of labour, wealth,
and skill," as Lord Bryce put it.[1] Growing up together in the first decades
of the nineteenth century, America and the railroad developed a remarkable friendship. As the nation grew, adding territory and population at a
fantastic rate, so did the iron web spun of railroad track. More mileage,
trains, and rail companies meant economic growth, commercial diversification, and the capability to tie far-flung American frontiers to commercial
and political centers.

Antebellum America, in particular, cannot be fully understood without
reference to railroads and the highly charged atmosphere surrounding
their construction and operation. Americans clamored for the progress
and prosperity that railroads would surely bring—to them and to their
communities, regions, and states. Promoters of small lines promised that
a ten- or twelve-mile track would revolutionize the commercial fortunes
of tiny villages on the outskirts of only slightly larger towns. Others
argued that railroads could accomplish what the fragile bonds of nation-
alism or paper assurances of the Constitution could not; that is, the ever-
widening network of railroad tracks would bind North with South, East
with West. Thus convinced, villagers pledged support and money to ensure
that the railroad would not pass them by. Corporate growth kept pace with
the increase in rail mileage: medium-sized rail companies gobbled up
smaller lines and were in turn swallowed by emerging business giants.

Such expansion in both the physical and the corporate realm astonished
foreign visitors and thrilled Americans.[2] The exuberance for railroad growth
seemed to epitomize the country's youthful and acquisitive spirit. By 1850,

all Americans?

1

nearly ten thousand miles of railroad track had been laid, and a great transcontinental railroad was being planned. This audacious scheme would push the railroad west to California. Across the Great Plains, through hellish deserts, and over the Rockies and Sierras, the "twin bands of iron" would come to the far western frontier. The nation would gloriously stretch itself full length.

Of course the transcontinental railway fascinated Californians. It was that second of imperial Spanish dreams that nineteenth-century Anglos had "discovered." First, James Marshall had spied gold in John Sutter's millrace in 1848; now the famed Northwest Passage had been found, not in some fog-enshrouded seaway but in the parallel lines of railroad tracks. The transcontinental railroad was, as Henry George described it, that "looked for, hoped for, prayed for" development which promised to transform the raw mining and farming society of the Far West into a mature civilization. Californians enthusiastically supported the project and made heroes, if but temporarily, out of the men who masterminded the "progress of the rails" across mountain and desert. And after the railroad's famed completion in 1869, Californians greeted its arrival with unprecedented celebration.

But excitement *about* the railroad and accommodation *to it* were often two very different phenomena. Adaptation to its presence was one of the attendant costs of the transcontinental, indeed any, railroad. The railroad forced individuals to make room for it in their lives. It was more visible and accessible than other technological innovations of the age; it also exuded a certain permanency, demanding that individuals accept the consequences of its fixed existence. Once laid, tracks virtually became part of the landscape. With use and the effects of environment, ties rubbed and scraped their way into ruts, rails dropped down further onto ties, and the earthen bed held fast the track. In the language of railroad engineers, the track became "traffic-tamped." A corresponding social process occurred as the railroad settled into the everyday rhythms of American communities everywhere. In both subtle and abrupt ways, the railroad changed people's lives just as surely as it affected the growth and development of their villages and towns. With the railroad's arrival, the sights and sounds of American life were forever altered.[3]

Americans—Californian or otherwise—did not adjust to railroads casually, inevitably acquiescing to the changes imparted by invention and innovation. How could they? Instead, the adjustment process was slow, troubling, and often complex. And that difficult process of coming to terms with the railroad—specifically, one massive railroad corporation—is the major concern of this book. For even a brief glimpse back at nineteenth-century California reveals the astonishing degree of antagonism directed at the railroad and the railroad corporation. *Railroad Crossing* is about that opposition, about its forms and shapes and meanings.

Why were railroads opposed? An easy answer would be that railroads were fought for every conceivable reason, from the singularly personal to the immensely political and everywhere in between. In fact, the sheer *range* of what I call railroad opposition is startling. Think about the process of laying railroad tracks across the local landscape of a tiny western village. Many villagers would regard the newly constructed railroad as a rude intruder into once-peaceful surroundings. Like Americans everywhere, nineteenth-century Californians expressed dislike for railroads simply because of such intrusiveness. First came the work crews—ethnic and racial invaders loudly disrupting the local peace in a myriad of fashions. Then came the trains themselves. Giant locomotives belching steam and smoke created an overwhelming physical and sensory presence. Sparks shooting from the rails and trains sometimes started grass fires or burned crops. Roaring, whistling, steaming railroads spoiled the pastoral calm of the countryside and disrupted the routines of walking cities and quiet neighborhoods.[4]

The railroad was also phenomenally dangerous, as hazardous an invention of everyday use as any in American history. Railroad work crippled countless thousands. Shop or yard foremen in the nineteenth century were said to be able to judge a job applicant's experience by the number of fingers he was missing. No missing fingers meant a greenhorn; a couple of fingers clipped off meant a seasoned vet; too many gone, and the man was so experienced as to become worthless. What is more, horrific train wrecks occurred with frightening regularity, maiming and killing pedestrians and travelers alike. There were any number of things that could go wrong, sending trains careening off tracks and bridges. Worse yet, trains could and did run head-on into each other—"telescoping," as it came to be neatly described in the daily papers, where one train swallowed up the other, passengers included.[5] Less catastrophic accidents—livestock smashed by locomotive cowcatchers, pedestrians run over at unmarked crossings, wagons splintered in town streets—became almost routinized as common occurrences. The railroad rapidly became a familiar intruder in everyday lives, but such familiarity could nonetheless come at high expense.

For many people, the machinery portended the arrival of aggressive American acquisitiveness and commerce. Certainly, for well-to-do Californians of Spanish and Mexican heritage, even for those Anglos who had energetically "Hispanicized" themselves, the iron horse contributed to the decline of a particular way of life. The state's "rancho period" could not long withstand the onslaught of railroads and all that they represented commercially and culturally. And as if they had not been battered enough by missions and friars and Anglo gold seekers, what remained of California's Native American population would face further ruin in the railroad-sponsored "next chapter" of the state's history.[6]

But the railroad could represent a different sort of intrusion as well, something perhaps even more sinister than the arrival of machined "Progress." Many a nervous Californian looked on railroad depots as dens of iniquity. Classes, races, and complete strangers mingled uncomfortably at rail stations; children and runaways passed the time, pickpockets and confidence men singled out their next victim among the tourists and immigrants. Prostitutes loitered, gamblers lingered. Each arriving train brought outsiders in: black Pullman car porters, Europeans speaking countless tongues, Chinese, the rare Native American. Even the railroad cars themselves could be viewed as inanimate confederates to crime: they supposedly brought sinister influences into previously insulated communities and provided the criminal element with easy escape.[7]

In addition to expressing wariness and fear over railroads themselves, Americans distrusted railroad corporations. Adjustment to the railroad's corporate identity presented different—and often more serious—problems from those posed by the technological, nuts-and-bolts expression of a particular transportation technology. In California, native and newcomer alike had already been introduced to the machinery of railroads by the time the great transcontinental railroad was completed in 1869; but massive railroad corporations were themselves new inventions. For a myriad of reasons, the railroad empire born of the massive transcontinental project elicited several generations' worth of profound antagonism.[8]

The Central and Southern Pacific railroad companies, the corporate combination that built the overland railway and presided over most rail operations in the state throughout the second half of the nineteenth century, faced seemingly incessant attack over a forty-year period.[9] Angry Californians charged that passenger fares were too high, inhibiting their own travels as well as the state's ability to attract tourists and settlers from the East. Farmers insisted that oppressive freight rates robbed them of hard-earned profits, while manufacturers in San Francisco demanded higher rates on competing goods imported from Chicago or New York. Few opponents failed to note with resentment the near-monopoly status enjoyed by the corporation.

Countless complaints were made about rail service and the skills of railroad personnel. Trains ran too slow. Trains ran too fast. Tracks, hastily thrown down in the frenzy of construction, were dangerous. Many Californians, professional and blue collar alike, denounced the railroad company for importing thousands upon thousands of Chinese laborers to build the overland railroad across the Sierras. Corporate executives, bloated by wealth and greed, proved easy targets, accused of jilting their once-adoring California constituency.[10] The attacks could be harsh. One fervent critic of Leland Stanford, journalist Arthur McEwen, chastised the Central Pacific official for not recognizing California's dislike of the corporation and its officers. According to McEwen, Stanford remained ignorant of public hostility because he paid "large annual salaries to men whose chief task is to tell him that he is great and good." As for the former governor's political aspirations, McEwen added that Stanford was "better qualified to be a candidate for San Quentin than the Senate."[11] Others remained convinced that railroad political power, reinforced by steel-strong webs of corruption, blackened the state's image and undermined its republican foundations. Rival entrepreneurs decried the unmitigated evils of monopoly; they charged the railroad with stifling free trade and making economic slaves of the state's population.

Californians offered diverse and often unusual explanations for their anger toward the railroad and the railroad company. A humorous but insightful example is a letter written at the end of the nineteenth century from Bay Area resident George Emerson to Collis P. Huntington of the Southern Pacific. Mr. Emerson knew why he and so many fellow Californians hated the rail corporation. After reviewing decades of opposition, Emerson believed that he had discovered the root of the trouble. The reason was simple: the men who worked for the railroad, especially those in the passenger depots, were incompetent, full of "petty meaness and embecility." And just as the problem sprang from an easily identifiable cause, the solution was correspondingly plain. Emerson advised Huntington, by this time president of the Southern Pacific, to send someone to the rail depots "with a club some time and beat some brains into some of your men."[12] Presumably then opposition to the railroad would melt away. It is doubtful that Collis Huntington ever followed Emerson's advice.

As Emerson's letter attests, proposed solutions to the "railroad problem" encompassed a wide variety of options. Much depended on how one defined the problem; nineteenth-century political tracts are full of articles on "The Railway Problem," as if there were only one! Some individuals chose purely personal action (like Emerson's letter writing); others lobbied for increased state or federal railroad legislation or regulation. Constitutional amendments and changes in law were proposed. For the sake of principle, civic obligation, or election-year expediency, a politician might refuse to patronize particular railroads.[13] Some Californians offered more radical solutions, destroying railroad tracks or blowing up bridges and trestles.[14] Others wrote anti-railroad novels. A few Californians threatened the lives of railroad employees; assassination threats also were made against high-paid railroad officials. Masked gunmen robbed trains—and sometimes were sheltered from the law in the homes of sympathetic citizens. Workers went out on strike. Women's organizations attacked the railroad corporation's influence on public affairs. Newspapers adopted unyielding anti-railroad positions. Political parties with anti-railroad platforms sprang up, flowered, and died. Voters elected candidates who said they were opposed to the railroad power. Rival capitalists, displaying their own railroad-hating credentials, built competing railroads to challenge the monopoly of the Central or Southern Pacific. Other Californians took their frustrations to court, looking for compensation for train-killed livestock or resolution of land and labor disputes.[15]

Although most anti-railroad actions were directed at a particular corporation and not a particular form of transportation, in a few rare instances railroad opponents attacked the physical components of railroading: ties and tracks most often, occasionally depots and trestles. Because "the railroad" existed as a loosely defined common denominator—embracing technology, transportation, and corporate entity all at once—such actions could in effect be both anti-corporate and anti-technological. In other words, the infrequent instances of industrial sabotage may have been (and in California were more likely to be) prompted by animus toward a particular railroad corporation and not toward railroad technology.[16]

Over the course of half a century, from the days of the transcontinental railroad's impending arrival to the first decade of this century, Californians grappled with the significant problems that, in their view, were created by the presence of the railroad in their lives.[17] Depending on what those in power would tolerate or could withstand, certain forms of opposition became legitimate at specific points in the state's growth. This book seeks to chronicle these various forms of opposition and to relate them to changes over time in the California of one hundred years ago. It also questions whether there actually was an all-powerful, monolithic railroad corporation or a cohesive railroad opposition.

From the exuberant years of cross-country railroad building to the construction of an explicitly anti-railroad political base in the Progressive gubernatorial campaign of 1910, the issue of railroad opposition helped define the ways in which Californians saw themselves and their state. Like California society itself, railroad opposition evolved; its methods, techniques, and objectives changed over time. These shifts help illuminate important changes in California from the middle of the nineteenth century through the first decade of the twentieth. Analysis of such change needs always to be placed against the giant canvas of Gilded Age and early-twentieth-century America. For in their interminable wrestling match with the railroad, Californians proved simply that they were—as Lord Bryce suggested—prototypically American: full of contradictions about the roles that technology and industrial capitalism would play, and be allowed to play, in their lives as they looked to the coming of the new century.[18]

Unlike Frank Norris, who wanted his classic novel *The Octopus: A Story of California* to "say the last word on the R.R. [railroad] question in California," I have a more modest goal in mind. The issue, not to mention the literature, is far too complex for this work to approach comprehensiveness. As Hubert Howe Bancroft, the nineteenth-century dean of California history, admitted regarding his study of the impact of railroads on California: "The constant difficulty has been an excess of matter, rather than a lack of material."[19] That observation rings with even more truth today. A generation after Bancroft did his work, Stuart Daggett titled his study of the Southern Pacific Corporation *Chapters on the History of the Southern Pacific*.[20] *Railroad Crossing* is offered in that same spirit: interpretive, thematic chapters that analyze change through an unusual historical prism. Intrinsically interesting in its own right, the story of railroad antagonism and its endless cycles of rhetoric, action, discourse, and behavior can also tell us a great deal about the coming of age of the nation's most important western state.

In wandering over this fascinating terrain, this book also encounters the chaos of industrial America. This world is both different and strangely familiar, one in which reform battles tradition, political parties square off in real or mock opposition, and lawmakers fret over the limits and reach of legislative control over giant corporations.

First we look at the excitement (and the hype) surrounding the audacious scheme to build a transcontinental railroad west across the nation. What did such a railroad mean? And, more in line with the purposes of this book, what did it mean in particular to California? From the laying of tracks, we turn in chapters 2, 3, and 4 to the years of the railroad's troubled honeymoon with anxious Californians, a generation's worth of debate, struggle, even violence—all of which attempted in different ways to define the precise meaning of the railroad in the lives of Californians. Chapter 5 explores the tricky relationship that the press established with the railroad as well as the railroad with the press. This chapter ("Pens as Swords") also investigates *The Octopus*, a turn-of-the-century best-selling novel that purported to be the last word on the "railroad question" in California.

The book closes with the success of the insurgents within the state's Republican Party, a group of reformers who recognized the political and sheer rhetorical power of railroad bashing and skillfully used that knowledge to seize the governor's mansion in the 1910 state elections.

Before any of this, though, there was a bold and breathtakingly ambitious idea, and it is to that idea that we turn our attention in the chapter that follows.

1 "What Is This Railroad to Do for Us?"

There was a time when it was the general feeling that all we wanted to usher in the millennial dawn in this State was railroad communication with the Atlantic, and that no sacrifice was too great to secure it.
——Newton Booth
Principles of the Republican Party, 1879

I am well aware that I have much to learn in railroad matters.
——Collis P. Huntington
Letter to Mark Hopkins, 1869

There is an often-told California story about the making of the first issue of the *Overland Monthly*. Designed to be a voice from the cultural wilderness of the American West, the magazine was in the final days of production in the spring of 1868. A distinguished group of editors and writers had gathered in San Francisco to work out the remaining editorial and artistic problems. A cover illustration had already been chosen: a growling young California grizzly bear, the mascot of the state. "As a bear," Mark Twain remembered, "he was a success; he was a good bear." Yet something was missing. Twain thought that the drawing depicted "an *objectless* bear—a bear that *meant* nothing in particular, signified nothing,—simply stood there snarling over his shoulder at nothing."

Bret Harte then did something that Twain regarded as "nothing less than inspiration itself." Taking a pencil, Harte hastily drew the parallel lines of a railroad track beneath the grizzly's feet; "behold he was a magnificent success!" wrote Twain, "the ancient symbol of California savagery snarling at the approaching type of high and progressive Civilization, the first Overland locomotive!"[1]

The cover of the *Overland Monthly* did symbolize an older California giving way before the none-too-subtle charms of advancing progress. But Twain's interpretation (satirical or otherwise) that the transformation was positive—"savagery" replaced by "progressive Civilization"—is but one of several possible ways of looking at the meeting between snarling Cali-

9

fornia and the oncoming railroad. For although Harte himself apparently welcomed the transcontinental railroad's arrival,[2] other Californians were much less convinced. Perhaps that grizzly had been lured onto the tracks only to be obliterated.

A Railroad to the Pacific

America in the mid-nineteenth century exhibited all the railroad-crazed enthusiasm of the "Locomotive Age." Small spur, main, and trunk lines spread out from town and city epicenters like the spokes of a wheel, as mile after mile of tracks crisscrossed empty land. The subject of countless speeches, paintings, and, as the science developed, photographs, the railroad became typecast as the ideal symbol of the young nation's headlong rush to modernity. What Emerson had said of New England in the 1840s was no less true for the entire nation ten years later: "The Railroad is the only topic for conversation these days. That is the only one that interests farmers, merchants, boys, women, saints, philosophers, and fools. . . . The Railroad is that work of art which agitates and drives mad the whole people."[3]

Not only did the railroad symbolize American energy; it rapidly came to be seen as critical to the nation's future. As the sectional crisis deepened through the 1850s, and the nation drifted toward civil war, anxious Americans looked for ways to bind the country and thus lessen the threat of disunion. The idea of a transcontinental railroad, tying North, South, East, and West together with a gigantic sash of iron, had been proposed much earlier, in the first decades of the nineteenth century, and often greeted with ridicule. Now, however, many naively thought that a transcontinental railroad might at least temporarily solder weak spots in the chain of national unity. Unlike those who had suggested the idea in the 1820s and 1830s as a way to bolster the American whaling industry or trade with the Far East, later transcontinental boosters looked to the proposed railway as a way to ease domestic sectional tensions.

The voices of enthusiastic Californians mingled with those of other Americans pushing for the building of an overland railway. They saw in the project union and peace as well as guaranteed and rapid prosperity for their isolated state. Despite the Gold Rush avalanche of miners, the state did exist at the furthest hazy reach of Manifest Destiny's gaze; it was the railroad that would bring California into the national fold, physically as well as otherwise. The railroad would increase the productivity of all workers, people believed, bringing markets, business opportunities, and the wherewithal of industrial capitalism to the Far West. "It will lend strength, nerve, motion, activity and purpose, to the minds and arms of toiling millions," gushed western enthusiast Henry Fitch.[4] The entire nation ought to promote the project and work together to ensure its completion. National prestige and, indeed, the future of the republic were at stake. "Shall we weave a starry girdle fit for liberty to wear?" Fitch asked from San Francisco, knowing full well that the answer was a re-sounding "yes."[5]

Yet not even the overland railway could escape the bitter rivalries soon to tear the nation apart. The transcontinental railroad and the sectional conflict were too important to the nation's future *not* to become inter-twined. In the mid-1850s, in the midst of rising political crisis, Congress sent four separate teams to explore the West in search of feasible railroad routes.[6] The various expeditions, which scouted potential passages stretch-ing from the Mexican to the Canadian border, ostensibly signaled Con-gress's lack of sectional favoritism. But the North was not about to put the transcontinental railway within the grasp of the South. In the end, Congress chose to bind the North with California, instead of trying to fend off the all but inevitable North-South sectional crisis by selecting one of the southerly routes. In June of 1862, with any Southern opposition dissolved by secession, Congress passed the bill allowing construction of the Pacific Railroad. The chosen route ran west of Omaha to an as yet undecided terminus on the California coast somewhere near San Fran-cisco.[7] What had been a far-fetched dream only years earlier had become expectation: "there must be a railroad to the Pacific; it must be financed by grants of public lands along the route; and it must be built by private interests which received those grants."[8]

In January of 1863, scarcely a week after the Emancipation Proclamation went into effect, hundreds of Californians gathered in Sacramento to witness ground-breaking ceremonies for the Central Pacific Railroad. For years, civil engineer Theodore D. Judah had tried to convince Californians that a railroad could be built across the Sierra Nevada. His persistence and vision finally paid off in the early days of the Civil War with the congres-sional go-ahead and the incorporation of the Central Pacific Railroad of California, the seed from which the mighty Southern Pacific railroad empire would eventually grow. Pushed along by the managerial aegis of four dour local merchants and Judah's impressive engineering skills, the tracks of the Central Pacific were to snake east from the state capital.[9] At some point between the California mountain peaks and the plains of Nebraska, the Central Pacific was to merge with the westward-building Union Pacific. At the Sacramento ground-breaking ceremony, orator New-ton Booth christened the railroad in the exalted tone found in many a mid-century railroad speech. This railroad would be far more than a mere transportation network:

> Hail, then, all hail, this auspicious hour! Hail this bond of brother-
> hood and union! Hail this marriage tie between the Atlantic and
> Pacific! Hail, all hail, this bow of promise which amid all the
> clouds of war is seen spanning the continent—the symbol, the
> harbinger, the pledge of a higher civilization and an ultimate
> and world-wide peace![10]

Although it would be nearly a year before any rails were laid, the massive project was under way. Six years of railroad construction followed, the likes of which the world had never seen.[11] Equally spectacular was the way in which Californians greeted the inevitable coming of the "thousand rushing chariots" steaming across "pathways of iron."[12] Californians wanted desperately to believe that the transcontinental railway would be much more than a commercial and transportation artery to and from the East. Many looked to it as an iron thread with which to stitch up the wound of disunion, a sentiment aptly voiced by the Reverend Israel Dwinnell in a special sermon before the citizens of Sacramento. "I think we must all feel that the mission of railroads is somewhere in the general direction of human peace, fraternity, unity," he declared. "Clearly these iron bonds which bind States, and in some cases nations together, hint a higher and warmer and purer brotherhood of mankind, and a snugger home-feeling beneath our common father's roof, for the race."[13]

Besides earthly union and brotherhood, the transcontinental railroad would yield spiritual as well as secular gain. Many saw in the enterprise fulfillment of the biblical obligation to "make straight in the desert a highway for our God." San Francisco preacher Charles Wadsworth cau-tioned his brethren not to expect spiritual tidings necessarily to spring from the coming of the railroad. At the same time, he suggested their inevitability.

> While it is proper, and even scriptural, for "our sons and our
> daughters to prophesy, and our young men to see visions, and our
> old men to dream dreams," it is still, perhaps, safest to dismiss
> from our minds the pleasing illusion that yonder iron road is, in
> our day, to bring New York over the Sierras that it may be a sub-
> urb of San Francisco, or that along it even now the New Jerusalem
> is coming down out of Heaven, and will "switch off" into
> Oakland.[14]

Stripping away deep layers of metaphor, Reverend Dwinnell echoed Wads-worth in making a startling prediction he must have thought certain to come true: "I cannot doubt that in time men will see that a wonderful change in the spiritual history of mankind dates from the railroad age."[15]

Those preachers who saw in the railroad a conduit to spirituality and godliness may have been stretching matters for the benefit of their flocks. But the minds of many a Californian were fertile fields in which to plant prophecy. As the Central Pacific made its way east and the Union Pacific worked west out of Omaha, Californians watched the construction of each mile with growing fascination. With each additional mile of track laid, they learned more and more about the mysteries of railroad building and the intricate maneuvers of railroad corporations.

The Big Four

Doubtless the Californians who learned the most, and who had the most to learn, were the top executives of the Central Pacific Railroad Corporation.[16] These men, who would sit atop one of the nation's greatest transportation networks, a modern engineering wonder, were not railroad men to begin with. Yet the Big Four, as they came to be known, were already successful before they took on the audacious task of building a railway across the Sierra Nevada.

Collis P. Huntington, a merchant-salesman in upstate New York, succumbed to gold fever in 1849 and joined the amazing migration of young men to the faraway Pacific Coast. A single day's struggle to free the precious metal from the earth's grasp was enough to convince the young Huntington that mining was not for him. Gold could be had easier: at one point during the Gold Rush, Huntington nearly cornered the California market on shovels. In partnership with taciturn Mark Hopkins, Huntington built "Huntington & Hopkins," the state's largest hardware business, on K Street in Sacramento. As the Central Pacific Railroad began to grow, Huntington took over the corporate fund-raising tasks, and Hopkins handled the company books.[17]

Leland Stanford, the best known of the railroad's senior executives, beat the Gold Rush odds and struck it rich on a mine in northern California. With newfound wealth, he settled comfortably into the life of merchant-politician in Sacramento. When Congress passed the Pacific Railroad Bill, Stanford was governor of California. Although not distinguished by intellect or political deftness, Stanford had been an early supporter of the infant Republican Party in the late 1850s, and his loyalty was rewarded as the party rose to prominence. He would long be identified as the state's Republican standard-bearer. At his death, in the words of an itinerant Russian visitor to the state, Stanford had become nothing less than "the terrible American Jupiter, who emerged from manure, passed through trials and tribulations, and tore himself out of the noose to, at last, win himself a position which many sovereign princes would rightly envy."[18] The description was hardly hyperbole: Stanford and his railroad partners became fabulously rich, thanks to the grand railroad scheme (and the generosity of the federal government).

Like Huntington and Stanford, Charles Crocker came from upstate New York to seek his fortune in the gold fields of the Far West. But true respectability and comfort came only after he became a Sacramento merchant and minor Republican Party officeholder. Crocker's company received the contract for Central Pacific construction, and during construction he proved invaluable as overseer and boss, driving his crews to lay track faster and faster.

The financing of the great project relied on a fairly simple scheme. The two rail companies were to build in opposite directions and meet, no one knew how many years later, somewhere in the middle. For each mile of track laid, the companies were to be rewarded by substantial grants of federal land and the loan of great amounts of federal funding. The money was to be parceled out depending on terrain. Flatland construction would be compensated at $16,000 a mile, desert mileage at $32,000, and mountain terrain at $48,000. In addition, the companies were free to raise money by selling stock and securing construction subsidies from towns along the proposed route.

Raising the requisite funds for construction proved difficult. No matter how excited they were about the possibility of the transcontinental railroad, Californians seemed little interested in backing the project with their own money. San Francisco residents proved especially reluctant to subscribe to railroad bonds, a hesitation that the Big Four were quick to assign to the machinations of rival capitalists.[19] Collis Huntington, who relocated to New York to handle financial matters, tried with mixed success to sell the project to eastern financiers and capitalists. Attempts to interest European backers simply foundered; as John Williams points out, "Central Pacific stocks and bonds were shunned like lepers in Europe."[20]

Fund-raising tactics, therefore, often required creativity, if not subterfuge. By convincing Congress that the Sierra Nevada range actually began farther west than was previously thought, for instance, the Central Pacific executives gained additional federal monies for mountainous construction. Leland Stanford's influence in state politics also aided the fledgling conglomerate: his stature and prestige helped convince the legislature to increase state allotments for construction costs.[21]

Building a railroad over the Sierras required a phenomenal amount of manpower. From an 1864 total of fewer than 2,000 men, Central Pacific construction crews grew to number nearly 15,000 by 1867. By then, white workers constituted only about 20 percent of railroad laborers, and they were primarily in skilled positions. The majority of the Central Pacific's track crews were Chinese immigrants, many of them shipped over from China expressly for railroad construction. Although the employment of such large numbers of Chinese workers would prove more and more controversial in the years to come, the Big Four were obviously pleased with their reliance on Asian labor. "I like the idea of your getting over more Chinamen," Collis Huntington wrote to a company official in the fall of 1867; "it would be all the better for us and the State if there should a half million come over in 1868."[22]

Just as the composition of crews would provoke the wrath of the non-Asian working class and Sinophobic Californians, the ways in which the railroad itself was constructed would eventually prompt outrage. With millions of acres of land and a king's ransom in federal loans at stake, speed was of the utmost importance: every mile not constructed by the Central Pacific was as good as money in the coffers of the Union Pacific. Therefore, work crews laid track as fast as possible, with only minimal regard for safety or quality of construction. The Big Four, especially chief fund-raiser Collis Huntington, knew exactly what had to be done to ensure the maximum windfall. "I am very glad to learn that you have made up your mind to go in for quantity of road instead of quality," Huntington wrote to Crocker at the beginning of 1868. Six months later, when Union Pacific crews were laying ten miles of track a day across the flat plains, Huntington's tone became less measured. "Work on as though Heaven was before you and Hell behind you," he urged his construction boss.[23] The advice was not lost on the severe Crocker. "Everybody was afraid of me," he later remembered. "I was just looking for someone to find fault with all the time."[24]

Central Pacific executives worked no less diligently to ensure a popular reception for the railroad once it was complete. To a significant degree, they could count on the popular groundswell in favor of railroads—all railroads—to sustain a positive environment for the Central Pacific. Californians saluted the courage of the Big Four, canonizing them as representatives of western entrepreneurial success. And as sections of the transcontinental railroad began to carry trains, public response was largely favorable.

This popular reception can be partly attributed to the railroad's inchworm progress through the 1860s. The periodic addition of ten- or twelve-mile railroad sections could hardly cause any major disruption or social upheaval. And northern Californians were already accustomed to railroads in the gold-mining country. Built shortly after the great rush of 1849–50, the Sacramento Valley Railroad ran twenty-two miles from the state capital to Folsom. By 1860, railroad tracks, "projected or in progress," crisscrossed a map of central California accompanying the annual report of one gold region rail company. Lines under construction included the California Central Railroad, connecting Folsom to Marysville, and another line running from Marysville to the San Francisco Bay Area. Mining towns—Rough & Ready, Long Bar, French Coral, and Cherokee—would all be drawn into the expanding iron net.[25]

Opposition, even to these small lines, was not unknown, however. For the most part, antagonism came from rivals who feared the competition a railroad would present to a stage company or a different railroad project. A longtime employee of the Central Pacific, for instance, noted in his memoirs that most of the early opposition to the line came from other transportation interests, including steamship lines, Wells Fargo, and other stage or freight companies.[26] Town loyalties also contributed to the antagonism. Sacramento residents resented neighboring Marysville for backing the construction of the San Francisco and Marysville Railroad. In a report to the little railroad's board of directors, chief engineer D. B. Scott referred to certain individuals, "tools in the hands of their employers," who "have endeavored, by chicanery and stratagem, to throw every obstacle in the way which would tend to cripple your resources, and retard the progress of the work." Antagonists attempted to disrupt the company's fund-raising by various methods, but the work on the ninety-mile railroad would go on.[27]

A few Californians voiced concern about the coming transcontinental railway's potential impact on the state. During the initial stages of Central Pacific construction, Albertus Meyer, a German immigrant living in Oakland, published a small pamphlet in which he pointed out the changes that the overland would surely bring. Relative prosperity had prevailed in Gold Rush California, Meyer suggested. The state's isolation, abundant natural resources, and moderate labor supply combined to foster an egalitarian environment. Would the coming of the railroad change all that? If the railroad did bring about an economic boom, what consequences could California expect? Would an economic underclass be created? Would immigrant laborers (Meyer expressed specific concern over Asians) rush in to take jobs previously held by Anglo-Saxon workers? And did Californians really want to help pay for the massive enterprise?[28]

Despite the thoughtfulness and even the prescience of such questions, publicly expressed concerns such as Meyer's were rare, and Californians paid such naysayers little heed. As the Central Pacific began the difficult assault on the Sierras, attention focused on the progress of the rails much more than on the potential impact of the railroad. It was eighteen miles from Sacramento to Roseville; that first leg of the project was completed in 1863. From there, track slowly snaked thirteen miles to Newcastle, another five on to Auburn, six to Clipper Gap. It was September of 1865 before the railroad reached Colfax, a scant fifty-four miles from Sacramento. Eight months would pass before the next twelve miles of track were laid to Secret Town.[29]

Crucial to the maintenance of a public pro-railroad disposition was corporate influence on the press. The directors of the Central Pacific, at first inexperienced, would eventually master this sort of lobbying. The Big Four did not single out California newspapers; Stanford and Huntington, in particular, took pains to create favorable eastern opinion about the American West, the Central Pacific, and rail travel in general. From his base in New York, Huntington directed Crocker to place articles in western newspapers and magazines about the favorable working conditions in the West; he would then make sure that the articles were reprinted in eastern journals.[30]

In exerting corporate influence on the press, Huntington and the others often relied on crude methods. "I have but little trouble to get favorable things said of us by any of the papers by giving the local editor a box of cigars," Huntington boasted in 1868. But time-honored practices evidently wore thin as the corporation (and its directors) increased in influence. As Huntington complained that same year, "We have grown so that old Bennett, of the 'Herald,' and others like him, think we are fat enough for them to gather tribute of, and so they forbid any one about these papers saying any good-natured things of us."[31]

Unfavorable articles in western newspapers dogged the railroad corporation as the transcontinental linkup drew closer. The Sacramento *Union* proved particularly troublesome, prompting the Big Four to contemplate buying the paper. Railroad executives explained journalistic opposition as simple jealousy and opportunism: the powerful editors of western papers wished to exert influence over the railroad's route and operation. Central Pacific officials saw little distinction between antagonistic journalists and what they viewed as an ungrateful public. "I notice that you write that everybody is in favor of a railroad until they get it built," Huntington wrote to Hopkins in the spring of 1868; "and then everyone is against it, unless the railroad company will carry them and theirs for nothing."[32]

The directors of the Central Pacific understood the inescapable connection between the press and a "correct" political environment. And in his efforts to secure a political climate receptive to the corporation's aims, Huntington proved particularly energetic, even Machiavellian. He and the other members of the Big Four quickly realized that their influence was difficult to ignore, and they displayed little timidity in throwing their political or financial weight around. As historian Richard Orsi has argued, such manipulation could be anything but subtle, especially in years following the completion of the transcontinental. "To preserve its near monopoly, the corporation entered politics on a massive scale, influencing political parties and elections and even on occasion dispensing bribes when necessary."[33] In earlier days, affairs had a certain specificity, particularly wrapped around the issue of fares. "I am sorry to notice that there is a movement in Cal. to reduce fares on the C.P.R.R.," Huntington wrote to Crocker in late 1867. "If we could get the rates fixed so that the Legislature could not change them, at about the present rates, it would be a good thing."[34]

The complex rate issue would prove to be a vexing and lasting arena of dispute between the railroad corporation and opponents. As sections of the Central Pacific opened up for traffic, complaints over artificially high prices increased. Farmers shipping produce through and beyond Sacramento were especially vociferous in their denunciations of the monopoly's ability to inflate the costs of transporting crops. And the vexing longhaul/short-haul battle—where the railroad corporation charged more for short-distance freight shipments than for long ones—arrived in California in the same stormy way that it had existed in states to the east. Despite farmers' angry complaints, the legislature proved unwilling to meet rate issues head-on and even passed a 5 percent subsidy law, which would tax counties as an inducement to further rail construction. The justification for such a hands-off approach to the fare question was simple. Wary of the precedent of state intervention into the marketplace, representatives claimed that they were acting to entice additional railroad and other corporate entrepreneurial activity. "Until our system of railroads is built up," read one report out of Sacramento, "we regard it as bad policy to interfere radically with the present legally established rates."[35]

The railroad corporation acted to maintain a favorable attitude on the part of the state's representatives. "We have always tried to prevent the passage of those laws that were going to ruin us just as any man would throw a bucket of water on a fire that had attacked his house," Charles Crocker explained pragmatically. To maintain its influence, the corporation proved extremely fickle in its loyalties. "Neither Cole or Johnson should ever be returned to Congress," Collis Huntington wrote bluntly to Leland Stanford in an 1868 memorandum regarding two on-again, off-again corporate allies. "Damn them with faint praise, but set in motion an undertow that will be sure to destroy them."[36]

Party affiliation likewise meant little. Although the railroad corporation generally supported Republicans, its officials would stump for Democrats who seemed friendly to the needs of the railroad. "He is the best man for us that has been in Congress from California," Huntington said of Democratic congressional candidate Samuel Axtell in 1868, adding that "'us' are whom we are working for, I suppose." In short, "while we would have a Republican, all other things being equal, I must say that for myself I would rather have Axtell returned than any Republican that has ever been in Congress from California, but whoever is returned should be our friends."[37]

The Big Four must have realized that they could gain a western railroad empire if their amazing success with the building and early operation of the Central Pacific continued. The federal government stood willing and able to provide the financial wherewithal to support construction, even throwing millions of acres of land into the bargain. And, in an almost exponential fashion, additional rail mileage brought in more and more revenue. Federal funds, land, some money gained from passenger fares, and, gradually, freight-carrying revenue piled up as the Central Pacific opened additional sections along its line. "We should control the west end of the three overland routes, and without much trouble we ought to control the whole railroad system west of the Rocky Mountains," Huntington confided to his partners as early as the summer of 1868. It would be almost a year until the transcontinental railway linked up, but Huntington was already initiating big plans for the future.[38]

Grandiose schemes—most of which they would eventually realize— kept the Big Four actively promoting the beneficence of the Central Pacific. Yet, as the transcontinental railroad approached completion, a few more Californians began to express doubts that it really would provide great tidings to every Californian, as the boosters claimed. Certainly the most prescient and important of these skeptics was a struggling California journalist named Henry George.

Henry George's Predictions

Years after the overland railway had been completed, Henry George recalled an event that helped shape his thoughts about it. On a New Year's Eve in the 1860s, following a disappointing mining foray into the gold country, George had gone to a theater. A new curtain had been strung up above the stage; and when it fell, members of the audience leapt spontaneously to their feet. Painted boldly on the new curtain was a picture of the overland railroad, "a dream of the far future." The audience cheered and cheered. But Henry George remembered hesitating ("after we had shouted ourselves hoarse"). What, he began to wonder, would the arrival of the railroad mean to workingmen like himself, "those who have nothing but their labour?"[39] Speaking nearly thirty years later, George paid homage to a miner who had given him a valuable lesson about the transcontinental railroad's imminent arrival and effect: "As the country grows, as people come in, wages will go down." From that seed grew a compelling critique of the railroad age in California.

During the most active years of construction on the Central Pacific, Henry George was an impoverished editor and writer. Little about him in the 1860s could have suggested that he would achieve lasting importance and fame as the author of *Progress and Poverty* and the single-tax theory of land reform. Yet George was profoundly moved by economic and political inequities. And using the spectacle of the transcontinental railroad, he set about questioning the promise of California's railroad-induced "millennial dawn." The clamor and excitement surrounding the building of the Central Pacific seemed to ring hollow—the rhetoric and boosterism exceeding any realistic expectations for the railroad's ability to uplift California.

In the lead essay of the *Overland Monthly*'s October 1868 issue, Henry George filled in with words what the journal's cover, that snarling grizzly poised in the railroad's path, could not fully convey. Amidst articles celebrating the this-and-that of California and the West, George wrote with deep concern over the impending completion of the transcontinental railway. The resulting essay stands as one of the most brilliant articles ever written about western railroading. "What the Railroad Will Bring Us" raised questions about nearly every point that railroad boosters celebrated.[40]

"What is this railroad to do for us?" George asked his fellow Californians, "this railroad that we have looked for, hoped for, prayed for so long?" Surely the "California netted with iron tracks" was to be a far cry from the California of more primitive transportation; that much was obvious, given the effect railroads had already had on other regions of the United States. Notions of time and space were sure to be altered ("annihilated" was the era's verb of choice). "We are so used to the California of the stagecoach, widely separated from the rest of the world, that we can hardly realize what the California of the railroad will be," George wrote pensively.

Doubtless the state would change. Like the railroad's unabashed supporters, George expected an era of "steady, rapid and substantial growth; of great addition to population and immense increase in the totals of the

Assessor's lists." But, unlike those uncritical promoters of the railroad and the railroad age, George questioned whether such change would be universally positive. "The new era will be one of great material prosperity, if material prosperity means more people, more houses, more farms and mines, more factories and ships," he wrote. Towns would spring up along railroad tracks, nursed through infancy by railroad-spawned commerce. Cities would grow as large as their counterparts at eastern railroad termini. San Francisco would mushroom first into the preeminent western metropolis, the commercial capital of the entire trans-Mississippi West. The city would then "grow up with the country" into an influential world power.[41]

"Yet we cannot hope to escape the great law of compensation which exacts some loss for every gain," George warned. The completion of the Central Pacific would bring more and more migrants to the state. Wages would fall. Class divisions would become more distinct, rigid. The egalitarian openness of Gold Rush California, "where the wheel of fortune had been constantly revolving," would fade with the railroad's arrival. "The truth is, that the completion of the railroad and the consequent great increase of business and population, will not be a benefit to all of us, but only to a portion." With the addition of the railroad, land values would increase, making it more difficult for the workingman to achieve independence. The inevitable crowding together of the poor would result in "courts, slums, tenement-houses, squalor and vice."[42]

"The locomotive is a great centralizer," George wrote. "It kills little towns and builds up great cities, and in the same way kills little businesses and builds up great ones." Accompanying its arrival would be a new class of rich and a further concentration of wealth in the hands of the few. "The 'honest miner' of the placers has passed away in California. The Chinaman, the millowner and his laborers, the mine superintendent and his gang, are his successors." The California of the Gold Rush would forever disappear once the Central Pacific met the Union Pacific. Connected to the East by an iron cord, California would no longer be protected from national disruptions, economic cycles, or social ills.[43]

With the decline in personal independence and corresponding rise in corporate power, the political situation in California would worsen. The railroad corporation would exercise increasing influence in state politics, Henry George predicted, consolidating its power and inevitably altering representative government in California if not the nation. The potential for coercion and tyranny would rise along with corporate expansion. In short, George argued that the railroad corporation would be too powerful to be honest and far too powerful to ignore.

Henry George understood, perhaps better than the railroad builders themselves, that the overland railway could not exist in a social, cultural, political, or economic vacuum. Railroad boosterism tended to place the railroad gently on the California landscape without grasping its concomitant integration into the political economy of the state. But the transcontinental railroad could not be separated from critical relationships: labor and capital, the federal government and the West, technology and the environment, the corporation and the individual. And George pointed out, too, that once the railroad arrived in California, once the long-awaited linkup took place, there would be no looking back. Rickety, poorly constructed track notwithstanding, the transcontinental railroad would come to California to stay.

Promontory and Its Aftermath

Henry George's cautionary knell could not accomplish the impossible. In spite of his interjection of sober realism into an atmosphere of unrealistic expectations, Californians continued to look to the arrival of the overland railroad with unbridled enthusiasm, more than willing to endow the iron horse with remarkable capabilities. The railroad promised unchecked economic growth, its vocal supporters declared. It would open a passage to the Orient (becoming, in the process, the long-searched-for Northwest Passage), encouraging lucrative trade and commerce with Asia. The Central Pacific would prove to be a powerful civilizing agent as well, transforming California from rude frontier to modern society. As one supporter declared, the "vigor, vice and lawlessness of border life" would be "made subservient to one of the greatest instruments of refined civilization." Indeed, the railroad was a miraculous thing, transcending the rigidly defined capabilities of mere machinery. It was "a work that unites two extremes of a great country, that links widely-separated States, that annihilates geographical and sectional divisions, that marries the business and society of the east and west, and establishes a new highway for the commerce of Asia."[44]

Seven years after the signing of the Pacific Railroad Bill, after Gettysburg, Appomattox, Lincoln's assassination, and at the dawn of Radical Reconstruction, the incredible project was complete. In May of 1869, gathered at a desolate and lonely spot in northwestern Utah called Promontory, representatives of the two railroad companies drove the ceremonial last spikes into the rails that tied the Atlantic with the Pacific. Photographers captured the scene for posterity, after the Chinese laborers were asked to step aside. Anxious not to offend the railroad czars' gentility, the photographers took two versions of the commemorative photograph: one with workers holding aloft liquor bottles, one without. An eyewitness described the "finishing blow to the greatest enterprise of the age": Central Pacific president Leland Stanford "stood with the silver sledge gleaming in the air, whose blow was to be heard further, without metaphor, than any blow struck by mortal man; the realization of the ancient myth of Jupiter with the thunderbolt in his hand." Stanford swung the mighty ceremonial hammer at the ceremonial spike . . . and missed. No matter: the telegraph wires attached to the mallet sent the signal out anyway, and simultaneous celebrations broke out across the nation. It was, recalled another eyewitness to the scene, "the greatest and most exciting event my eyes ever beheld. . . . We felt that the work there being completed meant more to this nation and to the advancement of civilization than anything else that could be imagined."[45]

The completion of the railroad prompted statewide celebrating up and down California. In Sacramento, the driving of the last spike—telegraphically transmitted—was met with a chorus of guns, bells, and steam whistles. A procession of fire companies, military and civil officials, and mounted butchers and draymen worked its way proudly through the city's streets. "We see His mighty Hand now clasp this iron band," sang Sacramento's breathless citizens.

Residents of Oakland, a small village on the shores of the San Francisco Bay, greeted the completion of the grand project with perhaps even more jubilation than other Californians. It was their town that would be the Central Pacific's western terminus, the end of the line in the great east-to-west railroad journey.[46] Before his parishioners in the First Congregational Church, the Reverend George Mooar embraced the coming of the railroad as a sure sign from heaven. In a Sunday sermon—"God's Highways Exalted"—Mooar declared that the railroad fulfilled the biblical prophecy regarding Christendom's unification with the Orient. The fabled westward passage had at last been found, not in some secret fog-enshrouded seaway but in the "twin bands of iron" now stretching across the North American continent. In fact, Mooar pointed out, the railroad had already fostered a blessed connection with the Far East in the human example of thousands of Chinese laborers at work on railroad construction gangs.

The "peculiarly Californian" energy that accompanied the laying of the rails fascinated Mooar and provided an apt analogy for Christian spirit and dedication. For the building of the railroad, the audacity of crossing mountain ranges and bringing civilization across the desert, offered a parable to all Californians. "Be enterprising christians," Mooar urged. "That is what the railway kings are teaching us. . . . Undertake great things, work for great things." The scale of the project itself was an inspiration: "Such kind of railroad building as that from Lincoln to Marysville will not do. It is slow, dull. Lay ten miles of track in a day. That tells."[47]

The arrival of the overland also would bring secular rewards. In a state well past the heady years of gold seeking and the forty-niners, the railroad would usher in a new age of prosperity and resurrect California's flagging economy.[48] Mooar described the future: he saw "very wonderful advances, before the generation of 'forty-niners' has passed away, before the first of their children have reached the middle of life." The coming of the railroad was unlike any other event that California or the nation had yet experienced. It was to be a momentous, even millennial, portent of magnificent things to come. Speaking to his parishioners in May of 1869, Reverend Mooar urged them to maintain their excitement and optimism, to be "jubilant" and "expectant." All were, he said, "except a few ravens."[49]

The exuberance of Mooar's sermon captured in miniature much of the nation's fevered excitement over the building of the transcontinental railway. In typical nineteenth-century fashion, Americans looked first to God, thankfully receiving the products of heavenly design. Whether it was to hasten the godless to religion or simply allow isolated Californians to "touch more closely our christian brethren," the railroad fit squarely into a body of Christian doctrine. And because the overland railway had been judged godly, it was legitimate to celebrate the economic prosperity that it would certainly bring; for, as Reverend Mooar noted bluntly, "nobody owns so much stock in this railway as [the] Lord." In short, the grand railroad project offered an undeniably powerful metaphor: for church building, for Christian enterprise, for thinking and dreaming on a mighty scale.

But what did the transcontinental railroad's arrival mean beyond symbol? Certainly the iron artery to the East revolutionized western commerce, manufacturing, and trade. And the railroad forever changed the scope and importance of western tourism and emigration. All these changes had been predicted and championed by the booster promoters of the overland railway. Furthermore, the arrival of the railroad clearly and immediately changed those California communities that lay along its route. Oakland, because of its strategic position as Central Pacific terminus, felt the railroad's influence sooner than most towns. Even by the early spring of 1870, the village looked very different than it had the previous year. "All of the great railway systems have already begun to center here," wrote one enthusiastic resident. "The foundation of an immense city has been laid."[50] Broadway, the town's major thoroughfare, had been extended to the base of the foothills three miles away. Telegraph Avenue now ran north all the way to the new state university (which would move to neighboring Berkeley in 1873). Construction crews graded and paved new streets, and the city's population swelled to upward of ten thousand. "So far this year about 80 houses have been put up in this place beat that if you can," boasted one Oaklander in a letter to a friend.[51] A year later, a young student at the University of California described Oakland for his mother back home in tiny Los Angeles: "You have no idea what a big city is. There is such a noise going on all the time and so much smoke and dust. *Oakland* is a very large place."[52]

But such enthusiasm reflects a skewed and unfocused view of the iron horse. Steaming placidly in the background of countless guidebook sketches and lithographs, the railroad seemed to fit pleasantly on the landscape. Orderly farms and quaint farmhouses nestled beside silent orchards, and beautiful vistas complemented the straight and true lines of railroad track. Railway expansion and American progress were one and the same. Railroads and sturdy American yeomen went hand in hand as the nation subdued and civilized the Wild West, drawing straight lines in the wilderness with their fences, roads, and railroad tracks. But this booster view of the railroad was as rose tinted as it was calculated. A railroad could not add quaint charm to a rural or small-town landscape. On the contrary, the railroad—an apt symbol of the blunt and violent "civilizing" process of westward expansion—overwhelmed its surroundings. And Californians were forced to deal with its ambiguous effects. Railroads were not unknown to Californians in 1869, but the transcontinental was strikingly different. Its presence, whether it was roaring down the streets of Oakland at fifty miles an hour to its San Francisco Bay terminus or steaming out of the shops at Sacramento, was simply (constantly) unavoidable.

At the outset, Californians had to adjust to the jarring effect the railroad had on the senses. No less an observer than Nathaniel Hawthorne had noted earlier in the century that the locomotive brought "the noisy world into the midst of our slumbrous peace."[53] Such an observation could be as true in the literal sense as it was in the figurative: in an era accustomed to keeping large machinery behind factory walls, railroads disrupted tranquil landscapes by their clatter and accompanying "reek of steam." Noisy, smelly, and smoky trains had perplexed Americans since the early days of locomotion experiments and tests, prompting what Leo Marx has termed railroad-induced "psychic dissonance."[54]

As legions of nineteenth-century writers remind us, there was a world of difference between knowing *about* the railroad and knowing it firsthand. Many people in Oakland and elsewhere in California probably had never before ridden in a railroad car. Railroad travel could be an experience of equal parts terror and exhilaration. From our late-twentieth-century vantage point, it is perhaps difficult to appreciate the psychic price exacted by a short ride at twelve or fifteen miles an hour.[55] As one early rail traveler anxiously described the experience: "It is really flying, and it is impossible to divest yourself of the notion of instant death to all upon the least accident happening."[56] The fear of railroad wrecks permeated the consciousness of early travelers and required a concentrated effort to dispel. Once travelers accepted wrecks as statistically unlikely, railroad journeys could be relatively trauma free. But the repressed fear could easily reemerge: let anything on the journey appear out of sync—a jarring lurch of the car, a shrill whistle, or a whining steam engine—and fears of imminent disaster returned with a vengeance.

The invention also brought about profound changes in the understanding of time and the relationship between time and space.[57] To nineteenth-century observers, at first unable to adjust to the changes wrought by the machine, the railroad simply "annihilated time and space."[58] They had to acquire a new understanding of distance and the duration of journeys; places that once were remote became, in effect, closer and more accessible. The contrast in such a short period of time was astounding. When the transcontinental railway was completed, there were many Americans alive who remembered the cross-country explorations of Lewis and Clark only sixty years previous.[59]

Reorientation of spatial concepts had a powerful physical dimension as well, expressed in the railroad's reshaping of the topography of the United States—urban, rural, and in-between.[60] As Shelton Stromquist has written, the "redirection of land settlement, townbuilding, and the flow of commerce and immigration along new rail lines restructured the pattern of urban growth."[61] By providing reliable and quick transportation to urban business districts, the railroad eventually created commuter suburbs. Residential stratification on class lines gradually increased as middle- and upper-class neighborhoods bubbled up along suburban spurs; downtown areas (the "wrong" side of the tracks) became the exclusive housing domain of the poor and working class. Suburbanization, in effect, "insulated the bourgeois peripheries from lower-class invasion."[62]

Despite enthusiastic claims from many nineteenth-century commentators that the railroad actually broke down class barriers, it did just as much to confirm them.[63] Suburbanization was only one method by which railroads tacked down the class hierarchies required of the energetically capitalist nation. In areas of managerial hierarchy, labor and government relations, and even day-to-day operations, the railroad corporation re-shaped large-scale American business, complete with strictly defined class boundaries. Furthermore, the creation of vast railroad fortunes helped increase the gaps separating working, managerial, and upper classes.[64]

As an agent bearing profound physical, psychological, and social change, then, the railroad represented an intrusion of astonishing proportion and variety into mid-nineteenth-century American communities. Not only was the effect of the technology extraordinarily diverse, but the railroad itself was no single entity or idea. Just as the physical expression of "the railroad" incorporated a system of many elements (track, cars, engines, etc.), the social meaning of "the railroad" was equally complex. Machine, corporation, set of entrepreneurs, even a horse-drawn car—the railroad was all of these things. And each representation carried with it deep and lasting change. Most Californians adapted remarkably well to the railroad-ordered transformation of their society. Emerson's surprised observation of railroad workers, toiling with unconcerned diligence as a locomotive thundered by, could just as easily describe California's accommodation of all that the railroad represented: "Strange proof how men become accustomed to oddest things."[65]

An Iron Empire

Accommodation to the physical expression of the railroad was one thing. Making sense out of the corporate side of railroad expansion required assimilation on a different scale. Californians, like Americans the nation over, had little experience with corporate conglomerates the size of the Central Pacific Railroad. Their day-to-day world was profoundly rural—rapidly changing, yes, but still built largely on the familiarities of localized commerce and petty entrepreneurship. The growth and mounting influence of the railroad company amazed and frightened these people.

Making good on their dreams of an iron empire, the Big Four began to rake smaller railroads into a growing Central Pacific pile. No other railroad consortium could hope to garner the funds or bureaucratic machinery to operate extensive rail networks to the extent accomplished by the Big Four. Even before the celebrated tie-up at Promontory Point, the best-laid plans of Central Pacific executives pointed to corporate expansion at a fearsome rate. Especially anxious for aggrandizement was Collis Huntington, likely the brightest of the Central Pacific's directors and surely the most ruthless. "I would control that Southern Road even if it took a very high figure," he wrote to Charles Crocker in June of 1868, referring to a transcontinental route cutting across southern California. From there the company could move on to monopolizing all rail transportation west of the Rockies.[66]

Such expansion required massive capital outlays. For the most part, the Central Pacific relied on Collis Huntington, now living in New York, to oversee the complicated financial ballet inherent to railroad capitalization. But there was plenty to be done in California as well. Towns and communities required coaxing to help defray the costs of railroad building through bond subscriptions; local governments and perhaps even the state could likewise be enticed. "You write of getting aid from the State and counties," Huntington wrote to Leland Stanford in early 1870. "I do hope you will get it from the counties; we expect it; and if you can get some from the State, do so, for God's and our sakes, for I am satisfied that unless we get much aid we better stop building roads."[67]

Despite the melodramatic tone of claims such as these, Huntington, no less than his partners, had little intention of quitting. The story of California railroading through the 1870s is largely one of consolidation into the massive conglomeration headed by the Big Four. Much of the gathering up of both rival and new railroads was done quietly: "We should . . . not let it be known that we control the organization," Huntington wrote of one scheme.[68] In any event, by the fall of 1870 the Big Four had gathered a gigantic collection of railroad companies into the protective arms of the Central Pacific. Into the pile went the Western Pacific; the California & Oregon; the San Joaquin Valley; and the San Francisco, Oakland, & Alameda railroad companies. The Central Pacific itself would later be folded into the giant parent holding company, the Southern Pacific, which ate up even larger railroads. Huntington even thought about obtaining a controlling interest in the Union Pacific.[69]

Although at times they petulantly threatened to retire from the railroad business for one reason or another, company officials concentrated much of their energies (Huntington stands out among his partners in this regard) on meticulous supervision of their railroad projects. Little escaped their attention. If an opposition newspaper got in the way, it might face a buyout or be forced to compete with an invigorated railroad-backed paper. Even the state constitution might be altered. When foreign investment in the Central Pacific slacked off, apparently because of a clause in the California constitution regarding stockholder liability, Huntington asked Mark Hopkins to work on deleting the offending stipulation. No one need know that the railroad corporation sponsored the change; in fact, the railroad should try to make it appear that company enemies sponsored the change. Perhaps Hopkins "could find some cowboy or Democrat to make the move—some one that has some interest in having it done, so that parties would not mistrust that we wanted it."[70]

Increasing Opposition and Disillusionment

Californians looked on the growing corporate railroad presence with trepidation. What would the exercise of monopolistic corporate power mean to individuals? As the decade of the 1870s began, antagonism to the railroad corporation surfaced with increasing regularity. A chief expression of such opposition occurred in the state's political arena, in the shape of debate over railroad subsidies. Anti-subsidy activists, strong in both major parties, demanded an end to what they viewed as financial coercion of local populations by railroad corporations. The corporation's ability to demand subsidy payments from towns or counties along its proposed route only strengthened the power of the monopoly.[71] Invigorated by the intellectual force of such leaders as Henry George, the subsidy issue quickly metamorphosed into a referendum on the merit of this new kind of corporate power.

Governor Henry H. Haight took a prominent role in opposing subsidies, a stance that helped sharpen and focus a vague yet growing disillusionment with the railroad. The people of the state had already paid dearly for the construction of the Central Pacific; and while that dedication had helped bring about the completion of the transcontinental railroad, it had also helped make the Big Four phenomenally wealthy. Haight opposed further legislation that would provide corporate subsidies, because he regarded such subsidies as an unjust form of taxation. His view prompted concerned advisers to urge caution. Haight also earned the enmity of the Central Pacific: "We must beat Haight some way," Collis Huntington wrote to Charles Crocker.[72] One Haight adviser, Edward Tompkins, insisted that construction subsidies and further railroad expansion were "absolutely vital to the development of California," and Haight's association with an ostensibly anti-railroad stance worried him.[73] "That the Rail Roads will add immensely to the prosperity and wealth of the State, no one questions," Tompkins wrote to Haight. "They are then much to be desired: That the People having the benefit, ought to bear a reasonable proportion of the cost, hardly admits of an argument." Any argument to the contrary was both illogical and reactionary and proved "the existence of a prior race, that has no affinity with the present, and . . . ought to be extinct."[74]

But Haight maintained a steadfast antagonism to the subsidy system, which he thought "so corrupting and so destructive of wholesome legislation." He had considered retiring from politics, but the subsidy contro-

versy prompted him to run for reelection in the 1871 gubernatorial campaign at his party's insistence. Haight wrote that he had little choice but
to run: the Democrats could come up with no other viable candidate, and
the "combination already formed in the interest of the Central Pacific R.R.
Co. would have a clear field and the state would pass under the control of
that corporation. This at last became my own conviction and induced [my]
tardy assent."[75] Such selflessness notwithstanding, Haight's Republican
opponent, Newton Booth, was also a confirmed anti-monopolist.

The issue to Haight was one of political and party independence. Would
hard-working Californians be forced to support the get-rich-quick schemes
of railroad builders? The question was simple: "whether the homestead
and property—large and small—acquired by industry and enterprise shall
be enjoyed by its owner subject only to taxation for legitimate govern-
mental purposes or whether it shall be in whole or in part wrested from
its owner to fill the coffers of those who for their own profit choose to
embark in railway construction and who have already at public cost ac-
cumulated colossal fortunes."[76] The positive effects of railroad construction
could not offset the evils of unfair taxation. "It is, to me, inexplicable that
men claiming to be imbued with the pure democratic principles of the
olden time should fail to denounce and resist this monstrous system of
taxing out of existence farmers and small property holders in order to add
to the surplus of those already enriched out of the public treasury and the
public domain."[77]

In what would in later years become a stereotypical California political
assurance, Haight was careful to distance himself from what he thought
of as radical railroad antagonism. "I am far from cherishing hostility to
corporations within their proper sphere," he insisted. "These combinations
of capital execute works of great public utility and ought to be fostered by
all legitimate methods but we object to their conversion into agencies for
public plunder and we also object to placing the government in the hands
of their managers and making the people their serfs and tributaries."[78]

Haight's opposition to subsidies would not prove vigorous enough as
far as voting Californians were concerned. As the 1870s began, more and
more Californians held the railroad responsible for the state's malaise, and
antagonism to rail subsidies did not satisfy their complaints.[79] Doubts had
of course been murmured about the railroad's capacity to uplift the entire
state ever since the transcontinental system had been proposed. But the
1870s witnessed the rise to prominence of political figures whose railroad
antagonism formed the basis of much of their popular support. The Republican Party latched onto Newton Booth as its gubernatorial candidate,
and Booth himself latched onto strident anti-railroad opposition. The

successful 1871 gubernatorial campaign of Booth (he who had welcomed the Central Pacific in glowing terms just a few years earlier) was based largely on opposition to railroad subsidies, corporate monopoly and the dangers it posed to the republic, and the railroad's ownership of huge amounts of land.[80]

A short time later, as the candidate of the hybridized People's Independent Party, Booth jumped from the governor's office to the U.S. Senate; again he made the "railroad issue" a crucial part of his campaign. In speeches before voters, Booth declared that the coming of the rails had revolutionized the state, that the "old order of things has been destroyed by the new." But that change was not all to the good. Couching his critique in classic terms, Booth argued that the railroad managers' overwhelming power threatened the independence and liberty of every Californian. Booth took pains to point out that he was not suggesting that the railroad officials were "different from other men, or that they have met together in a conspiracy to do a particular thing, and are methodically proceeding upon a fixed plan." But their control of corporate and technological capital necessarily placed them in positions inviting tyranny. "The means are in the hands of a power that claims to be, and seems to be, independent of law and public opinion."[81] It was as if the railroad itself, by allowing men like Stanford, Huntington, Crocker, and Hopkins to control it, had betrayed the people of California.

Booth even suggested at times that the government might need to take over some railroads, at least those that had been the greatest beneficiaries of federal land and money. Booth also recognized one feature of the "railroad question" that would dog railroad opponents throughout the nineteenth century: railroad supporters charged that anti-railroad sentiment equaled reactionary, even Luddite, behavior. Those who opposed the political strength of the corporation were accused of wanting to eliminate the railroad presence entirely from the state.[82] Booth and others argued that their railroad antagonism was not aimed at technology but rather at the dangers of monopoly and corporate bigness. "It is as easy as it is brutal to say, if you do not like 'our' railroads you can go back to ox-carts and pack-mules," he declared. But it was not the technological machinery of railroading that Booth and others like him bridled against; it was the corporate invention that they fought. The people of California, these early railroad opponents argued, must unite to oppose the threat posed by the railroad corporation and its owners, not the tracks and trains themselves. "God in heaven!" Booth thundered. "You are two hundred thousand— they are three!"[83]

The subsidy issue was but one of a growing number of complaints.

Land, too, was intricately associated with the railroad question. Of course, land had long been a critical and sensitive western subject, well before "the West" had come to mean the region beyond the Rockies, or even the Appalachians. But with the granting of gigantic plots of land to newborn railroad companies, the land issue took on a compelling urgency. In his 1871 book *Our Land and Land Policy*, Henry George had referred with surprise and wonder to the extent of the railroad land grants. "Just think of it!" George exclaimed. "25,600 acres of land for the building of one mile of railroad. . . . And this given to a corporation, not for building a railroad for the Government or for the people, but for building a railroad for themselves; a railroad which they will own as absolutely as they will own the land—a railroad for the use of which both Government and people must pay as much as though they had given nothing for its construction."[84] In the early stages of working out the theories that would find expression in *Progress and Poverty*, George realized that the state's economic inequities must be addressed; otherwise, the potential for social upheaval would only increase. And the state's future—good or bad—was intricately related to its dealings with the railroad.

William G. Morris and H. C. Bennett, in their 1872 tract *An Essay on the Manufacturing Interests of California*, had suggested a similar connection between the completion of the railroad, the state's economic problems (discussed in chapter 2 of this book), and the implicit threat of unrest. "It is neither just nor politic, under the existing state of affairs, to compel the working classes to bear all the effects of the change in business brought about by the completion of the trans-continental railway," they wrote.[85] Casting about for answers to the state's plight, Bennett and Morris settled on "sinister influences," which kept people, especially boys and women, from laboring in the manufacturing industries. Presumably, then, the mysterious and newly arrived forms of railroad-sponsored business and capitalist enterprise—and not the railroad itself—had caused the problems.

Part of the disillusionment over the transcontinental railway's completion and proposals for further railroad construction clearly resulted from the exaggerated expectations that had surrounded the building of the Central Pacific. The revolutionary effect of the railroad—the massive influx of tourists and settlers, the tremendous growth of cities and towns, the rising tide of prosperity—did not immediately follow the "marriage of the rails" at Promontory.[86]

Caspar T. Hopkins, president of the California Immigrant Union, wrote dejectedly of the railroad's failure to carry waves of new immigrants to the West. (Chinese laborers brought to the state by the railroad company did not count: the union wanted easily assimilable, hence white, immigrants.) "We are forced to stop and ask what there is in our civilization that is so shrunken and shrivalled by the magnetic current setting towards us through the iron conductor from the East." According to Hopkins, the solution required an almost metaphysical appreciation of California's railroad-produced connectedness to the national and international economy. "We are led for the first time in our existence—hitherto isolated—to look beyond the present moment, to study the past and contemplate the future, in order to derive from the experience of the remaining ninety-nine and a half percent of the world's population, the facts and figures wherefrom to work out our own destiny."[87]

The transcontinental railroad plainly could not meet the extraordinary expectations placed upon it. The mere introduction of a railroad to the California landscape was bound to produce problems and unforeseen consequences—features that we will address in later chapters. Moreover, the corporate and bureaucratic machinery required to keep a massive railroad operation running carried with it associations and meanings that were bound to provoke antagonism. Even the vaunted Big Four would increasingly come under the glare of less-than-admiring public scrutiny. They faced castigation for violating the trust of their fellow Californians; they had built the overland, but they could no longer claim motives of civic duty free from self-interest.

The railroad and the railroad corporation would always have their faithful supporters. But, just as certain, the railroad would always face opposition, and always for a multitude of reasons. Journalistic and political insistence that "the anti-railroad war is a profitless enterprise" and ought to be discontinued was but a vain and uninformed wish. "It will be a relief to the people of California to have this railroad excitement subside," the Oakland *Daily News* reported in 1872. "It keeps up a feverish, nervous feeling, injures business and retards the progress of permanent improvements."[88] But that "railroad excitement," whether prompted by debate over subsidies, terminus locations, fares, or routes, would not evaporate. It would be as easy to tear up railroad tracks as to squelch railroad antagonism. Even before the laying of the first rail on a wet January day in 1863, the railroad was simply too important and too powerful not to be fought over and fought with.

"The railroad has become almost a necessity to us now," a young California emigrant wrote to his mother early in 1872.[89] For trade, commerce, culture—even, as this letter writer described, for mail from home—the overland railroad had immediately become "almost a necessity" to Californians. Equally crucial, at least to certain groups in the society, was the necessity of railroad opposition.

2 "California Netted with Iron Tracks"

> You can get any man to be unfriendly
> with a railroad after it is built.
> —Charles Crocker
> Crocker Papers

In his memoirs, California journalist James Ayers wrote of a visit to Leland Stanford's Nob Hill mansion in the late 1870s. The proud railroad magnate guided Ayers around the two-million-dollar palace, showing him the innumerable works of art, famed Chinese room (a gift to Stanford from the Chinese embassy), and other treasures—all testimony to Stanford's *nouveau* and very *riche* status. Just as Stanford was showing off one of his prized possessions, a vase that Marie Antoinette had reportedly given to a favorite nobleman, a commotion erupted in the streets below. A crowd of men and boys had gathered outside, yelling and jeering at Stanford. The railroad executive treated the episode as a joke, Ayers writes, seemingly unconcerned with the rantings of ne'er-do-wells. But Ayers, perhaps more aware of the lessons of history (and certainly more melodramatic), thought the incident and its timing "ominous." To him, the scene conjured up images of regicide. Could the crowd below be a California version of the massed *Parisiens* who seized and executed the French queen in 1793? Ayers wondered if the street scene might foreshadow revolution: "Were the mutterings that reached us the first symptoms of an uprising that might some day blindly lead its cohorts into the very house where that fatal vase now stood?"[1]

Although Gilded Age California was quite unlike revolutionary France, Ayers was right to recognize at least some similarities, tenuous or not. California did possess its own monarch; Leland Stanford *was* the closest thing to a California king. The wealthy politician and railroad builder lived a life of influence and royal splendor.[2] Ayers was equally shrewd, though certainly overzealous, in his pairing of California political upheaval with revolutionary France. Although the California Jacobins stopped well short of regicide, they nonetheless altered the shape of their society by rearranging the state constitution; and many of their grievances against the California political, economic, and social status quo were not terribly unlike those of the eighteenth-century French citizenry. Yet the French revolutionaries did not face one question, inescapable in California: What was to be done about the railroad?

The transcontinental railroad had not lived up to its billing. It had not miraculously transformed the state into the Eden that its boosters promised—a shortcoming that few besides Henry George had dared predict. On the contrary, the arrival of the railroad coincided with local economic downturns: problems that would only worsen in the great national depression of 1873. Already caught in the volatile cycles incumbent to large-scale mining operations and bonanza agriculture, the state economy was now rail-linked to the East and Midwest; the result of such embeddedness could easily be seen in the crazy spirals and collapses throughout the early years of the 1870s. Instead of the dynamism that the railroad was supposed to herald, the state experienced economic stasis, even decline.[3] Many Californians blamed the railroad for failing to bring about the universal prosperity they had been led to expect. Lonely towns and empty town sites, motionless on the brink of success or failure, awaited the promised railroad boom. John W. Reynolds, an émigré from the Midwest, caught the feel of the era in a letter written in the spring of 1875: "San Diego is most awful dull now, nothing doing, and only the hope of future growth keeps most of the people here who are here—The place has been literally built upon hope."[4]

Traveling north to San Francisco, Reynolds observed faith take a desperate turn. A speculative mania gripped the city; speculation was "all the go here—even the mechanics [and] servant girls who get $100 ahead put it into Mining Stocks [and] either double it or lose it in a short time."[5] Hope had become vain hope. The state's critical financial capital was being undermined from within; rampant local speculation in stocks, land, and commodities further destabilized an already dangerously weakened economic foundation.[6]

The situation outside San Francisco was little better. Agricultural and mining regions of the state proved unable to absorb the state's new immigrants; there simply were not enough jobs, not enough gold, not even enough food. Land values skyrocketed, drought cut crop production, and western agricultural practices proved strange and unfamiliar to newcomers. Since the late 1860s, increasing single-crop specialization in wheat threatened to drown out the production of other agricultural staples.[7] "The whole country is poverty-stricken; the farmers shiftless, and crazy on wheat," wrote one state official. "I have seen farms cropped for eighteen years with wheat, and not a vine, tree, shrub or flower on the place. . . . The effect of going through California is to make you wish to leave it, if you are poor and want to farm."[8] Increased rainfall in the winter of 1871–72 led to a brief resurgence of agricultural production and the foodstuff economy, but the springtime crash of the San Francisco stock market then wreaked havoc in the state's rural districts.

Given the restricted opportunities in the countryside, migrants and natives gravitated to cities, especially San Francisco. But work in the city was likewise hard to come by, as foundries, machine shops, and ironworks all felt the pressure of reverses in the mining regions. But that was not all. Thousands of railroad workers were laid off after work on the Central Pacific slowed, and, in the words of one writer, "San Francisco was the Mecca toward which all feet turned."[9] Wages fell. By the early months of 1870, there were seven thousand unemployed in San Francisco.

Chinese laborers made up the majority of those idled by the completion of the transcontinental railroad. After being discharged, most of these workers traveled to the major northern California cities in search of family and work. Chinese populations in Oakland, Sacramento, and San Francisco increased dramatically in the 1870s. "The number of Chinamen here is great," a San Francisco visitor noted in the early 1870s. "One reason [for] the great prosperity of California is the cheap labor of John. He has done a great work here for a little pay and his employers have got rich."[10] The obvious wealth of these employers could hardly diminish the resentment of the thousands of non-Asian Californians struggling with the consequences of a severe depression. In an atmosphere already rife with Sinophobia, crowded Chinatowns exacerbated both racial and class tensions. Bitter denunciations against the Chinese increased (from all sectors of society), and antagonism toward the rail corporation and its top officials— for spilling large numbers of Chinese workers into an already tight urban labor pool—grew as well.[11]

Panic and Poverty in California

Doubtless the railroad brought prosperity to some, the most obvious beneficiaries being the railroad builders themselves. Their ability to equate their own personal success with the economic health of the entire state was nothing short of astounding. For instance, Mark Hopkins, noting in a letter to Collis Huntington late in 1873 that traffic on Central Pacific trains had been high, added: "We have not had here a single suspension or failure. The harvests of the year, in grain and gold, have been abundant. The general condition of the state and all its industrial interests were never better or stronger."[12] By the 1870s, California's Big Four and their top associates had learned the skill that most Americans of the era would neither acquire nor require, that of conspicuous consumption. Ostentatious displays of wealth heralded the arrival of this new West Coast aristocracy, surrounded by even more grandeur than the Comstock Lode silver kings.[13]

With fabulous wealth came displays of appalling arrogance. Crocker's "spite fence" is a prime illustration. Wishing to own all the land around his Nob Hill palace overlooking the city, Charles Crocker tried to buy out his neighbor, an undertaker named Nicholas Yung. When Yung would not sell, Crocker resorted to coercion. Failing at this, Crocker defiantly built a three-story, three-sided fence around Yung's home.[14]

Such ostentation was not without consequence. Once championed as archetypical examples of American entrepreneurial success, the railroad builders came to be seen by many a struggling Californian as perversions of the rags-to-riches tale: too greedy, too powerful, and too wealthy. Mansion-building railroad tycoons continued to live lives of fantastic opulence while thousands around them suffered in poverty. Because they did nothing to assist those thousands, the railroad kings were unable "to break the wave of suspicious dislike."[15]

By the mid-1870s, the words of Henry George had the ring of prophecy fulfilled. What had once seemed blasphemous to predict was now only honest observation: the railroad had not brought plenty and prosperity to all. Financial strain and panic had all but replaced the enthusiasm of railroad boosterism. The coup de grâce came in the fall of 1875, when the Bank of California temporarily closed its doors and mining securities plummeted $60 million in value in just a week's time.[16]

"Bankruptcy, suicide and murder and robberies were the order of the day," Frank Roney recalled.[17] A convicted revolutionary who had taken part in the rebellion of 1867, Roney fled Ireland for the United States after his release from prison. Arriving in San Francisco in 1875, Roney wandered about the city as an itinerant laborer, moving from job to job and one boardinghouse to another.[18] Following one long stretch without any employment, he landed a job at the Union Iron Works, whereupon he worked three straight shifts—day, night, day—to earn enough money to pay his debts. From firsthand experience, Frank Roney knew that San Francisco had little to offer the workingman; jobs were scarce, unemployment high. City relief agencies staggered under the demand for public assistance. "Business very dull and growing still duller," Roney lamented in his diary in the fall of 1875, uncertain whether he could throw off the "dark cloud of adversity."[19]

The new year brought little improvement. A stint loading coal for the Southern Pacific on the waterfront helped, but only temporarily. "Things look mighty blue at present," he wrote in January. "No money, rent due, nothing coming from the room to help to pay the rent, coal nearly out, little food in the house, and worse of all no prospects ahead either to pay what is due or to replace what is nearly out. Even if I get a job it would be a month before I could have any money. God only knows what I will or can do under such circumstances."[20]

John Reynolds, the Midwesterner who traveled the length of the state in search of a reason to stay, gave up and went back to Illinois. California offered little inducement to remain: the southern half of the state remained asleep, and in San Francisco "everything is so over-crowded . . . [and] every place full [and] so many others waiting to fill every vacancy that there is not a chance for a poor man."[21]

The depression continued through 1877. The Comstock Lode's Consolidated Virginia mines withheld a month's worth of dividend payments, amounting to a million dollars; mining stocks caved in yet again. Unemployment in San Francisco reached 20 or 25 percent.[22] As economic historian Ira Cross writes, the depression also impoverished "those who had invested their capital in the state's industrial and mercantile enterprises."[23] "This State has been through two years of disaster, [and] there is at present no bright outlook," wrote commission broker George Kelley in the summer of 1877. Not only was the business depression strangling the economy, but the weaknesses of a provincial and immature commercial system made the situation worse: "You see we have little or no back country," Kelley wrote to a friend, "[and] what there is, is at such great [and] expensive traveling distance, that the system of introducing goods or stimulating trade by travel is almost of a necessity unknown." Kelley confessed that he was in "a terrible business" and frankly did not "quite know how to swim in this maelstrom of speculation."[24]

California's hard times were caused by simple trade inequities and the deleterious effects of a nationwide depression. More than any other single development, the railroad ended California's—and especially all-important San Francisco's—isolated, provincial economic status. No longer could local industry or urban merchants escape competition from their counterparts in Chicago or even New York. This increased commercial activity between East and West generated by the railroad brought the city into closer economic contact with the crushing depression of 1873. Furthermore, the discharge of railroad workers, representing the largest labor force in the state, naturally put great stress on the local economy. The effects of a northern California drought, excessive single-crop agriculture, and rampant, hyperactive speculation only added to the difficulties. And with race and class tensions on the rise, California in the 1870s was poised on the brink of profound turmoil, if not the first stages of what could only be called a revolution.

In his July 4, 1877, oration before the citizens of San Francisco, Henry George had recognized the danger in the state's hardening class structure: "As we see the gulf widening between rich and poor, may we not as plainly see the symptoms of political deterioration that in a republican government must always accompany it?" Like others before him, George was careful to emphasize that his was a systemic critique. He did not necessarily mean to suggest that individual capitalists—the railroad builders were by far the most prominent—were to blame for California's plight. "I am talking of things not men," he assured his listeners.[25] But there were murmurings that men, and especially railroad men, were somehow in part responsible for the state's woes.

As he had been ten years earlier, George was again prophetic. The summer of 1877 brought the greatest class confrontation the nation had yet witnessed, as striking railroad workers clashed violently with federal troops and police in eastern cities. The sensational outbreak of violence threatened to touch off similar disturbances in the West. Workers, railroad and otherwise, had seen drops in wages over the course of the decade, and many blamed railroad corporations and railroad officials for much of the distress.[26]

But if we are to accept the later reminiscences of prominent merchant and civic leader William Tell Coleman, the San Francisco elite at first blindly ignored the outbreak of violence in the East. They apparently believed that the eastern episodes, having at their foundation railroad labor troubles, would be of little consequence in the West. After all, antagonism toward the Central Pacific had not by and large come from the ranks of railroad workers; it had emanated instead from farmers and manufacturers, who were concerned about rates, and from the politicians representing them. And the directors of the railroad corporation had wisely rescinded a proposed wage cut after learning of the outbreak of eastern troubles. Therefore, despite its notoriety, the Baltimore & Ohio strike would find little support in California. "Our people did not think that we would have serious trouble," Coleman remembered, "chiefly for the reason that they looked upon agitation at the east as more a railroad disturbance than anything else, and the Central [Pacific] Railroad and the system having never had serious trouble with their operatives, being generally in harmony, and all parties were satisfied."[27]

But Coleman and fellow pillars of the San Francisco mercantile elite were sorely mistaken and hopelessly naive. As would again happen in the 1894 strike against the Pullman Palace Car Company (to be discussed in chapter 3), an ostensibly narrow eastern labor dispute seemed to provide the impetus for widespread expressions of far western discontent. Much of that antagonism (in both episodes) would be aimed at the presence of the railroad and the railroad corporation on the California landscape and in California culture. What Coleman and other "society savers" failed to gauge at all accurately was the degree to which the railroad occupied the eye of a dangerously unpredictable social, political, and economic storm.[28]

Sinophobia and "Anti-Railroadism" in California Politics

The virulent strain of anti-Chinese racism that pervaded the nineteenth-century California labor movement (and society at large) has been sensitively analyzed in a number of excellent studies. Chief among these is the work of University of California historian Alexander Saxton. In *The Indispensable Enemy*, Saxton argues that the Sinophobia of California's white working class emerged as a defensive reaction to labor's position on the political and social margins of California society.[29] The presence of the poorly understood and easily ostracized Chinese presented whites with an ideal "other," an entire population to be defined out of the republic and declared ineligible for its privileges. By attacking the Chinese, then, one marginalized group could demonstrate that it did not occupy the furthest reaches of "the margin"; there was at least one other easily identified collection of people who deserved even greater insignificance.[30]

The Chinese issue did not make for ideal political capital, however, simply because it cut across so many political lines.[31] Sinophobia was safe terrain, hardly controversial enough to shake up the electorate or forge a partisan political front: everyone believed in it. Outside of the railroad magnates and other large employers, few in California disagreed with the strong bipartisan opposition to the presence of the Chinese. Even Henry George proved a dogmatic opponent of Asian immigration.[32]

Opposition to the railroad also came from all quarters. But what made such antagonism a political issue of greater latitude than Sinophobia was its elasticity. Anti-Chinese behavior and action existed in a realm of vague distinctions, with little separation between points of view or policy aims. Except for murder or arguments in favor of genocide, opposition to the Chinese was primarily of a type.[33] Immigration restriction or exclusion, segregation, commercial and political isolation were all measures that Sinophobes found little to disagree about.

Railroad opposition never had that sort of harmony in California or elsewhere in the nation. Individuals might agree that there was a "railroad problem" but disagree on just exactly what this supposedly singular problem looked like. One "anti-railroad" policy might get agreement across arbitrary class or political lines, and another might invite vociferous disagreement. Various groups could and did clash within the arbitrary confines of the anti-railroad position; the opposition bandwagon was wide enough and deep enough to admit diverse stances that shared, often in only the vaguest "common denominator" fashion, an anti-railroad perspective (a feature also evident in such twentieth-century political banners as anti-communism or anti-fascism).[34] But this weak glue rarely bound together groups that differed in more fundamental terms over the definition of the railroad problem (and, as critical, the definition of "the railroad") or the direction the state was to take toward these entities as the century progressed.

Fights beneath (and for possession of) the anti-railroad banner became, certainly by the early 1870s, one of the defining features of California political expression. Opposing groups even used their anti-railroad credentials or platforms as political calling cards. The battles between railroad antagonists and railroad supporters as well as between various anti-railroad groups were viewed as nothing less than momentous; fighting the railroad—on whatever terms—was a tremendously significant political and social act in California. Depending on ideological sway, "anti-railroadism" could be a righteous crusade or a revolution, the work of pure republicanism or communist agitation. Expression took wildly varied forms: attempts at surgery on the entire body politic or single political-party housecleaning, rhetorical attack on railroad officials, legislative and regulatory strictures, strikes. Since "the railroad" could be a speeding locomotive, a nameless collection of corporate officials, a bought newspaper, or an eminently powerful political lobby, opposition to that object (or objects) was equally varied. It would be misleading and wrong to lump myriad types of railroad opposition into the artificial category of like movements headed by like-minded people.

Taking on the railroad was an action fraught with difficulty. Although the Southern Pacific Railroad did not control events and individuals to the degree that both older and newer commentaries have charged, it *was* an extremely powerful entity nonetheless.[35] The Central/Southern Pacific (the Central Pacific would be swallowed by the holding company Southern Pacific later in the century) was the state's largest corporation, largest landowner, and largest employer. It had rapidly become California's lifeline of commerce and communication as well as the most recognizable symbol of California corporate capitalism. The Southern Pacific maintained an impressive political lobby, was adept at manipulating public opinion, and was itself presided over by wealthy, tremendously influential, and ambitious men.

Regardless of method, then, fighting the railroad corporation was a difficult task. The potential impact of almost any form of opposition could conceivably be blocked or blunted by some arm of the corporation. Even the mere presence of the railroad, its iron network connecting far-flung communities at all ends of the state, bespoke a certain immutable permanence. Rival transportation companies, as well as smaller railroads, faced crushing competition from the sheer economic power of the Southern Pacific. Opponents within the traditional political arena faced a conspicuous collection of railroad supporters possessed of often overpowering financial resources. Antagonistic newspapers faced daunting odds at success unless they made at least nominal concessions to the corporation or allowed their editorial policy to be dictated by corporate officials.

The railroad corporation had its defenders in California, none of course more loyal than the railroad builders themselves. The correspondence and public statements of the Big Four and their underlings are full of self-congratulatory praise as well as condemnation of those spouting anti-railroad sentiment. For the most part, railroad apologists feared that reformers would go too far. Because the railroad—and, again, one railroad in particular—was the prevailing symbol of corporate capitalism in the West, it was assumed that actions aimed at curbing the railroad's influence would naturally permeate through the society and touch every commercial activity in the state. Such symbolic sway only added to the perceived magnitude of railroad opponents' reform efforts. Not only did potential reformers have to confront corporate power; they had to overcome a powerful assumption on the part of many that railroad antagonism equaled economic if not political revolution. One way to overcome that assumption, as exemplified by a movement that sprang up among the working class in San Francisco, was to resort to a traditional rallying cry and a staple of American political culture: the imperilment of liberty.

Denis Kearney and the Workingman's Party

The story of the meteoric political ascension of both Denis Kearney and his Workingman's Party of California (WPC) has been told before.[36] In brief, Irish émigré Denis Kearney emerged from obscurity in the summer of 1877 to lead a vocal and active segment of San Francisco's workers in the creation of a powerful, if short-lived, third-party movement. Speaking from his improvised podium on the sandlots of San Francisco's not-yet-completed City Hall, Kearney attacked the Chinese, vilified capitalists, and blasted alleged political corruption of local and state officials.[37] Before long, the charismatic drayman and recently naturalized U.S. citizen found himself at the head of a potent political movement, which he named the Workingman's Party of California.

One critically neglected aspect of this drama concerns the role that railroad opposition played in formulating and sustaining the Workingman's Party. Railroad antagonism was nearly as crucial to the rise of the WPC as Sinophobia (the sine qua non of the party): the issue helped create Kearney's viable third-party institution and remained a source of potent political sustenance during the party's short life. Not only was railroad opposition a significant component in the makeup of the movement; it also helped bring about a fleeting political alliance between city and country. Foreshadowing later Populist campaigns in California and the nation, the largely urban WPC movement formed a tenuous coalition with the rural discontented. This alliance was to a large degree based on mutual antipathy toward the railroad corporation.[38]

The WPC was a potentially revolutionary movement, complete with prescriptions for racial and class violence. And it did briefly empower the segment of California's urban population that had suffered most from the downturns of the 1870s. The movement also introduced working-class politics and demands into California's mainstream political process.

The rise of the Workingman's Party can be traced to the resonance of two or three related issues in the lives of the urban working class during the "Terrible Seventies." One historian has argued that the typical Kearneyite "was a new social type—a man who had been victimized by the transformation of the economy."[39] Despite its overgeneralization, this assertion is largely true. Facing a stagnant economy, high unemployment, and hardening class lines, the city's working class formed a defensive political cocoon out of an ostensibly reformist agenda. There were many planks to this agenda, including opposition to Chinese immigration, support for various labor reforms, and restriction of corporate influence in the California economy.

But, as we noted earlier, an unavoidable feature of WPC political discourse was railroad opposition. The sheer rhetorical power of "anti-railroadism" as an issue was not lost on Denis Kearney and other WPC leaders. In short, arguing against the railroad would surely draw a crowd. And crowds could conceivably be persuaded to rally, to march, to vote. Given the railroad corporation's near-monopoly status (by the late 1870s, the Central Pacific and affiliate lines controlled more than 80 percent of

California rail traffic), its history of Chinese employment, the awesome wealth of its top officials, and the widespread disillusionment following its arrival, Kearney was wise to attack the corporation. Though the issue seemingly operated at times as little more than a drawing card for rallies, its significance cannot be explained away as merely rhetorical. Admittedly, the urban working class offered fewer specific complaints against the railroad corporation than did the rural discontented (who objected especially to what they viewed as unfair freight rates); nonetheless, railroad antagonism provided group cohesion in the face of what Kearneyites saw as potential tyranny. The railroad threatened the independence of the workingman, Kearney and other WPC spokesmen insisted.

When specific legislative demands were voiced, railroad antagonism often gave way to more traditional concerns of labor: insistence on the eight-hour day, abolition of the convict labor system, prohibitions against Chinese immigration, and popular election of political leaders. But antagonism toward the railroad was a critical facet of labor's republican opposition to monopoly and monopolists.[40]

Kearney specialized in large rallies and extravagant threats against the keepers of California's status quo. At a Nob Hill gathering in November 1877, he attacked the barons of railroad wealth, several of whom had shut themselves behind locked mansion doors only yards from the rally.[41] "The Central Pacific men are thieves and will soon feel the power of the Workingmen," he declared. "When I have thoroughly organized my party we will march through the city and compel the thieves to give up their plunder." Urging his followers to stand with him, Kearney promised to "lead you to the City Hall, clean out the police force, hang the Prosecuting Attorney, burn every book that has a particle of law in it, and then enact new laws for the workingmen. I will give the Central Pacific just three months to discharge their Chinamen, and if that is not done Stanford and his crowd will have to take the consequences."[42]

One instance of plutocratic arrogance especially provoked Kearney's wrath: the infamous "spite fence" that Charles Crocker had erected around hapless neighbor Nicholas Yung's home. Always quick to deliver an ultimatum, Kearney announced: "I will give Crocker until November 29th to take down the fence around Jung's [*sic*] house, and if he doesn't do it, I will lead the workingmen up there and tear it down, and give Crocker the worst beating with sticks that a man ever got."[43] "If I give an order to hang Crocker, it will be done. . . . The dignity of labor must be sustained, even if we have to kill every wretch that oppresses it," Kearney shouted to the two or three thousand people assembled at the Nob Hill rally.[44] Several days later, the scene was replayed. In Union Hall, men and women laughed as WPC members presented a play called "The Workingmen's Riot on Nob Hill," a burlesque on the Crocker family's terror the night of the rally.[45]

Despite the antagonism directed at Crocker, he and the other directors of the railroad corporation expressed, at least at first, little concern over the events. Crocker, in particular, thought that the working class could be bought off through philanthropy. "We are spending some three hundred dollars a day . . . for the benefit of the unemployed workingmen of San Francisco, and it is creating a good feeling towards us, and helping us here in the city, and with the Legislature," Crocker wrote Huntington in early 1878. "These workingmen had been making a great deal of fuss—marching in processions, and demanding 'bread, work, or the county jail.'" But charity had supposedly done its part: "You can have no idea how much good this move has done us."[46] Crocker's naive hopes notwithstanding, the situation in San Francisco looked grim. The Kearney movement remained strong.

"Kearneyism" was a complicated movement that ought to be viewed in a wider light than that cast by its dynamic, eccentric leader. Among the shrewdest of all observers of this movement, not surprisingly, was Henry George. Writing in *Popular Science Monthly* in August of 1880, George reviewed the life and importance of "The Kearney Agitation in California." He argued that the public perception of Denis Kearney was out of line, that Kearneyism did not in fact represent San Francisco's mimicry of the Paris Commune. Nor was California acting out of special regional agendas having to do with socialism or radical agrarianism: "it is yet a mistake to regard California as a community widely differing from more Eastern states." On the contrary, George regarded California, and San Francisco in particular, as quintessentially American. "There has been in California," he wrote, "growing social and political discontent, but the main causes of this do not materially differ from those which elsewhere exist."

George noted the power of the railroad corporation in the state's political economy: "the concentration of the whole railroad system in the hands of one close corporation is remarkable," he wrote. In short, California sketched again the old repressive outline of rich over poor; but in the Workingman's movement the state also exhibited the potential for significant upheaval. Perhaps most intriguing, George wrote that California was not unlike a social laboratory, testing the reaction to what was occurring nationwide: aggregations of capital clashing with rapidly expanding labor organizations. The Kearney agitation, he wrote, "is not the result of the importation of foreign ideas, but the natural result of social and political conditions toward which the country as a whole steadily tends, and its development has been on lines strictly American."[47] Watch California, George urged Americans, to see the arrival of the future, which would then move east. "We have great and increasing accumulations of wealth," George wrote; "capital is becoming organized in greater and greater masses, and the railroad company dwarfs the State." Yet such "progress" in the Golden State did not bode well, and George certainly knew it: "these are not the forces of stability," he cautioned. The state could not hope to prosper until both "the ignorant poor and the ignorant rich" ceased to exist.[48]

Despite his criticisms of the status quo and the burgeoning railroad-borne industrial era, George was no great supporter of the WPC. He suggested that most of the energy required for real social reform had been wasted on emotionalism and foolishness. And in the final analysis, he thought their efforts both naive and essentially conservative.

The 1878–1879 Constitutional Convention

Contrary to what their opponents charged, the WPC and its rural allies were not crazed neo-Luddites out to rip up railroad tracks.[49] The leaders of the movement and its constituent parts followed highly traditional paths by which to implement political aims: electoral success and eventual constitutional revision through coalition politics. Yet the railroad issues were far too significant not to occasion fierce partisan struggles—especially when it came to the rewriting of the California constitution.

By the late 1870s, the 1849 constitution had long since ceased to be effective. The state's population had increased greatly, industrial and corporate expansion had altered the economy, and the disruptions and upheavals of the 1870s added impetus to the necessity for a new constitution.[50] Following impressive political success at the local level (especially in San Francisco and other Bay Area communities), the WPC added to the insistent calls, coming from city and country alike, for a constitutional convention. Though much of their lobbying must be assigned to demands for exclusionary immigration clauses, WPC members also evinced significant antagonism to the railroad corporation—discontent that they hoped to remedy through constitutional innovation. In the spring of 1878, the legislature at last approved the calling of a convention to rewrite the California constitution.

Reactions to the upcoming convention illustrated the fissures separating widely varied political outlooks. The "prize"—namely, the chance to influence the constitutional direction of the state—was simply too dear *not* to provoke battles among opposing groups. Certainly the railroad executives saw little good in the prospect of rewriting the constitution. Confessing that he did not know what the convention would do about railroad matters, Leland Stanford nonetheless wrote that "there is a bad disposition there. Have done what I could to counteract it." Shortly afterward, having looked into the matter more closely, Stanford informed Collis Huntington that the convention "is a dangerous body, and it will not intentionally do railroads any good."[51]

Other conservative powers, or those working on behalf of the railroad, often through the San Francisco *Alta* or *Argonaut*, demanded that Republicans and Democrats immediately fuse in order to circumvent perceived WPC radicals. As the *Argonaut* declared in reference to the convention, "it is of the first importance that the men of intelligence and property, without distinction of party, control the organization."[52] The resulting hasty marriage between Democrats and Republicans produced seventy-seven Non-Partisan delegates, who entered the convention halls in the fall of 1878 with a significant majority.[53]

Even before debate began, it was clear that the convention would be hard fought. Conservatives feared that any revision of property and tax clauses would mean the end of outside investment in the state, or so they said both in public and in private. Checks on the power of the railroad corporation would likewise send an unmistakable message to the nation regarding the state's commitment to the sanctity of private property. In particular, proposals to establish a regulatory railroad commission frightened conservatives. If the commission were created, one editorial insisted, "it would instantly go abroad that California had fallen into the hands of an organization that declared war upon property; and thenceforth we should be shunned by all the world. The emigrant would avoid us. Capital would keep away from us. Real property would depreciate."[54]

To be sure, many delegates, including a few from the Non-Partisan camp, had recognizable anti-railroad or anti-corporation credentials and sentiments. Los Angeles delegate Volney Howard, for example, voiced suspicions of corporations in general, whereas his fellow delegate James Ayers, editor of the Los Angeles *Express*, maintained special hostility toward the Southern Pacific. As he wrote in his memoirs, its arrival in southern California had in many ways been a regional replay of the statewide reception of the transcontinental railroad seven years earlier. The Southern Pacific "had not come up to the rosy anticipations the people entertained when they voted for the subsidy. It was expected that the road would not only open near and distant markets for their products, but that its completion would be soon followed by a great rush of desirable population to their part of the State. They were disappointed in their expectations."[55] On the contrary, the expected stream of immigrants failed to materialize, and high freight rates antagonized local producers. "The feeling against the railroad corporation became very pronounced," Ayers remembered.[56]

When it convened in the state capital in the fall of 1878, the convention had already been sorted into three primary voting blocs.[57] The Non-Partisan group, mostly attorneys, occupied the conservative end of the spectrum, uneasy about any radicalism emanating from the perceived left. WPC delegates, overwhelmingly from San Francisco, made up another bloc. The third bloc was composed of delegates from the state's interior towns and rural districts. It was this third bloc, comprised mostly of farmers, that held the balance of power in the convention; though it generally split its vote or followed the conservatives, this bloc swung left on the "Granger issues," most of which were related to the railroad. Such a pattern allowed the urban WPC members and the rural element the opportunity to form an influential alliance.

Unlike the urban WPC delegates, whose pronouncements were often vague, the farmers formulated a powerful economic critique of the railroad corporation based on their opposition to the structure of freight rates.[58] Many were members of the Patrons of Husbandry, or Grange, an influential society first organized in Washington, D.C., in the late 1860s. California Grange organizations, loosely allied with one another and speaking through the pages of the *Pacific Rural Press*, attempted to attract non-agricultural workers to their organization by their powerfully worded critiques of railroad monopoly. The anti-railroad overlap, or potential overlap, between the dissatisfied in the city and the dissatisfied in the country could sustain a coalition. As Charles Beerstecher, WPC leader from San Francisco, argued shrewdly in the early days of the convention: "We recognize that the Granger element in this state has exactly the same fight to make that the honest artisan and mechanic in the City of San Francisco is making."[59]

Conservatives were quick to belittle the potential reformers and their agendas, eager as they were to cut the ties that might bind anti-railroad delegates. Fearful conservatives charged that those out to alter the ways in which railroad corporations did business were only backward-looking reactionaries, unwilling to accept railroad-borne progress. After all, every other region of the country had accommodated to the changes brought about by railroads, often with even greater disruption than that faced by Californians. Other states had worse railroad problems, delegates insisted. As one Non-Partisan tortuously tried to explain the difference, "The railroad system of this State, and which seems to cause so much anxiety, is like a single drop of rain that falls from the clouds in comparison with the deluge that descends from a Summer storm, when compared with that of other States."[60]

Yet in many ways, it was precisely that sort of comparison which prompted concerted anti-railroad action on the part of the WPC-Grange coalition. In their view, the history of railroad development in the United States, especially the concomitant growth of massive rail corporations, had always been tinged with tyranny. The wealth and arrogant power of the railroad builders threatened the liberty and republican independence of all citizens, yet those same despots remained insulated behind corporate walls. If constitutional provisions could be established to purge the body politic of such dangers to republicanism, all would benefit.[61]

One plausible reason for conservative fears of an anti-railroad jugger-naut, besides real concerns about property, had to do with violence. The specter of violence, which permeated the anti-Chinese movement in San Francisco and elsewhere, influenced the texture of railroad opposition as well. Echoing Kearney's sandlot pledge to hang railroad officials, some anti-railroad delegates in Sacramento's convention halls spoke of retribu-tive violence. Although their statements and promises seemingly sprang more from rhetorical motives than did the racist declarations of Sinophobia (wherein action often followed rhetoric), the violent pronouncements surely must have occasioned some concern. For example, William White of Santa Cruz offered a to-the-point scheme for keeping railroad commissioners—the men elected to supervise corporate conduct—in line: "I say if these Commissioners sell out and betray us, let the people rise and crack their worthless necks on the first tree they can find; that is the bond I want."[62] Similarly, WPC convention delegate Charles Kleine from San Francisco suggested that any railroad official found guilty of ignoring the commis-sion's directions ought merely to be "hanged by the neck until he be dead."[63]

This potentially violent component of the anti-railroad debate should not be surprising. After all, there were plenty of very public incidents that one could point to as examples of the rough side of even post–Gold Rush California life: the shocking assassination of oddly named James King of William in San Francisco, the wounding of Isaac Kalloch by Michael De Young, the subsequent murder of De Young by Kalloch's son, and the countless other instances, public and private, of violent personal attacks. There can be little doubt, then, that the specter of violence stalked the halls of the constitutional convention.

Above all, of course, the convention represented a tug-of-war over power. The state had undergone astounding change since the days of the

Gold Rush, a "rapid, monstrous maturity," as described by a San Francisco journal in 1855.[64] The apparent simplicity of Gold Rush California had disappeared forever. Extraordinarily powerful individuals, most prominent among them railroad magnates, now presided over California affairs to an unprecedented degree. Delegate White, speaking "simply as a farmer," opened a convention discussion by asking fellow delegates to "reflect . . . on the enormous power in the hands of Leland Stanford." White declared that the railroad corporation had overstepped its authority, had betrayed the public trust and support, and had to be stopped lest the foundations of republican government be threatened. A railroad commission, empowered with significant enforcement punch, would help keep corporations in line. White further stated that the position of railroad commissioner must come through election, not appointment by the state legislature or governor; otherwise, the railroad corporation would continue to manipulate affairs to its advantage by working through its supporters in the Senate and Assembly, legally or otherwise. In the most recent legislature, White charged, "there were forty-four men out of the eighty . . . who were always ready to jump on board the railroad car when the whistle blew, and in the Senate the majority was much larger who were pliant tools of the railroad."[65]

Conservatives answered such charges by declaring that it was merely the personal bearing and obvious arrogance of the railroad builders that prompted public ire. Non-Partisan delegates were quick to differentiate between the railroad barons and the corporation they controlled; the railroad company (and, as well, ties, tracks, trains) was above reproach.[66]

Clearly, what preoccupied delegates was the future of California's relationship to one railroad company and to corporations in general.[67] Convention delegates knew that they were hammering out the structure of state regulatory power, using the obvious example of the railroad to create a template. Some wondered whether such regulation could extend past the corporation to technological capital. By offering an unusual resolution, WPC delegate Clitus Barbour suggested the lengths to which railroad regulation could theoretically travel. Since the federal government had provided the wherewithal for the laying of the rails, and since railroad corporations had proven themselves inimical to the health of the republic, why not permit the government to take possession of the tracks? Then, utilizing the legal latitude inherent in the railroads' status as "public highways," the state could allow anyone to run railroad cars and locomotives on the tracks. Competition would thus be assured and the bloated monopoly felled at one stroke.

Morris M. Estee, chairman of the committee responsible for creating corporate regulatory measures, quickly steered debate away from Barbour's proposition: "I don't believe that anybody, outside the owners of the railroads, contemplates running cars upon any of the railroads in this State." Estee, who would in 1882 become the Southern Pacific's choice for governor, recognized that regulating the railroad corporation required a firm approach, but he believed that the state would have to rely on the corporation to police itself, at least partially. "The business is of such a peculiar character that it must necessarily be under the control of one company and one mind," Estee said. "I do not believe there will ever be any practical solution of the railroad problem by allowing people indiscriminately to place and run cars on other people's railroad tracks."[68]

Estee knew that he had to turn debate away from such proposals to more palatable innovations—notably, some sort of regulatory commission. In a number of recent decisions, particularly the "Granger cases," the U.S. Supreme Court had granted states the authority to regulate railroad freight and passenger tariffs. Using this precedent as leverage, WPC and Grange delegates wisely argued in favor of a California Railroad Commission. William White of Santa Cruz, later to be the WPC candidate for governor, told the convention that there were but two ways to control the power of railroad corporations in California: either the railroads should be bought out or a commission formed to regulate freights and fares. White himself had drawn up a draft constitution with a commission amendment before traveling to the convention.[69]

For years, California citizens had been complaining that fares and freight rates were too high; but the state's politicians proved extraordinarily wary of enacting any laws that could cap, or at least regulate, railroad tariffs. As one early report put it, the effect on further rail development would be disastrous, "a door . . . effectually closed against capital seeking this sort of employment."[70] But calls for some sort of regulatory body gained momentum throughout the 1870s. In early 1874, the San Francisco Chamber of Commerce attempted to convince the legislature to develop a railroad commission to set freight and fare schedules. The chamber, speaking through a specially constituted committee, hinted at railroad bribery of public officials and urged that a regulatory body be created to decipher complex railroad economics, since "no one outside the railroad employ knows anything accurately about the nature of that enormous and most complicated business."[71]

Yet there was a great deal of opposition to this early proposal as well. As one local newspaper argued presciently, a commission "would soon become a good thing for the railroad men, for they would readily capture the Commissioners, and matters would be worse than at present."[72] The state legislature of 1875–76 did create the Board of Transportation Commissioners. This body met with mixed success. It had taken the Southern Pacific to court for not divulging enough information about day-to-day operations and the mysteries of railroad economics. In its report to the legislature, the board had blasted stock-watering practices and the tendency toward horizontal integration in the building of the Central Pacific (the most notorious example being the award of construction bids to companies owned and managed by the Big Four). In January 1878, the board recommended four bills, one of which sought additional power for the board in dealing with intransigent railroad companies. The other bills proposed the regulation of freights and fares, prohibition of discriminatory rate practices, and organization of police power on the railroad lines. But, quite clearly at the bidding of the railroad lobby, the legislature responded to the report by essentially emasculating the regulatory agency. An even weaker regulatory option was turned to: a commissioner of transportation, who was little more than a puppet of the legislature and, opponents argued, of the railroad corporation.

The early commission did point to several crucial features of railroad operation and corporate influence in California. It first extolled railroad technology over other forms of transportation, because of its "almost unlimited capacity . . ., its superior speed, safety, and punctuality." The railroad also was "as much a permanent feature in the geography of the country as a river."[73] Furthermore, it did all those things that the American West saw as progress: it encouraged settlement, commerce, stability. Indeed, "the history of all the great West" was one and the same with the history of railroad-spawned communities and cities.

But with that growth and prosperity came an obligation. The railroad corporation must not be permitted to stop running trains to communities in which it had become an integral component. Permitting it to do so would be "differing only in degree, not in kind, from permitting it to tear up its rails and destroy its roadbed."[74] The early commission did, if only implicitly, recognize the railroad corporation's enormous power and influence in the state, a notion that few delegates at the constitutional convention needed to be reminded of.

Convention delegates did not disagree about the railroad's role in the planned growth of the state. All seemed to agree that railroads and railroad tracks were unquestionably positive aspects in California life. What delegates did clash over was how to control the railroad's corporate officials as they moved toward what many saw as despotic power. Conservative delegates were less antagonistic toward the railroad corporation, unwilling to hold it responsible for the state's malaise and fearful of a domino effect should it be attacked too stridently. Non-Partisan delegates especially expressed the fear that harsh anti-railroad measures, whether in freights and fares or taxation, would send a signal to capitalists around the globe that California would no longer tolerate entrepreneurial activity. Many of these delegates viewed the proposed constitutional checks on the railroad corporation's power as a barometer for the social, political, and economic future of the state. If the railroad and the railroad corporation were "shackled," conservatives feared, the entire economy of the state might be jeopardized.

In the period of a month, from early October to early November, convention delegates introduced twenty-seven resolutions regarding corporations.[75] Nine dealt directly with railroads. Morris Estee, as chairman of the "committee on corporations other than municipal," straddled the dividing line between those that supported a "hands-off" policy regarding railroads and those pushing for significant regulation.[76] Clitus Barbour was the only WPC member appointed from San Francisco to this all-important committee, and southern California was at first without any representation at all. Newspaperman and Southern Pacific opponent James Ayers fought to have southern California represented, arguing that "to the people of that end of the state the question of railroad discrimination is of vital importance. We have over four hundred miles of railroad . . . and we would like to have that portion of the state represented on the committee."[77]

The fight was successful: two southern California representatives were appointed to the committee, including parliamentary wizard (and anti-corporation leader) Volney Howard. The committee issued a majority report at the end of October. Several weeks later, two workingmen, representing a minority opinion, issued a report that promoted stiffer regulations for corporations.

Many of the proposed amendments revealed the level of delegate frustration with and anger at the railroad corporation. James Ayers, basing his suggestion on his experience with the Southern Pacific monopoly in southern California, argued that the best way to subvert the economic power of a monopoly would be to make constitutional provisions regarding rate structures. If, in the interests of driving out competition, a rail corporation lowered its rates, it should be required to maintain rates at that artificial level.

Non-Partisan delegates, for the most part, thought the Ayers amendment wrong-headed, if not dangerous. James Hale of Placer County spoke for fellow Non-Partisans when he said that it would be "a gross error" to harness the "engines of progress" in such a manner.[78] Samuel Wilson,

Non-Partisan delegate from San Francisco, echoed Hale's sentiments. Wilson declared that such a policy might invite the disappearance of California railroads altogether, since they might be unable to pay off their federal debt if their rate schedules were so manipulated.

At the same time, conservative opponents attempted to protect themselves from insinuations that they were "railroad lawyers." Non-Partisan Thomas Laine of Santa Clara County pursued a cautious route in voicing his opposition to a railroad commission. "Now, then, it seems to me, that one of the prominent objections to this—and bear in mind that my objection is not because it is too severe upon the railroad corporations—no, sir, I have no objection to that. My objection is not to that." Laine argued that the railroad corporation could easily subvert the commission. Hadn't the railroad already demonstrated that it could effectively control much of the state? "Why, from the year eighteen hundred and forty-nine up to the year eighteen hundred and sixty-five, our whole people were wild upon the subject of the Pacific Railroad. It occupied our thoughts by day and our dreams by night." The state had pledged its financial and political support. "We had all been on their side. We had fattened these corporations, and fawned at their feet, gave them dinners and grand receptions, and there was no such thought as regulating freights and fares. Such a proposition would have been scorned out of existence."[79]

Perhaps in recognition of its status as the lesser of potential evils, many Non-Partisans did support the proposed railroad commission. As delegate Hale argued, the commission would "remove this notorious source of vexation, excitement, and corruption from the halls of our Legislatures, and relieve us from the turmoil which it occasions among the people, and place it where there will be a wise, calm, and just exercise of the power of control by the people of the State over these railroad companies."[80] Another Non-Partisan, Thomas McConnell of Sacramento County, supported the commission in a harsh soliloquy against the Central Pacific. McConnell made it clear that his opposition was not based on any personal animosity toward the Big Four. Rather, he was opposed to the railroad corporation's record of monopoly, misuse of public funds, discriminatory rates, and corruption.[81]

Amid rebounding name-calling—delegates calling one another everything from Communists to corporation lawyers—and constant questioning of opponents' republican credentials, the supposed benefits and dangers of the commission were argued back and forth. If they could not defeat the railroad commission, conservatives at least wanted to retain the right to determine how the three commissioners would be selected. They argued that an elective body would be far too powerful, an extraordinary gift of authority to three individuals. The one clear way to prevent that, given the recent example of WPC and Granger electoral success, would be to make the three positions appointive and not elective. Otherwise, H. L. Barnes declared, the commission might well become "a weapon for the use of the demagogue, in some senseless crusade against capital." Thomas B. McFarland insisted that one would not even "try a Chinaman before such a one-sided tribunal as that." Byron Waters echoed McFarland, arguing that the commission supporters were simply "turning over the people of this State to this Board of three men."[82]

In a decisive ninety-two to twenty-eight vote, the amendment setting up the new regulatory body was accepted. Now it remained for the voters of the state to accept or reject the constitution. Lobbying for and against its passage was intensive. Again the railroad issue was prominent. Conservative opponents of the document, recognizing the popular appeal of the railroad problem, even argued disingenuously that the constitution did not go far enough in restricting the powers of monopoly. Taking a more familiar tack, the same groups insisted that the new constitution "killed" corporations instead of restraining them or that it would provide disincentives for competing railroads. On the left, the more radical wing of the WPC viewed the document critically as well. "A Constitution may be evaded by the rich," one pamphlet argued, "but it surrounds the struggling classes like the atmosphere, and it fits closely upon the laboring masses like knit under-garments." The potential power of the railroad commissioners disturbed many members of the WPC; if the railroad corporation could capture the new body, then the state would be hopelessly beholden to the railroad. The new commission, according to one WPC delegate, was as effective as "crowning Stanford king."[83]

Yet in the spring of 1879, the new constitution, complete with an elective railroad commission, was accepted by the California voting public. The constitution was accepted largely because rural California voted in favor of it.[84] Following ratification, many conservatives reacted predictably. To them, the ways in which the document purported to regulate and tax railroads (and, ostensibly, all corporate entities) sent dangerous messages to potential investors, migrants, and, no less important, other railroad builders. "I fear no one will touch [California] lands since the new Constitution!" wrote Edward Fitzgerald Beale in March of 1879. "I think it has diminished the value of [California] property fifty or seventy five percent. They had better let all the Chinese come that want to, as they will not get any whitemen to live in such a state, or at least to go to it as emigrants."[85]

Neither the fears of conservatives nor the hopes of reformers came entirely true. California did not fall into a stupor of nongrowth, and the considerable power of the Southern Pacific Railroad was not effectively curtailed by the new regulatory body. The railroad commission may have been a welcome weapon in the fight against the railroad, but it was surely not powerful enough to stifle all forms of dissent or to solve all problems. On the contrary, as events in the San Joaquin Valley almost immediately proved in brutal fashion, there were railroad-spawned difficulties that the new commission was woefully ill equipped to cope with.

Mussel Slough

The agricultural hinterlands of central California had been the scene of tensions between the railroad company and settlers for years. Farmers raised their voices in organized or individual protest over a wide variety of railroad ills: the corporation's rate structure, railroad routes that by-passed regional marketplaces, or the propensity for speeding locomotives to smash mercilessly into wandering herds of livestock. But as the 1870s drew to a close, the region around the small town of Hanford in rural Tulare County grew more volatile. There the focus of dispute concerned land and land ownership. In an area called Mussel Slough, increasing numbers of farmers had come to settle on lands ostensibly belonging to the Southern Pacific. Until title was officially transferred from the federal government to the railroad, the legal position of the settlers remained in limbo; they existed in a nether world between squatter and owner. No doubt many of the settlers in the Mussel Slough region were opportunistic gamblers. Betting that the railroad's title to huge tracts of land would be voided by the courts (because of corporate infractions of land-grant pro-visions), groups of settlers had begun moving onto the railroad-reserved sections in the early 1870s. As Richard Orsi has recently pointed out, the number of settlers on railroad land increased to hundreds in a few years; land businesses sprang up to answer the need for title assurances should the railroad lose its claim to the grant.[86]

Shepherded into a loose coalition by self-described lawyer John J. Doyle, settlers filed claim after claim with local and federal officials in their attempt to get the railroad's title to the land rendered void. But Congress declared that the title resided with the Southern Pacific.

In 1878, the Mussel Slough farmers formed the Settlers' Grand League to publicize their position and create solidarity; this organization, cloaked in patriotic rhetoric, served as a paramilitary secret society and demon-stration of resistance to the railroad. Anti-railroad rhetoric escalated; many in the region turned out to hear Denis Kearney speak on the evils of railroad monopoly when he visited in the spring of 1878. Armed Settlers' League members harassed railroad employees and land buyers and formed a cavalry contingent commanded by Confederate Army veteran Thomas J. McQuiddy.[87]

By the late 1870s, the situation in the Mussel Slough region had grown extremely tense. Assured of its legal title, the Southern Pacific began to grade, or evaluate, its landholdings as a step toward sale to other farmers or settlers new to the region. The corporation declared that all occupied lands would first be offered to those in possession. Southern Pacific officials attached price figures to the land, prices that reflected the region's great agricultural promise.

League members protested that the new prices were unfair, that the railroad ought to charge only $2.50 an acre, the price for government-owned public land. They claimed that the railroad corporation was levying upon them charges as high as $80 an acre for the land. The settlers, who by this time were squatters in the eyes of the law, refused to buy and continued to intimidate those who wished to purchase the railroad land. The railroad corporation, never quite certain what course of action to take, tried a conciliatory position one month and a firm, legalistic approach the next.

A major Circuit Court decision in 1879 again upheld the Southern Pacific's right to the land. Many squatters gave up their battle after the decision, but a militant core remained intransigent. The situation in the region deteriorated. In May of 1880, a U.S. marshal, Alonzo Poole, began to dispossess the squatters from the railroad land. On May 11, Poole—accompanied by the Southern Pacific's land grader, William Clark, and two recent purchasers of railroad land—was met by an armed contingent of squatters on horseback. The league members "arrested" Poole and demanded that the others surrender their weapons. Suddenly a horse reared, knocking Poole into the road. Shooting broke out immediately. Five farmers and one of those accompanying the marshal were killed in the shoot-out. Another man who had been in the marshal's party was later found dead in a field with a gunshot in his back. Five squatters were later convicted of obstruction of justice and served light jail terms.

The California Railroad Commission

The tragedy at Mussel Slough, an immediate cause célèbre, provided added ammunition to those who charged that the Southern Pacific had emerged from the reform-minded 1870s stronger and more tyrannical. The activities, or inactivities, of the infant railroad commission seemed to hint at a similar situation. After its formation, the commission dutifully set about its task of hearing complaints about railroad service, discriminatory rate structures, and exorbitant shipping charges. But the three-member group received a lukewarm response from the public. Commissioners Stoneman, Cone, and Beerstecher at first seemed enthusiastic about their responsibilities. They toured the state, taking testimony from farmers and merchants regarding Southern Pacific freight rate schedules. Yet, as the minutes of their meetings make plain, the commissioners were hardly overrun with complaints.[88] Many meetings were adjourned for lack of business; at other times, the body failed to act on complaints because of a confessed lack of expertise in railroad economics or out of strange fits of pique. In Stockton, for instance, a local farmer complained that local railroad employees thought him "a d—— fool" and told him that the railroad "cared nothing for the Commission." The commission refused to hear the farmer's case until he divulged the names of those who told him this story.[89] Not surprisingly, the railroad corporations expressed real hesitation in aiding the commission in any way whatsoever.[90]

Following the commission's slowed activity (news of which was certain to be published in anti-railroad newspapers), public attacks on the railroad corporation and railroad officials intensified. A leading public critic was the San Francisco satirical magazine *Wasp*. San Francisco had never been a friendly city as far as the railroad was concerned, and as the 1880s began, the city's antagonism intensified. Through sharply worded editorials and articles, the *Wasp* and other anti-railroad journals attacked the Southern Pacific for a myriad of transgressions. Crucial to this campaign were the efforts of political cartoonists, particularly the merciless pen of Frederick Keller. *Wasp* satire was not limited to judgments against land monopoly or inflated freight rates. Almost anything was fair game to Keller. One of his harshest cartoons appeared in March 1881: a cartoon depicting California as a cow being energetically suckled by Stanford of the Central Pacific and Crocker of the Southern Pacific. The cartoon was captioned "Sucking Her Dry."[91] Editorial comment on the railroad's power often rivaled Keller's drawings for bitterness: "Of the three vampires which have sucked the life blood of this State—stock gambling, Chinese labor and railroad extortion—the latter is certainly the chief. The miner digs, the farmer plows, the shepherd shears—and Stanford and Crocker take the proceeds."[92]

Wasp editorials even suggested that government ownership of the railroad might be called for.[93] The journal supported the formation of a new political party (not unlike that which had arisen in the early 1870s in opposition to railroad subsidies) or, "better still, the acquisition by the national government of all our iron highways, which might then be run in the interest of the people, and not for the purpose of adding additional millions to the already replete purses of a dozen selfish millionaires."[94] As another editorial argued,

> The Anti-Monopoly party in this State will be a tremendously successful one. The promise is so good that the shrewdest political managers will take hold of it, and in their own interest push it forward in a smooth path which the past has made ready for it. San Francisco has thousands of voters to whom the question needs but to be deftly put (for there are two sides to it) to gain thousands of converts and voters. The State, from Siskiyou to San Bernardino, is in bitter hostility to the Railroad. If proof be needed, the passage of the new Constitution, in the face of grand obstacles, is sufficient.[95]

The journal reserved venom as well for the seemingly paralyzed railroad commission. "The community was startled well-nigh into insanity last Friday morning by a report as incredible as it was novel, viz, that the Railroad's Commission had actually reduced a fare." Even so, this reduction, which took place on a little San Rafael line and not on the Southern or Central Pacific routes, was merely a "sop thrown to a nauseated public."[96] "This idea of a Railroad Commission might almost have been originated by the C.P. themselves," ran one editorial. "It is so obviously easier to—ahem—convince three men than a hundred."[97] The commission presented no threat to the railroad corporations, the magazine editorialized. It was, as one Keller cartoon depicted it, only an annoying, tiny dog yapping at the feet of unconcerned millionaires.

Historian Gerald Nash, in the only comprehensive analysis of the activities of the California Railroad Commission, argues that inexperience and lack of information proved to be greater handicaps to the commissioners than corruption or "corporate capture."[98] Although the railroad corporation did possess greater levels of expertise when it came to rate scheduling, corruption was no less a part of the story. Following the public outcry against the commission's inactivity, the California legislature launched an investigation, wherein it was revealed that not only was Beerstecher $20,000 richer since his appointment but that Commissioner Cone had recently made a $100,000 profit on a questionable deal.

Beerstecher came in for special attack, not only from the press, when he tried to explain away his sudden wealth. He at first declared that it had come by way of an inheritance from his parents. But when those same parents arrived from Germany, very much alive, that explanation for a

$20,000 windfall wore thin.[99] In the May 20, 1881, issue of the *Wasp*, a cartoon berating the railroad commission depicted California as an ass being ridden by the railroad magnates and a Chinese coolie. The ass has been bridled by the railroad monopoly and is being beaten with the twin clubs of "fares" and "freight rates." Astride the ass, Leland Stanford literally has the railroad commission in his hip pocket. A dangling cage contains "The Poor Mussel Slough Settlers," captured by the railroad company's supposedly unfair land policies in the Central Valley. Also at the whim of the magnates is the 1881 legislature and a headless constitution. The cartoon's caption asks, "When Will This Ass Kick[?]"; and the subcaption reads, "A Case for the Society for Prevention of Cruelty to Animals."

Legacy of the 1870s

Capitalizing on waves of popular antagonism toward the railroad corporation, both major parties trotted out recognizable anti-railroad leaders in the gubernatorial election of 1882. Democrat George Stoneman had been the only railroad commissioner to emerge untainted from the first term of the new regulatory body. Republican Morris Estee had achieved prominence in his role as chairman of the convention committee most responsible for the commission's birth. Both candidates stood on explicit anti-railroad platforms. Certainly the two parties differed on many matters relating to such control, but the legacy provided by the 1870s, and the lasting impact of the incorporation of working-class and rural California demands into the traditional party politics, promoted a real change of direction in political affairs. As historian R. Hal Williams notes, "no party could fail to include a vigorous denunciation of railroad oppression and a demand for increased government regulation of corporate affairs."[100]

One historian has termed the anti-railroad groundswell culminating in the new constitution "blind but grimly vindictive."[101] Yet such opposition was hardly blind or vengeful, although it may sometimes have been unfocused and unsophisticated. The constitutional solution of a railroad commission may have been simplistic. But its creation did symbolize the degree of power that had been mobilized by, at first, a working-class cross section of the society and, as regards the constitution's ratification, a sympathetic response from the countryside. As much co-optation as anything else, the mainstream adoption of the "Railroad Question" offered the Republican and Democratic parties a ready-made political package. It remained to be seen just what they would do with it.

3   A Volcano at Any Moment
The Pullman Strike in California

Industrial contests take on all the attitudes and psychology
of war, and both parties do many things they should never
dream of doing in times of peace. Whatever may be said,
the fact is that all strikes and all resistance to strikes take
on the psychology of warfare and all parties in interest
must be judged from that standpoint.
—Clarence Darrow
c. 1894

Railroads are good things. So are rivers, but not when
they rise above their banks and deluge and destroy.
—Thomas V. Cator
San Francisco *Weekly Star*, 1890

After the excitement of the constitutional convention and the Mussel
Slough murders faded, the 1880s witnessed a period of relative quiet
between the railroad corporation and its various opponents. Antagonism
to the railroad did not disappear by any means, but it seldom reached a
comparable level of influence or notoriety. In the political arena, both
major parties continued to adopt planks decrying the monopolistic actions
of the Southern Pacific and that corporation's concomitant influence in
the halls of government. Democratic victories in the 1880 and 1882 elections brought reform elements to the fore. Efforts to enact change, however, proved difficult. As California writer Rockwell Hunt grandly lamented long ago, "sincere efforts at reform seemed like the beating of the
feeble waves of a mill pond against Gibralter."[1]

The publication of the infamous Colton letters in 1883 accentuated the
railroad corporation's troubles. These exchanges between Collis Huntington and David D. Colton, an important railroad official (the fifth of the
"Big Five," or the "Half" of the "Big Four and a Half"), detailed lobbying
and political efforts of the Central Pacific during years of rapid consolidation and growth in the 1870s. The letters were made public after Colton's
death in the course of legal proceedings begun by Mrs. Colton to recoup
assets from the Big Four. They not only divulged Colton's own shady
derrings-do as a financial officer in the corporation but also revealed

questionable behavior—including hints of bribery, influence peddling, and corporate meddling—at all levels of government. Newspapers and political figures responded all across the state, as well as in Washington, with collective "I told you so" declarations of outrage.[2]

The Southern Pacific had further trouble when it challenged California's tax system. As part of the legacy of the new constitution of 1879, railroad capital had been taxed differently from capital held by other corporations or individuals. In the early 1880s, the Central Pacific went to court with constitutional challenges to the state taxing system and also withheld its tax payments. The courts initially decided against the corporation; it was not until the relevant cases reached the California Supreme Court that the railroad's position was upheld. The controversy did not stop there, however, as angry Californians, Governor George Stoneman among them, blasted the Central Pacific's cheek as well as the state's timid response to such corporate aggressiveness.[3]

Despite these events, the relationship between the railroad corporation and the people of California eased in the 1880s—partly because the company relaxed its monopolistic grip on transcontinental freight and passenger traffic, at least in southern California. The Atchison, Topeka & Santa Fe Railroad broke through the S.P. barrier first in southern California, arriving in that region in 1885. The resulting (if temporary) rate war between the two transportation giants helped spawn and sustain a population and growth boom. "You would have thought all the United States and a part of Canada were on the move," remembered one railroad employee.[4] By the fall of 1886, newcomers to Los Angeles had to line up for rooms to rent, as tourists and immigrants alike discovered the "semi-tropic" paradise of the southland. "The town is just bursting with tourists," wrote one Angeleno in the fall of 1886; "for the last five days they have come in excursions nine or ten sleepers full at a lick. Every thing is full to over flowing and people who live here are just coining money." Prosperous times no doubt helped lessen railroad antagonism; the Atchison, Topeka & Santa Fe, in particular, was hailed as the savior of southern California.[5]

Important, too, to a somewhat changed railroad climate was the state's inability to do anything about rate schedules and structures. Not even the findings of a massive federal study in the late 1880s, which reported on the railroads' manipulation of freight rates, prompted concerted action in California.[6] In an era just prior to bureaucratic courting of expertise, the railroad commission remained handicapped by a lack of accounting acumen and experience with railroad economics: expert opinion usually came from company employees. Such shortcomings the railroad corporation could, and did, easily exploit.

Apparent lessening of railroad antagonism helped to cut the feet out from under the state's reform Democrats. The creation of the federal watchdog Interstate Commerce Commission at the close of the 1880s only furthered the decline of anti-monopoly politics in the state. With supposed federal intervention, as well as the expectation that competing railroads would continue to arrive in the state, many Californians apparently put their faith in the power of the invisible hand of open competition. The battle cry and political platform of reform Democrats did not disappear— they would resurface on the political left bank with the rise of California Populism. But during the 1880s, issues and platforms changed, and the form of railroad opposition changed along with them. All the while, the railroad and the railroad corporation continued to settle deeper and deeper into the state's economy and political culture.

Also during the 1880s, the state's agricultural prosperity gradually returned. California's farm output increased as more settlers arrived and expanded the range of regional market crops. Irrigation brought water to the desert interior; California's agricultural bounty grew to include a wider variety of vegetables, nuts, wines, and citrus fruits. Such growth relied upon the railroad; and, as in the Los Angeles real estate boom, it is reasonable to suppose that economic expansion went hand in hand with a relaxation of railroad antagonism.

The 1890s and Resurgent Railroad Opposition

But the 1890s brought major changes and new problems. A nationwide depression rocked California, and, as had happened before, the disruption seemed again to rekindle fierce railroad opposition. In depressed times, one could mount almost any political stump, to the right as well as the left, and blast the railroad for a variety of logical, tried-and-true reasons: the company's officials made too much money; the railroad charged too much; inequities between workers and management were too extraordinary; the Southern Pacific hired the wrong workers. In short, the common refrain surfaced: the railway corporation kept California and Californians down.[7] Besides these hardly dormant seeds of discontent, very different types of antagonism appeared: the strident anti-monopoly campaigns of People's Party populists, the reformist whispers of the major parties, the utopian pleas of organizations like Bellamy Nationalist clubs, and the increasingly militant voice of labor unionism. The 1890s came to be a staging ground for determining California's twentieth-century relationship with the railroad and the railroad corporation. Eruptions of the 1890s would force Californians to rework that unsolved equation describing the state of affairs existing between the multitentacled railroad and the state's political economy.

One such eruption, the Pullman strike of 1894, shattered the traditional form and shape of anti-railroad thought and behavior in California. The strike produced a degree of railroad antagonism not before seen in the state's history. The sheer scale of the strike, not to mention its real potential for violence, marked a departure from the various anti-railroad political movements of the 1870s and early 1880s, where expressions of discontent had been largely reserved for varieties of platforms and campaigns. What is more, the Pullman strike arrived in California ostensibly through the efforts of workers, particularly those affiliated with the American Railway Union. Not since the days of Denis Kearney and the assembled crowds of unemployed workers in San Francisco had a worker-centered affair so captured the attention of the state or so provoked the concerns of the rail corporation. The strike in California was in reality far more than a workers' boycott; the Pullman strike signaled the arrival of an especially turbulent period in the state's complex relationship with the gigantic Southern Pacific.[8] With the exception of affairs in Chicago itself, where the strike originated, the Pullman boycott had as great an impact on California as anywhere else in the entire nation. Through an examination of the strike, we can learn a great deal about such critical western issues as insurgent, third-party political movements, the increasing role played by the federal government in western affairs, the specter of anti-railroad violence, and the ever present influence and muscle of corporate power. We can also begin to see better how events of the 1890s suggested patterns and directions for the new century.

Origins and Background of the Pullman Strike

The Pullman strike began in May of 1894 in the "model" industrial town of Pullman on the outskirts of Chicago. Among other duties, workers at Pullman manufactured the luxurious private railcars that insulated well-to-do travelers on railroad journeys throughout the nation. Faced with a considerable wage cut that spring, the Pullman employees initiated a strike. After failing to attract support from more conventional labor unions (generally not about to support unskilled laborers, railroad or otherwise), these laborers appealed to a newly formed labor organization, the American Railway Union (ARU), in a bid for solidarity. Begun in 1893, the innovative ARU admitted railroad workers of all skill levels, thus departing from the hierarchical example of the various railroad brotherhoods. Directed by its founder and president, Eugene V. Debs, the egalitarian union agreed to support the striking workers.[9] The support would be more than token: in late June, Debs ordered all ARU members to boycott trains pulling Pullman cars.

It was generally thought at first that the strike would have little effect in California. "Pullman's Fight Not Expected to Extend to Coast," ran a headline in the Oakland *Enquirer* on June 26, 1894. California nonchalance sprang from equal parts logic and naiveté. Because the ARU was an underground organization, few realized its actual strength, and its numbers were said to be very small. Known ARU members were mostly railroad shop workers, and therefore thought unable to pose any serious threat to the movement of trains, Pullman cars or otherwise. In addition, the Southern Pacific owned outright most of the Pullman cars attached to its trains. It did run cars belonging to the Pullman Company (as did the Atchison, Topeka & Santa Fe), but most people thought that the relatively small number of cars in this category would naturally blunt the impact of any organized boycott of the Pullman Palace Car Company.[10] Finally, few people thought that the strike—ostensibly prompted by an industrial wage dispute thousands of miles away and *not* by the grievances of actual railroad workers—would be sustained by California's more than ten thousand railroad employees, who were commonly believed, at least by railroad management, to be well paid and content.[11]

In hindsight, the "Pullman strike moment" looks remarkably like that of the summer of 1877, when Californians apparently expressed little concern that the Baltimore & Ohio rail strikes of the East could possibly be met by equal trouble in the Far West. Hindsight being perfect, it seems almost unbelievable that shrewd observers did not sound the alarm. Like tinder awaiting a spark, widespread discontent *did* exist in the early 1890s. Popular opinion against the railroad corporation, specifically the Southern Pacific, continued to run high. Struggling again with the effects of a crippling national depression, much worse than that of the 1870s, Californians did not hesitate to blame the railroad corporation for many of the state's woes. The 1880s may have been fairly quiet, but the tide was turning by the 1890s. "We have the slowest railroads, the most stupidly managed, the greediest, in the whole Union," declared one prominent Southern Pacific antagonist at the beginning of the decade.[12] Third-party Populist campaigns, arguing that the conventional party system could no longer adequately address the railroad problem (among other issues), gained momentum in state and local elections in the early 1890s. Thomas V. Cator, one of the state's most influential Populists, played a prominent role in opposing the railroad through his writings and speeches.[13] Populist rhetoric often sketched the state's future as an inevitable struggle between the people and the railroad corporation. If Californians could not lessen the power of the Southern Pacific, one Populist writer declared, "we are politically doomed to serfdom and lasting degradation."[14] Pushed left in part by the example of the Populist platform, both major parties ostensibly supported railroad nationalization in their state gubernatorial platforms of 1894.[15] Other "railroad issues" provoked public outrage; and recriminations against the ineffectiveness or outright criminality of the California Railroad Commission, allegedly corrupted by the railroad corporation, continued to be journalistic stock-in-trade.

Just beneath the surface of such dissent lay an unmistakable potential for violent conflict, or again so hindsight suggests. In an 1891 public letter to Collis Huntington, San Franciscan William Cubery declared that the Southern Pacific had for too long controlled political affairs in California, thereby earning the lasting enmity of the people. Cubery explained in some detail why the people of California "so bitterly dislike you and yours, and why a volcano is forming to burst at any moment." "You are now alone," Cubery ominously warned Huntington. His partners and associates, "as well as the Mussel Slough martyrs, are under the sod. You are an old man." No longer would California meekly acquiesce in the face of individual or corporate railroad authority. "Free men of this State have registered a vow that the Railroad shall infringe no longer on their rights, and that the company must go out of politics, or there will be very serious trouble in the land."[16]

Trouble in the land became personified when, in the winter and spring of 1893–94, ragged and weary "regiments" of Coxey's Army made their appearance in various towns and cities across the state, frightening other citizens and invariably denouncing the railroad corporation and its officials as toadies to greed and anti-democracy.[17] Though the unemployed men presented a scene deserving more of pity than fear, local leaders nonetheless greeted the perceived threat with force, apparently fearful that destitution could easily spawn revolution.

In a different camp, business and other organizations increasingly took to opposing the monopolistic authority of the Southern Pacific. In 1891, a wealthy collection of merchants formed the Traffic Association of San Francisco to lobby for a competing railroad through the Central Valley.[18] In southern California, the Los Angeles Chamber of Commerce constituted a powerful anti–Southern Pacific organization throughout the decade, especially in the controversy over the location of the region's deepwater harbor (discussed in chapter 4). Even business organizations with boundaries extending across state lines took stances against the Southern Pacific.[19]

The rise of such institutional opposition often made for strange coalitions, united by little more than shared antipathy toward the Southern Pacific.[20] For instance, by the mid-1890s, coalitions had arisen to lobby against passage of federal legislation that would refund the Central Pacific Railroad's outstanding debt to the government. Such collections of groups and individuals often had little in common except their opposition to the railroad corporation's insistence on continued federal financial support. And though mutual antagonism united them temporarily in an anti-railroad camp, these tenuous coalitions fell apart once affairs became slightly more complex (or momentous). More than any other single event, the Pullman strike fractured such coalitions, along class and programmatic lines, casting into high relief the discrepancies and differences in the respective anti-railroad stances of diverse groups.

A Train Is Not a Train: The Strike, the Law, and Language

Los Angeles railroad workers formed the first California local of the American Railway Union in the fall of 1893. By the time the Pullman strike broke out seven months later, the ARU in southern California had an estimated one thousand members.[21] Other powerful ARU chapters operated in the railroad cities of Oakland and Sacramento. Although open to all railroad employees, the ARU membership was drawn primarily from the ranks of low-skilled workers; the elite railroad brotherhoods (firemen, brakemen, and engineers) shunned the union and rejected its experiment in labor egalitarianism.

The strike rumbled through California like a massive earthquake. The railroad, which had so effectively "sped up" life in post–Gold Rush California, was now the agent of shutdown, almost pushing the state back in time because of strike-induced inertia. In late June, acting on orders from Eugene Debs in Chicago, rail workers in Oakland refused to make up trains carrying Pullman cars. The boycott spread quickly to other rail centers in Los Angeles (where the Atchison, Topeka & Santa Fe was boycotted as well), Sacramento, and the California interior. When the railroad companies began to fire workers for not making up complete trains, the boycott turned into a general strike; "we were compelled to fight the Southern Pacific itself," the president of the ARU in Oakland declared.[22] That proved to be a momentous transition: by July 1, rail traffic in the state was paralyzed: overland trains did not run at all, local trains ran only intermittently. "The California roads are all tied up and the railroad company is having its death struggle," Sacramento ARU leader Henry Knox wrote exultantly to Debs.[23]

An ironic incident occurred in the summer heat of 1894. Jane Lathrop Stanford was traveling the northern portion of the state in her private railcar. Trapped in her ornate car well north of the Bay Area, she wanted to go home, strike or no strike. Southern Pacific railroad workers warned her that she would be in danger if she attempted to push through the blockade. But Mrs. Stanford insisted that she must get to San Francisco. She also declared that Southern Pacific railroad employees would honor her late husband's memory by kindly complying with her wishes. Surely the strikers could relent long enough to let her party through, if only as tribute to the late and great railroad builder. "I have no fear whatever to continue my journey," she wrote to Southern Pacific officials. "I find the strikers are anxious to signify their allegiance to my husband's memory by carrying me safely to San Francisco. I have this assurance from them."[24]

Granted a meeting with officers of the striking American Railway Union in Dunsmuir, Mrs. Stanford was nonetheless told that she could not break the strike unless the railroad workers received permission from Eugene V. Debs to run her train. And even if that permission were forthcoming, the workers cautioned, the union could not guarantee Mrs. Stanford safe passage in the wake of track sabotage and trestle fires.

The redoubtable Mrs. Stanford telegraphed Debs in Chicago. "Most of the men in your organization are old [and] devoted friends of my husband," she wrote, "and it is to testify their respect for his memory that they are anxious to take me safely over the Road to my home."[25] Would the union official allow her train to break the boycott? Remarkably, Debs granted the unusual request, instructing Mrs. Stanford to present his telegram to the trainmen as proof of his official dispensation.[26]

Arriving in Oakland, where strikers controlled the yards and depot, Mrs. Stanford's train resembled a huge pro-strike banner, which is probably just what Debs hoped for, if not expected. Bunting and streamers waved from the locomotive, and flowers on either side of the engine spelled out ARU in giant letters. Strikers cheered as the train steamed in, and a grateful Mrs. Stanford appeared at the window of her car and bowed regally. "It would have pleased you to have seen the joy in the faces of the Representatives of your Organization here to carry out your sanction of their desire," she wrote to Debs.[27] But when asked about her view of the strike, Mrs. Stanford, now safely home, admitted that her sympathies were with the Southern Pacific and not the striking workers.

Strike leaders made sure to disavow violence, surmising correctly that any public support for the boycott would be jeopardized if strikers committed violent acts.[28] Initially, the only apparent violence was symbolic (though ominous): nonstrikers and strikebreakers hanged in effigy.[29] Yet the threat of more potent action permeated the tense atmosphere, which supporters and detractors alike were quick to call a war—even though it was not yet clear what constituted loyalty to one side or the other. Responding to a truculent message from Southern Pacific official Alban N. Towne, the Oakland chapter of the ARU published a communiqué modeled after the Declaration of Independence, stating that the corporation's intransigence "can be interpreted only in one way, namely: a declaration of war."[30] The union further stated that "Mr. Towne is an employe of a corporation which claims that every man who is not with them is a scoundrel, . . . a black sheep and an anarchist."[31]

The conduct of the strike itself, despite the best efforts of ARU leaders, was laced with violence. Strikers yanked nonstrikers and scabs from railcars, men fought in the railroad yards, railroad tools found new uses as weapons. One nonstriking engineer at Oakland refused to move several empty Pullmans, for fear of "having my head caved in with a coupling pin" by strikers. Worried citizens fearing armed rebellion called in turn for repressive, violent, and speedy action against railroad employees.[32]

The Southern Pacific, though clearly caught offguard by the magnitude and initial success of the boycott, adopted an unyielding stance from the start. In private and public statements, corporation officials displayed their unwillingness to waver on what they saw as principle and, more important, precedent. In their view, the strikers were operating in violation of good faith; since they had as yet no stated grievance with the Southern Pacific, their actions were an inexcusable inconvenience to the public. The strike had nothing to do with affairs in California, officials believed. Once the people of the state voiced their displeasure, the strike would melt away in the glare of popular disapproval. In the meantime, the corporation could try to enhance its image by chipping away at public tolerance for both trade unionism and, equally important, anti-railroad sentiment in general. The strike was certainly no blessing to the Southern Pacific, but it *was* an opportunity.

Southern Pacific official Henry E. Huntington declared that the railroad would not violate its contract with the Pullman Company or willingly enter into a labor dispute in which it was not directly concerned. In private correspondence, Huntington urged other Southern Pacific executives to discover the hidden opportunities the strike offered. "We are going to break this strike," he wrote to his uncle in early July. "This is the first strike we have ever had here and as we are making history, [I] think we ought not to take a step backward and make such concessions that we will hereafter regret them."[33] In other words, inconvenience and daily losses of $200,000 aside, the corporation should seize the initiative and mold the public relations capital the strike offered.[34]

The Pullman boycott simultaneously offered railroad officials an un-precedented opportunity for aggressive in-house action. Troubled by the influence of the ARU over his employees, the president of the Southern Pacific saw the dispute as a way to begin wiping the slate clean. "When this strike is over," Collis Huntington wrote his nephew, "I think we should get men on our own line who do not belong to any union, and follow this policy persistently until we do not have a union man on our line." Huntington advised his nephew to look into the possibilities of importing huge numbers of African American workers from the South, much the same way as the railroad had delivered Chinese by the thousands to construction camps in the 1860s: "I think we should almost immediately commence getting some colored people from the South for our yard men all over our lines, doing it in a quiet way, putting a few here and a few there until the change is made."[35] Huntington's motives were twofold. He had indeed established worthy credentials as a supporter of black educational and vocational training, particularly through ties to Booker T. Washington. But there were more "practical" concerns as well, made all the more pressing by the Pullman stalemate. The rail magnate apparently believed that African American employees would not "have that desire to destroy capital that white laborers do, who belong to the Communists and anar-chists of our country."[36]

The Southern Pacific's refusal to run trains without Pullmans attached amounted to a colossal mistake in corporate judgment. Backed by an influential anti-railroad San Francisco press, large numbers of Californians simply refused to blame the striking employees for the blockade. After all, the strikers insisted that they had no complaint with the Southern Pacific and that they would run trains if the Pullman cars were cut free. Ever suspicious of the railroad's actions, the public appeared to side with the strikers. As the San Francisco *Call* pointed out, the Southern Pacific's decision to hold back trains "was done in the interests of Pullman, so that by inconveniencing the public in a most distressing way sympathy may be withheld from the strikers."[37] Certainly that is the way that many

Californians saw the dispute, at least in its early stages. An editorial in the Oakland *Railroad Men's Advocate* declared that the ARU simply wanted to "place the refusal to carry the mails and passengers where it belongs—on the railroad companies. Will the people sustain us? We think they will."[38]

These first waves of public opinion, which seemingly supported the strikers, ought properly to be interpreted as negative reaction to the Southern Pacific rather than positive support of the ARU and its goals.[39] The Southern Pacific's notoriety and supposedly dastardly role in state history plainly made it a far more viable public enemy than the ARU made a public friend. Powerful newspapers stood ready to take an opposing stance to nearly every action the corporation proposed, and railroad officials were well-known (and equally mistrusted) public figures. As one observer from rural California commented, "the railroad company has made a grievous mistake in this matter. It has tried to draw the public into this fight and prejudice the case of the men; but the effect has been just the opposite."[40] Furthermore, public aggravation could potentially be channeled into real policy aims, such as railroad nationalization or support for competing lines. California never had a shortage of available anti-railroad entrepreneurs, political or otherwise. As an editorial in the San Francisco *Call* declared early on: "The advocates of paternalism have never given as good reasons why the Government should take charge of the transportation service as the railroad companies are now giving."[41] Henry Huntington's hopes to turn the tables on the strikers proved, initially at least, painfully naive.

At the same time, Californians eyed Eugene Debs, the union's mysterious and charismatic leader, with a mixture of suspicion and wonder. The ARU's agenda was unknown. If railroad officials did not understand the union objectives, neither did the public. The state had never offered a tolerant environment for unionism, and the militancy of the infant ARU was bound to bring out deep-seated antagonisms. Public support for the union hung by a thread of anti-railroad tradition and little more. Once the California population determined, rightly or wrongly, that the Pullman strike was not about railroad opposition but was instead the opening shot of a potentially violent revolution that would fundamentally change their society, what had at first seemed popular support for the ARU quickly evaporated.

Even in the midst of early, ostensibly supportive, public opinion, anxious voices declared the strikers to be the vanguard of class revolt. Southern Pacific officials spoke publicly and privately from this rostrum, as did others less willing to appear too tolerant of the corporation. One observer chose to blame exaggerated and misguided anti-railroad sentiment in northern California on San Francisco's partisan newspapers. The press refused to recognize the implicit threat of the strike, he claimed, a calamity "which prostrates the entire business of the State and points to revolution." "Mind you," he insisted, "I am not a Southern Pacific man—I am simply a law-abiding citizen, who sees in this sympathetic strike a menace to the welfare of the community."[42]

The Southern Pacific's defiant posture toward the strike and strikers relied on and even required eventual government support. The railroad's political and propaganda muscle could not by itself push the problem aside; the strike simply posed too great a challenge for the corporation to handle on its own. Railroad officials quickly recognized that they would need federal aid—first in the form of legal weaponry and then, if necessary, actual military force. But the corporation had to act quickly, lest by some twist of fate the government spring to the aid of the strikers. As always, the corporation enjoyed the presence of significant legal talent on the company payroll. "I think refusal of trainmen to make up our Interstate Commerce trains with pullman cars is a crime," corporate legal counsel William F. Herrin wrote attorney John Bicknell in Los Angeles. "I suggest that you see U.S. Dist. Attorney with a view to having arrests made in the Federal Court of guilty parties under this law."[43]

Southern Pacific legal expertise, never to be underestimated, did not stop there. A potentially more powerful legal lever existed in regard to United States mail shipments. As the boycott continued, undelivered mail piled up amidst other goods and merchandise at depots and railroad storage facilities throughout the state. Strikers insisted that they would run mail cars if the railroad companies would not attach Pullman sleepers to the trains. The Southern Pacific refused, arguing that a mail train had always been a regularly composed collection of railcars, Pullman included. As the San Francisco *Call* pointed out, with a great deal of simple truth, the trouble existed "all because Mr. Huntington refuses to acknowledge that a train without a Pullman car is a train."[44]

The interstate commerce and mail questions were two-edged swords. The strike obviously interfered with mail shipments, and interstate commerce was definitely obstructed. But if the federal court ruled that the Southern Pacific had to ship the mails on trains with or without Pullmans attached, the strikers would gain a crucial victory. If it decided that a mail car was essentially whatever the railroad company said it was, the strikers would face charges of obstruction. The strike could then be met head-on by judicial orders or, potentially, by a United States military force.[45]

The Southern Pacific won this all-important legal and semantic dispute and, in doing so, won also the partnership of the federal government in breaking the strike. In a decision reached in early July, Judge Erskine Ross of the U.S. District Court in Los Angeles agreed with the railroad corporation. A train was not a train unless the railroad company said it was. As the rightful owners of the property, the stockholders of the railroad were "legally and justly entitled to determine how many and what cars and engines shall constitute their trains."[46] Armed with the court's decision, Southern Pacific officials demanded that federal and state authorities act to arrest ARU leaders, disperse strikers, and regain control of depots and train operations across the state. But although the rail corporation gained the military and legal backing of the federal government—the most critical "prize" of the Pullman strike dispute—the strike was not thereby dissolved. As events in Sacramento quickly showed, breaking the strike and alienating public support for it would prove a difficult task indeed.

The Sacramento Fair and "Bloodless Battle of the Depot"

"This looks more like a fair than a desperate strike," the U.S. marshal, Barry Baldwin, remarked on his arrival in Sacramento in early July. [47] And he was right. Some three thousand people—men, women, and children—milled about the Southern Pacific depot and grounds, where they had lived since seizing the property in June. But appearances could be deceiving; despite the apparent festivity, the atmosphere was hardly tension-free. Baldwin did not know how strong the strikers really were, how many guns they had, or whether they planned to act with violence. Rumors abounded: the strikers were going to blow up two massive powder kegs, guns were streaming into the depot, and armed sympathizers from other parts of the state were on their way to Sacramento.

Baldwin failed in his attempt to convince the strikers to run trains out of the depot. After apparently getting ARU cooperation for sending a mail-carrying train out of the yards, Baldwin tried to permit the attachment of Pullman cars. In the resulting confrontation, strikers knocked the marshal down several times; he finally came to his feet brandishing a pair of pistols.[48] Realizing that he was outmatched, and possessed of little faith in local authorities ("peace officers here are in thorough sympathy with strikers"), Baldwin called on Governor H. H. Markham for support from the state militia.

Markham responded by ordering the guardsmen into the field. Convinced that a large show of force, including a declaration of martial law, would dissolve the strike in Sacramento, Major-General W. H. Dimond assembled militia units in San Francisco on July 3.[49] Veterans from the Civil War who offered their services were politely turned away, told that the fight was to be left to a younger generation.[50] Militia officers urged their men to take their task seriously: the threat was real. The young guardsmen were ordered to "impress the enemy that we mean business. . . . Remember that your own lives are at stake, and you will fire low, and fire to kill."[51] Given twenty rounds of ammunition each, and accompanied by artillery units hauling a Gatling gun, the soldiers marched down Market Street in San Francisco to both the jeers and cheers of a large crowd.[52] From there they took a ferry to the Oakland train station, boarding thirty cars bound for the occupied depot in Sacramento.

Because of the blockade and fears of sabotage, the train took an absurdly roundabout route, arriving in Sacramento some eight or nine hours later. The exhausted guardsmen disembarked on the morning of July 4 at Twenty-first Street. There they were served a meager breakfast while they were still standing in the hot sun. The assembled regiments marched first to the armory, where they met up with the contingent of Sacramento militia already deployed. Commanding officers canvassed the ranks to determine whether the guardsmen would perform their duties. All units responded favorably except Sacramento Company A; the men of that unit informed their superiors that, should matters come to it, they would not fire on their friends and relatives assembled at the depot. This news ought to have given militia officers some idea of what they were in for at the railroad yards. The hesitant guardsmen were left standing at the armory as the other soldiers marched away in a single column toward the depot.[53]

At their approach, the piercing whine of a factory whistle summoned strikers from their homes, and soon crowds of people lined the streets of the city. (One local citizen was mortally wounded when a guardsman's gun went off accidentally.) The nearly one thousand men of the guard reached the front of the Southern Pacific depot at high noon. A large body of strikers and sightseers, including women and children, blocked the eastern entrance of the station and steadfastly refused to give way. Militia commanders ordered their men to fix bayonets. Chaos reigned, "a scene of confusion almost indescribable."[54] The strikers carried and waved numerous American flags, and many wore miniature versions in hatbands and lapels. Inexplicably, the two militia regiments at the head of the column were both Sacramento units; many of the guardsmen wore ARU buttons themselves and knew the men and women they faced across the arbitrary line separating striker from soldier. Strikers urged the guardsmen to join them. The heat bore down on the hapless and, by this time, thoroughly frightened militiamen, many of whom collapsed from the heat and strain and had to be carried away.

Sacramento Guard commander Timothy Sheehan—Irish émigré, Civil War veteran, ex–carriage painter, and manager of a local newspaper— pleaded with the strikers to surrender the depot.[55] Unsuccessful, Sheehan reported to his commander, Major-General Dimond, that he could not gain entry without the use of force. Dimond then ordered Sheehan to charge and fire if necessary; Sheehan requested that Dimond get the order in writing from Marshal Baldwin. Baldwin refused to give such an order unless he were given control of the guardsmen, which Dimond allowed. Baldwin then ordered Dimond to charge the crowd but hold fire until another peaceful attempt was made to dislodge strikers and warn the women and children.[56]

The units at the front, the guardsmen from Sacramento, continued to stand face to face with the strikers as all this shuffling went on. Strikers and their families mingled with the amateur soldiers, urging them to retreat. "Frank, if you kill me you make your sister a widow," one striker casually informed a guardsman.[57] The militia units wilted; men began to unload their weapons. The Sacramento guardsmen refused to disperse the strikers when given orders.[58] They lowered their guns and wandered away, sent ostensibly on an errand to guard nearby railroad bridges. The strikers cheered and embraced the guardsmen. Some militiamen apparently surrendered their weapons to the railroad workers.[59] The Stockton contingent next in line also gave way, retreating to shade (and ARU-supplied lemonade and ice) 150 yards away.[60] Left at front were San Francisco guardsmen, spoiling for a fight.[61] Marshal Baldwin, accompanied by several flag-waving strikers, mounted a locomotive and pleaded again with the workers to disperse.[62] To the cheers of the striking ARU members, Baldwin negotiated a truce until 6 P.M. The dispirited guardsmen withdrew, defeated in "The Bloodless Battle of the Depot."[63] The strikers' occupation of the depot would eventually stretch into weeks.

Rumors of statewide support for the Sacramento strikers were in part true. Several hundred ARU members in Dunsmuir and Truckee, many of them heavily armed, left for Sacramento on July 4. Throngs of people along the way turned out to greet them with bonfires, crowds, and parades. A band in one location serenaded the union men with "See the Conquering Hero Comes."[64] In the northern California town of Chico, according to an officer in the National Guard at that place, many "prominent and wealthy citizens" not only encouraged the strikers but supplied them with guns as well.[65]

The Blockade in Oakland

Like Sacramento, Oakland was the scene of a rail blockade. Within hours after receiving Debs's shut-down order, ARU members had halted rail traffic in and out of the Oakland yards. Freight and passenger traffic ground to a standstill, prompting another worried exchange of telegrams between militia officers and state officials. Strikers slipped past squads of deputies and deputized railroad employees to cut brakelines of trains and kill locomotive steam engines. In order to stop moving trains, some went so far as to lie down en masse on the tracks. Many nonstriking engineers, brakemen, and firemen gave in to the great pressure (and threats of physical violence) from massed ARU members and joined the strike. Meanwhile, stranded travelers and commuters milled about Oakland's depot, "killed time and swore at the railroad company at frequently recurring intervals."[66]

Support for the strikers was high in Oakland, naturally so. The Southern Pacific's Bay Area yards and shops employed hundreds of men, many ARU members among them. At a strikers' solidarity meeting, a member of Oakland's city council received cheers when he declared that "your cause is a just one and you will win. Keep cool and as long as you pursue your present course you will secure the sympathy of the people of the State."[67]

The strikers' action also elicited support from nonrailroad unions as well as expressions of solidarity from the countryside. At one Oakland rally, prominent union official John Gelder of the Federated Trades celebrated the cohesion of urban and rural discontent, not seen in Oakland to such a degree since the days of Denis Kearney and the Workingman's Party. "After many years of hard fighting we have prevailed upon the farmers of the lands to unite with us, and Mr. Plutocrat, look out or something will fall."[68] At the same gathering, the head of Oakland's ARU chapter declared that the Southern Pacific wanted civil authorities to call on federal troops because the militia would not fire on the strikers. If the guardsmen arrived at the Oakland depot, Roberts said, "we will give them three cheers."

Under the direction of Mrs. Thomas Roberts, wife of the local ARU leader, a Strikers' Sympathetic League was formed in Oakland. Composed entirely of women, the league held its own meetings, raised funds, and played a prominent role in attempting to make the strike more palatable to the surrounding community. Part of that role included well-publicized ritual, as when the president of the league draped black crepe over a Southern Pacific locomotive that had been "killed" in front of her house.[69]

League members distributed white rosettes fashioned by Mrs. Eugene V. Debs to local women. The members of the league clearly believed that their support for the strike would help obviate community fears of violence and revolution. Drawing from the activist example of the women's suffrage movement, which was then trying to get a suffrage ballot before the voters, Mrs. Roberts insisted that "women can have the most important influence in keeping such a movement as this within the bounds of peace and dignity."[70]

Strike leaders, men and women alike, shrewdly recognized that many people would evaluate the strike's legitimacy simply by observing the behavior of strikers; a rigid adherence to standards of conduct perceived to be correct would presumably gain allies from the nonstriking community. Consequently, at a large public meeting in San Francisco, strikers and their supporters passed a resolution prohibiting acts of overt violence and offering aid to the railroad company should fires or other acts damage property or equipment. Temperance, too, was an important part of ARU strategy, a crucial component of the group's presentation of itself as a patriotic, peaceful, legitimate, and sober organization. According to one report, a striker involved in the seizure of rail operations at Oakland carried with him a huge jug of wine. But when he started to open it, a strike leader intervened and ordered the jug broken to pieces. This was done, apparently without objection.[71]

Early press accounts of the strike leveled a great deal of antipathy at the Southern Pacific for its stubbornness in refusing to run trains minus Pullman cars. The Oakland *Tribune* reprinted an editorial from the fervently anti-railroad San Francisco *Examiner*, which declared that the Southern Pacific "has done a service of extraordinary value to this State. It has rubbed into the minds of the people of California the realization of their helpless dependence upon the whims of a single corporation." The strike illuminated profound statewide tensions, the resolution of which would set California's direction for the future; the railroad's "stupid, blundering, malicious" stubbornness occurred "at precisely the moment when an aroused and enlightened public opinion can be most effective in securing a permanently satisfactory alteration in the relations between the railroads and the people."[72] The article ended with a call to nationalize all transcontinental railroads—a proposal that was by then a staple of Populist thinking (and one gradually adopted, in sometimes weaker language, by both major parties).[73]

Matters in Oakland took on a new hue in mid-July with the return of the mayor (and future governor), George Pardee. When the strike had broken out, Pardee was vacationing outside the city and unable to return immediately. Once back at the mayoral desk, however, Pardee took charge with a show of force that dwarfed even his exaggerated response to the earlier presence in the city of hapless members of Coxey's Army.[74] Before a gathering of like-minded citizens, the mayor declared that Oakland would be defended at all costs against depredations by the striking workers and their supporters. One man conveyed his approval of this iron-glove approach by affirming that the "only way to put down mob violence is with a Gatling gun."[75] The same meeting witnessed a dramatic confrontation between Thomas Roberts of the ARU and Pardee. Amidst cries that Roberts be arrested, hung, or dynamited, Pardee and the union official traded interpretations of the strike. Roberts denied that he had ordered his men to beat scabs and nonstrikers. He also denied involvement in the destruction of corporation property. Pardee closed the meeting by warning the union official that the city of Oakland would hold him personally responsible if further trouble broke out.[76]

Workers and conservative officeholders obviously had different agendas and different ideas of the public good. In particular, they disagreed about the role to be played by the government—in the strike as well as in western affairs generally. What degree of federal intervention was called for? Conservatives viewed the strike as an assault on property. The strikers not only had unlawfully seized possession of railroad yards and trains but also had demanded that the operation of railroads be fully turned over to, instead of regulated by, the government. For their part, strikers severely tested the government's strikebreaking capability. In building an alliance with Populists and affiliated labor unions—as well as cementing apparently strong ties with large sectors of the public—the strikers presented a front with the potential of undeniable political clout.

Fearful of such power and the ever present threat of violence, conservatives closed ranks with the railroad corporation in defense of property rights. Yet taking sides was not always a simple act of political or ideological loyalty. Many political figures, Mayor Pardee among them, feared the political muscle of organized labor and attempted to place themselves between the workers and the rail corporation. (In this respect, they anticipated twentieth-century Progressive maneuvering between the hard place of Labor and the rock of Capital.) For instance, at a public gathering that he called to demonstrate public censure of the strikers, Pardee read a damning letter from city official Warren Olney. Pardee's editing of the letter is illustrative: he crossed out the most reactionary passages, choosing not to call the strikers a "mob" but referring instead to a general spirit of "lawlessness."[77]

Olney's letter itself is interesting. He believed that the strike had driven a wedge between groups formerly united on "the railroad issue." He wrote that Californians "do not love the railroad, nor do we love the railroad managers. We have no reason to love them. But the strikers, with most surprising dullness of apprehension, are compelling the great public, in sheer self-defense, to take sides with the railroad managers in the conflict now going on." And despite fears that such an alliance would allow the railroad to exert "a still stronger grip on us," Olney supported swift repression of the strike: "Rioting [Pardee substituted "Lawlessness"] must be put down in the interests of the people, not of the railroads." Olney declared it "strange that men do not stop to think that in these days railways are, in a very large sense, public corporations. They are the highways of commerce. They are an absolute necessity of modern civilization. No set of men has the right to block them. The man who does it is a public enemy, and should be treated as such."[78]

The labeling of the railroads as "public corporations" struck at the heart of the debate. Conservatives saw the railroads as crucial and emblematic functions of corporate capitalism that required only the guiding hand of regulation. Those consciously outside that loop, including the third-party Populists and their potential ballot-box allies, saw the matter differently: they wished to make the corporations' "public" status official through public ownership or nationalization. Herein lay the crux of the debate over the public good.

At the strike's conclusion, Pardee again revealed a desire to stay somewhere between angry radicals and frightened reactionaries. Accompanied by other middle-class businessmen, the mayor crossed San Francisco Bay to call on top railroad officials at the Southern Pacific's main office. There he pleaded that Oakland's striking workers be allowed to return to work, excluding those, of course, who had committed acts of violence or been ARU leaders. A number of Oakland's workers bitterly resented the paternalistic intervention, branding it a brazen attempt to fashion a false and misleading truce between capital and labor. The Oakland *Times* blasted the mayor as "A Pretended Friend to Labor" and accused him of "Misrepresenting the Strikers to Serve Political Ends." Pardee's delegation represented the cause of labor "as much as Coxey is the incarnation of Jesus Christ." Thomas J. Roberts declared that the city's workers could speak for themselves; furthermore, as far as he was concerned, the Pullman strike was still in effect in Oakland.[79]

Tensions in Southern California

Affairs in southern California were hardly less tense than in the north. There people displayed a fascination with the strike as intense as anywhere in the state. In Los Angeles, large crowds gathered on a downtown street in front of a stereopticon that depicted views of the strike in cities across the state and the nation. ARU members in Los Angeles had struck the Atchison, Topeka & Santa Fe Railroad first, when that line fired employees who refused to run trains pulling Pullman cars. Southern Pacific employees quickly followed suit for the same reason. As they did across California, local strikers affirmed their patriotism by wearing small American flags above their ARU badges.[80] U.S. Attorney George Denis telegraphed Attorney General Richard Olney on June 29 to inform him that there was "considerable feeling in favor strikers."[81] Olney, a former railroad attorney, urged Denis to act, assuring him that he had the law on his side. Southern Pacific attorney John D. Bicknell wrote to corporation counsel William F. Herrin that the strike had "assumed such magnitude" that making arrests of only a few strikers (using the anti-trust provisions of the elastic Sherman Act of 1890) would prove of little help in halting the strike. Bicknell instead recommended wholesale firing of ARU employees.[82]

Harrison Gray Otis, editor and owner of the Los Angeles *Times*, left little doubt about where he and his influential newspaper stood in the matter of the strike. The insolence of the ARU, and its petulance in inconveniencing the public, amounted to a slap in the face of the American people. But, as the *Times* warned at the start of the boycott, "the people will strike back, and they will lose no time in doing so."[83] Though the *Times* self-righteously declared that it had long been an opponent of the Southern Pacific's autocratic power, the specter of Eugene Debs presiding over rampant labor activism presented a far greater evil. "This is not a dispute between a railroad company and its employees," a typical editorial read, "but between the great masses of law-abiding citizens on the one hand and a small faction of lawless men on the other."[84]

Despite directions from the attorney general, U.S. Attorney Denis, overestimating local support for the strikers, was reluctant to take overt legal action. In a telegram to Olney, he worried that the "strikers' sympathizers, mostly called People's Party men, have been arriving here for ten days; have from two to three thousand guns and are organizing."[85] In part because of exaggerated claims like these, Olney authorized sending United States troops to Los Angeles.[86] Accordingly, six companies of 320 men, equipped with enough rations, weapons, and ammunition for a month of field service, departed San Francisco for Los Angeles on July 2.

Dispatching troops to ensure order smacked to many of federal privilege unjustifiably granted to private corporations. As one northern Californian wrote in a letter to the Oakland *Daily Report*: "The Government had better be careful in using United States troops in this matter. The people have been downtrodden by the corporations for the last fifteen years and

. . . forcing or intimidating men seeking redress for real or imaginary wrongs is neither democratic nor within the spirit of the Constitution." Roberts of the ARU, in an odd juxtaposition, agreed, pointing out that the striking railroad employees were not "coal-mine strikers or hoodlums, but respectable American citizens making an honorable fight for our rights."[87]

Some soldiers, like their counterparts in the militia, balked at the prospect of putting the strikers down by force. "If we had to fight Indians or a common enemy there would be some fun and excitement," one soldier remarked candidly, "but this idea of shooting down American citizens simply because they are on a strike for what they consider to be their rights is a horse of another color. All of the boys are against it from first to last, and many are in sympathy with the strikers."[88]

On its way to Los Angeles, the martial caravan passed through notorious anti-railroad territory in the Central Valley. At a stop in Kings County, not far from where the Mussel Slough shoot-out had taken place years earlier, a newspaper correspondent was surprised to see the region less demonstrably anti-railroad than he had anticipated: "Remembering the bitter struggles of the past people are not friendly to the cause of the railroad company, but they did not express the hostility that might have been expected." As in other communities, the San Joaquin Valley seemed willing to support the strike and the strikers as long as the conflict remained peaceful. "It was clear that the general sentiment favored the men, but that violence was not regarded as justifiable."[89]

In Los Angeles, U.S. Attorney Denis found himself pulled between duty on one side and regard for the legal rights of the strikers on the other. Despite his real fears of armed rebellion, Denis clearly respected the strikers and the degree of local support for their actions. "They are in deep earnest in what they have undertaken to do, and it must be confessed they are backed by the sympathy of a large portion of the community."[90] Denis's publicly expressed sentiments prompted a flurry of private exchanges between Southern Pacific officials, who were convinced that the U.S. attorney cultivated anti–Southern Pacific sentiments in southern California out of either a simple lack of comprehension or, worse, calculated loyalty to the Atchison, Topeka & Santa Fe.[91]

What followed was a sort of cat-and-mouse game played between the Southern Pacific and the U.S. attorney. After getting assurances from the ARU members that they would run mail trains provided there were no Pullmans attached, Denis fully expected that the Southern Pacific would begin to make up and send its trains out from Los Angeles. But the railroad company hesitated, presumably in order to weaken the union both by not giving in and by lengthening the public's strike-induced frustrations. Denis reacted by threatening to take the Southern Pacific to court for violating the provisions of the Interstate Commerce Act and for obstructing the mails.[92]

The Waning of Public Support

In many ways, Denis's actions and understandings mirrored those of many Californians. To some extent, they supported the strike because it threatened to emasculate the Southern Pacific, at least temporarily; at the same time, they expressed fears that the strike would at any moment erupt into revolution. If the strike was not settled peacefully, Denis apparently believed, one of two things would happen: the federal government would totter or the railroads would be nationalized.[93] "We are in the midst of the greatest crisis in our history," he wrote to Olney.[94]

Rather than dismissing such fears as ridiculous hyperbole, we need to analyze them at face value. The Pullman strike, in California and across the United States, terrified those who were convinced that it represented nothing less than the first salvo of terrible revolution. Ignoring ARU disclaimers (which reiterated the strike's narrow objective—namely, redress for Pullman employees), fearful Californians insisted that the strike threatened the very foundations of the republic. Expressions of solidarity from other labor organizations, as well as critical support from the Populist Party, heightened fears that the strike was the first blow in a conspiracy to overthrow American institutions.[95] A guardsman who had taken part in the Sacramento farce described the strike in terms no less momentous than those of U.S. Attorney Denis: "Never before, in the history of the country, with the exception of the Civil War, was the United States ever menaced by a movement so fraught with danger and terror as this. It had become something of far greater importance than a mere quarrel between railroad corporations and their employees over a matter of wages; it amounted to an armed rebellion against the laws of the United States."[96]

Conservatives feared that the situation in California would eventually erupt much the same way it had in Chicago and elsewhere back East. Certainly anti-strike newspapers (particularly the *Post* in San Francisco, the *Times* in Los Angeles, and the *Record-Union* in Sacramento) did their utmost to convince Californians that a Debs-inspired revolution would soon reach the West if the strike was not swiftly put down.[97] Debs himself was viciously lampooned, in cartoons and in print, as a violently unstable anarchist, madly preaching class warfare. Even the message from the state's pulpits suggested that class revolution lay just around the corner unless cooler and more Christian heads prevailed.[98]

Public sympathy for the strike, though fleeting, nonetheless indicates the degree to which the Southern Pacific was hated in California: a largely—sometimes rabidly—nonunion state backing a railroad strike pushed for by radical labor unionists operating at the orders of a non-Californian. But the realization that the state could not long tolerate the dangerous machinations of Debs and allied labor unions, despite the common enemy in the Southern Pacific, had long lain just beneath the strike surface. Such worries had initially been drowned out by the enthusiasm of apparently potent antagonism toward the Southern Pacific. An Oakland newspaper editorial in early July hinted at such wariness, as well as public reluctance to side with the railroad, when it lamented that "it has become difficult to say anything that even squints at taking sides with the Southern Pacific without the newspaper or individual doing so being open to the charge of being subject to ulterior influence." The editorial went on to chastise the strikers for "carrying matters to such an unjustifiable and ruinous extreme."[99]

As the strike wore on, other voices called for arbitration, often with undisguised frustration at the strike's disruption of commerce and travel. The San Francisco *Call*, a staunchly pro-strike paper, began to back down after the debacle in Sacramento. "It is, we believe, within the power of the business men of this city, professional men of high standing, conscientious men whose counsels carry commanding convictions, to induce the Southern Pacific Company to adopt a policy that will leave the Railway Union without an excuse for further interference in our local affairs."[100]

Certainly there were many who despised the action of the strikers from the start. One representative statement of opposition, expressing nearly palpable fear, came in a letter from a San Francisco man to a friend in the East. James Lloyd La Fayette Warren hated "these wretched, unfortunate strikes, that [have] so much deranged all *Business* and *Prosperity*, and we might say all *Internal safety*. I can hardly remain self possess'd when I *see*, *hear*, and *know* of the *sad* reckless and *villainous conduct* of so many men who should *know*, and *should do Better*."[101]

Warren's fears were shared by those who saw the strike as nothing but the dangerous ferment of the mob. "I would yield much to the honest wageworker [and] would advise the Company to do so," wrote Collis P. Huntington, "but will yield nothing to the mob which is wantonly destroying our property and seriously injuring the business of our patrons."[102] One concerned Oakland citizen echoed Huntington's prejudices in a letter to the Oakland *Tribune*: "I would much prefer to live under the most despotic of despotic despots than under mob rule."[103]

The strikers lost much of their initial support when they began to embrace just what conservatives feared: the explicit language of radicalism. At some point in the strike, varying from community to community, ARU leaders (as well as, especially in the Bay Area, their Populist advisers) faced increasing difficulties in moderating those who promulgated a more general "capital versus labor" dichotomy.[104] And given the fear and threat of violence that had permeated the strike from the start, many people now regarded the striking workers as revolutionaries out to reorder society by force.[105]

A railroad switchman, speaking before a crowded Metropolitan Hall audience in San Francisco on July 6, declared that the original goal of the ARU fight had been lost sight of: the struggle now pitted labor and capital against one another. Arthur McEwen, noted anti-railroad activist and journalist, wrote a long article in the San Francisco *Examiner* two days later beneath the incendiary headline "The Gigantic Struggle Between Capital and Labor." Such sensationalism may have sold newspapers, but it likely did not help keep the thin thread of community strike support intact. McEwen did not mince words: "Thoughtful men in general side against the railroads for reasons that are patriotic and infinitely higher than any bearing on a question of wages—side against them to the point of revolution, if need be." Another northern California newspaper editorial declared that "the accursed monopoly should be made to understand that California has received the last straw and the people are ready for open rebellion and war to the knife."[106]

Such rhetoric was anything but precise, but it was prescriptive enough to startle the public out of its temporary indulgence of the striking railroad employees and their labor union allies.[107] The diminution of support for the strike drove a wedge down the center of the formerly more cohesive anti-railroad forces in the state's political arenas; what had been a tenuous coalition united in anti-railroad action fractured over the question of which direction the strike ought to take following the boycott; what did it mean to society at large?[108]

An interesting illustration of this fracture could be found in the pages of the San Francisco *Examiner*, where William Randolph Hearst guided the paper's virulent anti-railroad editorial policy. Affiliated with the *Examiner* or on Hearst's staff were several men who caused the Southern Pacific no end of torment in the latter years of the century, including editor T. T. Williams, satirist Ambrose Bierce, and railroad-bashing Arthur McEwen.[109] Yet the Pullman strike obliterated the fiction of common anti-railroad positions shared by the three men.[110] While McEwen wrote ostensibly in support of revolution, Bierce rose to the support of Collis Huntington. Of the strike, Bierce wrote that "there can be no doubt whatever that the object sought by these otherwise ludicrously and hideously senseless proceedings is the absolute and final subjugation of every interest and every will to the interest of the labor class and the will of its leaders. That may or may not be reform—it is indubitably revolution, and if it come, must come by the sword. From the point of view of reason and right Mr. Huntington's argument seems to me impregnable at every point to dissent or depreciation."[111]

Events of mid-July convinced many a Californian that perhaps Bierce was right. "Pacified" by the presence of federal troops, strikers permitted Sacramento train operations to resume on July 11. But only minutes after leaving the depot, the first train out of the city since the strike crashed. Bolts had been pried from the rails on a small trestle two miles outside of town, and the train careened into a shallow ditch. The wreck killed the locomotive's engineer and four soldiers. The resulting furor completed the cycle of dwindling public support for the strike. "By this outrageous crime the strikers lost more than they ever could hope to regain," wrote a perceptive observer from the state militia. "Public opinion and press, which had largely supported them, now, when they saw what such support resulted in, turned against them. The public recognized that a strike that carried with it destruction of property and life must not be tolerated. Even the regular had sympathized with them in their struggle against the thieving monopoly—the railroad. But now, woe to the striker who would rub up against a regular." The act not only vindicated the worst fears of those who had long predicted the outbreak of violence but terrified many who perhaps otherwise would have supported the strikers. Train-wrecking terrorism was not likely to mobilize much grass-roots support: the sheer randomness of the act, its "anytime, anywhere, anyone" destructiveness colored the entire strike black. No longer was the strike's violence contained within the prescribed boundaries of rail yards and depots. The sabotage was, a guardsman wrote, the "most cold-blooded train wreck and murder ever perpetrated in the West."[112]

This violent denouement ended any chance for the strikers to garner additional support from the nonstriking constituency. Equally if not more important, the violent act contributed to the Democratic Party's ultimate rejection of alliance with the strikers and supporters on a railroad reform bandwagon. Just as the train fell off the tracks, so too fell the substantive issue of redressing the railroad's place in California society. The Pullman strike had for an instant seemed to put the question on a track headed toward the major political parties, but it stopped well short of that destination.

One way to gauge the Democratic Party's disfavor with the strike (beyond noting that a Democratic president, Grover Cleveland, had ordered U.S. troops into the Pullman fray) is to examine the views of

Stephen Mallory White, California's Democratic standard-bearer in the U.S. Senate. White vehemently and unapologetically opposed the form the strike took; the affair was, in his view, "without reason and had nothing to commend it whatever." Though he was "disposed to criticize the railroad people as much as anyone" (White was too shrewd a politician not to emphasize his anti-railroad credentials), White found the actions of California's ARU members "so revolting to my ideas of right, so contrary to accepted principles regarding the ownership of property and the privilege to attend to one's own affairs, that I cannot bring myself to countenance it for a single moment."[113] After a friend wrote him that people in Los Angeles supported the strikers, provided no violence was committed, White wrote:

> I sympathize with labor people for they usually get the worst of
> it and I will do anything at any time to alleviate their sufferings;
> but if I have to submit to tyranny, the last form of oppression
> which I will choose, is that which results from the mob. No strike
> based upon the absurdities of this one can be carried on without
> violence, and in this case every crime between murder and arson
> has been committed wherever the strike prevailed.

White regarded the strike as little better than revolution, and he welcomed the arrival of troops in Los Angeles (and said so in a letter to President Grover Cleveland). Like many who opposed the strike, White equated the strikers with revolutionaries, anarchists, and the "dangerous classes."

White defended the decision to put U.S. troops into the field against the strikers. "When we have to choose between a lot of irresponsible anarchists, who are tearing up trains, imperiling the lives of innocent people, and ruining those who are trying to get their material to market, and the law-abiding portion of the community, I shall certainly join hands with the latter. . . . I am sure that our wives [and] children slept better because of the presence of troops in Los Angeles, whose only mission was to prevent outrage and crime."[114]

The Democratic stance was summed up in a later article in the *Overland Monthly* by John P. Irish, San Francisco editor and influential Democrat. Entitled "California and the Railroad," Irish's essay amounted to little more than a polemical attack on those anti-railroad forces that threatened to stretch dissent too far. In a sense, the essay was an answer to Henry George's prophetic "What the Railroad Will Bring Us," published in the same journal thirty years earlier (see discussion in chapter 1). Irish sketched out his party's stance toward the railroad, expressing little tolerance of those who crossed that arbitrary line dividing legitimate from illegitimate opposition. Cleverly manipulating language, Irish blurred the distinction between railroad technology and railroad corporation. Those who harbored resentment of the Southern Pacific failed to take into account all the good that the railroad had done in thirty years. "The Californian who is not a railroad man," Irish belligerently declared, "and who does not wish to see a track laid in the service of each thirty-mile strip of our dazzling rich soil, should take his pack-mule and go into the wilderness."[115] Progress, the future, the new century, and the railroad all went together. Railroad antagonists might as well slip back in time.

Dissolution of the Strike

By the middle of July in Los Angeles, the Pullman strike had dissolved, with "strikers falling over each other to get back to work."[116] In northern California, the presence and prodding of U.S. troops helped convince strikers in Oakland and Sacramento to end their occupation of depots and yards. The dissolution of the strike in those places was not without violence; in mid-July, soldiers fired upon and killed several strikers in Sacramento. In Oakland, infantry and cavalry units charged strikers, "using bayonets to good effect," according to a relieved Henry Huntington.[117]

Yet, despite the strike's obvious failure, there seemed, for a brief moment, a small chance for strike-induced railroad reform—this time with the government on the side of the strikers instead of as corporate ally. Granted permission by Attorney General Olney, U.S. Attorneys Denis and Joseph Call in Los Angeles prepared to file suit against the Southern Pacific for unlawful combination with the Pacific Mail Steamship Company and others in restraint of trade.

Call explicitly tied his actions to the strike atmosphere in southern California: Los Angeles citizens had expressed grave displeasure with the government during the tense period of the strike; the city had been on the "eve of an open rebellion." "This intense feeling against the Government," Call informed Olney, "was owing to a conviction among much the larger portion of the people, that the laws of the United States were being enforced with great severity against laboring people and not against the corporations." As redress, Call filed suit against the railroad corporation and thirty-four other railroads owned or leased by the Southern Pacific for alleged violation of the Sherman Act of 1890. Such an action was necessitated by law, Call explained, and would send a message to the people of the West that the government understood their plight with the railroad corporation. "Nothing has, in my opinion, done so much to alienate the people of the Pacific Coast from the Government of the United States as the oppressions of this monopoly upon these people." If the federal government did not step in with legislative or enforcement aid, Call believed, it would be forced to station troops in the West solely to keep the people down.

Southern Pacific officials, on hearing that the suit was about to be filed, sought out witnesses to testify to the corporation's good faith during the strike. They also sought information regarding the conduct of Denis and Call, especially toward the striking ARU employees. On July 19, top Southern Pacific attorney William F. Herrin knew the suit would be dropped: "Have information from Washington that Attorney General will probably order withdrawal of suit filed on 16th instant but do not give anyone this information."[118] And, in fact, Attorney General Olney swiftly dismissed the action with an expression of exasperation that it had ever been filed.[119]

"The fight is won," Henry Huntington wrote to his uncle on July 21. For the railroad corporation, the strike had proved to be an expensive and unsettling disruption of normal operations. Yet it was not without its benefits. For one, the corporation could proceed with its hidden agenda to stamp out unionization in the ranks. Huntington assured his uncle that the company would henceforth refuse to hire any ARU members, although such blatant discrimination would have to remain secret. To do otherwise "would make us liable as the law states that we shall not discriminate against any order, but our Superintendents are privately informed that they must not under any circumstances employ any man that is a member of the A.R.U."[120]

Corporate leaders also realized that the completion of the strike presented them with the chance to massage California's collective memory of the strike for corporate and political ends. In other words, the legacy of the strike could both be manufactured and manipulated. The railroad corporation had been in the public relations business too long not to realize the opportunity. "If the people of the State use this terrible experience that they have had as a lesson and heed it properly," Collis Huntington advised his nephew, "it can be worked to the benefit of the State and every interest therein."[121] By August, with affairs quieted down and the strike a clear failure, Collis Huntington could brag that the company had weathered the storm of the strike by subtly guiding the actions of the strikers: "Sometimes in dealing with mobs you have to join them and then lead them, which is often better than to try to drive them."[122]

Yet shaping favorable political and public prestige out of the ashes of the Pullman strike required concerted and quick action. "Defences must be built in time of peace," one top official wrote to Collis Huntington. "The labor element of this country stands amazed at its own success. . . . It will repeat the experiment."[123]

Making sense of and explaining the Pullman strike remained a highly charged task, for both the railroad corporation and the general public. Despite their obvious relief at the strike's failure, railroad executives expressed pointed incredulity at the level of public support for the strike. And they feared that such support would not simply evaporate, post-Pullman. In a letter to Collis Huntington, Charles F. Crocker referred to the "bitter feeling" Californians had for the railroad. "A settlement of the strike will not wipe out this feeling," he cautioned. "It will slumber."[124]

High-ranking Southern Pacific official William H. Mills was likewise astounded at the state's reaction to the boycott; it was "an uprising as sudden as spontaneous combustion and was in effect spontaneous anarchy" and "met with practically universal approval at first of the people of California."[125] Mills expressed fears that the Pullman strike had stirred up a hornet's nest of popular opposition, certain to spill over into the fall elections of 1894. To counter the threat, perhaps the Southern Pacific could establish or buy a metropolitan newspaper from which to dispense pro-railroad opinion, a tried-and-true practice from the corporation's bag of tricks.[126] "There is a practical unanimity among political parties that the railroad is a wrong-doer and that its subjection, control and suppression is the burning issue of the campaign," Mills wrote to Huntington. Before the campaign ended, "each party will try to outdo the other in radical, violent and malignant antagonism toward the Company." If only the railroad could "come down from the clouds" and take its natural place "as a simple implement of the movement of persons and property from one place to another," Mills wrote wistfully.[127]

California Politics after the Strike

Three major problems faced the Southern Pacific Corporation in the aftermath of the Pullman strike. First, the nagging question of federal refunding of the massive Central Pacific debt—over $25 million plus interest—continued to be the focus of much popular and governmental interest. The corporation faced countless attacks in the press and political speeches over its thirty-year outstanding debt to the government. Many Californians simply hoped that the Southern Pacific would not be able to pay the debt and would thus lose control over this important chunk of the conglomerate.[128] Finally, in 1899, a repayment schedule was set up; and the company's favorite-son financial relationship with the government ended once and for all. Second, the fall elections, specifically the gubernatorial race, occasioned much concern from Southern Pacific officials. Third, the question of railroad nationalization continued to be spoken of in political circles, although the issue generally produced more heat than light.[129]

In analyzing the gubernatorial election of 1894, and the general state of anti-railroad sentiment, Southern Pacific officials naturally embraced a conservative outlook. Their understanding of the state's political situation was colored by the belief that the Democratic Party's watered-down reform platform threatened to undermine the state's political and social stability. Democratic politicians pandered to the rabid anti-railroad interests of the population, they charged, trying to win votes from the Populists. But this policy offered perennial Republican candidate Morris M. Estee an opportunity to rise above the fray. As Southern Pacific watchdog Mills put it in a letter to Collis Huntington, "there are two tickets vieing [*sic*] with each other as to which shall have the best certificate of anti-railroad idiocy; that may divide the anti-railroad sentiment and let Mr. Estee in on a plurality."[130]

The Southern Pacific took Estee under its sheltering corporate wing, convinced that his candidacy was the most palatable of the possible alternatives.[131] In order to capitalize on the anti-railroad political climate and weaken the efforts of Democratic opponent James Budd, Estee spoke from an apparently reformist platform, including statements in support of nationalization of telegraph and telephone. It seems clear that such rhetoric was little more than a vote-getting ploy, since the Republicans (and Estee's railroad company advisers) recognized the importance of maintaining at least the appearance of railroad reform attitudes.[132]

The success of the Populist Party in state elections in 1894—the apex of that party's political success—has been interpreted as a direct result of the Pullman strike.[133] Undoubtedly the strike did help elect Adolph Sutro mayor of San Francisco. Sutro had campaigned energetically on a Populist "destroy the Octopus" ticket and, because of his anti-railroad credentials, likely would have "won on any ticket."[134] Populist support also aided Democrat Budd in his successful campaign against Morris Estee.

Although such victories did occur immediately after the strike, some historians have argued that the Southern Pacific, chastened and chagrined at the avalanche of public disapproval during the Pullman strike, simply redoubled its efforts at political mastery following the elections of 1894.

Hence, in the long run, the strike had a negative effect on "the direction of politics in the final years of California's railroad domination."[135] In particular, according to this line of reasoning, the Democratic Party's failure to place a candidate in the governor's seat for another forty years following Budd's victory over Estee is evidence of the Southern Pacific's effectiveness.

Such an interpretation is flawed for several reasons. For one, it places far too much confidence in the Southern Pacific's ability to control the political loyalties of California's citizens. Although the railroad corporation may have *wanted* to see a particular candidate elected, it could not guarantee that such would occur. Politics is surely a more complex game than that. This one-dimensional understanding also neglects to take into account the long-range influence of the Pullman strike on voters. Given the violent nature of the strike, and the subsequent labeling of the strikers and all their supporters as dangerous anarchists, the state might well have moved away from the perceived threat of radicalism on its own volition. Fleeting flash-in-the-pan Populist victories, mostly in rural elections, absorbed about all the reformist energies the state had—in tenuous urban-countryside coalitions formed by mutual hatred of the railroad corporation.[136] What remained was the power of conservatism, aided by the influence of the railroad corporation and its undisputed ally: the state (in both its California and federal expressions), complete with its own potential for repression and violence.

In early 1895, R. B. Carpenter, whom Collis Huntington had hired to keep abreast of political affairs in California, expressed utter frustration about the situation in the state. "The events of the past year have left the S.P. Co. in a [state] of moral siege with the whole State as the attacking force." Carpenter blamed company policy for the antagonism—specifically, bribery, favor granting, and permission for Estee to take an anti-railroad stance in his unsuccessful gubernatorial campaign. Such kow-towing could only worsen the political climate, Carpenter claimed. What was needed was an aggressive, pro-railroad public relations drive to counter the corporation's poor standing with the public. "In the present conditions and temper of the public, the social, political and moral elements in human nature must be considered in connection with great vested interests as well as purely commercial desires."[137]

Despite the worried tone of Carpenter's letter, the railroad corporation and its conservative allies not only had weathered the Pullman strike but had clearly benefited from it.[138] The Southern Pacific had survived the potentially perilous days of the strike, witnessed the turning of public opinion in the wake of violence and feared revolution, and gained an all-important ally: the legal and military punch of the federal government. Never again would the power and presence of the railroad corporation be challenged to the degree that it was in the summer of 1894. As Eugene Debs himself wrote, the strike had "shocked the country and jarred the world." California and Californians felt that earthquake more than most places.[139]

Something of the busy atmosphere of the train station is captured in this 1876 Carleton Watkins photograph of the terminus of the transcontinental line at the Oakland waterfront. Courtesy of the Huntington Library, San Marino, California.

Omaha through to San Francisco in Less Than Four Days: The transcontinental railroad is finished! Courtesy of the Bancroft Library.

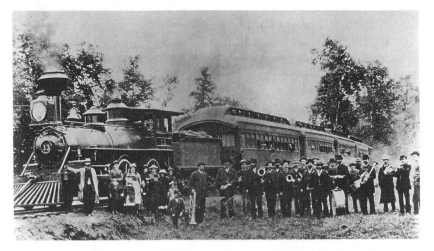

The Southern Pacific arrives amidst fanfare and music, Los Angeles, 1876. Courtesy of the Huntington Library, San Marino, California.

The Southern Pacific's ticket offices in downtown Los Angeles in the early twentieth century. Courtesy of the Huntington Library, San Marino, California.

The Southern Pacific depot in Los Angeles, circa 1900. Courtesy of the Huntington Library, San Marino, California.

The Los Angeles yards of the Southern Pacific idled by the Pullman strike in the summer of 1894. Courtesy of the Huntington Library, San Marino, California.

This summer 1894 cartoon from San Francisco's *Wasp* satirizes, among others, the National Guardsmen who failed to displace Pullman strikers and their supporters from the Sacramento Depot. The burning trains in the background were a popular symbol of anarchy and social disruption, conflicts which could apparently be addressed only by military force (in this case United States troops). Courtesy of the Huntington Library, San Marino, California.

The Crocker (left) and Colton mansions on Nob Hill. Courtesy of the Bancroft Library.

Leland Stanford's residence on Nob Hill. Courtesy of the Bancroft Library.

This crash of two Bay Area trains, just months after the celebrated linkup, proved that the railroad's arrival would be a more complicated affair than many had thought. Courtesy of the Bancroft Library.

Railroad wrecks proved to be extremely popular public spectacles. Although at
first the railroad may have seemed incapable of malfunctioning, things could go
wrong and often did. Courtesy of the Bancroft Library.

Rules and Regulations for Employees.

1. The clock of G. M. Parker, 34 K street, is the time by which trains are to be run. Conductors and Enginemen will compare their Watches with it daily, when practicable.

2. No person will be passed free unless they have a pass from a proper officer of the Company.

3. No person employed on trains, or at Stations, will leave his place or change with another without permission from the Superintendent or Train Master.

4. Conductors, before leaving terminal points, will ascertain if all Trains due of an equal or superior class have arrived.

5. All trains will be under the control of the Conductor and will be run as nearly to Card time as possible, under no circumstances leaving a station earlier than the Card time, and remaining at a station only as long as necessary to transact the business of the train.

6. Conductors, Enginemen, Baggagemen and Brakemen will be at their trains at least 20 minutes before starting time, and see that their trains are in order.

7. Conductors, Baggagemen and Brakemen on trains conveying passengers are required to wear badges as prescribed by law.

8. Conductors of Freight Trains will be held responsible for the faithful performance of duty of the Brakemen on their Trains. They will require the doors of all Freight Cars in their Trains to be closed, and will in all cases when ascending or descending grades, station themselves on the rear part of the Train and see that their Brakemen are at their posts. In no case must a Car be left on a grade without the Brake being set and the wheels blocked.

9. Conductors will report in writing to the Assistant Superintendent all injuries to persons caused by their Train, giving number of Train and Engine; the names of all employees on their Train; also, the names of others witnessing accident, and all other information that may be useful as a matter of record.

10. Conductors will see that Switches, after being used, are left turned to the main track. Any employee leaving a switch turned from the main track, or unlocked, after using will be dismissed from the serviceof the Company.

11. Although the Conductor has charge of the train, the Engineer will not therefore be considered blameless if he run any unnecessary risk on the road, without all the prescribed precautions being observed which are necessary to perfect safety. Nor will he be relieved from all blame if he proceeds in violation of instructions or orders, even should the Conductor, from negligence or misapprehension, direct him so to do.

12. West bound trains will have the right to the track against East bound trains until they are twenty-five minutes behind their card time, after which they will lose all their right to the track.: East bound trains will wait twenty-five minutes for West bound trains, after which they will have the right to the track indefinitely, against West bound trains, keeping twenty-five minutes behind their card time at each succeeding station until the expected train is met. Always allow five minutes for variation of watches, but the five minutes so allowed must not be used for running; if a train cannot reach a station on time to meet another, all the necessary precautions must be taken to prevent accidents. Note Rules 13 and 14.

13. **Through Freight** trains will keep entirely out of the way of passenger trains, but will have the right of road over way freight trains.

14. **Way Freight** trains will keep entirely out of the way of both Passenger and Through Freight trains.

15. A Red Flag by day, or a Red Light by night, displayed on the front of an Engine, shows that another Train is following, which has precisely the same rights as the Engine or Train b a ng the signal. The trains following when running West, if they cannot reach a station within the twenty-five minutes as allowed by rule No. 12, to meet an East bound train, must keep entirely out of the way of the East bound train and rains following it under a red flag

16. A White Flag by day or a White Light by night, displayed on the front of an Engine, shows that another Train is following, but will keep out of the way of all regular Passenger and Freight Trains; but Work Trains and Track Parties must be kept entirely out of their way and give a clear track to them. Engineers and Conductors of Trains bearing a White Flag or White Light, will be particular and call the attention of **meeting Trains, Station Agents**, and all others concerned, and explain the meaning of it.

17. **Freight Trains must in all cases keep 10 Minutes out of the way of Passenger Trains.** If **Freight Trains** are at any time obliged to keep the Main Track at a Station where they are to meet a **Passenger Train**, a man with a Red Flag, by day, or a Red Lantern by night, must always be sent a sufficient distance in the direction of the approaching Train to give suitable warning for it to approach carefully.

18. **Construction, Wood and Extra Trains** will keep ten minutes out of the way of Passenger and Freight Trains, with the following exception, viz:

Construction Trains will have a right to work on the Track **whenever Freight Trains are Thirty Minutes late**, (except when an Engine passes bearing a White Flag or White Light, as per Rule 16), by taking care to keep a man stationed, with a flag, in the direction of approaching Trains, a sufficient distance to prevent accidents; and Freight Trains will run with great care whenever they are behind time.

19. Construction Trains must notify Train Master in the morning between what points they will work during the day, and if it should be necessary to go outside of those bounds, will proceed with great caution, and at the first Telegraph Office ask Train Master if there is any risk in proceeding.

20. Enginemen will not start with the Train until they are directed by the Conductor.

21. Enginemen must sound the whistle when within one half mile of a Station, and ring their bell when within eighty rods of a highway crossing and continue ringing until it is passed.

22. Enginemen will enter all Tunnels with great caution, and no Train or Engine shall cross any bridge or trestle work at a rate of speed exceeding six miles an hour.

23. Dampers of ash pans **must in all cases be closed** while Engines are crossing bridges and passing wood yards.

24. Enginemen must see that their engines are provided with a pair of screw-jacks, which must at all times be kept in good order, extra spring hangers, flags, lanterns and all tools necessary to meet casualties. They will not allow any person to ride on their engine, excepting the Superintendent of Repairs on their own sections, or the Conductor of the train, without an order from the Superintendent, Train Master or Master Mechanic.

25. Great care should be taken to prevent the killing of stock. If an Engineman kills stock when it is apparent that he might avoid doing so, the value of stock so killed will be deducted from his pay. Trains must come to a **full stop**, if necessary, to avoid doing so. When a case occurs, the Engineman must report in writing to the Assistant Superintendent, giving number of Engine, number of Train, names of Conductor and Fireman, and all other information which may be useful.

26. Approach all Stations slowly; pass all Stations carefully, and be sure the switches, by their levers, are seen to be right.

27. Enginemen and Firemen are particularly directed not to throw any wood from the Tender while in motion. If any wood is found too large for use it should be thrown off at the next Station. Wood must not be piled on Tenders in such a manner or quantity as to be liable to fall off.

☞ The attention of Enginemen is called to rule 11.

28. **A Brakeman** must always be stationed on the rear car, and must not leave his position without permission from the Conductor; and the brakes of that car must be ascertained to be in perfect order.

29 When the Engineman shuts off steam at Stations where the Train is to stop, the Brakemen must apply their brakes, and, using judgment, endeavor to stop at the Station without the necessity of the Engineer sounding his whistle—too much sounding of the whistle impairs its value as a signal of danger. Brakemen must not **slip the wheels**, and it is the duty of the Conductor, and a very important one, to see to this matter.

30. When it is necessary to back a Train, a Brakeman must be stationed on the rear of the car, where he can have a full view of the track, and have a brake under his control; and the Engineer and Fireman must so station themselves as to see any signal given to stop. Back up slow and have Train under control.

31. Passenger Trains will not run faster than twenty-five miles an hour, except on special order, over any part of the road, and Freight Trains will run as near to Time Table as practicable.

32. Any Train following a Passenger or other Train, will proceed with great caution, keep at least six minutes in rear of it; whenever an Extra Train is to follow another, notice must be given the forward Train, and the Conductor of that Train must notify the Station Agents and all the Conductors whom he meets, besides carrying the proper signal; and the Extra Train must approach all Stations and Wooding Places with great care.

33. Night Trains must in all cases carry a red light on the rear car.

34. Too great care can never be taken to ascertain precisely the meaning of every signal given intended to indicate danger. Notice must be taken of all violent signals.

34. In case of accident or stoppage upon the main track, from any cause, Conductors must always, and immediately, station men with red flags by day, or red lights by night, and as an extra precaution, if foggy or storming, two torpedoes must be clasped to the rails, half a mile distant in both directions, and have no right to assume that there are no trains approaching from either direction. Special care must also be taken in case a train gets behind time and liable to be overtaken by a following train, to guard against accident. Disabled cars left at Stations must be reported to Train Master.

35. No Extra Engine, with or without a Train, will be allowed to pass along the road without permission from the Superintendent or Train Master. In case it is necessary for an Extra Train or Engine to be flagged, permission to have it done must be obtained from the Train Master, or other person authorized to give such orders, and no Train will carry a flag for an Extra without orders, and any such Engine or Train being flagged, on arrival at its destination must immediately, if it is a telegraph station, report its arrival to the Train Master.

36. In all cases, either by day or night, when the track is obstructed, by reason of repairing or otherwise, so as to endanger the passing of Trains, a red flag by day or a red light by night must be placed in both directions so as to be plainly seen by an approaching Train at least one half mile.

37. Station Agents will be held responsible for the proper security and position of the Switches, and must in no case allow them to be removed from the main track, except when a Train is to leave or enter a turn out.

38. When a Flag (red or white) carried for a train following is taken down at a Station, the Agent will be particular and not let any Train pass towards such Flagged Train, unless it has rights over it, according to the Rules.

39. Station Agents are required to see that the doors of all cars on the side tracks are securely fastened and that the brakes are set and the cars far enough from the main track as not to endanger passing trains, and that the wheels of all freight or other cars on side tracks are properly secured and blocked.

40. Cars must **never** be allowed **to stand on the Main Track**, but must be placed on a siding, and the wheels must be securely blocked.

41. No wood, freight, timber, or other material of any kind, will be allowed to be piled within four feet of the track.

42. All property found on the Road must be forwarded to the Assistant Superintendent, or notice given him of being found.

Carefulness is enjoined to prevent accidents when taking Wood and Water in obscure places. A man with a Red Flag by day, or a Red Light by night, must be stationed a sufficient distance in the rear to warn approaching Trains. In such cases, TRAINS MUST ALWAYS BE EXPECTED.

DIRECTIONS CONCERNING SIGNALS AND FLAGS.

A Red Flag by day or a Red Light by night or an explosion of a torpedo on the track is a signal of danger, and the train must be brought to a full stop and meaning of it ascertained. A Green Flag by day or a Green Light by night, displayed at a Station, denotes that a Telegram is waiting and the train must be brought to a stop. A Blue Flag by day or a Blue Light by night, signifies caution, and Enginemen will govern themselves accordingly.

One Sound of the Whistle is the signal to apply the Brakes. **Two Sounds of the Whistle** is the signal to let go the Brakes. **Three Sounds of the Whistle** is the signal to back. **Four Sounds of the Whistle** is the signal to call in a Flagman. **Several Short Sounds of the Whistle** is the signal of danger.

Night Signals.—A light swung over the head is a signal to go ahead; when swung across or at right angles with the track, is a signal to back up, and when moved up and down is a signal to stop.

Early Los Angeles. Note the horse-drawn trolley in the center of the photograph. Courtesy of the Bancroft Library.

The photographer somehow convinced this group of Native Americans to pose alongside Central Pacific tracks in the early years of transcontinental construction. Despite the inherent dignity of the group, the clash of cultures is epitomized by both the hunter's aim with his bow and the nearby intrusive presence of the railroad. Courtesy of the Bancroft Library.

The horizontal meets the vertical as the railroad arrives. Courtesy of the Bancroft Library.

Western industrial capitalism in the railroad era: Wells Fargo, the Central Pacific, and town building. Courtesy of the Bancroft Library.

Hiram Johnson takes on "The Octopus," 1910. Courtesy of the Bancroft Library.

4   The Los Angeles "Free Harbor Fight"

> The question with me is whether we shall live long enough
> to get any returns from our investment and our labours.
> It has been a long and hard road to travel. . . . We think
> the community of Los Angeles owe something to us and to
> themselves.
> —Terminal Railway official Richard C. Kerens
> Letters to Thomas E. Gibbon, 1893–94

As the Pullman strike paralyzed rail traffic and worried Californians in the summer of 1894, a different sort of railroad battle began to take shape in southern California. This dispute, known as the "Los Angeles free harbor fight," pitted two railroad factions in a bitter tug-of-war over the location of a southern California deep-water harbor. The controversy helped to determine much about the commercial future of Los Angeles; it also marked the coalescence of a new group of opponents to the Southern Pacific.

In geological terms at least, a southern California harbor problem originated eons ago. Ancient shifting of the North American continent created two magnificent harbors along the California coastline. The natural deep-water bays of San Diego and, especially, San Francisco offered safe and accessible anchorage to ocean-going ships and helped both towns attract sea commerce and international trade throughout the nineteenth century. But the coastline off Los Angeles had no natural deep-water harbor. Yankee and other traders in mid-century were forced to make do with nature's whims. Ships anchored offshore in one of several bays, transferring cargo and passengers to smaller vessels that could navigate the shallow waters near the coast. San Pedro Bay handled much of the region's shipping, either at San Pedro or at nearby Wilmington, where Phineas Banning built southern California's first railroad in the late 1860s. As time passed, Redondo, Santa Monica, and Balloona bays had shipping activity as well. But no location could overcome the shortcomings of natural inheritance. None offered the capabilities that burgeoning Los Angeles sought. What was needed was a deep port. And that necessitated vast outlays of money that only the federal government could provide.

The harbor controversy, beginning in the early 1890s and continuing for the better part of a decade, centered on whether federal funds should be appropriated for harbor improvements at San Pedro or Santa Monica. The Southern Pacific Railroad Corporation lobbied for the Santa Monica appropriation. In the end, San Pedro won out. This outcome is ordinarily viewed as a victory for the "people" of southern California. Frustrated by the greedy and unfair practices of the railroad company, the people of Los Angeles banded together in the face of a common enemy: the Southern Pacific "Octopus." Their victory, local histories tell us, was both a vindication of regional vigilance in the face of corporate tyranny and a symbol of the entire state's railroad-hating vox populi.[1] The controversy and its outcome have also been interpreted as a formative instance of Progressive reform in California, emblematic of early-twentieth-century anti–Southern Pacific successes. Additional studies have pointed to the harbor fight as an example of the railroad corporation's less-than-monolithic power in determining the state's commercial or political direction.[2]

Although studies that demythologize the "Octopus" are important, it is also important not to oversimplify the harbor fight. Most analysts have discussed the role of Collis P. Huntington; the actions of other participants seldom receive close scrutiny. As a result, the conventional interpretation—that the harbor fight was a battle between a powerful corporation on one hand and an almost nameless collection of "the people" on the other—has been bolstered, and a skewed version of this important event has been presented.

There were many principals in the Los Angeles harbor fight. On one side, the Southern Pacific Railroad and Collis P. Huntington stood as the most powerful proponents of locating the harbor in Santa Monica. The influence of this corporation and its officials can hardly be denied. Yet the railroad company was not alone in its support of Santa Monica; others favored that place as well. On the other side stood those in support of San Pedro, many of them involved in businesses or possessed of motives hardly less mercenary or self-serving than those of the Southern Pacific. The most prominent of these San Pedro supporters were the officials, stock-holders, and employees of the Terminal Railway Company. Perhaps above all, the harbor controversy pitted one railroad corporation against another; both companies courted the approval of "the people." The aim of the following analysis of the Los Angeles harbor fight is not to offer an apology for the motives, influence, or actions of the Southern Pacific. It is rather to add complexity and skepticism to what has previously been interpreted largely as a morality play of good citizens, bad railroad officials, and one dangerously powerful transportation corporation. By the 1890s, certainly, opponents of the Southern Pacific could appeal to thirty years of public mistrust, suspicion, and anger to generate support for their aims. And that is precisely what the opponents of the Southern Pacific did in the Los Angeles harbor fight. What emerges from this "revisioning" of the harbor fight is not quite the victorious struggle of an exasperated populace. Although the controversy *was* about opposition to the Southern Pacific, it was also about the cunning manipulation practiced by that opposition.

The Los Angeles Chamber of Commerce and the "Southern California Gospel"

Much of the publicity and lobbying efforts for a deep-water harbor originated in the meetings of the Los Angeles Chamber of Commerce. This organization actively embraced the idea of a harbor and maintained a prominent role in the controversy for the better part of a decade. Originally founded in the 1870s but reorganized in the midst of the incredible boom period of the late 1880s, the chamber energetically went about its self-appointed task of ensuring southern California's ascendancy.[3] Part business association, part gentlemen's club (though a few women became members in the 1890s), the chamber attracted a cross section of Los Angeles business and social elites.[4] Some members had come to California with the Gold Rush, a few were native sons, most had arrived sometime after the Civil War. Membership included prominent merchants, newspapermen, railroad officials, ranchers, politicians, and lawyers. Conspicuous by their absence were members of Californio families of Mexican land-grant wealth: the chamber was almost uniformly an Anglo businessmen's gathering.

The entire membership met together infrequently; most of the group's programs were decided upon by the board of directors in regular meetings. Topics discussed mirrored the wide-open, energetic nature of southern California's growth, as well as the diverse interests of the membership: cloud-seeding schemes might get the attention of the board one day, ostrich farms another, sugar beet factories the next.

Ironically, in light of their eventual estrangement over arguably the single most important issue relating to the future of Los Angeles, the harbor question, the chamber and the Southern Pacific (as well as the Atchison, Topeka & Santa Fe) worked together in spreading the tantalizing southern California gospel that promised equal parts health and wealth. The success of such a campaign was readily evident in the boom years of the late 1880s, as the population of southern California swelled with ever-increasing numbers of tourists and settlers. Members of the chamber received complimentary railroad passes from the Southern Pacific, and both organizations blanketed eastern papers and periodicals with glowing accounts of southern California's prospects.[5] From the start, however, because the Santa Fe line enjoyed the reputation in Los Angeles of "monopoly breaker," that railroad received special praise from the chamber. For instance, upon the death of Santa Fe president Alan Manvel in the early 1890s, the chamber passed a special resolution lamenting the passing of southern California's "best and most powerful friend."[6] Such accolades could not conceivably have been directed at Collis P. Huntington in life or death, and this difference in opinion about the respective railroad moguls (and the two corporations) is an important feature of the harbor fight. If all railroads were equal in the eyes of the civic boosters of the Los Angeles Chamber of Commerce, the Santa Fe was more equal than the others.

By the late 1880s, the Southern Pacific owned much of the land surrounding the waterfront at San Pedro. Southern Pacific trains ran into the area, and Southern Pacific firms did the harbor's lighterage business. The community was a small but bustling seaport, its shoreline warehouses stockpiled with the material of railroads and railroad building: lumber, coal, and other commodities. There was much talk of getting an appropriation from Congress for building a tidal breakwater (a tiny one had been built fifteen years previous) and deepening the harbor to permit the anchorage of larger ships. Local business groups, as well as the Los Angeles Chamber of Commerce, supported these plans. The Southern Pacific apparently backed such efforts as well. Doubtless the increased capabilities of an improved deep-water port would enhance the Southern Pacific's position in the area and bring the corporation added revenue. The company extended its rail line in 1888 and started building a wharf out to sea. But construction was halted shortly thereafter. And when Collis Huntington became president of the Southern Pacific in 1890, he quickly made it clear that the company's San Pedro operations did not suit his plans. Instead, he turned his attentions to Santa Monica, the quiet resort village to the northwest.

The Santa Monica Faction

Huntington's motives for making this move remain somewhat clouded. Yet several things are clear. First, he had been buying up land in the Santa Monica area for years. Second, the advantages to the Southern Pacific at Santa Monica were potentially greater than at San Pedro. For if the government decided to build a deep-water harbor at Santa Monica (thereby turning much of the commercial activity of Los Angeles away from San

Pedro), then surely the railroad's fortunes would be impressively advanced. And if the Southern Pacific could get a jump on its competitors—namely, the Atchison, Topeka & Santa Fe—it could establish a literal beachhead at Santa Monica, which rival lines could not easily penetrate, if they could penetrate it at all.[7]

Collis Huntington's decision to reorient emphasis to Santa Monica necessarily relied on several eventualities, the outcome of which was hardly known in 1890. First, he had to acquire sufficient property to run his railroad in the area. Through an agent, he had purchased large parcels of land above the beach on the bluffs overlooking the ocean, but the potential rail route lay on the beach itself.[8] That land belonged to the partnership of Senator John P. Jones of Nevada and California pioneer Robert S. Baker. Despite later charges to the contrary, the relationship between Huntington and either man was hardly one of complete amicability. Second, Huntington had to overcome the opposition of his own business partners to a switch from San Pedro to Santa Monica. As he wrote to his agent Abbot Robinson: "Some of our people want to go to San Pedro [and] I have kept them from going there for a long time."[9] Finally, Huntington did not know whether the government would make an appropriation for a deep-water harbor and, if so, where those funds would be spent. To be commercially viable, Santa Monica required better harbor facilities. Such an improvement would cost several million dollars. Could the government be convinced that Los Angeles's deep-water harbor belonged in Santa Monica and not at San Pedro?

Founded in 1875 by Jones and Baker, Santa Monica in 1890 was a quiet beach community and resort. Although the town had grown rapidly during the boom period of the late 1880s, it retained its flavor of genteel, well-to-do refinement. This ambience was in large part due to the Jones family. Senator Jones, who had made a fortune in the Comstock Lode, built his palatial home, Miramar, near the ocean in the late 1880s. Presided over by Georgina Jones in her husband's absence, the mansion was for decades one of the prominent social centers of southern California. There visiting dignitaries, magnates, and foreign tourists mingled with the local gentility. The community cultivated a playful, relaxed atmosphere revolving around tennis, polo, beachfront walks, and teas. Tourists came out from Los Angeles to gape at Miramar's gardens and prominent guests. In short, Santa Monica was just the sort of paradise that southern California's boosters had promised travelers they would find in the Far West.

Jones was by far the largest landholder in the Santa Monica area, since he had purchased three-quarters' interest in the land from his partner, Baker. The remaining quarter was retained by Baker and his wife, Arcadia

Bandini. By virtue of his status as majority partner, Jones received the overtures of Collis P. Huntington, who desired land and a right-of-way for Southern Pacific tracks.

Jones felt a good deal of bitterness toward Huntington, because of soured business dealings in the past. When he founded Santa Monica, Jones had also built the Los Angeles & Independence Railroad, a small line that went east from the sea to Los Angeles. Santa Monica's slow growth, business competition from San Pedro Bay, and reverses in his personal fortunes—all combined to force Jones to sell the railroad in the 1880s to the Southern Pacific, an event he long regretted.[10] Jones viewed both Collis Huntington and the corporation he controlled as arrogant and greedy, best dealt with at arm's length.[11]

Not surprisingly, then, both Jones and his wife expressed hesitations about doing business with Huntington and the Southern Pacific. Although Huntington's offer was no doubt tantalizing—he proposed to buy a large portion of the estate as well as take an active interest in the development of Santa Monica—the railroad magnate's dubious reputation was enough to make Jones wary. For her part, Georgina Jones was extremely suspicious of Huntington ("He ought not to be trusted farther than you can see him") and the railroad, warning her husband to get everything in writing and "*beware* of them as I would of a snake."[12] Both husband and wife shared concerns that a beachfront railroad would detract from the beauty and ambience of the seaside resort. After all, the Southern Pacific operations at San Pedro, primarily coal and lumber, had done little to enhance the beauty of that town.[13] Jones tried to determine whether the beach could accommodate a double track near the bluffs and still have room enough for serene bathing and driving. Georgina Jones worried that "a railroad at the foot of the bluff will ruin all the homes on Ocean Avenue; there will be more or less smoke [and] soot, [and] the wind will blow it right over in our direction." A wharf might even destroy Santa Monica as a beach resort (unless, she added, the railroad were to build an iron pier that would benefit the area's many yachtsmen).[14]

Jones and his wife were not alone in their suspicions. According to Georgina Jones, Robert S. Baker and others in Santa Monica looked upon the railroad "as a great ogre that will devour everything, and never even say 'by your leave.'" As for the president of the Southern Pacific, "there is only one thing that is sure [and] that is that Huntington seems to be generally hated by everyone even employees of the road [and] he has a very bad reputation—no one seems to trust him."[15]

Yet, for all their doubts, both Jones and his wife saw something of promise in the Southern Pacific's offers. A railroad did foreshadow commercial advancement of the community. That much had been proven in countless other towns over the years. And, as Jones pointed out, if any railroad company was to build in Santa Monica, he "would rather have the Southern Pacific than any other road because it is richer [and] stronger than . . . others [and] could if it would do Santa Monica more good."[16] Most important, the chances that the government might be convinced to build a Santa Monica breakwater would feasibly be increased if the Southern Pacific was allowed to build its tracks. "My sole view in negotiating with the Southern Pacific Company is to pave the way for the building by the Government of a breakwater which would cost probably two million dollars," Jones wrote. He believed that the railroad corporation could somehow convince the government engineers to recommend Santa Monica over San Pedro.[17] Once a favorable recommendation from the engineers was received, the congressional committees in charge of making appropriations (Jones was conveniently a member of one of these committees) could go about making Santa Monica "the greatest [and] safest harbor on the Pacific Coast not even excepting San Francisco." With an improved harbor and a breakwater, as well as the eventual completion of the Nicaragua Canal, the village could become "the important commercial city of Southern California."[18]

Jones eventually accepted Huntington's offer to buy up much of his land. With the acquisition of land and a right-of-way, the Southern Pacific had taken the first important step toward making Santa Monica a first-class port. Yet the crucial problem of getting a government appropriation for making a deep-water harbor at that place had now to be addressed. But in December of 1891, the Army engineering report recommended that San Pedro receive the government appropriation designed for harbor improvements. The harbor fight was on.[19]

Congressional and Commission Hearings, 1892

Although the engineering board returned a virtually unqualified recommendation in favor of San Pedro, the matter defied a simple conclusion. At a congressional hearing on a San Pedro appropriations bill, Senator William Frye of Maine introduced a telegram from William Hood, the Southern Pacific's chief engineer. Hood declared that the holding ground at San Pedro was far too rocky to allow for suitable harbor and wharf facilities; he insisted that this fact alone accounted for the Southern Pacific's move to Santa Monica.

Hood's revelation about San Pedro's harbor capabilities, later shown to be an exaggeration at best, prompted the convening of a new harbor commission (and earned both Frye and Hood the lasting enmity of San Pedro supporters). By the order of Secretary of War Stephen B. Elkins, a new board of military engineers was directed to examine San Pedro and Santa Monica and report on each location's capacity for harbor development. The new board, headed by Colonel William Craighill, was to hold open meetings in Los Angeles in order to assess regional opinion on the matter. The forum was scheduled for the fall of 1892, to be held in the meeting room of the Los Angeles Chamber of Commerce.

In the meantime, the Southern Pacific was building a massive wharf stretching far out into the sea from its rail line at Santa Monica. This "Long Wharf," as it came to be called, was a 4,500-foot engineering triumph. The existence of this wharf, itself something of a make-do breakwater, seemed proof enough that the Southern Pacific was confident that the appropriation would be awarded to Santa Monica.[20] Once the government saw the energy and money that the Southern Pacific brought to its enterprises, many believed, the appropriation for a breakwater would be forthcoming.[21]

But the other side of the budding controversy had equally firm opinions. In September of 1892, the new engineering board assembled in Los Angeles. There the commission heard the opinions of the Los Angeles citizenry. Scientific, engineering, and safety matters were discussed, but the hearings especially concentrated on commercial aspects: how would a deep-water harbor at either place affect local or regional commerce?

At the outset of the meeting, C. M. Wells of the Los Angeles Chamber of Commerce made clear that "in this matter of selecting the best site for a harbor upon this coast at one of the points named, the Chamber of Commerce is not taking a part; is not throwing its influence in favor of any one position as against another."[22] Nonetheless, the hearings marked the first public instance when such impartiality was beginning to disintegrate.

In testifying before the board, the representatives of both San Pedro and Santa Monica emphasized the advantages, commercial or otherwise, of each location.[23] For instance, James de Barth Shorb, a wealthy and influential local vintner, relayed the details of personal conversations with both Collis Huntington and Leland Stanford. The two railroad officials had agreed that a harbor was needed near Los Angeles, so that trade connections could be established with the Orient. Shorb believed that these two men were speaking of San Pedro (or adjacent Wilmington) and not Santa Monica. Indeed, the Southern Pacific's actions at Santa Monica, in pulling down the old wharf of Jones's little Los Angeles & Independence Railroad, seemed to indicate an initial attachment to San Pedro. Subsequent actions at Santa Monica only proved to Shorb that the Southern Pacific saw an opportunity to establish a harbor-front monopoly.[24]

On the second day of public testimony, San Pedro supporters called Charles Monroe to testify. Monroe, an attorney representing Jones and Baker, was asked to ascertain "what means other railroads have of getting into the harbor [at Santa Monica]." Monroe replied that "the main idea with Jones [and] Baker was that they wanted to leave plenty of room there so that other railroads could get in, and we believe that we have done that, and I think it has been done. There is plenty of room there. And their anxiety all the time was that other railroads should get there. They are very anxious to have as many roads there as can come."[25]

Following the testimony of Monroe, J. M. Crawley, assistant freight and passenger agent for the Southern Pacific, testified that Santa Monica enjoyed commercial and other advantages that San Pedro could not match. Thomas E. Gibbon, vice president of the Terminal Railway, which operated a line to San Pedro, questioned Crawley closely about the reasons behind the Southern Pacific's change of venue. "Isn't it a fact," Gibbon asked, "that the motive, the leading motive in the construction of this wharf at Santa Monica, arises from the desire to take from the Redondo wharf [of the Santa Fe railroad] the business which they have taken from the San Pedro wharf?" Crawley replied that he did not think that was necessarily correct, but that Santa Monica did enjoy certain commercial advantages that neither San Pedro nor Redondo could match.[26] Gibbon's examination of Crawley marked the redoubtable attorney's first public foray into the battle; in the future, he would play a growing, if more private, role.

William Hood, chief engineer of the Southern Pacific, was also called to testify before the board. He too was asked whether other railroads would be able to run track on the Santa Monica beach. Hood assured the board that there was plenty of room within the reach of the proposed breakwater to allow other lines to lay tracks and build wharf facilities. Gibbon pressed Hood about the monopoly issue. Would competing lines be forced to cross Southern Pacific track? How much room would remain on the beach once Southern Pacific track had gone in? Would there be enough space to service several wharves?

Hood's testimony angered those favoring the San Pedro site for the harbor. Local newspapers—particularly the Los Angeles *Times*—had for weeks been pointing out that the Southern Pacific favored Santa Monica only because the railroad possessed a monopoly on the waterfront.[27] But when a member of the audience at the hearing dared mention that assertion (and its source), Chairman Craighill gruffly replied that "We don't care a copper for what the newspapers say."[28] Apparently the board was to separate truth from fiction—not a simple task in what was fast becoming a battle of rhetoric and propaganda.

Hood closed his testimony by defending the Southern Pacific's move to Santa Monica. The corporation had millions of dollars at stake in the decision, "more millions than we care to go into at present." With ample facilities at San Pedro, the company required an extremely good reason to move to Santa Monica and build the "Long Wharf." Doing so, he asserted, was purely a timely business decision. Any other considerations were distinctly secondary to the corporation's aims: "we are building without any reference to any breakwater proposition or deep-sea harbor proposition whatever, a wharf at Santa Monica on the site that has been discussed, which will ten months of the year take safely, we think, any sea going vessels, any coasting vessels or any other vessels that choose to come there."[29]

Terminal Railway executive Gibbon's cross-examination of the two Southern Pacific officials marked a turning point in the harbor controversy. The exchanges seem fairly clear: an official of one railroad asking pointed questions of the employees of a rival railroad. Yet, almost from this point forward, the harbor controversy became something other than simple competition between competing railroads over the location of a commercially valuable deep-water port.

The San Pedro Faction

Formed in 1890, the Los Angeles Terminal Railway Company operated a small rail line between points in Los Angeles and the San Gabriel Valley as well as south to San Pedro.[30] The financial backers of the railroad belied its appearance as a seemingly modest local rail network. They included the likes of Stephen B. Elkins of West Virginia (who as secretary of war had appointed the Craighill board), St. Louis railroad builder Richard C. Kerens, and several prominent Los Angeles businessmen, ex-mayor W. H. Workman among them. These men banked on the fact that another overland rail line loomed in southern California's future. If the hoped-for transcontinental railroad through Salt Lake was ever completed, the Terminal Railway would be just that, the western terminus of the line.

The prerequisites had been accomplished: wharf and harbor facilities had been obtained at San Pedro, land bought, additional railroad routes scouted. A congressional appropriation for harbor improvement at that location would seemingly ensure prosperity for the little railroad and its backers. As Kerens wrote to Gibbon, outside investors (himself included) had "invested millions of their capital in Los Angeles." Any success on the part of the Southern Pacific "to overthrow the Terminal Company . . . will be far reaching and permanent." The blame for the expanding controversy lay with Collis Huntington and his ability to deflect any form of railroad competition, Kerens believed. "It is too bad that the community, and the interests of Los Angeles, which have such a splendid prospect, should be retarded as they always have been by this sort of work. Had Los Angeles been out of the clutches of the S.P. ten years ago, she would to-day have double the population she has, and perhaps twice the wealth. A railroad from Salt Lake, opening up the coal and iron fields and bringing it to So. California, would double the value of every man's property in the San Gabriel Valley." Each commodity Kerens listed—land, coal, iron— would, if the new transcontinental railway were completed, be as money in the pockets of the Terminal's stockholders.[31]

The principal officers and stockholders of the Terminal Railway, together with San Pedro businessmen and property holders, labored tirelessly to garner the federal appropriation for San Pedro. And one of the most effective, and simplest, ways to accomplish that was to argue against Santa Monica's strongest supporter: the Southern Pacific. If the motives, behavior, and tactics of Collis Huntington and the S.P. came to light, San Pedro supporters believed, the harbor issue would be settled in their favor. "I do not believe Mr. Huntington's manipulations in this direction will do him any good, and it ought to at once settle the question in favor of San Pedro," Kerens confided to Gibbon.[32]

Until the controversy was resolved, Gibbon kept the harbor issue—or at least the San Pedro side of the battle—before the chamber of commerce. As a result, he and the other supporters of San Pedro eventually turned the chamber's somewhat amorphous opposition to the Southern Pacific into support for their position. At the same time, these men recognized a regional mistrust of the railroad, which, if similarly cultivated, could potentially be turned into "the voice of the people." Whereas their own opposition was based primarily along lines of business competition, they recognized a latent antagonism to the Southern Pacific that existed in Los Angeles. Regardless of the origin of such sentiment, Gibbon must have realized that the Terminal Railway's fortunes could be advanced on the heels of the public's distaste for Collis Huntington and the S.P. Because the Southern Pacific was powerful and often ruthless, it suffered from a long-standing poor public image. In short, the Southern Pacific was the perfect scapegoat. And Thomas Gibbon and others knew from the start that opinion, public feeling, and image were important features of the harbor fight.

This strategy was of course not lost on the officials and friends of the Southern Pacific. As early as the Craighill Commission's hearings before the chamber of commerce, Santa Monica supporters attacked the motives of San Pedro's backers as self-serving. Judge R. B. Carpenter proved particularly hostile, his words a challenge to the opposition's patriotism, masculinity, and understanding of the state's glorious railroad past. Those in favor of San Pedro, he fumed, "seem to rest their case chiefly upon abuse of and distrust and denunciation of the Southern Pacific Railroad."

> What that has to do with the question before this commission I do not comprehend. . . . If the Southern Pacific was on trial it could show that its iron horse came over the Sierras when this was a dense forest of wilderness and a sheep pasture and developed almost the entire interest. . . . And this is the gratitude that republics give to their savior. . . . We stand upon our manhood and our rights. We can defend Santa Monica without aspersing or lying about or abusing San Pedro or Redondo or any railroad under heaven. . . . And that is a platform, sir, that will stand when all these miserable insinuations, with their authors, are buried in eternal oblivion.[33]

In January of 1893, Thomas Gibbon, who had joined the Los Angeles Chamber of Commerce just as the harbor issue was becoming the focus of controversy, addressed its directors on behalf of the Terminal Railway. In the opinion of that company, San Pedro was the best location for a deepwater southern California port. Furthermore, Gibbon asked the chamber to appoint a delegate who would go to Washington and represent the company's position to Congress. Accordingly, the directors voted to send Charles Forman to meet with California's congressional delegation and work toward that end.[34] Gibbon himself was to accompany Forman to the capital, to better shepherd the cause.[35]

A month later, Gibbon again appeared before the chamber. He urged that the group's president write a letter to the chairman of the House Committee on Rivers and Harbors, urging the passage of a San Pedro appropriation. In a letter to the chamber two weeks later, Richard Kerens followed up Gibbon's address with his own views in support of San Pedro.[36]

In response to Kerens's views, and those of Forman in Washington, the chamber wrote to Senator Stephen Mallory White in Washington and suggested that he find himself a position on the Senate Committee on Commerce (which oversaw harbor appropriations). White, a Los Angeles attorney who had only recently been elected to the Senate, may have seemed a strange ally to the San Pedro backers. In the 1880s, in partnership with John D. Bicknell, White had been an attorney for the Southern Pacific, working closely with that organization's legal division. Once he stopped practicing with Bicknell, however, and drifted away from railroad patronage in order to pursue political ambitions, White increasingly found himself in conflict with the railroad corporation. As a powerful Democrat, he was often at odds with the railroad, which generally (although by no means always) supported Republicans. Since he was the U.S. senator from southern California, with a home in Los Angeles, White's views regarding the harbor fight were of obvious importance; encouraging White to favor San Pedro was smart politics. As Terminal Railway official Richard Kerens noted, "it will do no harm to keep a strong pressure from his home friends in the interest of San Pedro." In fact, there is some evidence that White landed his position on the important committee through the efforts of Terminal Railway supporters.[37]

Concurrent with lobbying efforts in Washington, the factions supporting San Pedro counted on local opposition to the Southern Pacific. In Kerens's words, "I think it would do well to stir the people up and let the emphatic demand that the interests of San Pedro should be looked out for come thick and fast."[38] Accordingly, the Southern Pacific's monopolistic actions in northern California were pointed to as indications of things to come if Santa Monica garnered the harbor appropriation. The history of the corporation in the state was unfavorably reviewed, especially in the pages of the Los Angeles *Times*. As the attacks on the S.P. continued, some people worried that the level of antagonism toward one railroad might be read as a generic indictment of all railroads. In an address before the chamber of commerce, outgoing president C. M. Wells warned members that they ought not be too strident in their anti–Southern Pacific statements, lest that antagonism keep rival lines out of the region or state. Wells also warned against dissension within the chamber ranks, itself an indication that the harbor issue fostered strong opinions on both sides.[39]

Controversy within the chamber ebbed as the year passed, and—for a number of reasons—support for San Pedro grew accordingly. First of all, Terminal Railway officials occupied positions of influence within the organization. In addition, T. E. Gibbon's reports from Washington kept members informed about the progress of congressional action. As important, if not more so, was the fact that the San Pedro side of the issue enjoyed the support of one of the most influential men in all California: Harrison Gray Otis of the Los Angeles *Times*.

Bombastic, arrogant, and undeniably powerful, Otis ran his paper with the iron will of a martinet. From the start of the controversy, the *Times* championed San Pedro over Santa Monica; Otis's impact in popularizing that position over the course of a decade can hardly be underestimated. As one Southern Pacific official candidly admitted: "We should not deceive ourselves with regard to Col. Otis or his influence."[40]

The reasons for Otis's interest in the harbor question remain unclear. He may, as Southern Pacific officials suspected, have had business dealings with the Terminal Railway; perhaps he owned land in San Pedro. As Southern Pacific official William H. Mills wrote Collis Huntington, the newspaperman's interest in the controversy had "all the ear marks of one who has a personal and private interest." Mills added, "The Times will never be friendly to the project of establishing a harbor at Santa Monica. . . . I have lately come to the conclusion that H. G. Otis is in the pay of the Terminal Company."[41] In any event, Otis and the *Times* served in tandem as leading propagandists of the San Pedro campaign. And Otis's personal prestige within the chamber of commerce was high; he was one of the group's founding members and maintained a high profile throughout the controversy. His devotion to the San Pedro cause even provoked the devoutly Republican newspaperman to eloquent support of Democrat Stephen White. In fact, Otis retained White as an attorney; the influence of his powerful client may have prompted White to lean to the San Pedro side of the issue.[42]

In addition to Otis, the Terminal Railway had another strong ally in John Tracy Gaffey. Like Stephen M. White, Gaffey would perhaps at first seem a more likely supporter of the Santa Monica side of the controversy. He had married into the Bandini family; his wife, Arcadia, was a niece of Robert Baker's wife. Gaffey and his wife maintained ties with the Jones and Baker families, and Gaffey was a well-known local figure in and around Santa Monica. In 1891, he even made arrangements to buy land just to the north of Santa Monica, hoping to capitalize on the Southern Pacific's activities in the region.[43]

But most of Gaffey's property and interests were in San Pedro. There, through his wife's familial ties to other Mexican-era land grantees, he controlled large amounts of land. An enthusiastic opportunist, Gaffey spent much of his time speculating on mining properties, buying and selling land, trying to build roads, even doing business in Mexico for the Santa Fe railroad.[44] To Gaffey, the possibility of a deep-sea harbor in San Pedro (where the main street still bears his name) undoubtedly signaled potential wealth. (Turn-of-the-century maps in the Stearns-Gaffey Papers at the Huntington Library also show Otis Street, Patton Avenue, Gibbon Avenue, and White Street.)

As Stephen M. White's campaign manager and trusted adviser, John T. Gaffey occupied a position of great influence, both with the senator and in southern California. He played a prominent role in local affairs in San Pedro as well as in Los Angeles business circles, joining the chamber of commerce in the spring of 1893. Aided by White, Gaffey garnered the post of customs collector at San Pedro during the most volatile years of the controversy and became president of that town's chamber of commerce. And Gaffey apparently did much to influence his powerful friend in the U.S. Senate: his daughter remembered that he put "great pressure on Stephen White to have San Pedro chosen."[45]

In the spring of 1894, Stephen M. White, who had by then indicated that he might indeed support San Pedro, sent a telegram to certain members of the chamber of commerce. White admitted that matters were not going well in Washington. He wondered whether or not the people of Los Angeles would perhaps agree to a "double appropriation," one that would allot funds to both San Pedro and Santa Monica.

Despite some support within chamber ranks for such legislation, the most powerful San Pedro backers would not agree to such a plan. If the double appropriation were to pass, both the Terminal and the Southern Pacific would gain improved harbor facilities, and the larger railroad would enjoy a distinct advantage over the smaller. Before it could be read to the entire chamber, White's message was apparently burned.[46] To resolve the question of the chamber's stance on the matter, a vote of the entire membership was called for.

That prospect of a straw vote prompted a flurry of public relations efforts. T. B. Burnett, vice president and general manager of the Terminal Railway, sent a long letter to chamber members. In the letter (which included a pass to ride the Terminal line out to San Pedro), Burnett made several points about San Pedro, the Terminal, Los Angeles, and, not least, the Southern Pacific.

The Terminal Railway was formed, Burnett said, just after the initial recommendation was made by the engineering commission in favor of San Pedro. (This was not true. The Mendell board submitted its report in December of 1891. The Terminal Railway had been incorporated the previous January but had been in operation for many months prior to incorporation.)[47] Burnett wrote that the Terminal was projected to be the western terminus of a proposed transcontinental line, which would come to California from the mining regions of Utah. But all the corporation's plans had been delayed by the harbor controversy.

Like other San Pedro supporters, Burnett emphasized that the government never ignored the reports of its engineers. The Terminal "has always considered this harbor question a matter of very much greater importance to the people of Los Angeles than it is to any single company," he insisted.

But if the harbor were built at Santa Monica, where the Southern Pacific had gained a waterfront monopoly, the new transcontinental railroad would not be built, and Los Angeles would not have access to cheap fuel from Utah.[48]

The membership vote—a nearly three-to-one margin in favor of San Pedro—left little doubt about the chamber's position. Following that vote, the group became an explicitly pro–San Pedro organization. Soon afterward, the chamber voted to send another delegate to Washington to represent himself as the people's proxy in favor of San Pedro. Sherman O. Houghton, a friend of several Terminal Railway backers, including Stephen B. Elkins and Richard Kerens, was initially proposed as the organization's delegate. Some members were apparently opposed to Houghton, perhaps because of his ties to the Terminal Railway.[49] Houghton had been instrumental in obtaining the original 1871 appropriation for the San Pedro–Wilmington breakwater. But since he was unable to make the trip, George S. Patton, Sr., was selected to go in his stead.

San Pedro supporters could hardly have desired a more appropriate representative. Related by marriage to the wealthy Banning clan of Wilmington (on San Pedro Bay), Patton himself owned property in the area of the proposed breakwater, and one of Patton's closest political advisers was none other than John T. Gaffey. Accompanied by the ever present T. E. Gibbon as an adviser, Patton went east to Washington in the spring of 1894.[50]

The Shaping of Congressional and Public Opinion

As Patton soon discovered, matters in the nation's capital were entirely unpredictable. Strong arguments were presented on behalf of either side of the controversy. Collis Huntington appeared in person to defend the Southern Pacific and its move to Santa Monica; Gibbon, Patton, and Kerens responded with equally firm arguments—and inevitable attacks on the Southern Pacific—in favor of San Pedro. The Los Angeles press hardly steered clear of events. Harrison Gray Otis was dispatched by the chamber of commerce to inform Congress of public opinion in Los Angeles, and Joseph Lynch of the Los Angeles Herald was there to do the same for the other side. Many important congressmen had not decided where they stood on the matter. Even Stephen White showed signs of wavering; Senator Jones thought that White "would like to straddle the question," and Collis Huntington remarked privately that he thought White "will be all right on Santa Monica, I am quite sure."[51] Spokesmen for each side insisted that they alone knew, understood, and represented the vox populi of southern California. As Senator Jones wrote to his wife, the testimony of Gibbon, Patton, and others favoring San Pedro "dwelt with *much* emphasis on the statement that the citizens of Los Angeles were a hundred to one in favor of San Pedro."[52]

Doubtless the officials of the Terminal and Southern Pacific railroads watched the proceedings in Washington with great interest. But the Atchison, Topeka & Santa Fe was hardly less concerned. The president of the line, J. W. Reinhart, corresponded directly with Stephen White and met with him on at least one occasion.[53] In July of 1894, Reinhart sent a telegram to Richard Kerens in Washington. Harbor matters appeared to be going poorly for San Pedro's supporters. Reinhart wished Kerens to wire all senators on the Commerce Committee, expressing concern that the Southern Pacific ("whose prayers if granted would shut Atchison and create absolute monopoly") seemed on the verge of obtaining the appropriation for Santa Monica. The telegram ended with a juxtaposition of corporate and popular interest, an association that the officers of the Terminal no doubt understood: "If the appropriation goes to Huntington it throttles all chance for competition and besides permanently injuring growth of California and adjacent States and Territories; most serious damages Atchison interests, which it must be apparent are those of the people."[54]

Late in 1894, San Pedro supporters seized a great opportunity to influence Los Angeles opinion. After months of planning and several lost chances, a consortium of southern California Democrats, including White, Patton, Gaffey, and at least one important stockholder of the Terminal Railway, purchased the Los Angeles *Herald* from its Republican owners.[55] Thomas Gibbon had initially wished to have the wealthy officials of the Terminal buy up the paper's stock. But those officials, at first intrigued, backed out of the project for fear of alienating Otis of the *Times*. In any event, the Terminal's backers urged Gibbon to pursue the acquisition with other investors, which he did with notable success.[56] John Gaffey was installed as the *Herald*'s managing editor, and the overnight change in the paper's position on the harbor issue soon earned him the enmity of Santa Monica.[57]

San Pedro's supporters also used other methods of marshaling favorable opinion. The chamber of commerce made much of the support that other civic and commercial interests, in Los Angeles or elsewhere, gave to San Pedro. Among these interests, the chamber often pointed to the support given San Pedro by the Trans-Mississippi Congress. That body, an important commercial group composed of delegates from western chambers of commerce, met in St. Louis in the fall of 1894. There it pledged its support for San Pedro. Two Los Angeles delegates attended the meeting, and the San Pedro endorsement came at their suggestion. Richard Kerens and George Leighton, president of the Terminal Railway, both St. Louis residents, were the Los Angeles delegates. As Kerens wrote to Gibbon, "there was not the slightest difficulty" in getting the resolution passed.[58]

By the fall of 1894, regional political affairs in and around Los Angeles were saturated with the harbor question. Both parties adopted pro–San Pedro platforms. Campaigning for Congress, George Patton adopted an explicit anti–Southern Pacific stance. Stephen White became for Democrats and Republicans alike the leading light of the harbor battle, apparently a San Pedro stalwart.[59] Fighting the Southern Pacific, long an effective method of winning votes, had become a crusade.

Certain San Pedro supporters worked to enlarge the scope of the issue's political capital. At the discretion and direction of Charles Dwight Willard, secretary of the chamber of commerce, a letter was sent to various U.S. congressmen in January of 1895. The letter outlined the history of the harbor fight, emphasizing both the Southern Pacific's holdings at Santa Monica and its various actions in California. The Southern Pacific, Willard noted, "rules the commerce of . . . portions of California with an absolute despotism" and was in the process of accomplishing the same in southern California. Unless Congress acted—by supporting a San Pedro appropriation—California would come under the complete commercial control of the voracious corporation.[60]

Even with efforts such as the circular letter, some felt that the crucial arena was not being well attended to. "It is all very well to unite the people of Los Angeles, and flash around with letters and telegrams," Richard Kerens observed, "but a little effort in the Senate Committee on Commerce, or the floor of the Senate, or still better, before the River [and] Harbor Committee, would be a more effective exhibition of sincerity than speeches to the galleries." Kerens plainly suspected that Stephen White was being drawn in by the Southern Pacific and could not be counted on. "Do not," he warned Gibbon, "proceed on any other theory than that Mr. W. belongs to the S.P."[61]

San Pedro supporters also believed that, despite the backing of an increasingly pro–San Pedro membership,[62] the Los Angeles Chamber of Commerce was not doing enough to drum up local support. Harrison Gray Otis and the officers of the Terminal Railway felt especially constrained by what they saw as the chamber's limited institutional backing of their position. Accordingly, with Otis as president, the Free Harbor League— an extended but autonomous wing of the San Pedro contingent of the chamber of commerce—was established in late 1895. Other members included Harry E. Brook, a staff writer of the *Times*; Lewis Blinn, general manager of the San Pedro Lumber Company (which leased property from the Terminal Railway); John T. Gaffey; the Terminal Railway itself; the Kerckhoff-Cuzner Mill & Lumber Company of San Pedro; Charles Weir, manager of the Southern California Lumber Company, also in San Pedro; F. K. Rule, auditor for the Terminal Railway; and former mayor W. H. Workman.

Otis kept a Free Harbor League petition at the offices of the *Times* and encouraged citizens to add their signatures in support of "the people's harbor." Tallies of the number of signers were continually reported in the paper, as were references to the representation of local opinion within the 300-member league and 1,000-member chamber of commerce.[63]

The chairman of the Free Harbor League's Committee on Congressional Action was T. E. Gibbon. At that committee's urgings, the league sent four delegates to Washington to appear before the House Rivers and Harbors Committee in February of 1896: W. C. Patterson, H. G. Otis, W. D. Woolwine, and William Kerckhoff.[64]

Southern Pacific officers recognized the hand of the Terminal Railway behind almost every public instance of pro–San Pedro support. Henry Huntington wrote to his uncle that, because of its holdings around San Pedro, the Terminal had "naturally been fighting us hard against Santa Monica harbor and in favor of San Pedro." The little railroad was "a constant menace to us, and if we could get it on reasonable terms, we ought to take it in." Buying the railroad would change the whole complexion of the harbor controversy: "If any trade was made, I presume all the terminal people would turn in and help out our Santa Monica breakwater." Collis Huntington replied only that he would bargain with Kerens or Elkins (now a United States senator and a member of the Senate Commerce Committee) when the opportunity presented itself.[65]

Given the self-righteous conflict-of-interest charges leveled at the Southern Pacific and at Santa Monica supporter Jones, it seems odd that the Southern Pacific management did not publicly exploit the tactics of the San Pedro–Terminal crowd. Certainly many of the supporters of San Pedro wished to mask their interest in the issue with a veil of privacy, if not secrecy. As Kerens wrote to Thomas Gibbon in early 1895 of his support for San Pedro: "If I lived in Los Angeles I would proclaim it from the house-tops; but I do not, and my interest being an investment, and a personal one, I am embarrassed and greatly at a disadvantage." Earlier, Kerens had urged Gibbon to "not say too much about the St. Louis influence, or the So. Pac. will take up the cry that foreign influence is interfering in California affairs."[66] Yet the Southern Pacific apparently made little political capital out of the Terminal Railway's involvement in the harbor fight. Perhaps the corporation did not want to get itself into a potentially embarrassing scandal; the corporation's public footing was already tenuous enough. It was also fighting on other political fronts: perhaps in the midst of, among other things, the protracted contest over refunding of the Central Pacific federal debt, the railroad simply could not spare the public relations and propaganda horses.

Collis Huntington did return some of the Terminal's charges, though in a very private manner. In a letter to Senator Matthew Quay of the Senate Commerce Committee, Huntington insisted that Santa Monica was the best choice for a deep-water harbor and suggested that the pro–San Pedro sentiment emanating from Los Angeles might be somewhat misleading. Huntington wrote that Kerens of the Terminal "capitalized his road for a very large sum, and has been very liberal with his shares to some of the people in and about Los Angeles." Such a practice would tend to make "active partisans of men who, perhaps, would not otherwise be so."[67]

In the early months of 1896, San Pedro supporters made public a change in strategy. Either in recognition of the strapped conditions of the treasury, or out of respect for the lobbying power of Huntington and the Southern Pacific, the proponents of San Pedro backed down from their initial aim. Whereas they had long insisted that they wanted a congressional appropriation for both the outer and inner harbors of San Pedro Bay (the outer harbor to be made into the deep-water port, the inner to be improved), they now said that they would accept funds for the inner harbor only.

The change in strategy appears simply to have been one of expediency. The country was in the midst of depression; Congress seemed in no mood to be lavish. The inner harbor had received appropriations in the past; if that sort of precedent could continue, San Pedro supporters thought, future development of the outer harbor—leading to the establishment of the deep port—would naturally follow.[68]

But Congressman James McLachlan was uncomfortable with the changing demands of his constituents. McLachlan had always pledged to support the government engineers' findings in favor of San Pedro's outer harbor. But the new insistence that he favor the inner harbor—and that alone— left him in a curious position. He had been elected on a platform that explicitly pledged support for the outer harbor appropriation; if he were to go back on that pledge and support the inner harbor only, he would look foolish. But that is precisely what the Terminal Railway people now wanted him to do.[69]

Reports from Washington created worries that perhaps San Pedro would not get any appropriation at all. Disappointment was masked by anti–Southern Pacific vehemence, at least in the editorial pages of the *Times*: "Better San Pedro as it is for the next twenty years than that this people should be placed at the mercy of a corporation which never has shown mercy to any man or any community that it has been able to cinch."[70]

The Double-Appropriation Plan

In March of 1896, the House Committee on Rivers and Harbors released a surprising recommendation. Several hundred thousand dollars was appropriated for San Pedro's inner harbor—just what that location's backers had been asking for. But nearly ten times that amount was accorded Santa Monica for development of its outer harbor.[71]

The news of the recommendation fractured the San Pedro campaign. The Free Harbor League stumbled; its president resigned in the midst of heightened controversy. Evidently some San Pedro supporters wanted to take what Congress had offered and let the controversy go at that; at least San Pedro had received some funds and could improve its inner harbor. But the Terminal Railway, amply backed by Otis, cried foul. Any harbor appropriation at Santa Monica, especially one of the size offered, would effectively kill the Terminal Railway and all plans for a competing transcontinental line. The fight for a free harbor meant a fight for a harbor at San Pedro or none at all.

In early April, McLachlan informed San Pedro supporters that Congressman Binger Hermann of the House Committee on Rivers and Harbors had approached him about the dual appropriation. If the city of Los Angeles would unite on the double-appropriation scheme, with a clause allowing all competing railroads to lease S.P. track at Santa Monica, the funds would in all likelihood be forthcoming.

But the Free Harbor League maintained its fervent opposition. The plan was only a trick perpetrated by Collis P. Huntington, Otis declared with characteristic vehemence. If that sort of scheme passed, Los Angeles would become more and more like Oakland, where the Southern Pacific held a tight rein over the waterfront. But the people of Los Angeles could be counted on: "Los Angeles is not Oakland. Our people have not grown up accustomed to the Southern Pacific yoke."[72]

After McLachlan refused to go along with the double-appropriation scheme, Hermann struck the southern California appropriation from the rivers and harbors bill.[73] Caught between campaign promises on one hand and the power and influence of Otis and the Terminal Railway on the other, McLachlan complained that he was "damned today if I do" and "damned tomorrow if I don't." Even Santa Monica's supporters hammered the congressman: "The railroad people are denouncing me for misrepresenting my people in throwing away $2,800,000 that had been offered my district," he wrote Otis.[74] Now the district had nothing. Any chance for success seemingly depended on Stephen White's actions in the Senate Commerce Committee, where it was commonly assumed that Collis Huntington wielded great influence.

As attention focused on White and the Senate, San Pedro supporters stepped up their denunciations of Collis Huntington and his role in the controversy. Cartoonist Will Chapin viciously lampooned Huntington in the *Times* as a roadside bandit robbing Uncle Sam, a hunchbacked miser, and a cowboy tightly cinching up a horse representing California. "Are the citizens of Los Angeles slaves and curs that they should permit themselves to be whipped into line by Collis P. Huntington?" the paper asked.[75]

The *Times* and Otis enjoyed the quiet fraternity of Stephen White. In long letters to the mercurial newspaperman, White wrote of the plans "we" have for San Pedro, "our success," and the supporters in "our ranks." The Santa Monica appropriation looked unlikely; "In no event can that succeed," White wrote. Otis took it upon himself to advise White, going so far as to suggest the "following line of policy," which included restoration of funds for San Pedro's inner harbor as well as capture of the several-million-dollar appropriation designed to go to Santa Monica.[76]

Georgina Jones, faithfully reporting on local affairs to her husband in Washington, decribed the atmosphere in the spring of 1896. "Everyone is much excited over the harbor question," she wrote.

> There is such a feeling against Mr. Huntington + the Times tells
> such lies about the S.P.—that they have a complete monopoly here
> + no other roads can get in etc. etc.—that many people who do
> not know the truth are prejudiced. To mention the S.P. is like
> shaking a red rag in front of a bull to many people. It is absurd but
> it is a fact. The Chamber of Commerce of L.A. is composed of a
> few men who are interested in the Terminal road + own a few
> lots at San Pedro + they *pretend* to represent the people of
> Los Angeles.[77]

In a similar vein, an editorial in the Santa Monica *Daily Outlook* observed that the "San Pedro schemers and Terminal Railway sharps seem to have [the chamber of commerce] completely under control. They have inoculated its leading members with the Huntington-phobia and the poor fellows don't know what it all means."[78]

Both sides fought for regional support, and both were quick to send even a hint of such support on to Washington (and especially to White). Otis and the Free Harbor League wrote to McLachlan in late April, telling him that the double appropriation was against the "popular wishes" of the people of Los Angeles, that the people had decided "emphatically in favor" of San Pedro.[79]

Calling Collis Huntington the "worst enemy labor has in these United States," the *Times* courted the petitions and testimonials of the city's laborers. And for the *Times*, notoriously anti-labor even before the celebrated 1910 bombing of the *Times* building, such a campaign signaled extraordinary circumstances.[80] The *Times* emphasized the inglorious history of the Southern Pacific's labor relations, pointing out that it hired Chinese or Mexican laborers to displace Irish and other working-class groups working on the line.[81]

Both sides of the controversy held mass meetings in early April in Los Angeles. The San Pedro supporters met in front of the courthouse on New High and Temple streets; the Santa Monica contingent held its meeting two blocks away, in Illinois Hall. Special trains ran from San Pedro and Santa Monica to bring in partisans. Bands played in the city streets all day, and a carnival atmosphere reigned. At the San Pedro meeting—which probably did not attract the "seven thousand of God's free people" that the *Times* claimed in its April 7, 1896, issue—people chanted "S-a-n P-e-d-r-o, Free Harbor, Let the S.P. go." Banners—"No More Monopoly," "Rally for the People's Harbor"—were held aloft as a succession of speakers presented the case for San Pedro. Most of the speeches lambasted the Southern Pacific's actions in the harbor controversy, in southern California, in the whole state. W. H. Workman denounced the Southern Pacific's excessive freight rates. Ex-mayor Harry Hazard, acting as president of the meeting, insisted that it was absurd for the government to award a dual appropriation to one region of the country. The harbor issue had to be resolved in favor of San Pedro or not at all. The city must stand by the decision of the harbor engineers. After finishing his speech, Hazard was greeted with three cheers from the crowd and serenaded with "Marching through Georgia" by one of the bands.

W. C. Patterson spoke next, not as the president of the chamber of commerce, he insisted, but as a private citizen.[82] He, too, said that the double-appropriation scheme was little more than a trick (the crowd responded with "San Pedro or Bust!"). The "foreignness" of the Southern Pacific and its leadership was mentioned; one man questioned C. P. Huntington's citizenship, "for who knows where Huntington resides?" George S. Patton informed the crowd that "Huntington has not a friend in California. He is not entitled to one." One speaker compared Collis Huntington unfavorably to Satan. Another assured the crowd that the working-class vote belonged to San Pedro. And the ubiquitous T. E. Gibbon reiterated the harbor's importance to the proposed Salt Lake transcontinental railroad.

Following the meetings, both sides claimed that their rally represented the true sentiments of southern California. Santa Monica supporters wrote White, telling him that the Illinois Hall meeting attracted at least five thousand citizens and was the "largest mass meeting ever held in Los Angeles." They urged White to support the double appropriation.[83] The Los Angeles *Evening Express* belittled the San Pedro rally as the "Otis-Gaffey meeting" and "the Gaffey-Patton crowd."[84] Henry Huntington wrote to his uncle that the Santa Monica meeting "did not have the mob, but the people were with us."[85] White received telegrams in favor of the double appropriation. One writer, G. Montgomery, urged him vaguely to "get the most money possible for the working classes." Another constituent, frustrated by years of harbor controversy, insisted that White obtain congressional funding, "even if it is to go to Arroyo Seco," an exasperated reference to the dry canyons slicing through the eastern edges of Los Angeles.[86]

Not to be outdone, San Pedro's supporters blasted the Southern Pacific as "a foreign corporation" inimical to the future of California and demanded that White work toward a "free harbor for a free people at San Pedro, or none at all." George Patton encouraged White to "Stand to your Guns."[87]

By mid-April, matters had reached a fever pitch in Los Angeles. Petition campaigns canvassed the electorate; results were hurriedly sent on to Washington. White admitted that his position in "the railroad situation" was "anything but a bed of roses." Support for Santa Monica appeared to be gaining on the eve of the Senate hearings. The apparent change in public opinion made White's position more difficult and caused him to "use 'cuss words' occasionally." "The public blames a representative when he flops about, and yet the public itself is the boss flopper of the age."[88]

John D. Bicknell wired his former law partner that the San Pedro supporters had only "brass bands" and "a loud noise" going for them and did not represent true regional opinion. White replied that, although he personally favored San Pedro, he did of course "wish to properly represent my constituents."[89] Robert F. Jones, a nephew of John P. Jones and president of the Bank of Santa Monica, wrote to Walter Trask (an attorney in practice with Bicknell), asking him if he could perhaps exercise his influence in the matter. Jones wanted Trask to oversee a telegram campaign in favor of Santa Monica. He hoped that White could be convinced to let any appropriation for Santa Monica stand, regardless of what Congress decided to grant San Pedro. Jones was confident that matters were going smoothly: "We have captured the situation down here as you no doubt know. Every thing is going on all right and every body seems satisfied. We have no doubt cut off all further opposition to our interests down here."[90]

Senate Debates and Commission Findings, 1896–97: Defeat of "the Octopus"

Hearings before the Commerce Committee, complete with impassioned testimony from both sides, took place in mid-April. The committee returned a 9–6 vote in favor of keeping the three-million-dollar appropriation for Santa Monica. Several key committee members, including Senators Elkins and Arthur Gorman, voted for Santa Monica, much to the surprise of White.[91]

The harbor controversy hardly ended with the Commerce Committee's vote. The entire issue could conceivably be placed before the assembled Senate for debate. As Collis Huntington observed in a letter to Charles F. Crocker, "Steve White is making a great rumpus and says he is going to knock it out on the floor of the Senate." Huntington admitted that he had uncharacteristic second thoughts about pursuing the harbor matter given the controversy it had created, but the Commerce Committee's vote had created momentum in favor of Santa Monica. "If we withdraw it now a few wild men in St. Louis will say that they beat us."[92]

Georgina Jones commented on the vehemence of the newspapers covering the controversy (especially the *Times*): "How uncalled for, how vulgar + low the personal abuse is, which the papers in favor of San Pedro, or I should say, against the S.P. have resorted to."[93]

Washington affairs replicated the Los Angeles excitement. Both sides viewed the coming debates in the Senate with optimism; both thought that their position would triumph. Last-minute attempts to encourage White to favor Santa Monica failed.[94] In several days of speeches on the Senate floor, he brilliantly analyzed the history of the harbor fight and of the Southern Pacific's actions in California. In particular, he pointed to a possible connection between expert harbor testimony and Southern Pacific employ, referring to the apparent conflicts of interest as "the sinuosities of the situation."[95] The senator also resorted to time-honored methods of opposing the Santa Monica appropriation. The bucolic seaside resort would wilt beneath industrial development: "Its beauties will fade if its beach is devoted to railroads and locomotives." And what of the danger involved?

"Can boys and girls, women and children, nurses and babies safely be trusted upon a shore thus devoted to commercial uses?" Clearly Senator White thought not.[96]

White succeeded in getting yet another commission appointed to examine the two locations. The recommended port would receive the three-million-dollar appropriation. Santa Monica's backers thought the plan a "contemptible trick." Cornelius Cole declared that the "opposition to Santa Monica, in our *public men*, is instigated by hatred of the S.P.R.R. + Huntington and so they go against public interest."[97]

The Southern Pacific attempted to mollify local opinion and mend fences in Los Angeles, in the vain hope that the commission might be persuaded to recommend Santa Monica. Henry E. Huntington suggested to his uncle that granting Los Angeles businessman and Santa Monica supporter J. S. Slauson ten thousand dollars to be used in a hotel project could influence local opinion. Huntington thought the loan "might be a politic plan, just at this time when there is such a feverish controversy among the people of that city in regard to the harbor. . . . It would show that we feel a keen interest in the welfare of those people and might help us in throwing the right kind of influence around the Government Commission."[98]

Other fences were mended in the business arena. In order to protect interests in the eventuality of either port's victory, the Southern Pacific and the Atchison, Topeka & Santa Fe reached agreements in the spring. In addition to dividing southern California territory between the two lines, the agreements included a prohibition against one line's buying the Terminal Railway without the consent of the other. The Southern Pacific agreed to allow the Santa Fe to run its cars over S.P. tracks in Santa Monica in exchange for a Santa Fe pledge to lobby for Santa Monica.[99]

The Southern Pacific tried to cover political bases as well. Writing to a company official, Collis Huntington hinted that George S. Patton, again running for Congress, might receive the powerful backing of the railroad if he were to support Santa Monica (which he did not do).[100]

The new engineering board, like its predecessors, held public meetings in Los Angeles to assess the citizenry's opinions about either location. The climate of opinion was yet again clouded with rhetoric. The *Times* greeted the public meetings by printing a history of the harbor controversy. The battle was marked by "corporate greed, arrogance and treachery on one side, [and] a determined and tireless struggle by the people on the other side."[101]

The hearings, though not without sharp exchanges between the two sides, consisted primarily of technical arguments pertaining to the nautical capacities of either port.[102] Each side paraded before the engineers a series of ship's captains, master mariners, and sailors who testified that one harbor was somehow a better or safer place than the other. The San Pedro defenders introduced the 1894 Trans-Mississippi Congress endorsement of San Pedro—without, of course, noting that the Los Angeles delegates to that gathering were both officers of the Terminal Railway. W. C. Patterson, soon to become a member of the Terminal's board of directors, appeared for the Los Angeles Chamber of Commerce (he was then that group's president). Patterson presented a petition of southern California businessmen in favor of San Pedro. T. E. Gibbon emphasized Collis Huntington's holdings in and around Santa Monica and scoffed at the clause that would allow other lines to lease S.P. tracks. Such a clause could easily be invalidated by Santa Monica local government, he declared.

William Hood questioned both Patterson and Gibbon about their knowledge of Santa Monica property ownership. Patterson, in particular, revealed that he did not know much more than what the newspapers (i.e., the *Times*) alleged. Both sides engaged in rebuttal (largely on technical matters); John Muir of the Southern Pacific pointed out that the qualifications and experience of some of the San Pedro witnesses were suspect if not clearly falsified.

The board adjourned in mid-December. As in every other head-to-head engagement in the history of the harbor fight, both sides claimed to have emerged from the hearings the victor. Both insisted that they truly represented the sentiments of the region.

Before leaving southern California, some members of the harbor commission were entertained by Georgina Jones at the Jones mansion in Santa Monica. William Hood related a curious (but telling) story of the affair to Collis Huntington. The wife of ex-senator Cornelius Cole, a Santa Monica supporter, informed the commissioners that Collis Huntington actually wanted San Pedro to be chosen as the deep-water port because of his and the Southern Pacific's holdings at that place. For that reason alone, Mrs. Cole offered, the choice ought to be Santa Monica.[103]

Goergina Jones, on the basis of a private conversation with a member of the commission, informed her husband that Santa Monica was likely to get the board's recommendation. Joseph Lynch, formerly of the Los Angeles *Herald*, also thought that the commission would choose Santa Monica. Writing in his new journal, *Greater Los Angeles*, Lynch commented on the battle. The claims of Santa Monica's supporters had been unfairly attacked, particularly by the *Times*: "taking advantage of a sentiment which has been drummed up in favor of San Pedro it has assumed that the overwhelming preference of this section is in favor of San Pedro."[104]

The commission, reporting in March of 1897, did decide in favor of San Pedro, prompting Lynch to write: "You can give odds to-day that the man wearing a cherubic expression of peace and good-will . . . is a Terminal railway man." As if taking the cue, Thomas Gibbon wrote exultantly to Stephen White that San Pedro went "wild with delight and you may suppose that I was not among the least demonstrative of the populace."[105]

For all intents and purposes, the harbor fight ended with that recommendation. There would be no more engineering boards, no more public hearings. The Southern Pacific and its officials, especially Collis Huntington, continued to support Santa Monica and were able to block construction of the breakwater at San Pedro for another two years. The delay provoked many San Pedro supporters, who impatiently awaited the commercial windfall that harbor improvements would invariably bring. In the fall of 1897, a friend wrote to John Gaffey (some people only half-jokingly suggested that San Pedro be renamed "Gaffey") that he was "sorry to hear that your dreams of San Pedro's greatness had not been realized, as I sincerely hoped definite action would have been taken ere this, and yourself made a multimillionaire."[106] But the breakwater was eventually constructed, and the story of the harbor fight drifted comfortably into legend and local pride: "the people" had defeated "the Octopus."

An Opening Blow for Progressivism?

Historians have recently analyzed the harbor fight in one of two related ways. The first and simplest recasting of the story is as much a resurrection as it is a revision. Rejecting the oversimplification of the "Octopus school" of California historiography, which sees the railroad much as Frank Norris described it, some historians have pointed to the harbor controversy as proof of tangible, potent, and successful opposition to the supposed domination of the Southern Pacific. The defeat of the railroad corporation alone sustains this analysis. Despite its somewhat superficial nature, the argument is important for adding complexity to an older and no longer viable tradition, which regarded the railroad as all-powerful.[107]

Other historians have sought to place the harbor controversy into the context of Progressive reform. In these analyses, the harbor fight politicizes a coalition of civic-minded leaders who battle the S.P. This formative nineteenth-century reform experience is thus seen as crucial to the Progressive movement of the early twentieth century, especially the anti-railroad gubernatorial campaign of Hiram Johnson in 1910. These analysts point to the common enemy of both eras, the Southern Pacific, and to the fact that many of the principal actors in the harbor fight became active and important Progressives.[108]

Yet there are significant problems with this argument. As Robert Fogelson has pointed out in his fine history of Los Angeles, the powerful forces favoring San Pedro subscribed to a more complicated agenda than most historiography suggests: "the so-called 'free harbor contest' was actually a struggle for speculative profits and not commercial freedom."[109] Manipulation of public opinion, patent self-interest, even the suggestion of outright deception on the part of San Pedro backers—all raise significant questions about means, ends, and the definition of "Progressive" reform. None of this is meant as an apology for the actions, motives, or mercenary tactics of the Southern Pacific Railroad Corporation. But the self-righteous gleam that covers many of the San Pedro supporters cannot withstand serious scrutiny.

Fortified by a web of interconnecting ties, the influential proponents of San Pedro constituted a formidable anti–Southern Pacific force. This coalition drew sharp distinctions between private aims and public pronouncements. Public stances rarely revealed self-interest, and private exchanges infrequently resorted to propagandistic railroad bashing. As Stephen M. White confided revealingly to Harrison Gray Otis: "There is so much in this matter that one cannot afford to publish, that the embarrassments are very greatly augmented when we come to make public explanations." White later wrote to Otis that all care must be exercised in harbor matters "because some of our friends charge that you and I are engaged in a very dark and fearful conspiracy."[110]

As for the larger question of "the Octopus" and railroad power in nineteenth-century California, the free harbor fight demonstrates that the Southern Pacific Railroad was not the all-powerful entity it has been made out to be. It did at times face significant opposition. Yet scholarly inquiries must critically assess the motivations of those who battled the railroad corporation. Matching the harbor fight personnel with later Progressive-era reform movements in itself proves little. Nor does painting the pro–San Pedro activists as selfless urban populists tell us much about their actions or motivations. Those who battled the Southern Pacific in the Los Angeles harbor fight had learned well the lessons of California history and shrewdly massaged a public predilection to view anti-railroad activists in an uncritical light. As long as they did not stretch discontent into radicalism (symbolized as the crazed revolutionary ripping up railroad tracks), the anti–Southern Pacific coterie in the harbor fight had accomplished what would become standard political behavior of the next century:

emptying anti-railroad pronouncements of all but rhetoric. To be sure, Terminal Railway capitalists did not want to rip up railroad tracks: they wanted merely to be allowed to build their own and to do so quietly.[111]

We must therefore reexamine the inclusion of San Pedro's supporters into the Progressive fold. Perhaps we need to reassess our working definition of California Progressivism, at least insofar as opposition to the Southern Pacific Railroad is concerned.[112] Chapter 6 of this book makes such a reassessment, exploring the relationship between the railroad corporation and Progressive reformers in the early years of this century.

5 Pens as Swords

Fiction, Nonfiction, and Railroad Opposition

> It is impossible to control the newspapers in their items.
> They will write and publish what they please, in spite
> of everybody.
> —Charles Crocker
> Letter to Collis Huntington, 1878

> This is practically a fight for the control of public opinion.
> Public opinion is the sovereign of this country, and adverse
> public opinion can rise to a condition of menace which
> would eventually destroy the rights of property.
> —William H. Mills
> Letter to Collis Huntington, 1896

In my discussion of railroad opposition in California, I have relied on the press as an important historical informant. But such reliance entails considerable risk, since the press cannot speak for the majority of people in any particular society: it offers at best only a hint of what the behavior (to say nothing of the thoughts) of great numbers of people left out of the journalistic "loop" may have been. Except for what can be vaguely teased out from between the lines, daily or weekly newspapers tell us only what a tiny number of reporters and editors—overwhelmingly male, obviously employed, at least somewhat educated—wanted to tell their literate readership. Furthermore, there is little guarantee that what was printed in the nineteenth-century press is at all "correct." The institution hardly resembled the press of today; in fact, the two are wholly separate enterprises, linked only by crude mechanistic parallels of putting ink to paper and regularly turning out thousands of newspapers.

What separates journalism in the past from that of today can be described in three rough categories: objectivity, professionalism, and impact. Journalism was, in California no less than any other region of the nation, an enterprise firmly enmeshed, nearly synonymous, with politics. Of course the twentieth-century American press is also a political institution, but newspapers are no longer vehicles for the opinions of their editors to the degree that they were in the nineteenth century.[1] Reportage and editorializing once were inextricably linked in "party organ" newspapers. As Thomas Leonard has bluntly pointed out, the "confidence in one's ability to get the facts and to keep a prejudice is the most striking difference between journalists before and after the turn of the century."[2]

That prejudice inevitably shades and colors the journalistic documentation of California's relationship with the railroad corporation. It is simply hard to figure out whom to believe and what to believe. As chief Southern Pacific propaganda officer William H. Mills candidly admitted regarding his own duties, "Something of abstract truth must sometimes be [sacrificed] when the necessities for assault or defense call for that sacrifice."[3] Nonetheless, in any serious discussion of a subject as important as railroad opposition, the role and power of the press must be evaluated.

This chapter also discusses California railroad opposition as expressed in fiction. For just as there is much that is subjective, overtly political, and false in journalistic reportage, there is much that is "true" in ostensibly fictional works about the railroad and its role in California history. We must of course start and finish with *The Octopus*. Frank Norris's turn-of-the-century novel remains today the best-known work, fictional or otherwise, on California's peculiar relationship with the Southern Pacific railroad. The novel's lasting fame, not to mention its often strange reception by historians, requires that we give the book a close reading.

The Press and the Railroad

Looking back on California's ambivalent relationship with the Southern Pacific railroad, the distinguished San Francisco journalist Fremont Older minced few words. Of politics in the 1890s, Older wrote that the "entire state . . . was politically controlled by the Southern Pacific Railroad." The phenomenally powerful corporation dominated "the Legislature, the courts, the municipal governments, the county governments." It also had "as complete a control of the newspapers of the state as was possible, and through them it controlled public opinion."[4] Few editors dared criticize the railroad, Older wrote, lest they risk the wrath of the "Octopus." A contemporary of Older's viewed the corporation in a similar light. Southern California journalist Thomas M. Storke, who devoted six chapters of his memoirs to "S.P. Rule in California," wrote that no "newspaper publisher who was active from the early 1880s until Hiram W. Johnson became Governor in 1911, could wholly escape the effects of the operations of the Southern Pacific's political machine in molding the life and character of his newspaper."[5]

What was the relationship between the press and the railroad corporation? Where did the balance of power lie, and how did it shift across the course of several generations? Was it as amazingly all-powerful as these contemporary observers (who were not fools) insisted?

As we have seen, the railroad enjoyed favorable press long before there was a Central or Southern Pacific. Throughout the antebellum period, countless writers, politicians, and newspapermen championed the idea of a transcontinental railroad. Breathlessly awaiting the reports of various survey parties, eastern writers spared few adjectives in describing the potential impact of the railroad on western society.[6] Neither the discordant voices of worried Southerners (sure that any but a southern transcontinental railway meant more power to the North) nor the prophetic cry-in-the-wilderness cautions of Henry George could effectively dilute the overwhelmingly positive reception granted the transcontinental railroad scheme. And once the four diligent businessmen of Sacramento inaugurated the Central Pacific, they naturally received the jubilant praise of writers expecting railroad-borne progress. The ambitious project made for a perfect fit with mid-century expectations of Manifest Destiny and American prosperity. It was a technological antidote to the Civil War's tragedies.

But that glowing reception would not and could not last. In California, despite the rapt attention given the beginning of transcontinental construction and operation, discontent fairly quickly became part and parcel of railroad dialogue. Railroad-sponsored tracts and travel accounts continued to heap accolades on the Central Pacific and its directors, but stage whispers of skepticism could be heard above the din.

One of the earliest and most emphatic challenges to the railroad corporation came in the pages of the powerful Sacramento *Union*. Initially supportive of the eastward progress of Central Pacific track, the paper shifted its policy early in 1868. In explaining the policy change, the paper's owners pointed to the railroad corporation's subsidy demands of towns and counties lying in the Central Pacific's proposed path. "In ordinary matters we can respect shrewdness in an enemy," a February editorial declared, "but such shrewdness as is being practiced upon the people of California by the corporation known as the Central Pacific Railroad Company is simply execreble."[7]

Railroad executives apparently believed that the paper's hostility sprang from less civic-minded sources. Mark Hopkins thought that the Union Pacific was to blame, a not unreasonable assumption given the fierce competition between the two rail companies. Charles Crocker thought otherwise. In a statement given to California historian Hubert Howe Bancroft, he blithely insisted that the overnight hostility of the paper resulted from an altercation between *Union* editor James Anthony and a Central Pacific employee. Out for a day of hunting, Anthony boarded a train with his dog. A conductor balked, insisting that Central Pacific policy forbade dogs in passenger cars. Anthony's protests were unsuccessful, and immediately thereafter "the Union changed its tone, and assaulted the company in every way possible."[8] Probably apocryphal, surely absurd, such an explanation is really as good as any for explaining the *Union's* turnabout regarding the railroad. In any event, the antagonistic tone of the paper and its strategic location in the state capital, coupled with an increasingly hostile Bay Area press, forced the railroad corporation to act.

No doubt in reference to the *Union* and political affairs in Sacramento, Collis Huntington confided to Charles Crocker in early 1868 that it "is really unfortunate that so nearly all the California Press are down on us, but at this late date I have no doubt you can handle the committees better than you can the press." It is clear that journalistic criticism vexed Huntington. "I wish we could come nearer controlling that paper than we do," he admitted; not only was the *Union* exercising influence in California, but equally worrisome was the fact that eastern papers picked up and printed *Union* stories.[9] In his attempts to promote expansion of the Central Pacific, Huntington was then conducting energetic and somewhat sensitive negotiations with the federal government and eastern investors.[10] The *Union's* antics conceivably threatened such plans, and by the spring of 1868, a strategy had been sketched out to blunt the paper's impact.

The railroad corporation began by backing the Sacramento *Record*, setting it up as an opposition paper.[11] But more emphatic action was required. "You suggest that I buy out Fuskin's interest in the 'Sacramento Union,'" Huntington wrote to Crocker. "It would seem to me much better, if you wanted to control the 'Union,' that you should buy out the parties in California that really control the paper."[12] By the mid-1870s, the corporation had done just that, merging the two papers into the *Record-Union*, from then on a partisan pro-railroad newspaper.[13] The company had discovered an effective way to eliminate "bad" press and fill the void with "good."

Most papers did not adopt the Sacramento *Union's* hostile attitude in the late 1860s. Like all Californians, journalists and editors needed time and experience to come to grips with the transcontinental railroad's impact on their state. Consequently, they tended to give the technology and the corporation the benefit of the doubt, initially at least, rather than questioning their presence. For instance, when two passenger trains smashed head-on into each other only days after the first overland arrived in Oakland, killing more than a dozen people, the local *Daily News* stoically admitted that "so long as railroads are used accidents will occasionally occur." The paper expressed only slight ambivalence about railroads, curiously referring to the fated passengers as "inmates" and noting that "the cause of our congratulations becomes the instrument of our grief."[14] An accompanying editorial merely suggested that perhaps overland trains traveled faster than necessary. And when a rival, out-of-town paper dared suggest that the railroad corporation deserved to be held responsible for the wreck, the *Daily News* scoffed that such finger pointing was "the sheerest ignorance or envenomed spite."[15]

But as corporate power increased, so too did public and press hostility. "Richardson, the correspondent of the 'Tribune,' has just returned," Collis Huntington wrote to Mark Hopkins in the summer of 1869. "He says we are very unpopular in California; that we talk as though we owned the country. . . . He said that Mr. Crelish, of the 'Alta,' told him that he could not stand us much longer . . . that we know nothing about operating railroads, and much such talk."[16]

The Crédit Mobilier scandal concerning the financing of the Union Pacific, which became public in 1872, did little to endear the press to the Central Pacific. "Since the [congressional investigation] that portion of the press naturally inclined to be unfriendly are very bold in every species of assertion and innuendo tending to identify the C.P. as a part of the great Pacific R.R. fraud," wrote Mark Hopkins in early 1873.[17]

The increase of journalistic grumbling coincided with the rising importance in California of anti-railroad politics. Editors anxious to stake out partisan terrain, increase readership, and possibly earn political favors became vocal opponents of the railroad corporation. By the mid-1870s, other important newspapers followed the path blazed by the Sacramento *Union*, often leaving behind old alliances for new. For instance, George Fitch and Loring Pickering, owners of two important San Francisco newspapers, had originally been enthusiastic promoters of the transcontinental railway. That support waned, however, amid the controversies over railroad subsidies and federal and state gifts of large parcels of land. Consequently, Pickering and Fitch shifted the point of view of their two papers, the *Call* and the *Morning Bulletin*. This change apparently caused no small amount of consternation at the highest echelon of railroad management. In December of 1875, Fitch and Pickering met with several top Central Pacific executives, including Leland Stanford and Mark Hopkins. The railroad officials, not averse to pressuring the journalists by hardball politics and rerouted philanthropy, were assured that "we did not want any further trouble."[18] Nonetheless, the two papers, and George Fitch especially, continued to attack the railroad conglomerate.

The railroad corporation attempted to fend off the attacks of the press by distributing free passes and blank railroad tickets. Editors of many a small paper would happily accept annual passes to travel on S.P. lines in exchange for favorable railroad press; free rail travel would be a valuable economic boost for any hardscrabble journalist. As editor Storke remembered of the local Southern Pacific agent in Santa Barbara: "Jack Harrington always carried a pocket full of railroad passes. If you had an opportunity to do a friendly act for the Southern Pacific, Jack would hand out passes to you and your family to go anywhere on that railroad. If you happened to be a city, county or state office holder, all that was necessary for you to do was to ask Jack, and free passes would be forthcoming."[19]

The California legislature, responding to public outcry against the free pass, passed resolutions in the mid-1870s forbidding their use. But company officials clearly found ways around the obstacle. "When you want to come to San Francisco," Charles Crocker wrote to southern California businessman Charles Maclay in 1877, "write me in a few days and I will fix it for you. I am very sorry that I cannot issue you a pass; the law was passed on purpose to prevent us from favoring our friends, or, rather, to prevent us from having any friends!"[20]

As discussed in chapter 2, one of the railroad's sharpest critics through the 1870s and into the 1880s was the Republican San Francisco journal *Wasp*. Supportive of reform measures aiming toward freight and fare reductions, abolition of the free pass, and the establishment of a new railroad commission, the *Wasp* lampooned railroad officials and bemoaned the growth of corporate influence in California affairs. "Without doubt, one of the greatest dangers which threaten this country," cautioned an 1881 editorial, "is the immense power of these wealthy railroad corporations. . . . Not only can they force the unfortunate farmer and merchant to pay whatever they choose to ask for transportation, but there will, we fear, be few members of our legislative bodies, able to resist such temptations as they can well afford to offer."[21]

By the mid-1880s, *Wasp* publisher E. C. MacFarlane had at least a temporary falling out with the Republican leadership because of his objections to the railroad corporation's machinations within the party. In a letter to journalist Ambrose Bierce, MacFarlane wrote: "The more I think of the proposition to abandon the Republican Party, so far as my paper is concerned, the more I am satisfied of the wisdom of such a move. In the first place, we cannot be sincere and [consistent?] in our Rail Road fight, if we are willing to join hands with the Republican Party, when Crocker [and] the whole rail road gang are controlling the movement of the Party."[22]

Yet disassociating the journal from the party, not to mention the Southern Pacific, proved no easy task. The 1885 campaigns, including Leland Stanford's attempt (eventually successful) to get the Republican Party's nod in filling a vacant seat in the U.S. Senate, complicated affairs immeasurably. The interplay of matters personal with matters political frustrated MacFarlane, prompting him to seek the advice of Bierce. "I am in a peck of trouble [and] begin to wish the d——d campaign was in hell," he wrote. "I have so many complications to contend against and so many personal interests to reconcile with political ones, that I don't know which way to turn at times." The editor wanted to support anti-railroad candidates for public office, but conflicts inevitably arose. Revelations about any particular candidate's ties to the railroad or some other "interest" might be made at any time. "If I should support Jesus Christ, if he were a candidate for office, I believe they would spring something on him at the last minute," MacFarlane lamented.[23]

By the volatile 1890s, the railroad corporation had had several decades to make enemies, and make enemies it did. Fremont Older, who charged the Southern Pacific with Octopus-like hegemony in the 1890s, was wrong. On the contrary, the corporation was mired in conflict and fighting a veritable laundry list of foes. In the arena of state politics, Senate and gubernatorial elections preoccupied railroad officials forever fearful of "communists" and hated "agrarians." The brief but powerful Populist movement in California crystallized railroad antagonism into a viable and moderately successful third-party force. The harbor fight in southern California represented a major challenge to the Southern Pacific's ability to direct both regional development and federal backing of pork barrel projects. The Pullman strike temporarily crippled the railroad, bringing with it much Southern Pacific handwringing over the public's apparent tolerance of and support for the militant tactics of the ARU. In the mid-1890s, the controversy over the refunding of the Central Pacific debt, like the harbor fight, engaged and enraged people on both coasts, as the railroad sought with mixed results to manipulate state and federal policy as well as public opinion. Internal strife hurt the corporation as well: Stanford and Huntington's long-simmering dispute erupted at the beginning of the decade with Huntington's succession to the presidency of the Southern Pacific. Stanford's political ambitions, including his clumsy courtship of farm and labor organizations with a history of railroad opposition, added fuel to the fires of corporate squabbles.[24]

The Southern Pacific met each of these various challenges combatively, always cognizant of the power of the press. The corporation did run a well-oiled, if crude, propaganda machine, forever strident in its defense of the aims, policies, and history of the railroad company in California.

Toiling hand in hand behind the scenes with the corporation's "political bureau," press propagandists worked to satisfy the wishes of Collis Huntington, who spoke for the railroad when he insisted: "We must do something to get better men in public places than we have had before; and I think we must keep out of politics." Given the contradictions in such a policy, Huntington recognized that "all these matters should be kept from the public, as they are so liable to be misconstrued."[25]

California's chief supervisor of Southern Pacific propaganda was William H. Mills, faithful servant to Collis P. Huntington. "In your position you can do a great deal to put things right," Huntington assured Mills in 1891, "as I think there is no other man in California so near the public press as you are or who would have so large an influence over them. In that direction I think you can do very much to keep the public mind quiet. It seems to me that our position is very strong when we say we are going to keep aloof from politics."[26] Machiavelli lives! In other words, Mills had the unenviable duty of keeping his right hand busy meddling with the press while constantly denying his manuevers with his left.

Corporate detachment from the political arena rarely progressed any further than Collis Huntington's rhetoric. Recognizing the political power of "anti-railroadism," the railroad corporation might even urge friendly candidates to borrow from that camp while out on the stump. A prominent example of such politicking occurred during the gubernatorial campaign of 1894. Despite his ostensible support of railroad nationalization, Democrat James H. Budd apparently represented little threat to the Southern Pacific. Henry Huntington assured his uncle in late 1894 that Budd "feels very kind toward the Southern Pacific Company notwithstanding his assertions to the public to the contrary. The copy of his letter the other day was written at our suggestion."[27]

Promotion of such superficial opposition hints at the political power of both the anti-railroad press and the voting public. For his part, Henry Huntington thought the press crucial to the formation of anti-railroad factions throughout the latter decades of the nineteenth century. In an unusual and highly revealing letter to Southern Pacific official Thomas Hubbard, Huntington sketched the history of railroad opposition in California from before Promontory through the mid-1890s. Railroad antagonism was a national phenomenon, Huntington argued; California's experience differed from eastern states only in chronology and the compression of like events into less than half a century. Completely blind to the real causes behind all varieties of railroad opposition, Huntington insisted that such antagonism was first and foremost a singular and malleable political issue, not a grass-roots affair. Antagonism periodically raised its head "through the instrumentality of the hungry politicians and the black-mailing demands of the venal press."[28]

Yet the reasons for journalistic antagonism toward the railroad and rail company varied from paper to paper and editor to editor and defy railroad executives' penchant for simple explanations. Collis Huntington often wrote that the media's antagonism came only after the corporation cut off payments to the various papers' owners. "The *Argonaut*, I see, is as nasty as usual, but I don't blame [editor Frank] Pixley for being mad, as I cut off his $10,000 a year; although it is not as bad for him as it would be if Stanford was not at this time paying it out of his own pocket, which I have no doubt he is."[29] Stanford's alleged distribution of cash for political favors especially infuriated Huntington. "I have an impression that no-body ever made more mistakes than our people have made in handling matters political in California. I think they have paid out large amounts of money [and] paid much of it on the street corners, although of that of course I am not certain. We were paying some vampires, like The Argo-naut, Bassett's Standard [and] others, whose pay I cut off [and] of course they snarled back at me like so many hyenas."[30]

Huntington's logic may of course have been reasonable, given the specifics of any given case or any given paper. But that does not explain the body of press opposition, which, despite their invariable attempts to explain it away, railroad executives could never really understand. The net result of press opposition was a cluster of antagonistic opinion, which doubtless helped harden public reaction against the corporation for a wide variety of reasons. Several key papers, editors, and journalists played especially prominent roles in the 1890s. In northern California, the "Dear Pard" letters of journalist J. M. Bassett, which often viciously attacked the character and actions of Collis Huntington, became notorious by century's end.[31]

No less notorious a critic of the Southern Pacific was William Randolph Hearst's *Examiner*. Hearst's motivations for his opposition are doubtless complex. Certainly his own political ambitions and support of prominent Democratic candidates often placed him at loggerheads with the likes of Stanford and Huntington, usual supporters of the Republican party. Too, Hearst supported and held stock in sugar magnate Claus Spreckels's "Peo-ple's Railroad," begun in 1893 to compete with the Southern Pacific in the Central Valley. What is more, Hearst's father, George, had been an active anti-railroad force in state Democratic circles since the early 1880s. Not surprisingly, given their penchant for reductionist explanations, railroad officials thought the root of Hearst's antagonism much easier to discover. Sometime in the early 1890s, the Southern Pacific and the San Francisco

Examiner had entered into an unusual contract agreement. The railroad corporation agreed to pay the newspaper $30,000 in monthly installments; the company would in turn "receive certain advertising and also fair treatment at the hands of the paper." But of course the advertising space was purely secondary to the contract's aims. As Southern Pacific chief counsel William Herrin wrote to the *Examiner*'s business manager, "There can be no question that the chief consideration to inure to the Southern Pacific Company in this transaction was the fair treatment to be accorded by your paper; that it would not have entered into an agreement to $30,000 for advertising merely, as the benefit to accrue from such advertising alone was grossly inadequate to the sum of money involved." In this, Herrin was certainly right: the railroad could float its own advertising magazine for far less than the money exchanged with Hearst. Before long, however, a dispute arose over the fulfillment of the contract, and the monthly payments to the paper halted. In ordinary business arrangements, such a situation might lead to legal and at least mildly public arbitration. But, as Herrin noted matter-of-factly: "That method of determination in this instance would not be satisfactory to either party."[32]

The dispute likely did little to endear the already hostile Hearst to the Southern Pacific (or vice versa). At the probable direction of their employer, journalists Ambrose Bierce and Arthur McEwen and cartoonist Homer Davenport turned their acidic pens on Collis Huntington and his company throughout the remainder of the decade. Davenport caricatured Huntington as a paunchy, probably Jewish, gnome and shylock.[33]

Arthur McEwen, brilliant and cantankerous in the mold of Bierce, though politically much further to the left, wrote intemperate columns for Hearst as well (and published his own anti-corporate *Arthur McEwen's Letter*). McEwen reserved most of his venom for Leland Stanford. Stanford's tenure as U.S. senator was, McEwen charged, "an indictment of the intelligence and moral character of the people of California." Unlike Bierce, McEwen pledged allegiance to a definite political platform. "Mr. Stanford lacks either the breadth or courage to be logical and accept the Socialists' aim of a cooperative commonwealth, in which there would be no competition—and no Stanfords." The combative journalist agreed that Stanford and his partners deserved credit for taking on the transcontinental railway project, but their business acumen and ruthlessness alone did not make them worthy of public canonization. After all, Stanford and company did not invent the railroad; they merely reaped the benefits brought about by the ingenuity of others.[34]

The *Examiner* held sway in northern California as the major Democratic organ of railroad opposition. Even Senate hopeful Stephen M. White felt compelled to write the *Examiner* and emphasize his credentials as an anti-railroad man. Shortly before his 1893 appointment to fill a vacant Senate seat, White wrote to Loring Pickering of the San Francisco *Call*. Because he had at one point crossed William Randolph Hearst, White expected to be labeled a railroad lackey by the paper. But such was not the case, White insisted. As a member of the state legislature, he "ardently and persistently" argued that the Central Pacific be forced to pay its state taxes. Charges that he was tied to the Southern Pacific were "utterly and absolutely ridiculous." Unlike others, he did not accept railroad passes. And though he explicitly distanced himself from the more radical Populists, who supported railroad nationalization, White emphasized his anti-monopoly credentials.[35]

Part of the *Examiner's* success at irritating the Southern Pacific lay in a clever strategy of diversified assault. The corporation's actions—political, technological, local, statewide, routine, and extraordinary—were all attacked. Even the character of Southern Pacific officials was not above criticism: their meanness, spite, and aloof bearing "made the railroad a hated thing in California," the paper insisted.

The decade-long dispute over the refunding of the Central Pacific debt presented the perfect opportunity to attack the railroad on several fronts. The funding crisis revolved around a single question: When should the federal government "call in" its massive loans made to the Central Pacific during the early days of transcontinental construction? From that simple query was spun an immensely complicated legal and financial web. For their part, the railroad officials requested (somewhat sheepishly) that the entire debt be forgiven, since the transcontinental had done so much for the nation. Failing that, they wished the government to claim its money by gobbling up railroad land-grant parcels—parcels that were originally gifts from the federal government to the railroad!

The debt controversy, not finally settled until 1899, gave Hearst's *Examiner* a terrific cause célèbre; the paper reviewed over and over again the history of railroad abuses in California, and Hearst gave Bierce the plum assignment of covering the controversy—and "railrogues"—in Washington as debate heated up. Bierce's regular installments were masterful examples of his trademark invective and sarcasm. Along with other major papers in the state, the *Examiner* urged that the railroad corporation meet its federal debts or face a government takeover. Hearst urged Bay Area residents to sign anti-funding bill petitions at the *Examiner* offices. The final defeat of the bill in 1897 prompted the governor to proclaim a holiday of statewide celebration. "San Francisco Wild with Joy at Downfall of the Huntington Lobby and the Funding Iniquity," the *Examiner* declared triumphantly.[36]

In southern California, the harbor fight prompted a similar propaganda war. Southern California newspapers, most notably the Los Angeles *Times*, covered the funding bill closely but emphasized the local importance of the harbor dispute. The juxtaposition of the two conflicts did the railroad corporation little good in the southland. To the north, the *Examiner* tried to combine forces with those battling the Southern Pacific in southern California.[37] As George Miles, lobbying on the Southern Pacific's behalf in Washington, noted: the harbor fight "crystallized . . . the sentiment, already a bit shaky, on the Funding Bill into a more or less compact body of opposition."[38]

As shown in chapter 4, the powerful supporters of San Pedro displayed a shrewd appreciation for the press in their dispute with Huntington and the S.P. Terminal Railway officials exchanged thoughts and schemes about Los Angeles newspapers and "expenditures for educating the people in favor of San Pedro Harbor." "I think it would be well to stir the people up and let the emphatic demand that the interests of San Pedro should be looked out for come thick and fast," Terminal Railway executive Richard Kerens wrote to Thomas Gibbon, adding: "You know how to do this." Anti-railroad propaganda no doubt played a role: "Please consult with Mr. Burnett and quietly adopt a policy of raising your voices against the oppression and methods of the S.P.," Kerens requested of Gibbon in 1893. The effort required caution. Kerens did not want San Pedro supporters to be accused of adopting the same tactics as the Southern Pacific (nor did he want his personal interest in the affair to come to light). Consequently, Gibbon's behind-the-scenes newspaper-buying actions were accomplished with sensitivity and secrecy.[39]

The Southern Pacific clearly tried to fight back, not willing to let propagandistic tables be turned. The Los Angeles *Express*, under the editorship of H. Z. Osborne, did the railroad company's bidding in the harbor fight. Until its sale to a consortium of pro–San Pedro Democrats, the *Herald* did likewise. But faced with the increasing power of Harrison Gray Otis and his *Times*, the Southern Pacific would lose its fight for favorable press in Los Angeles.

In northern California, the *Examiner* and other papers took the battle directly into the enemy's camp, by sensationally reporting on the day-to-day dangers of riding Southern Pacific trains and trolleys. Railway—particularly streetcar—accidents occurred with frightening regularity across the country during this period. Safety regulations were few, streetcars ran perilously close to pedestrian and carriage traffic, and operators were often poorly trained. Furthermore, many accident victims—visitors to the city from the countryside or reckless children—clearly did not appreciate the speed or power of all manner of urban trains and trolleys.

Mixing yellow with investigative journalism, the *Examiner* splashed the grim details of train and trolley accidents across its front page, nearly always concluding with an indictment of the Southern Pacific or Henry Huntington, who sat atop the company's Bay Area trolley management. "Grim Death Waited for Hundreds" read one headline following a collision between two passenger trains that seriously injured two travelers. *Examiner* editors began to keep and publish accident statistics. The paper also pushed for better safety measures, including fenders at the front of cars to scoop up anyone caught in the train's path. Hearst even commissioned cartoonist Thomas Nast to draw a famous cartoon depicting "Death, the Gripman" at the helm of the city's trolleys.[40]

"Little Frankie Mohr Run Down Yesterday by a Fenderless Motor," the paper reported after an accident involving a young boy. Frankie, his body now "Mangled by an Electric Car," had gone out to search for loose chunks of coal along the tracks of the street railway. His mother had sent him out to scavenge because his father lay at home nursing a crushed arm, the result of an accident involving a Southern Pacific train a month earlier. The father, reported the paper, had received no assistance from "Mr. Huntington's agents."[41]

Although the *Examiner*'s melodramatic tactics provoked the wrath of both the railroad corporation and many of its employees, the sensationalism proved infectious.[42] The previously timid *Call* even joined in. One notable cartoon in the paper depicted a car from the Southern Pacific–controlled Market Street Railway. Passengers seeking life insurance policies were asked to inquire of the motorman upon boarding; they were further "Requested to Keep from Under Wheels if Possible."[43]

A cost-cutting measure by the railroad corporation furthered its troubles with the antagonistic press. The Southern Pacific, like most large railroad companies of the day, employed teams of men to walk sections of track, looking for potential problems or obstacles on the rails or in the railroad bed. In an attempt to streamline operations, the railroad company began to cut its trackwalking operations in the mid-1890s. The S.P. instead strapped men onto specially fitted track velocipedes that allowed for faster survey of rail lines. The opposition press blasted the decision, arguing that the elimination of trackwalkers was both heartless and dangerous. "Death and Disaster are Laid at the Southern Pacific's Door," charged the *Examiner* after one fatal wreck.[44]

Despite the Southern Pacific's impressive resources and energetic efforts at manipulating public opinion, events in the mid-1890s produced surprise and consternation among the corporation's elite: Californians continued to raise their voices (and cast their ballots) against the Southern Pacific. To the S.P., the public clearly was "misguided, misdirected, and miseducated." The deep concern of propagandist William H. Mills reveals company perplexity. In 1895, Mills had boasted to Collis Huntington: "My relation with the press is such that I exercise a direct influence upon public thought." Such arrogance quickly melted away. A year and a half later, Mills complained: "it is perfectly apparent that there is some fault somewhere in producing a good relation between the Company and the public." All the energy expended by Mills and others to ensure favorable press seemed, in light of the 1896 elections, the harbor fight, and the funding bill, for naught. Sounding much like a late-twentieth-century political spin doctor, Mills lamented that the "newspapers in short do not appear to create public sentiment or produce results." But instead of searching for the roots of the public's anti-railroad thought and behavior (treating the phenomenon, in other words, as if it were real), Mills concluded that the Southern Pacific "does not do business with the right kind of men."[45] The problem lay with individuals, not method or theory or, it seems, reality.

Consequently, and with the blessing of Collis Huntington, Mills redoubled his efforts with an eye toward the elections of 1898. The Southern Pacific especially feared the potential power of California's farmers, primarily those gathered loosely into the state's rapidly disintegrating Populist Party (an "agrarian army" and a "party of communists," Mills called them). By October of 1897, he could write to Huntington that the farmers of California had begun to "regard me as their friend."[46] Propaganda work on behalf of the Southern Pacific clearly *coincided with*—much more than brought about—the decline of short-lived anti-railroad political movements such as the movement that gave rise to the People's Party.[47] Nonetheless, after the polls closed in 1898, Mills and other railroad servants gleefully took the credit for turning away the tide of popular discontent. "Good government has been established," Mills gloated. "The obstructing forces of communism and socialism have been swept away."[48]

High corporate officials believed that they had vanquished their anti-railroad enemies in the elections of 1898. In an end-of-the-century letter to a New York banker, Collis Huntington looked back at his nearly fifty-year involvement with the transcontinental railroad in the American West. In his view, railroad opposition in California was merely a reflection of similar opposition in other states—precisely what his nephew had decided in an earlier summing up. But in a remarkable example of reductionist thinking, Huntington also wrote that antagonism pointed at his company was "almost altogether created" by San Francisco newspapers.[49]

William H. Mills believed that Republican and railroad company success in the 1898 elections meant peace for the Southern Pacific for "at least ten years." He was wrong. Opposition to the Southern Pacific was far too diverse a feature of California society to be put to sleep by the defeat of the Populists. Furthermore, Collis Huntington's indictment of San Francisco newspapers as the source of such antagonism—clearly pointing his finger at Hearst and the *Examiner*—revealed an equally simplistic understanding of California's railroad problem.

Only a month after the 1898 election, Mills complained that the corporation was again fending off the slings and arrows of angry Californians. By the early years of the twentieth century, with the Southern Pacific implicated in the corrupt antics of San Francisco power broker Abraham Ruef, the corporation faced increasingly influential hostility from the press. By the time Mills's naively predicted ten-year hiatus had ended, an even more powerful journalistic juggernaut was set to be loosed on the Southern Pacific. Under the direction of shrewd newspapermen such as Chester Rowell, E. A. Dickson, and E. T. Earl, the Lincoln-Roosevelt League lassoed well over a hundred state papers—small, medium, and large—and put them to work championing the anti-Southern Pacific campaign of Hiram Johnson for governor, which we will examine at length in chapter 6.[50] Realizing that their candidate's most important hurdle was the Republican primary, Rowell and company made sure that loyal papers throughout the state saturated their readership with pro-Johnson coverage very early in the campaign. The strategy worked. Even the opposition of Hearst's papers in San Francisco and Los Angeles (Johnson's anti-railroad credentials could not overcome his Republican roots as far as Democrat Hearst was concerned) proved of little moment in the end.

Frank Norris, Historian

> It's possible to cut and slice history really any way you want to. . . . That's probably why history belongs more to the novelists and the poets than it does to the social scientists. At least we admit that we lie.
>
> —E. L. Doctorow
> *Essays and Conversations*, 1983

Any discussion of "the railroad" and "pens as swords" in California history begins and ends with a single novel. The role of the press in standing for or against the railroad in California, regardless of its significance, has been completely overshadowed by this single work of fiction. When he set out to "just say the last word on the R.R. question in California," Frank Norris went first to newspaper accounts purporting to explain much about the railroad's role in California history. Then Norris went those papers one further in his turn-of-the-century best-selling novel *The Octopus: A Story of California.*

Frank Norris was not the first to attack the railroad in the pages of a western novel. Others had taken the story of railroad opposition, especially the bloody drama of the Mussel Slough affair, as their subject well before him.[51] William Morrow, in his 1882 novel *Blood-Money*, furthered the martyrdom of the settlers killed in the notorious 1880 shoot-out. C. C. Post's *Driven from Sea to Sea* followed several years later with a similar theme. Anti-monopoly tract *The Squatter and the Don* (1885) put the railroad problem in startlingly millennial terms, confessing that "we . . . must wait and pray for a Redeemer who will emancipate the white slaves of California."[52] In *The Monarch Philanthropist* (1892), a pastoral California existence is destroyed by the venality and crushing power of railroad official "Eland Lanford." Portrayed in the novel as a corrupt capitalist who lived off other people's money, refused to pay his debts, and polluted the republic by the manufacture of liquor, Lanford was caricatured as the quintessential railroad magnate.[53] Other books, too, depict a frustrated and angry California population, anxious to do something about the state's perennial railroad problem or problems. But none do it so powerfully as *The Octopus*, and it is Frank Norris who has emerged as the unquestioned champion of the anti-railroad genre, far bigger than arguably more important figures, such as journalists Arthur McEwen and Ambrose Bierce.

At the end of the nineteenth century, Norris described to a friend his latest book project. "I've got an idea thats as big as all outdoors," he wrote excitedly. The new book would "be all about the San Joaquin wheat ranchers and the Southern Pacific, and I guess we'll call it The Octopus.—catch on?" The young writer would travel to California from the East to do research and study "the whole thing on the ground." He would then return to New York and "write a hair lifting story."[54]

Norris knew what would make a dramatic story, and in the outlines of the new book lay the potential for a great, if not *the* great, American novel. "There's the chance for the big, Epic, dramatic thing in this," he declared, "and I mean to do it thoroughly—get at it from every point of view, the social, agricultural, & political."[55]

Frank Norris approached the writing of his most famous work with auspicious ambition: he wanted the book to be a major literary success, and he hoped to "just say the last word on the R.R. question in California." *The Octopus: A Story of California*, the result of this attempt to satisfy the two muses of history and literature, appeared in 1901. Since then, neither historians nor literary scholars have been quite sure what to make of it.

Reading uncritically, many historians have accepted *The Octopus* as a faithful depiction of the power, even menace, of the Southern Pacific Corporation. But naming the ostensibly fictional work as a companion to history—if not history itself—is extremely problematic.[56] If the novel is to be viewed as such, it ought to be subjected to the same scrutiny and evaluation that other historical works are subjected to. That assessment requires first an understanding of intention. What sort of book did Norris set out to write?

Many historians view Norris as a muckraking reformer and argue that *The Octopus* is a progressive tract of social criticism, whereas literary scholars have long ceased to read the novel in this light.[57] Historians for the most part persist in describing *The Octopus* as California's version of Upton Sinclair's *The Jungle*.[58] We can see the tendency in the texts assigned in California or western history courses: one typical textbook affirmed that the novel "impressed men's minds and spurred reform efforts. This timely account of the famed Mussel Slough incident conditioned the minds of people to the Progressive reform crusade after 1910."[59] Another book declares simply that Norris "had a profound desire to correct social ills."[60]

But *The Octopus* was *not* written as social criticism. Readers looking for "a Thomas Nast cartoon in prose" might uncover one in the pages of the novel, but not because of any deliberate action on the part of the novelist.[61] For one thing, Norris did not have the concerns of a reformer.[62] Responding to a letter shortly after the novel's publication, he wrote to an inquiring newspaperman: "You ask if I shall attempt any solution of the problem [of the power of trusts in American life]. I hardly think so. The novelist—by nature—can hardly be a political economist; and it is to the latter rather than the former that one must look for a way out of the 'present discontents.'"[63] The thoughts of Presley, the major character in *The Octopus*, might have echoed those of Norris himself: "These matters, these eternal fierce bickerings between the farmers of the San Joaquin and the Pacific and Southwestern Railroad irritated him and wearied him. He cared for none of these things. They did not belong to his world."[64] Frank Norris wanted simply to write a great novel. The truth he was interested in portraying was not the truth embedded in the minutiae of historical fact.[65] Having drunk reverentially from the cup of French writer Emile Zola's naturalism, he claimed that his work was as true as life; as writer, he merely held a mirror to the face of man, transforming the reflection into language.

How good a historian was Frank Norris? Aside from questions of philosophical consistency or literary skill, how "real" or "truthful" is *The Octopus* as a depiction of nineteenth-century California? Can the novel legitimately cross the boundary that separates fiction from nonfiction and stand as the representative work of an important tradition in California history? And is the novel worthy of citation not only as a work of history but, as many continue to insist, as a historical document itself?

Quick study of Frank Norris's approach to and work on *The Octopus* leads to the impression that the novel would provide a reliable depiction of railroad conflict in nineteenth-century California.[66] After declaring his intention to pursue his research "from every point of view," the twenty-nine-year-old novelist left New York for California in the spring of 1899. Like John Steinbeck and Carey McWilliams a generation later, Norris would do his work "on the ground," surrounded by his subject. Once in San Francisco, Norris threw himself into research with characteristic abandon. "I'm having such a bully good time," he wrote to friends. "Feel just as if I was out of doors playing after being in school for years."[67]

Norris's enthusiasm sprang partly from his happiness in returning to California. He had spent his adolescence in the Bay Area and had gone to college at the University of California.[68] In the mid-1890s, he had served a journalist's apprenticeship on the staff of the *Wave*, a high-toned, pro-railroad San Francisco weekly magazine under the editorship of John O'Hara Cosgrave. The Bay Area had formed the backdrop for Norris's dark novel *McTeague* (1899), which, like *The Octopus*, was based on actual events and characters.[69]

Frank Norris spent four months in California. In the Mechanics' Library in San Francisco, he pored over old newspaper and journal accounts of the notorious Mussel Slough shoot-out. Through Cosgrave of the *Wave*, he contacted John P. Irish, then editor of the conservative, pro–Southern Pacific *Argonaut*. Upon learning that Irish "would be kind enough to give some information in the matter of the controversy between the California farmer and the S.P. Railroad," Norris arranged a meeting with the important Democratic journalist.[70]

Assuming that the two met, Irish doubtless provided Norris with a great deal of information. Several years earlier, he had written an article in the *Overland Monthly* entitled "California and the Railroad," in which he cast himself as the conservative response to anti-railroad politics and sentiments.[71] This essay, which we looked at in chapter 3, was in many ways the alter ego response to Henry George's "What the Railroad Will

Bring Us" (discussed in chapter 1). In effect, Irish argued that George's pessimistic prophecies had not come to pass. The railroad's effect on the state had been incontrovertibly positive. Opinions and declarations to the contrary he dismissed as self-serving rhetoric.[72]

Norris contacted others familiar with California history, railroads, and the Mussel Slough incident. As he wrote to journalist Isaac Marcosson, "You've no idea of the outside work on [the novel]. I've been in correspondence with all kinds of people during its composition, from the Traffic Manager of a Western railroad to the sub-deputy-assistant of the Secretary of Agriculture at Washington."[73] He even spent about half of his California visit on the Santa Anita Rancho outside Hollister, where he took part in a wheat harvest and likely observed many of the farming and ranching rituals later to appear in the novel.[74]

Gathering up his notes, Norris reluctantly returned east in the late summer. His work continued. An interview was apparently arranged with Collis P. Huntington of the Southern Pacific, one that possibly changed the entire thrust of the novel.[75] Although we do not know what transpired between the two men, or whether the meeting took place at all, we can surmise what Huntington's perspective would have been. In a long letter to banker James Speyer at century's end, Huntington had analyzed the reasons for the railroad's unpopularity in California. While admitting that mistakes were made, Huntington defended most of the corporation's activities. "The law of self-preservation and of self-defense was not made for individuals any more than it was for corporations," he wrote. Sounding like his fictional counterpart, Shelgrim, in Norris's novel, Huntington declared that the Southern Pacific was but "a business proposition pure and simple; and the people will sooner or later recognize that no other company can, or will, do more for the development of the industries and resources of the State than will the Southern Pacific Company."[76]

In the fall of 1900, Frank Norris wrote to a friend that "the Squid is nearing completion."

> Hooray! I can see the end. It is the hardest work I have ever done in my life, a solid year of writing and four months' preparation— bar two months—and *I* think the best thing far and away I ever did.[77]

Doubleday published *The Octopus* in the spring of 1901. The novel became a best-seller. Less than two years later, the second work in a planned trilogy, *The Pit*, was published and received wide acclaim. Set primarily in Chicago, where Norris had lived as a boy before moving to California, *The Pit* chronicled the worldwide distribution of the wheat grown in the first novel. Norris planned to make *The Wolf,* dealing with the consumption of the wheat, the last book in the trilogy. But his sudden death at thirty-two left the book uncompleted.

Reviewing *The Octopus* shortly after it appeared, critic Wallace Rice thought that Norris overestimated the power of the railroad corporation (naming the Southern Pacific as the model for the novel's Pacific and Southwestern)—so much so as to undermine the entire work. Rice wrote that Norris "raises his rate so high [an interesting railroad image itself] that it is certain to be rejected at the bar of public opinion. If his novel be one with a purpose, and that the exposure of infinitely corrupt corporation methods, it is self-defeated on the instant."[78] Although Rice made the mistake of inferring that Norris wanted to write social criticism, his comments about the unbelievability of the railroad's power are insightful. They in many ways foreshadow the suggestions of current revisionist historical scholarship.[79]

Rice's evaluation notwithstanding, historians and literary critics persist in calling the novel a true representation of the force of the Southern Pacific in California.[80] Such power was apparently not limited to mere political influence; the octopus seized in its tentacles everything and everyone that blocked its path. Seen in this light, the novel's helpless ranchers symbolize the plight of all California, unable to fight the relentless railroad corporation.

In a catalog description of the railroad corporation's evildoings at the novel's end, Norris describes the awesome power of "the monster": it has seized the ranches, it has imposed high freight rates "like a yoke of iron." The "Railroad" had killed five men. It had widowed women and killed the unborn baby of Annixter and Hilma. It had "beggared Magnus and had driven him to a state of semi-insanity" after destroying his honor. It had corrupted Lyman Derrick. Mrs. Hooven starved to death because of the railroad, and Minna Hooven was driven to prostitution.[81] Even though Norris followed this depressing litany with the ecstatic affirmation "But the WHEAT remained," such a philosophical turnabout did not diminish the evil portrait he had painted of the nearly animate railroad.

The novel's depiction of the circumstances surrounding the outbreak of violence at Mussel Slough is woefully inadequate as history, and it is both unfair and misleading to term the novel a history of that particular conflict. Combining novelistic license with popular legend and misunderstanding, Norris produced real drama but a sketchy and unreliable version of events. In the first place, Norris peopled the novel with characters that did not exist in the San Joaquin Valley of the 1870s and 1880s. His characters may have indeed been modeled on real individuals, but they were only artistic types. Descriptions of Annixter, Magnus Derrick, or Presley are not biography. Attempts by historians to label these fictional characters as representations of historical actors in the actual confrontation are misleading.[82] Even patent parallels to real figures—Shelgrim as Collis Huntington, for example—cannot be read as biography.

The setting of the novel is deliberately confused. In telling "A Story of California," Norris compressed geography to the whims of fiction. A Spanish historical presence, complete with a rustic mission, migrates from the California coast to nestle in the San Joaquin Valley. Vast seas of wheat grow where small fruit and vegetable farms historically predominated. Like geography, chronology is telescoped in *The Octopus*. The Mussel Slough shoot-out took place in 1880, but the novel's time sequence is vague by design; it is clear that Norris wanted to make the novel representative of more than a single year's events, to shrink history to "one *fin-de-siècle* moment," in the words of one student of Norris.[83]

In his fictional account of the Mussel Slough controversy, Norris mimicked much of what he had discovered in his research. Reading through old issues of the San Francisco *Chronicle* at the Mechanics' Library, he was bound to get a slanted picture of the struggle between the settlers and the railroad. The *Chronicle* of the 1870s and 1880s was notoriously anti-railroad, and it catapulted the Mussel Slough settlers to heroic stature. Even Norris's short stay in San Francisco was likely to color his research; the city was abuzz with preparations for a rival railroad down the Central Valley to break the Southern Pacific's monopolistic hold on trade.[84]

The story line of the land controversy and path to violence is, at least superficially, quite simple. Settlers move into the region to take up lands made valuable by the presence of the railroad. Some take up government land, paying for and receiving clear title. Others choose railroad land, content to settle with the corporation after the railroad's title clears the hurdles of the government's land-grant bureaucracy. The Southern Pacific welcomes the settlers and promises that, once it can legally dispose of the land, the settlers will pay reasonable prices for the land they occupy. Thus assured, the settlers set about clearing, plowing, and irrigating their land. Crops, mostly wheat, are grown and marketed in San Francisco and beyond; the railroad and the settlers create a supposedly benign and mutually beneficial commercial partnership.

But, as novel and myth argue, the railroad company double-crossed the settlers. Once it received clear title to the land, the Southern Pacific regraded the value of the improved acreage. It notified the settlers that they would be forced, in effect, to pay for their own improvements. Acreage that the railroad had promised could be purchased for as low as

$2.50 an acre would now be sold for as much as thirty or even forty times that amount. Railroad-supported individuals stood poised to buy the land and homes out from under the hard-working settlers.

Such blunt divisions between good and evil—the controversy was never so simple, nor were the good and evil ever so distinct—make the myth a good story. The controversy pitted independent, hard-working ranchers against a menacing corporate giant. At the climax of the struggle, the railroad corporation acted to force the settlers off the land they had worked so diligently to improve. Railroad agents, backed by a U.S. marshal, began systematically to claim homesteads in the name of the corporation. Possessions were forcibly removed from homes, property rights trampled on. On one bright sunny day, the indignant settlers, most of them armed, rode out from a county picnic and intercepted the marshal and his party. A confrontation took place. Heated words were exchanged. A horse reared, knocking a man into the road. Shooting broke out. Five settlers and two railroad agents died.

Such is the understanding of the struggle that Frank Norris encountered in his research. And it is very close to the tale told in the pages of *The Octopus*. Norris added the intrigue of a bribery scheme, but in the confrontation, the story is much the same as the legend declared it was. Pushed to desperation by the actions of the insidious railroad corporation, the settlers are forced to defend their homes at gunpoint. Their defeat costs them their lives; the soulless railroad corporation lives on, driven by the deterministic force of supply and demand.

As outlined by historian Richard Orsi and described in chapter 2 of this book, the Mussel Slough incident looks very different from the comparable story in *The Octopus*; Orsi points out that Norris "misrepresented practically every facet of the actual Mussel Slough tragedy."[85] Norris's account, if taken as the scholarly presentation that many have declared it to be, is undeniably one-sided. If the novel is to be a history of the Mussel Slough affair, it is little more than hagiography, a sentimental vindication of the martyred squatters' righteousness in the hopeless battle against the railroad. Even though Norris clearly portrays the settlers as greedy and opportunistic, perfectly willing to resort to their own treachery to defeat the railroad, it is undoubtedly the railroad that receives the blame for their downfall and death.[86]

In short, the novel fails at what many historians have claimed it to be, a reliable depiction of the railroad corporation's ruthlessness and an extraordinary instance of anti-railroad conflict. But that shortcoming, something Norris would himself have admitted, does not mean that the novel is useless as a tool for adding to our historical understanding. On the contrary, Norris's failure as a monographic historian of the Mussel Slough affair merely allowed him to succeed in other arenas.

Norris did write truthfully in describing California and the railroad— not by making the railroad a virtually animate being or the technological mascot of an immensely powerful corporation but, rather, by making the railroad pervasive. As a tangible and unavoidable introduction to the landscape, the railroad haunts the pages of *The Octopus*. It is plainly everywhere and cannot be ignored. From the first page of the novel, a map depicting the locale, the railroad is a powerful presence in the physical and psychological setting. Ironically, such ubiquitousness helps to demythologize the Octopus: the railroad is not a sinister corporate or political influence, although it is no less intrusive. As everything from a frightening machine to a disturbing sexual presence, the railroad assaults the minds and senses of the novel's characters.[87]

Norris details that presence (and his own obvious fascination with trains) in a variety of ways. The railroad is foremost a physical addition to the landscape, often dangerous and threatening. It reorients patterns and understandings of time, space, and velocity. The first major action in the novel centers on a locomotive plowing mercilessly into a confused herd of sheep that had wandered onto the tracks. Only seconds before, the train had narrowly missed running down Presley, lost in contemplative repose not unlike the hapless sheep. In addition to its heavy-handed foreshadowing of the novel's climactic violence, this "massacre of innocents" graphically describes the dangers accompanying railroad technology. Furthermore, Norris has placed a pastoral way of life at odds with a burgeoning, railroad-borne industrialism—with devastating consequences.[88]

Norris brilliantly describes the meeting between California and the railroad by paying rapt attention to the technology's ability to shock the senses. The overland roars by on an overhead trestle: "It stormed by with a deafening clamor and a swirl of smoke, in a long succession of way-coaches and chocolate-covered Pullmans, grimy with the dust of the great deserts of the Southwest. The quivering of the trestle's supports set a tremble in the ground underfoot. The thunder of wheels drowned all sound of the flowing of the creek."[89]

At other points, the railroad may be less threatening but is still intrusive, unavoidable. Annie Derrick is afraid of the railroad, in both its corporate and its machine forms; she fears the "tentacles of steel" and the railroad as a "symbol of a vast power."[90] Characters and readers can hear trains throughout the novel. Several chapters end with the railroad roaring, whistling, or steaming in the distance. That sort of sensory intrusion can symbolize "menace and defiance" or peacefulness or mournful repose.

Regardless, the description rings true with what nineteenth-century California, city and countryside both, must have sounded like, given the railroad's ubiquitous presence—at times comforting, at times troubling.

In the novel, the railroad could also initiate sexual tensions or suggest the intrusion of unwanted male attention. Hilma Tree, sitting peacefully alongside a creek beneath a railroad trestle, thinks about cooling her feet in the water and begins to remove her shoes. But she hesitates. "Suppose a train should come! She fancied she could see the engineer leaning from the cab with a great grin on his face, or the brakeman shouting gibes at her from the platform. Abruptly, she blushed scarlet. The blood throbbed in her temples. Her heart beat." Well before early motion picture directors made sure to tie their heroines to train tracks, scenes replete with sexual and violation imagery, Norris anticipated the genre.[91]

Furthermore, the railroad often defines orientation on the vast California landscape: people are on one side of the tracks or another; even the railroad trestle marks a real boundary. Presley's opening bicycle ride—which virtually traces the novel's frontispiece map—introduces readers to the landscape, a region intimately affected by the presence of the railroad.[92]

The technology even manipulates language, giving the novel's characters words and phrases to express their new thoughts, as it did in California of one hundred years ago. At one point, the ranchers discuss whether or not their scheme of bribery will do any good in their battle with the railroad corporation. "I don't know," Harran Derrick says, "maybe it just wants a little spark like this to fire the whole train."[93] Again, Norris uses the railroad to foreshadow the violent climax: Derrick is, at least metaphorically, talking of train wrecking, a capital offense in California.

In another sense, at least as brilliant as the depiction of the railroad's sheer intrusiveness, Norris "got it right." By making his characters align themselves with various forms of opposition to the railroad corporation, Norris encapsulated much of nineteenth-century California political history. The novel can be read as a struggle between characters over how and why to oppose the railroad and the railroad corporation. Should they be violently opposed? Can the railroad commission help citizens take on the corporation? Should city unite with country in mutual antagonism toward the railroad company?

Such divisions among the characters reflect in archetypical fashion the social, political, and cultural fissures that Norris was no doubt familiar with. And reading the novel as an allegory of railroad conflict is one way to use the novel as "history." In other words, it is possible to see the railroad and the railroad corporation in the center of conflict between facets of society, rather than as simply the focus of unified antagonism.

The Octopus opens with an introduction to a cast of characters. Most of these several dozen individuals represent archetypes of nineteenth-century California social or occupational groups. Well-named Magnus Derrick, for instance, is a looming and influential gubernatorial presence, identified with the first generation of California political figures. Greedy and ambitious, Derrick symbolizes the wheat barons who desire little but profit from their fields, men who "worked their ranches as a quarter of a century before they had worked their mines."[94] Though antagonistic to the railroad corporation, Derrick will not take a radical path, choosing instead to mortgage his own integrity in the battle with the Pacific and Southwestern. The railroad corporation may be corrupt and all-powerful, but it is still part of a productive laissez-faire order, in which "fairness to the corporation is fairness to the farmer."[95]

Dyke is a blacklisted engineer on the railroad, a romanticized and stereotypical version of the workingman. He was blacklisted because of a pay dispute, not because of any strike or union activity on his part. His path to radical opposition against the railroad corporation forms a central, if melodramatic, subplot of the novel. Apparently guaranteed a reasonable freight rate for shipment of his produce, Dyke makes the transition from railroad employee to proud yeoman. Yet harvest time brings news that the railroad corporation has upped the freight rate for hops, thereby evaporating all of Dyke's expected profits. What follows is Dyke's tortured transformation into outlaw and bandit, feebly striking back at the corporation by individual acts of train robbery and murder.[96]

Caraher, a crossroads country grocer, is an anarchist. Radicalized by his experience as a striking worker and by his wife's death in a strikebreaking riot, Caraher preaches violent confrontation with the Railroad Trust: "It can't last forever. They'll wake up the wrong kind of man some morning, the man that's got guts in him, that will hit back when he's kicked and that will talk to 'em with a torch in one hand and a stick of dynamite in the other."[97] With his red face, red tie, red beard, and the red glint in his eyes, Caraher is unmistakably the representation of an overdrawn and crudely caricatured radical.

Presley, the novel's protagonist, represents not a distinct political or social type but, rather, generic public opinion. The others in effect are trying to enlist his support in their struggle against the railroad corporation. At first, he is apathetic, uncaring: "These matters, these eternal fierce bickerings between the farmers of the San Joaquin and the Pacific and Southwestern Railroad irritated him and wearied him. He cared for none of these things. They did not belong to his world."[98] Yet Presley undergoes a transformation. Listening to Caraher enlist Dyke into an-

[handwritten marginal note:] not the writer himself?

archism, Presley is moved by "a blind demon of revolt."[99] Thus inspired, he immediately returns home and writes his great poem, "The Toilers," a celebration of the common man. Later, after witnessing the shootings at the irrigation ditch, Presley suffers an apparent breakdown. "By God, I too, I'm a Red!" he declares.[100] He commits an act of anarchistic violence (throwing a bomb into the home of railroad agent S. Behrman). But following a meeting with the charismatic president of the railroad corporation, Presley disavows this radical position, going nearly full circle to a confused and fatalistic acceptance of the immutability of supply and demand.

A real contribution of the novel to historical insight, then, is its illumination of the forms of railroad opposition among various social groups. If students of California history read the novel less as an accurate account of focused events than as an allegory of social and political conflict—with the railroad and the railroad corporation as the inescapable centerpiece—then it can indeed add to an understanding of California's past. Read in this fashion, the novel can even be used to demythologize preconceptions about the "Octopus." The railroad is more than a huge corporate power; it is also an intrusive physical and even psychological presence. And opposition to the railroad and the railroad corporation is hardly a monolithic stance—either socially or politically. On the contrary, different opposition positions themselves both reflect and delineate class and other divisions within California.

The Octopus: A Story of California cannot replace conventional works of California history. Its chronology is flawed. It presents a misleading portrayal of a notorious incident, and it should not be evaluated as a historical document pertaining to railroad conflict. Yet Frank Norris did get certain things "right" in his famous work. He knew of the railroad's intrusiveness in people's lives; he understood the extraordinary impact of a remarkable technological innovation. Often sinister, dangerous, and troubling, this new technology invited opposition. Coupled with an undeniably powerful corporate superstructure, the railroad forever changed the lives of Californians. A product of that power was opposition—influential, vibrant, and extremely diverse. This opposition created and exacerbated social and political fissures in California society.

6 "Let Us Agitate and Agitate"
Progressives and the Railroad

To get at the real basis of the California insurgency and its
contemporary rise all over the United States in the first
decade of this century, you, of course, go back first to what
is known as the "Roosevelt policies." When you get into
that literature you will find that William Jennings Bryan
claimed that "Roosevelt stole his clothes" while he was
swimming. Bryan took his platform from the Populists of
the early Nineties who had theirs from the Greenbackers
of the Seventies and Eighties who got their ideas from the
contemporary Grange movement of that era.
>   —William Allen White
>   Letter to Alice Rose, 1941

Let us simplify our Platform by cutting out everything
except the anti-railroad corporation plank and whatever is
incidental to that, and let us agitate and agitate, and keep
the minds of the people on the subject incessantly.
>   —Thomas R. Bard
>   Letter to Chester Rowell, 1908

Historians have long recognized that opposition to the Southern Pacific
Railroad had a great deal to do with the origin and subsequent growth of
Progressivism in California.[1] Anyone making even a cursory examination
of California Progressivism in the early twentieth century will come across
references to the Southern Pacific Railroad again and again in Progressive
writings, speeches, and campaign platforms. And many a historian has
thus viewed the S.P., through the filter of Progressive rhetoric, as the
great corporate evil stalking the state. What has *not* been sufficiently
analyzed, however, is how the state's Progressives shaped their political
campaigns around the "railroad question" and "railroad problem," what
their aims were, and how they were able to gain impressive popular
support with an ostensibly single-issue platform. Nor have many histo-

rians closely examined the connections that California Progressivism shared (or claimed to share) with earlier anti-railroad movements.

Looking back on the Progressive era in California, which we can bracket between the turn of the century and 1920, journalist Chester H. Rowell wrote that the Progressives owed their success to the frustrations of the voting public and the specific strategy followed by the Progressive reformers. Rowell, who had been a guiding intellectual force behind the movement, noted vaguely that the early twentieth century marked the correct "psychological time" for a concerted reform effort: the people of California were ready for change. He further declared that the special nature of the Progressive campaign influenced that outcome as well. Progressives apparently offered the voting public a chance to follow a new political route. "We were the first who had gone at it in this spirit," Rowell remembered.[2]

In explaining his remarks, Rowell emphasized that he was comparing Progressivism only with other reform efforts in California's Republican Party. Earlier attempts by reform-minded Republicans "made one reserve," according to Rowell. "They would fight the battle [against the Southern Pacific] up to the point when it meant the defeat or injury to the Republican party. At that point they would stop." But the early-twentieth-century Progressives "did not have this reserve, and openly announced that we were going to reform the Republican party even if we had to smash it in the process."[3]

When did California Progressivism begin? Certainly the 1910 gubernatorial victory of Hiram Johnson proved a benchmark in the political housecleaning effort begun by the Lincoln-Roosevelt Republican League, an insurgent wing of the Republican Party. Most historians have pointed to this campaign and this electoral success as the beginning of organized, statewide Progressivism in California.[4] As we have seen, the Democratic Party waged (and usually lost) various campaigns with anti-railroad candidates from the end of the nineteenth century through the 1910 gubernatorial election. Despite obvious similarities to later Republican platforms and programs concerning the railroad, Democratic political aims are rarely included in descriptions of the "Progressive movement" in California.[5] Progressivism as a coherent political response has instead been largely characterized just as Rowell saw it: a political reform springing from within the Republican Party alone.

Studies of California Progressivism have formerly provided insight into the basis of national Progressive political reform. In his pioneering study *The California Progressives*, George Mowry offered a group portrait of the elite Progressive reformers of California, a profile that many other historians utilized in their analyses of Progressivism across the United

States. Middle-class, independent, WASPish businessmen, fearful of the Scylla of organized labor on their left and the Charybdis of massive corporations to the right, Mowry's Progressives offered a perfect template for Richard Hofstadter's invention of status-anxious reformers out to make the world safe for Americans just like themselves.[6]

But more recent studies have called into question the existence of a coherent, nationwide Progressive movement.[7] Furthermore, regional studies have raised significant questions about Mowry's conclusions. As Michael Rogin and John Shover have pointed out, interpretations of California Progressivism have in large part been drawn from problematic sources: "The interpretation of progressivism as a political movement of a disaffected middle class, frightened by the power of monopolistic corporations and fearful of organized labor, rests upon inferences drawn from public statements and, in a few instances, private thoughts, of a leadership elite."[8] Quantitative research by Rogin and Shover, although likewise not immune to flaws, indicates a higher level of working-class support for Progressive candidates than Mowry implies, as well as a genuine commitment to labor and labor policies following election.[9]

Despite the importance of such revisionism, much about the traditional understanding of California Progressivism remains compelling. Politics in the Progressive era—whether marked by the existence of a coherent movement or a shifting and fragmented collection of reform efforts—was a significant departure from earlier politics. And California Progressivism did have an impact on the national political arena, a development best indicated by Theodore Roosevelt's choice of Hiram Johnson as his Bull Moose running mate in 1912, only two years after Johnson's victorious campaign in the California gubernatorial election.

Yet what of the Progressives and their *bête noire*, the railroad? The anti-railroad Progressivism espoused by Hiram Johnson has been interpreted as the culmination of a long-standing anti-railroad reform tradition. Yet Progressivism in California offered a narrowly prescribed type of railroad opposition, expertly cultivated and advertised. This chapter examines that feature of the movement, as manifested in the state's most important Progressive campaign. Did Johnson's success in the gubernatorial campaign of 1910 represent the closing bell of a fifty-year bout with the railroad corporation in California? How and why?

Origins of California Progressivism

If anything is clear about California Progressivism, it is surely this: if the railroad did not exist, the Progressives would have had to invent it. As we have seen in earlier chapters, "The Railroad" could be many things to many people, but to the California Progressives, the railroad was an ideal opponent, a culprit in the public eye, the soulless Octopus. The California Progressives perfected railroad antagonism and channeled it through their carefully crafted organization better than any comparable political movement in state history.

If anything, the corporate behemoth loomed larger at the turn of the century. With Collis P. Huntington's death at seventy-nine in 1900 (last to die of the original Big Four), the direction and control of the western railroad empire was in question. Huntington passed on most of his great wealth and Southern Pacific stock to his widow, Arabella, and nephew Henry Huntington (these two would themselves wed a dozen years later). But, as expected by the financial and railroad communities, Arabella and Henry had few qualms about selling their railroad holdings. Into the breach stepped E. H. Harriman of the Union Pacific. Over the next several years, Harriman was able to acquire a controlling interest in the S.P. In effect, then, what had been literally linked at Promontory long ago in the 1860s became, as the new century arrived, one even more gigantic corporate entity.

The Progressives' ostensible attachment to railroad opposition implies a commonality with earlier anti-railroad actions and groups stretching well back into the nineteenth century. Many Progressives would insist that the movement was simply the victorious end to a decades-old battle. But that argument boils down to the simplistic notion that "railroad opposition is railroad opposition is railroad opposition," which clearly was not the case in California or elsewhere in the country. The invention of tradition aside, California Progressivism, at least that expressed by the state's Republican renegades, represented a particular and specific type of railroad opposition, one that emerged out of the divisiveness of the 1890s. The 1894 Pullman strike had driven wedges between anti–Southern Pacific moderates and striking railroad employees and had ended any chance for cross-class cooperation among reformers out to challenge the railroad status quo. The organizations devoted to what can be called "rivalry opposition"—such groups as the Traffic Association in San Francisco, the similarly composed coalition pushing for a competing railroad through the Central Valley, citizens' leagues opposed to the refunding of the Central Pacific debt, and the powerful "free harbor" advocates in Los Angeles—seemed to have sprung from the same constituency (at least as far as leadership is concerned) as the Progressives of the early twentieth century.

Also important was the internal reformation of the Republican Party that occurred at the end of the nineteenth century. Long the home base of Southern Pacific influence, the party surprised even itself when it appointed anti–Southern Pacific stalwart Thomas R. Bard to the United States Senate. Of equal parts conservatism and independence, Bard stood at the head of a small group of Republicans who sought to limit the railroad corporation's influence in the party.[10] Bard's single term in the Senate exposed a weak link in the railroad corporation's thick political armor (and assured Bard political sainthood among the Progressives who came to power shortly thereafter).

Yet despite the importance of these somewhat scattered and unfocused instances of antagonism, the snowball that became California Progressivism began in earnest with the early-twentieth-century activities of specific individuals and groups.

Who were California's political Progressives? According to Mowry's group profile, the state's most prominent reformers shared such identifying characteristics as religion, middle-class occupations, political amateurism, and commitment to limiting the influence of corporations in local and state government. This characterization has its drawbacks. It ignores exceptions to the profile (exceptions such as Jewish Progressive leaders Meyer Lissner and Harris Weinstock or millionaire reformer and San Francisco capitalist Rudolph Spreckels) and can be applied to political leaders who were not Progressives (men such as Democrat Theodore Bell; J. Stitt Wilson, Socialist candidate for governor in 1910; and Job Harriman, 1911 Socialist candidate for mayor in Los Angeles). It also ignores other issues of concern to Progressives—issues such as women's rights, the plight of minorities and the poor, educational reform, and more explicit moral reform (although Mowry does suggest that Progressive politicians believed their actions against corporations in general and the Southern Pacific in particular had a definite moral component). Yet, despite its drawbacks, Mowry's characterization does help to locate Progressives along a political spectrum and to determine the context within which Progressivism grew.

There was a similarly composed contingent of reformers concerned (at least initially) with a wider agenda than simply opposition to undue corporate power. In turn-of-the-century San Francisco, for instance, a coterie of well-to-do business leaders began to gather regularly at the Commonwealth Club, a private organization for men, to discuss major events and issues of the day: tax reform, women's suffrage, immigration, conservation. The club's first president, Democrat Harris Weinstock, would go on to play a prominent role in the California Progressive movement. It was a far cry from the comfortable meeting rooms of the Commonwealth Club to the trenches of California electoral politics, but the breadth of the club's interests nonetheless indicated the arrival of new outlooks and players on the twentieth-century political scene.[11]

To be sure, those who attended these conversational gatherings were also concerned with the role of the corporation in California life. As Franklin Lane, a prominent San Francisco Progressive, observed in 1905: "It does look to me as if the problem of our generation is to be the discovery of some effective method by which the artificial persons whom we have created by law can be taught that they are not the creators, the owners, and the rightful managers of the government."[12] Yet Lane, a Democrat who would go from San Francisco city attorney to a seat on the Interstate Commerce Commission and later an appointment as secretary of the interior, also believed that government intervention in corporate affairs entailed considerable risk. Any missteps in regulatory policy "will lead . . . to the wildest kind of a craze for government ownership of everything."[13] In short, Lane (like his Progressive colleagues around him) was no radical bent on jeopardizing the ability of any corporation, especially the railroad corporation, to continue business as usual.[14]

A series of sensational criminal trials early in this century galvanized the emergent Progressive movement in northern California, catapulting it from the paneled drawing room into the street. San Francisco mayor Eugene Schmitz came under criminal investigation along with union boss Abraham Ruef and United Railroads official Patrick Calhoun. Also implicated was the Southern Pacific Railroad and its chief counsel, William F. Herrin.[15] The investigation and subsequent trial accomplished several things. First, they brought to light the extent of graft and political corruption, not only in San Francisco but at the statewide level. Once a promising, highly touted civil servant, Ruef was pinned to influence peddling, kickback schemes, and vote selling in local as well as state elections.[16] Throughout the trial, the shadow of the Southern Pacific and chief counsel Herrin loomed large.

The graft trials also marked the coalescence of local businessmen and attorneys around a loosely defined "good-government" organization, which deliberately stretched reform beyond the realm of social club dinner-hour agendas. Under the primary leadership of crusading newspaper editor Fremont Older, these reformers provided much of the momentum, moral as well as political, behind the prosecutions.[17] The proceedings also spotlighted rising political star Francis J. Heney, a special U.S. attorney called in as prosecutor. With bulldog tenacity and corresponding tactlessness, Heney threw himself into the trials with abandon and an often reckless regard for procedure. Before long, he had become the most recognized figure in California reform circles, a veritable St. George out to slay the dragon of corporate corruption.

But Heney's bright future faded the day that he exposed a prospective juror as a convicted felon. Morris Haas retaliated in court by pulling a gun and shooting Heney in the back of the head. Although he eventually recovered, Heney could no longer continue as chief prosecutor in the trials. His duties were handed over to his assistant, Hiram W. Johnson.

A brash San Francisco attorney, Johnson was no stranger to the machinations and political clout of corporate interests in the state, especially of the Southern Pacific Railroad. His father was Grove Johnson, arguably the state legislator most friendly to the Southern Pacific during the latter years of the nineteenth century. What to others might have been adolescent rebellion became for Hiram Johnson a career, as he fought the railroad and his father's bond with it at virtually every turn.[18]

Southern Pacific executives had long known of Hiram Johnson. In the volatile 1890s, when the railroad corporation found itself scrambling for friends, Henry Huntington looked unkindly on some of the younger Johnson's views. Johnson continued to represent clients in damage suits against the railroad, and he seemed intent on breaking the family tradition set by his father of loyal political service to the Southern Pacific. In a letter to his uncle, Huntington stated that Hiram Johnson "has been doing considerable talking against our interests, saying that his father made a mistake in standing in with the railroad, that he had prostituted himself before the people by doing so, and had ruined himself politically." Huntington wished that Grove Johnson would exercise a little paternal discipline: "Hiram is a bright young man, of considerable ability, but is unsound in his judgment, and his father should give him a little advice on the lines of conservatism."[19] The younger Johnson had apparently not learned his lesson, however. By the winter of 1907, he had ably taken over the graft prosecutions and in the process emerged as the leading light of reform in northern California.

At roughly the same time, civic-minded citizens in southern California congratulated themselves on an apparently successful campaign to clean up Los Angeles city government. Under the direction of a small group of middle-class reformers and a sprinkling of wealthy patrons, a collection of "good-government" organizations had sought to reform municipal politics. Chief among these was the Non-Partisan City Central Committee of One Hundred, organized in the summer of 1906.[20] Overwhelmingly Republican, conservative, and well connected, the Non-Partisans quickly outflanked other municipal reform organizations.[21] The group's organizers convinced a slate of candidates to run for local office beneath a clean-government banner. Although the mayoral candidate at the head of the ticket did not specifically attack the Southern Pacific, supporting newspapers did, and it was clear that opposition to the railroad was the sine qua non of the reform effort. At the head of machine politics in the city was Walter F. X. Parker, an important Southern Pacific agent for all of southern California. As good-government leader Meyer Lissner saw it, the voters of Los Angeles previously "had no choice. . . . No matter who was elected, it was for the benefit of the Southern Pacific." Faced with the opposition of organized labor as well as tremendously powerful Harrison Gray Otis and the Los Angeles *Times*, the Non-Partisan slate nonetheless garnered three-fourths of the city offices in the municipal campaign.[22]

Thus inspired, the leaders of the movement looked to expand their success statewide. "I am glad you are finding that all the political virtue in the State is not included in the exterior boundaries of the City of Los Angeles," Meyer Lissner wrote to fellow reformer E. A. Dickson in early 1907 (Dickson, a journalist for the Los Angeles *Express*, was then covering the state legislature in Sacramento). "I hope that two years hence we can not alone send some respectable representatives from this end of the State but that we will start the animals up and show the S.P. and allied corporations here that the People have at last 'got onto their jobs.' . . . I don't see why it can't be done. All that it needs is intelligent work, work, work. The only question is, have we got the workers[?]"[23]

Reformers and potential reformers in the Central Valley were also important to the emerging Progressive movement. Physician and newspaperman Chester Rowell had for years used the pages of the Fresno *Republican* to oppose the Southern Pacific's excessive economic authority in that important agricultural region.[24] Rowell's nephew, Chester H. Rowell, came to Fresno after extensive travel and education in the United States and Europe. Under his uncle's tutelage, the younger Rowell turned his hand to journalism and discovered a life's work in reform. He would become the most significant thinker of the California Progressive movement.[25]

Oakland also contributed its share of Progressive ideas and leaders. As we have seen, Oakland understood the mixed blessings of the transcontinental railroad's presence perhaps more than any other city in the state. During the 1890s, at the height of legal battles with the Southern Pacific over the ownership of the city's waterfront, Oakland's voters elected an eccentric pseudo-Populist as their mayor. John L. Davie's administration of the city was disastrous (he raised virtually zero civic funds), but his anti-railroad tenure presumably helped convince local businessmen and lawyers to coalesce around a good-government agenda not unlike that of the reformers in Los Angeles. With Davie safely retired, Oakland attorney William R. Davis stood with Mayor George Pardee (who had so vehemently opposed the Pullman strike in 1894) at the head of the local reform effort. During the ongoing waterfront dispute, a group of citizens, with Pardee in the lead, tore down a Southern Pacific fence and pulled up piles that the company had driven into the waterfront's edge. Taking his campaign and anti–Southern Pacific credentials on the road, Pardee ran for governor in 1902, barely defeating Democratic challenger Franklin K. Lane.[26]

Like Pardee, Oakland's William R. Davis epitomized the inherent conservatism of turn-of-the-century California Progressivism. Davis made it clear that he and others like him opposed the political power of the railroad, but corporate business affairs were not their concern. In other words, their cultivated antipathy was largely company specific: society need not fear any retributive anti-corporation behavior from them. Such reassurances did not, at least as far as the rhetoric extended, obviate the potential for deep trouble. The Southern Pacific had a right, Davis argued, "to every wheel and rail of its system." But if the corporation failed to act responsibly, a terrifying spectacle loomed on the horizon. Step away from politicking, Davis warned the Southern Pacific, or the people of California "will sweep over that line that divides property rights and become a frenzied and unreasonable mob."[27] That terrifying threat of class upheaval would prove to be a recurring Progressive nightmare. Despite the obvious sensationalism of the language, the message was clear: either play by our rules, Progressives warned the railroad, or we will all lose.

California Progressives also found inspiration in certain national political figures. Many Progressives—especially those who leaned left of the Republican Party–centered Progressive spectrum—looked with nostalgia on the generic anti-corporate stance of William Jennings Bryan.[28] But the central national figure was President Theodore Roosevelt. Many of California's leading reformers felt an evangelical call to action by Roosevelt's very public example of energetic, apparently trust-busting, reform; and they set about to emulate him.[29] The president occupied an international political stage, but when he spoke of corporate reform, many Californians believed he was speaking directly to them. "I am a radical who most earnestly desires to see the radical programme carried out by conservatives," Roosevelt preached; California's Progressives took the charismatic TR at his word, looking to him for guidance, direction, and even interference on their behalf.[30]

The Lincoln-Roosevelt Republican League

As the California legislature met in session in early 1907, E. A. Dickson and Chester Rowell sat side by side covering affairs for their respective newspapers. In their view, the Southern Pacific's heavy-handedness—which reformers were convinced included bribery and other forms of corruption—demanded a coherent response. Dickson and others from southern California had been encouraged by the Non-Partisan Committee's notable success in the recent municipal elections. As Los Angeles attorney Meyer Lissner saw it, the railroad corporation was only accelerating its corrupt efforts in hopes of administering "a sort of political spanking to the people here for not being good." "They may think it is pretty smart politics," Lissner wrote Dickson, "but it looks to me like damn foolishness on their part. I believe they are generating an immense amount of resentment in the breasts of intelligent respectable people here that will manifest itself the very next chance they have . . . at the polls."[31]

Dickson and Rowell, along with men like Lissner, agreed that a Republican Party housecleaning was in order, one that would eliminate the Southern Pacific's influence at the statewide level. In a meeting at the end of April, several like-minded leaders spent several hours discussing ways to elect anti-machine state senators and assemblymen and thereby rid the party of corporate influence. This small group planned to have another brainstorming session in Los Angeles, a meeting to include recognizable reformers from all parts of the state (including "a couple of good men from San Francisco if we can find them").[32]

In an effort to gauge and broaden opinion on party reform, Dickson sent a letter to several dozen journalists and political leaders in the spring of 1907. Gone were any attempts at nonpartisanship; gestures in that direction may have been workable at the local and municipal level but not when state offices were at stake. "The next campaign will have to be carried out by fighting the organization within party lines, and this preliminary conference will be a conference of Republicans only," wrote Lissner.[33]

In early May, about fifteen men met at Levy's Cafe in Los Angeles. Participant A. J. Pillsbury confided to his diary not long afterward that he had gone to Los Angeles "to help organize an anti-organization movement to redeem California from Corporate domination. Don't know what will come of it. Hope something worth while." Marshall Stimson remembered that the men stayed "until long after midnight, discussing plans and principles to be advocated by the group." Taking a cue from an anti-railroad civic reform organization in New Hampshire (under the direction of novelist Winston Churchill), Dickson suggested that the infant group be called the Lincoln League.[34]

Several months later, its ranks swelling, the group met at the Hotel Metropole in Oakland. Principles and platforms were again discussed. Muckraker Lincoln Steffens, like Roosevelt a favorite of the nascent reformers, talked of Rhode Island and the phases of railroad domination that that tiny state had weathered.[35] Questions arose. Would the infant political league take on other corporations besides the Southern Pacific? Some felt that the central focus of opposition to the S.P. must be maintained but that the group also should spell out its antagonism to rampaging corporate authority, whatever the source. Former governor Pardee declared the Southern Pacific to be the root of all evil in California's body politic; he was seconded by another attendee, who thought, not surprisingly, that there was little need to antagonize other corporations. Meyer Lissner agreed, stating that the people of California would follow the lead of those who stood defiant before the Octopus. Others, future railroad commissioner John Eshleman among them, felt that a statement declaring the league's opposition to any corporation inimical to popular government would be appropriate. But Eshleman's suggestion was shot down by those wary of appearing too radical or too ambitious: taking on the Southern Pacific would be challenge enough. Francis Heney—one of the few Democrats in attendance—requested that the league be graced by the name of patron figure Theodore Roosevelt. With a war chest of $500, the Lincoln-Roosevelt Republican League was launched.[36]

The sense of excitement and optimism created by the founding of the league rings clear in the letters that the group's leaders exchanged with one another. "You may be sure that this movement is bound to be a winner," Lissner wrote to a supporter in the fall of 1907. "It is the first time that there has been a thoroughly organized attempt made within the Party to wrest control from the railroad machine, and within a couple of months every Assembly District in the State will be thoroughly organized." Just a month later, Chester Rowell boasted: "We are already recognized as the band wagon, and while that is a poor reason, it behooves everybody to get aboard."[37]

Like any insurgent political organization, the Lincoln-Roosevelt League faced severe opposition from party regulars. Stalwart Republicans ("standpatters") charged that the league exaggerated the role of the Southern Pacific in the state's political affairs. Taft Clubs (or Roosevelt-Taft Clubs) were begun by Republican Party regulars to counter the insurgents. Harrison Gray Otis of the Los Angeles *Times*, as bitter a foe of reform as he was of organized labor, used the pages of his newspaper to attack the

novice political organization. League leaders faced charges that their organization was actually the railroad-sponsored wing of the party masquerading as a reform movement. At one juncture, Meyer Lissner felt
moved to respond to the editor of the Riverside Press that the Lincoln-
Roosevelt Republican League's leadership did not enjoy the perquisites of
the railroad lackey and did not accept free rail travel. "These men not
alone do not travel on passes but do not intend to, and unless I miss my
guess never will," Lissner wrote. "They are not that kind of 'cattle.'"
Furthermore, Lissner pointed out that the league's officers traveled on the
Santa Fe and not the Southern Pacific.[38]

A surprising statement of opposition to the league came from Thomas
R. Bard, the Republican rebel and railroad foe who had served a turn-of-
the-century term in the U.S. Senate. Writing to a prominent Lincoln-
Roosevelt member in Los Angeles, Bard declared his support for the major
plank of the league's platform, that of eliminating Southern Pacific influence in the Republican Party. But Bard added that he could not countenance Theodore Roosevelt's policy favoring Asian immigration nor could
he abide plans to elect U.S. senators by popular election (instead of legislative appointment). "The Republican Party cannot be made a Revolutionary Party through any man's ambition or cranky policies," Bard wrote.
Lincoln-Roosevelt officer Lee Gates answered Bard with an assurance that
he could still be an important member of the organization, since he stood
on the correct side of the crucial question: "whether or not one stands for
machine domination in the Republican Party in the State of California.
On either side of that line all Republicans must align themselves."[39]

Lincoln-Roosevelt leaders set about pulling together a grass-roots organization to usurp power from the regular Republican political machine.
The league did not neglect rural California: loyal country newspaper
editors proved particularly valuable. "The places where there is no local
railway machine to fight are the very places whose help we need," Chester
Rowell shrewdly recognized. Yet the concentration was on the state's two
most important cities. "If we have San Francisco and Los Angeles, with
any considerable part of the interior (and with the prestige of the cities we
will get most of it) we become the one commanding political power in
California," master strategist Rowell correctly believed.[40]

From its inception until the 1910 gubernatorial victory of Hiram Johnson, the Lincoln-Roosevelt Republican League intended its anti-railroad
stance to be both sensational and narrow. The group may have pledged
continuity with earlier anti-railroad groups and policies, and it may have
recited a litany of railroad abuses, but in tone and format it was tied to a
very narrow approach to the nagging "railroad question." Thomas R. Bard,

by now a placated member of the insurgent camp, articulated the league's philosophy in a letter to a supporter in Oxnard. The league had been begun "not for the purpose of punishing the railroad, but to protect the people against the harmful influences which are exercised by the railroad in politics." The league hoped to bring about reform "by striking at the organization of the two great political parties in the State, and letting true representatives of the people control the Republican Party." Bard added, "I believe that there is no disposition on the part of the people to treat the railroad interests unfairly." In other words, the Lincoln-Roosevelt League made a better example of a Republican Party movement than an anti-railroad movement fitting some state model from the past.[41]

Gentleman farmer and prominent Progressive Philip Bancroft con-curred with Bard, though with a passing nod to democracy. "We weren't in there to try to upset the world or anything of that kind, and the great fight we were making was to try to get the control of the government back into the hands of the people instead of being in the hands of the Southern Pacific." League members saw themselves charting a new course between the party stalwarts and the third-party movements of the past. "We weren't radicals and yet we were progressives," Bancroft remembered proudly.[42]

The League's Entry into California Politics

The league's first major victory in its attempt to derail the railroad cor-poration occurred in a Sacramento mayoral race. League functionary Rob-ert Waring remembered staffing a table near the polling place. As Sacra-mento citizens arrived at the polls, Waring tried to hand them flyers endorsing the league's candidate, Clinton White. But most took the flyers from the regular Republican worker sitting at a table nearby. Waring thought all was lost. He said later, "I remember very well that the whole population of Sacramento was so dependent financially on the Railroad that folk could not pay their bills to the grocer and butcher and baker until the Railroad pay car came to town and paid off its employees."[43] But the machine official laughed and told him that the voters, mostly Southern Pacific employees in this case, were only masquerading as pro-railroad. Once in the polling place (a barn in this case), they would consult Lincoln-Roosevelt flyers, copies of which had been mailed to them earlier, and vote the league's ticket. Much to Waring's surprise, White defeated the Southern Pacific candidate.

Lincoln-Roosevelt success in this race emphasizes how quickly and effectively the Republican insurgents had organized. White's candidacy had been promoted by the use of the mails, by friendly and influential journalistic support, and by the energetic work of dedicated staffers (one apparently successful gimmick included distribution of blank "All White" buttons). Such highly developed electioneering expertise helped the league gain the necessary momentum to carry it through to major success in 1910.

By the fall of 1907, the league had begun to generate substantial publicity (especially in friendly Republican newspapers). In one typical cartoon published in the San Francisco *Call*, the league was graciously lampooned for its anti-railroad derrings-do. California (and California political virtue), portrayed as a Gibson girl ingenue, lay on the Southern Pacific railroad tracks, with chief counsel Herrin about to run her over. League president Frank Devlin stood at the switches nearby, frantically trying to change the train's direction and save the state's life and virtue.

After the 1908 elections, the league lapsed sleepily into public inactivity. Behind the scenes, however, the leaders of the insurgent movement remained extremely busy. Despite 1908 electoral success, they knew that the ultimate test would come with the gubernatorial contest of 1910. Consequently, league leaders began to narrow their list of possible candidates. Several men stood out prominently, among them Chester Rowell, William R. Davis, Francis Heney, Hiram Johnson, Harris Weinstock, Oakland mayor Frank Mott, and Charles Belshaw. Rowell enjoyed perhaps the most stature: many league members wished him to throw his hat in the ring, which he refused to do. In one early 1909 reply to a supporter, Rowell reiterated his aversion to becoming a candidate but added that it was "extremely important that we all get together on some one man and I think it is none too early to begin picking that man now."[44]

Much of the planning depended on projections of whom the regular party members would put up against the Lincoln-Roosevelt candidate in the Republican primary. League strategists were forced to do what now comes second nature to California political strategists; that is, consider geography as much as any potential candidate's qualifications and perceived voter appeal. Rowell firmly believed that no northern Californian could beat Frank P. Flint, the man most likely to be put forth by the regular Republicans. But if the Republicans put Secretary of State Charles F. Curry up for governor, Rowell believed that the railroad machine might fall in line behind the league's candidate (a prospect that apparently did not concern him). "Whichever we nominate," he wrote, "the higher-up part of the machine is likely to get aboard the band wagon and help us elect him." William F. Herrin was supposed to have "issued orders" that if Curry were the regular Republican nominee, the machine was not to support him. "Evidently Herrin has concluded that he must give us good government or lose the privilege of governing us," Rowell reasoned.[45]

Next to Rowell, Francis Heney enjoyed perhaps the most prestige of any of the prospective candidates. But Heney also worried many important league members. For one thing, he was a Democrat who had been taken in by the insurgent Republicans primarily because of his heroics in the San Francisco graft trials. Heney's loyalty to the Lincoln-Roosevelt brand of political reform was in doubt; he had flirted with and ostensibly supported public ownership of utilities. Such a stance was bound to make many Lincoln-Roosevelt leaders nervous. Philip Bancroft remembered the discomfort he had regarding the fiery Democrat:

> I think Heney would have been much more radical than [Hiram] Johnson. . . . One of the very strong points in favor of Johnson was that he was going into politics to kick the Southern Pacific out of politics in California. He never said that he would try to kick the Southern Pacific out of California or that he would attack the Southern Pacific as a railroad and try to destroy it, anything of that kind. He just wanted to get them out of the control of politics. . . . Now, my opinion of Heney is that he would have been extremely radical against a concern like the Southern Pacific and would have tried to have injured them commercially or economically, which Johnson never did.[46]

With Heney thus handicapped, Hiram Johnson fairly quickly emerged as the league's most viable candidate. A northerner, Johnson enjoyed a wide reputation as the man who stepped in to complete Heney's work as prosecutor in the graft trials. He was a strong speaker, and his public estrangement from his father could only help his reputation as an anti-railroad candidate.[47] But Johnson refused to run. No amount of pleading by Rowell and other league strategists seemed likely to change his mind. Apparently Johnson was also influenced by his wife, who had no desire to live in Sacramento. In any event, the situation looked bleak. "Johnson swears he will not run," Rowell wrote to Lissner in late January, 1910. "I would be willing to do almost anything short of murder to compel him to do so, but I fear it is hopeless."[48]

Rowell did all he could to "drag Johnson into the fight"; he even arranged a newspaper barrage which demanded that Johnson announce his candidacy.[49] At the same time, he wrote Heney that he was not out of the running yet: he might be the only choice the league would have. Probably at the request of Chester Rowell, Lincoln-Roosevelt members wrote to Johnson, pleading melodramatically that he announce his candidacy. "We cannot stand defeat now," wrote an attorney from Fresno. "We must win this battle or go down to utter failure and give up the fight in California and confess that we are unable to govern ourselves but must submit to the domination of one of the most corrupt political forces that ever cursed any State of the Union."[50]

Grove Johnson's position as an important lieutenant in the Southern Pacific political organization certainly gave the younger Johnson reason to hesitate. Years after the campaign, Hiram Johnson asked Rowell if he had thought about what it meant for a son to oppose his father politically. Rowell replied that he had, whereupon Johnson shot back that Rowell could not possibly appreciate the tremendous pain the matter had caused him.[51]

Hiram Johnson's Campaign

In February 1910, Johnson acceded to the pleadings and agreed to become the Lincoln-Roosevelt candidate for governor. With uncharacteristic modesty, Johnson wrote that the position had been thrust on him and, like Cincinnatus, he felt he must serve. "I didn't think that I would ever be a candidate for office," Johnson wrote, "but the matter came to me in such a way, that I really believed, if I intended to do my part, that it was my turn, so I yielded, and I am in it, and I will do the best I can."[52]

As soon as he announced his candidacy, Johnson was bombarded by optimistic political forecasts. "You will win," a supporter in southern California wrote. "Los Angeles will prove to you that it is big enough and broad enough and sane enough and discriminating enough to choose wisely between its local push [i.e., railroad machine] pet and a real man."[53] Other supporters affirmed that the regular Republican hierarchy viewed Johnson as "exceedingly dangerous"—a good sign as far as the insurgents were concerned. One Lincoln-Roosevelt supporter thought that Johnson's announcement had thrown the railroad camp into disarray: "there are weeping and wailing and gnashing of teeth in the S.P. Political Bureau," D. M. Duffy wrote to E. T. Earl, owner of the Los Angeles Express. "They are fighting and growling and denouncing and villifying one another;— at all of which we can afford to laugh."[54]

In announcing his candidacy, Johnson clearly felt the painful presence of his father. "I heard the other day from father," he wrote to his sister in late February. Grove Johnson had informed Harris Weinstock that, should Hiram become the Lincoln-Roosevelt candidate, he would oppose him "in every precinct in the state." "I am unable to comprehend this spirit in him," the younger Johnson remarked. "I presume the most disagreeable feature of the campaign will be my own father."[55]

Progressive organizational experience played a profound role in shaping the Johnson campaign. Men like Meyer Lissner, E. A. Dickson, and Chester Rowell proved to be expert political handlers. Lissner's close friend Charles Dwight Willard remembered him as a man who "runs things," surrounded as he was by "card catalogues, telephones, type writers, clerks, clips, proofs, letters, memorandum slips."[56] Adhering to an essentially nineteenth-century platform—at least as far as the rhetoric is concerned—Johnson campaigned in a decidedly twentieth-century fashion. Loyal journalists, editors, and newspapers were herded into the fold, and Johnson espoused a direct and easy-to-follow political strategy. Beneath the effective organizational umbrella provided by the Lincoln-Roosevelt League, Johnson's supporters set out to ensure his success in the gubernatorial contest.

Johnson left many of the strategic details of his campaign to his political handlers. He delivered himself into the arms of advisers in the league, especially his Lincoln-Roosevelt "team" in southern California. "I am entirely in the hands of you gentlemen, from the south," Johnson informed Meyer Lissner, "and will do exactly as you shall determine I ought to do." Once the campaign was under way, Johnson occasionally asked for guidance. "I would give anything I possess, to have you gentlemen here in command of this fight," he wrote (perhaps disingenuously) to Lissner after a campaign swing through Los Angeles and southern California. "You know how to do things, and you do them. We know neither."[57]

Johnson attempted to decipher what he was supposed to be standing for at the head of the Lincoln-Roosevelt League ticket besides railroad opposition. The official league platform itself was simple to understand: according to the organization's Declaration of Principles, the league's primary objective was to emancipate the California Republican Party "from domination by the Political Bureau of the Southern Pacific Railroad Company and its allied interests."[58] Just after agreeing to run, Johnson sent a fact-finding letter to several supporters throughout the state. "I do not wish to make any statement during the campaign that is not accurate, and above all, I do not wish to be unjust even to the S. P.," he wrote. Perhaps his supporters could "give me something of an idea of the methods of the Company, in dealing with its shippers, of the desire, if it exists, on the part of the Company, always to take advantage and the like."[59] Unsophisticated and poorly versed in substantive issues, Johnson returned again and again to focus solely on the railroad question, which is precisely what canny league officials wanted. As Lincoln Steffens wrote to Francis Heney, "Hiram doesn't understand, and he knows it and wants to. You must help him. We all must."[60] Platitudes and empty rhetorical flourishes—complete with gratuitous references to Theodore Roosevelt and Wisconsin Progressive Robert La Follette—made up most of Johnson's nonrailroad comments. Above all, his approach was blunt. As Johnson later recalled, "My only method of doing politics has been to state what I wanted to do and then, with a club, go out and endeavor to put it over." Thrusting his fist in the air, Johnson promised the Republican voters of his state that he would slay the railroad dragon.[61]

By the early spring of 1910, Johnson boldly predicted victory. He believed that southern California would support him, and he recognized the strides that had been made by the league's extensive efforts in the north. "The fight is already won, and unless something transpires in the next few months, which we cannot foresee, our success is certain."[62]

League officials such as Rowell and Lissner realized that Johnson's first, biggest, and most critical hurdle would be the Republican primary in August, in which Johnson faced four other Republican candidates: Philip A. Stanton, former speaker of the Assembly; Alden Anderson; Charles F. Curry; and state engineer Nathan Ellery. Even though campaign gossip suggested that Curry would not get much support from the top people in the railroad machine, Johnson believed that Curry would be his toughest opponent in the primary.[63]

In the six months before the primary, the league worked diligently to promote its man throughout the state. Californians had never seen so energetic a campaign.[64] Driven from the Oregon to the Mexican border in a fire-engine red automobile, Johnson visited hundreds of communities and gave countless speeches (or, more accurately, gave countless versions of the same speech). The entire Lincoln-Roosevelt ticket for high office usually traveled together, although Johnson disliked having to share the platform out on the stump. The ticket included Senate candidate John D. Works; prominent Los Angeles prohibitionist and president of the Anti-Saloon League Albert J. Wallace, running for lieutenant governor; and brilliant attorney John Eshleman as the league's candidate for railroad commissioner. Johnson's personal style emphasized aggressiveness and confrontation, a bearing that his advisers promoted.[65] His handlers surrounded their candidate with all the festivity of a country fair as he campaigned throughout the state.

Judging the degree of opposition to Johnson is difficult. Certainly many thought that his single-issue campaign bordered on the superficial. A "Down with Johnson" flyer anonymously distributed around the Sacramento Southern Pacific shops in the spring of 1910 listed many reasons why railroad workers ought not vote for the Lincoln-Roosevelt ticket. "Mr. Hiram Johnson is a society man and will put California 20 years behind the time if elected." Johnson would "fight the laboring class . . . from hand to foot." Johnson was wrong, the leaflet declared, in claiming that all railroad employees followed the Southern Pacific's dictates with mindless devotion. Similarly, a letter from the American Railroad Employes and Investors' Association in San Francisco urged "fellow railroad employees" not to vote for Johnson, because he insulted rail workers' intelligence by implicitly charging that they were so many sheep led around by the all-powerful railroad management.[66]

On the other hand, Johnson's Republican rivals, forced to play catch-up, usually reacted to Johnson's success the only way they could, by charging that he was a radical. In a speech in the Central Valley, Charles Curry declared that if elected he would not seek to pull up railroad tracks with his teeth, the obvious implication being that Johnson planned to destroy the farmers' all-important commercial highway. Curry remarked that, as far as he was concerned, a Pullman car was a far better way to travel than a mule.[67] Some Johnson criticism was more acrobatic than others; the Selma *Irrigator*, for instance, a small Central Valley newspaper, attacked Johnson for being both a railroad opponent and a railroad lackey:

> If [Johnson] persists in persecuting the [Southern Pacific], they may have to shut up shop and leave the state and then we'd all have to walk and it would be particularly disappointing to [Johnson] himself because he wouldn't be able to make any use of the free pass which Mr. Herrin doubtless sends to his address.[68]

Next to Secretary of State Curry, Alden Anderson represented the greatest threat to Johnson's candidacy from within the Republican Party. Interestingly, Anderson chose to take a blasé railroad position in his battle against Johnson. Anderson dismissed the so-called railroad problem as "nearly all buncombe." "There was a time, under the old constitution, when the railroads were undoubtedly perniciously active and when they secured special and improper legislation." But, Anderson insisted, all that had been done away with by the 1879 constitution. For his part, Johnson answered charges that he was an anti-railroad fanatic with characteristic aggressiveness (and, of course, without acknowledging that Anderson might be more right than wrong): "If it is fanaticism to resent the control of the government by William F. Herrin and the Southern Pacific political bureau; if it is fanaticism to fight with all one's energy to take this government away from the men who have disgraced and shamed it . . . I am a fanatic, and accept the characterization with no small degree of pride."[69]

But as the spring of 1910 waned, so did a measure of Johnson's confidence. Although he felt certain that he had southern California in his pocket, the farming communities of northern California worried him more and more. "The past week has convinced me that my sphere of action is north of Tehachapi," Johnson wrote to a close adviser, "and that my every effort in this campaign must be devoted to the *farmers et al* of the rural counties." The strength of his Republican opponents in the countryside, he confessed, "chilled my confidence, perplexed and confused me."[70]

Johnson did enjoy a high degree of southern California support, aptly demonstrated at a Lincoln-Roosevelt rally in Los Angeles in early June. After being introduced by local Progressive leader Marshall Stimson, Johnson received a five-minute ovation from the crowd. His speech was vintage Johnson, forever "harping on one string."

> In this campaign I am simply a Californian, fighting for my State.
> My residence in this campaign is just as big and just as broad as
> my California; and my allegiance is limited only by the boundaries
> and confines of my State. . . . You couldn't, even with a gatling
> gun, shoot enough spine into any of my opponents to have him
> even mention the saintly names of William F. Herrin, Walter Par-
> ker [S.P. political boss in Los Angeles], or the Southern Pacific
> Railroad Company.[71]

The Southern Pacific had grown bit by bit into the most insidious power in the state, Johnson claimed: "it seems as if its tentacles reach into every community, however small." Johnson referred vaguely to the anti-railroad antecedents of his campaign: in the past, in "sporadic, spasmodic instances, brave and patriotic men . . . made the attempt to overthrow [the railroad corporation]; but never with any real hope of success." Only now did the voters of California have any hope of regaining their political independence. Johnson made sure to add the obligatory disclaimer that the movement he headed did not condone any radical solutions to the railroad problem. "We are not seeking in this contest to tear up railroad ties or to destroy rolling stock." The aim of the Lincoln-Roosevelt League was not to "seek to put the Southern Pacific out of business, but to kick it out of politics." Johnson further insisted to the city's working class that his victory meant the emancipation of the laboring man, though he was less than clear about how that was to come about.[72]

A week later Johnson addressed a standing-room-only crowd at San

Francisco's Dreamland Rink. This meeting was an overwhelming success as well. From that point onward, Johnson's election seemed assured.

On August 16, 1910, voters cast their ballots in the first statewide primary election in California history. Hiram Johnson emerged the Republican victor by a nearly two-to-one margin over his closest competitor, Charles Curry. Johnson carried fifty-three of the state's fifty-eight counties. As expected, Johnson's strength lay in southern California, where the strong prohibitionist credentials of both his running mate, Wallace, and John D. Works were of likely benefit.[73]

Following the Republican primary, Meyer Lissner sent a pamphlet out from the Republican State Central Committee, urging the party to stay together to defeat Democrat Theodore Bell. Entitled "How to Do Effective Political Work for Good Government," the pamphlet was essentially a primer on political organization. In it, Lissner told Republican staffers how to get the vote out, keep track of voters, use automobiles for drumming up support, watch that correct tallies were made, and generally keep Republican momentum high.[74]

Three months later, Johnson defeated Bell in the general election. Neither Bell's declarations against the Southern Pacific ("The emancipation of California from the Southern Pacific rule overshadows every public question") nor his broader platform ("California Needs a Change, A New Deal, A Fair Deal") was enough to derail the Johnson juggernaut.[75] A comparison of the voting returns with those of the 1906 gubernatorial election reveals an almost rigid adherence to already determined party loyalties.[76] Bell received his support from loyal Democrats and pulled in votes from those who had voted for the fringe Independence League in 1906.[77] Johnson, again doing extremely well in southern and rural California, relied on the state's Republican majority to propel him into office. Socialist candidate J. Stitt Wilson, polling better than 12 percent of the votes cast, did not "take" votes away from either Bell nor Johnson; his support came predominantly from those who had voted Socialist in the 1906 election.

The Narrowing of Railroad Opposition

Johnson's myopic concentration on the Southern Pacific was hardly accidental. Progressive leaders had raised other substantive issues at earlier Lincoln-Roosevelt strategy sessions ("traditional" Progressive issues such as suffrage, racetrack gambling, workers' compensation, and conservation), but these were jettisoned in favor of sole emphasis on the railroad.

Progressive adherence to a single-issue campaign stood in stark contrast to the much wider reform agenda embraced by other groups to the left of the insurgent Republicans. "All he had to say," remembered one of Hiram Johnson's campaign workers, "was that if he was elected Governor, he'd kick the Southern Pacific out of politics. That was all he said; he just varied that theme."[78] But there *were* other issues out there in the political arena. In southern California, for instance, the platform of the municipal Public Ownership Party included a wide-ranging program of social reform. Municipal ownership of a gas plant, the construction of local railways to aid in the construction of an aqueduct, fireproof school buildings, fair wages on public works, and statewide implementation of the initiative, referendum, and recall, were all publicly supported by this group.[79] Although the Johnson administration eventually passed legislation in many of these areas, the 1910 Johnson campaign was marked by at best lukewarm support for any significant social program.[80] Johnson's position on the railroad issue was deemed enough to attract a voting majority (and it worked). Only after he had defeated his Republican rivals in the August primary did Johnson add, albeit vaguely, some complexity to his platform.[81]

Whether by design or accident, the Progressives effectively stole the political thunder—the rhetoric if not the substance—of the left. By campaigning against the political power of the Southern Pacific, insurgent Republicans also "borrowed" a significant platform plank from the Democrats. As one prominent Democrat observed in 1909, referring specifically to the Lincoln-Roosevelt League, "There does not seem to be any line of demarcation between [a] Democrat and a Republican these days."[82] For the most part, Johnson and his advisers seem to have believed that the railroad truly was the crucial issue in state politics and that the Southern Pacific, as king of the "interests," was as powerful as they claimed. As prominent Progressive A. J. Pillsbury confided to his diary in the summer of 1908: "truly free government is slipping away from the American people and especially so in California. The Railroad have got us."[83]

The traditional interpretation of Johnson's victory is that it marked the end of a long and shameful era in California history. The state could, with Johnson at the helm, become a democracy again. Egalitarianism would return. And such a change need not, and most emphatically did not, emasculate the railroad corporation. As Spencer Olin has written: "Emancipation of California from railroad rule—this is the most publicized and perhaps most significant contribution of the Johnson administration; for the liberation *was* accomplished, and without damaging the economic position of the railroads. In fact, those corporate enterprises enjoyed continued and increased prosperity." Johnson did not unleash the dogs of anti-trust, anti-railroad legislation; he did not have any to turn loose. The Progressives resuscitated the California Railroad Commission and did grant it significant power, but the railroad corporation hardly chafed at regulation.[84]

Olin argues further that California Progressives placed more faith in notions of individual moral standards than in specific group or class loyalties. Seeking to prevent class conflict, the Progressives created (and epitomized) a balance between labor and business that implicitly relied on the pluralistic political system to reward each of its members in turn.[85] In its refusal to place the Progressives on one side or another, however, such an interpretation suggests too great a degree of Progressive civic disinterest and selflessness. The California Progressives may have steered a central path between labor and capital, but they certainly leaned right. Their reforms were aimed more at a rational reordering of the state's business and entrepreneurial playing field, a designed effort to let the smaller company compete equally with the larger. As Olin notes, the transportation laws enacted by the Johnson administration fit the description of regulatory legislation "but certainly not antibusiness."[86]

Asked how the railroad corporation long managed to maintain its significant power, Southern Pacific chief counsel William F. Herrin is supposed to have answered: "By controlling reform movements." This disarmingly blunt statement anticipated an interpretive focus of historians of American Progressivism, who suggest that the era often marked the "corporate capture of dissent."[87] California Progressivism, in its opposition to the railroad corporation, was essentially a reform effort that did not require control or capture. That battle had been fought and won in the previous century; the railroad was going to stay an independent corporate entity. The powerful anti-railroad rural and working-class movements of the nineteenth century—most notably, the rise of the Workingman's Party, rewriting of the state constitution, short-lived Populist movements, and the Pullman strike—had sought with varying degrees of success to restructure the state's corporate environment, beginning with the railroad. Unlike those movements, Johnson Progressivism plainly posed little threat to the Southern Pacific. Given the structure of the 1910 campaign, the railroad issue clearly offered an opportunity for insurgent Republicans to stand on a reformist political platform. The transition from the powerful, if episodic, radicalism of anti-railroad events and moments in the 1890s to the tame conservatism of Progressivism in the early twentieth century was indeed striking. Lincoln-Roosevelt architects of Johnson's political victory made sure that he followed a carefully choreographed public ritual: first building an octopus of a railroad corporation, then promising to destroy it. It worked magnificently.

Epilogue:
Building an Octopus

There's many a man been murdered by the
  railroad, railroad, railroad
There's many a man been murdered by the railroad
And laid in his lonesome grave
    —Nineteenth-Century American Folk Song

There is a creature lurking amidst the pages of California history, a beast stalking the good people of the state, stealing their money, threatening their political virtue, and endangering their lives. This is the dreaded Octopus, the invincible railroad in all its guises: technological menace, political fiend, corporate behemoth. Wrapped around this monster is an entire interpretation of California history, one that spins off from the horror story of the railroad's quasi-animate existence. We can quickly describe the stages of this monster's life by reviewing the well-known story.

This railroad was born at a time of national crisis. A strife-torn people hoped that it would stitch the country together or, at the very least, encourage universal prosperity, good will, civilization. Sectional tension exploded, railroad or no railroad, but the Central Pacific—a symbol of God's hand on Earth, it was said—grew. Miles of track climbed out of Sacramento, inched across the Sierras, and then raced the length of the desert to meet up with the Union Pacific in northwestern Utah. Railroad adolescence proved troubling, especially when prosperity did not immediately visit California on the new tracks. Railroad guardians, those doting uncles Stanford, Hopkins, Huntington, and Crocker, began to pay much more attention to themselves than they did to either their railroad ward or the people of California. They had too much money, wallowed in arrogance, and ruthlessly threw around their power. They charged exorbitant rates, they cheated the government, they manipulated public officials. It was the railroad that had made all this possible, but the people of California (Henry George being the notable exception) had not anticipated these developments.

Of course the railroad did some or most of the positive things that people had expected of it. It did invite what the nineteenth century quaintly capitalized as "Progress": it moved people and freight and produce around, it created markets, it employed people (thousands and thousands of them), it built towns. All the while, the Central Pacific added size and track and bureaucratic fat until it grew into the full-sized Southern Pacific. But there was an awful lot of unforeseen *bad* in the railroad equation as well, ominous counterparts to every railroad enthusiast's boast. The railroad bypassed many towns and expectant cities, assigning them to a kind of urban Purgatory. Gigantic locomotives pulling car after car of passengers and goods shattered local calm and—all too often, it seemed—pulverized hapless livestock herds frozen by fear or ignorance in the path of the onrushing trains. People, too, became common railroad victims, losing fingers, limbs, and lives at a fearful clip through unlucky railroad work or travel or both. At the more mundane level, the approach of the train into a community, any community, meant the simultaneous arrival of coal dust, soot, noxious smells, piercing whistles: the sights and sounds of late-nineteenth-century American industrial might. It also meant the reorientation of space, time, and the physical layout of towns and villages.

None of these changes and forced accommodations happened without opposition. On the contrary, a historical constant of railroad-age California is antagonism. But, as the preceding chapters have tried to make clear, the forms of that antagonism could be breathtakingly varied. People could band together to urge the town council to make trains slow down as they passed through neighborhoods; others could come together to vote for an anti-railroad office seeker; still others might collectivize in a railroad strike. These and countless other actions were all ostensibly "anti-railroad" in design, but they were all perhaps as different from one another as they were the same.

Yet many historians would have us believe that there was a seamlessness to all this opposition. In their view, California history is a microcosmic example of the American march to progress: the state's people eventually triumphed over the iron beast by electing straight and true railroad-busting politicians. Opposition prior to 1910, although led by important Progressive precursors, was essentially puny and ineffective. Then Hiram Johnson (invariably cast in the drama as the state's heroic dragon slayer) took his gubernatorial campaign to the center of the tracks and cried "Halt." It supposedly worked. Thus, Johnson became for many a Californian (and many a California historian) the West's version of Teddy Roosevelt, the courageous answer to Thoreau's seventy-year-old call.

"That devilish Iron Horse, whose ear-rending neigh is heard throughout the town, has muddied the Boiling Spring with his foot," Thoreau grumbled, "and he it is that has browsed off all the woods on Walden shore, that Trojan horse, with a thousand men in his belly, introduced by mercenary Greeks! Where is the country's champion, the Moore of Moore Hall, to meet him at the Deep Cut and thrust an avenging lance between the ribs of the bloated pest?"[1] Hiram Johnson, backed by his Lincoln-Roosevelt minions and astride his automobile steed, was able to kill this soulless Railroad. Thus ends the heroic western story, a compelling tale of good's triumph over evil.

Yet this story of the railroad's power and demise, planted and cultivated by Progressive politicians and historians, is unsettling and, in tried-and-true historian's phrasing, "not without its problems." By labeling the enemy Invincible, Progressive actors and historians and journalists made Johnson's political victory more remarkable than it really was. Additionally, by their assumption of a monolithic railroad power (a misleading and simplistic thesis to begin with), they assigned railroad opposition to a similarly one-dimensional scheme.[2] In other words, they viewed all opposition movements as part of a seamless and uncomplicated progression of reform, in which goals are clearly articulated and always in sight. Railroad opposition thus becomes a long parade in which Hiram Johnson is the last, and most important, actor—the hero who answered the Far West's 1885 millennial cry for deliverance from railroad evil: "we . . . must wait and pray for a Redeemer who will emancipate the white slaves of California."[3]

But railroad opposition in California was far more complex than the "Octopus school" allows. The history of railroad-induced conflict reflects in miniature many of the social, political, and cultural cleavages inherent in any rapidly industrializing society. Reasons for railroad antagonism varied widely, and methods of opposition both cut across and helped delineate class lines. Hiram Johnson's brand of railroad opposition was not that of Denis Kearney or Eugene Debs, and it is misleading to speak of Johnson's success as the culmination of the earlier reformers' campaigns. And, of course, Johnson's Octopus and Henry David Thoreau's Iron Horse were clearly not the same beast. Johnson attacked the railroad's influence on political affairs—his was the corporate railroad. Thoreau, at least in the above passage, was wary of the railroad's physical intrusion on (and destruction of) the landscape (a problem that—given recent railroad accidents where toxic chemicals were spilled—America has still not adequately solved).

In such concerns, Thoreau was ahead of his time. His contemporaries thought that the purely technological problems and challenges of railroading had been solved. What remained to be worked out were, in the words of one long-winded theorist, those tricky and "more abstruse negative theorems determining the voluntary and legislative relation of the railways and the public to each other."[4] Those relationships did need to be worked out. But what deep thinkers like this seemed to ignore is that "abstruse negative theorems" often revealed class fissures. One cannot speak of railroad opposition in nineteenth-century California, or anywhere else for that matter, without referring to class and class conflict. Historians know that any lessening of railroad power and railroad domination did not come about, as Lord Bryce theorized wistfully, as part of inevitable western maturation or modernization.[5] It came instead at the hand of compromise and, perhaps especially, conflict—much of it explicitly class related.

An examination of the complexities of railroad opposition can help us understand class positioning in nineteenth- and early-twentieth-century California. From the simultaneous outbreak of the Pullman strike and the Los Angeles free harbor fight, for instance, we can readily recognize two different constituencies squaring off against a common Southern Pacific opponent. Goals, outlooks, and strategies differed wildly; but when Progressive hopefuls explained such events fifteen years later, they lumped Pullman strikers (or at least strike supporters) with harbor activists: brothers and sisters in the combined struggle against the railroad. But Pullman strikers and San Pedro harbor fighters did not necessarily view the railroad in the same light or even in a similar light. This "strange bedfellows" school of politics ignores their respective positions and motives and waters antagonism down to a common, anti-railroad denominator.

New scholarship has tempered many of the myths about railroad domination in California. Even our understanding of the railroad's corporate nature is gradually expanding. Closer study of California politics and a fuller appreciation of the Southern Pacific Corporation's internal affairs— not to mention the insights gained from two decades of exploration into social history—have enabled historians to see much more than a dramatic tale of railroad oppression when they write about nineteenth-century California.[6] We are learning, for instance, that the railroad was far more than the all-powerful, all-seeing Big Four; the Southern Pacific was a huge, extremely complex industrial enterprise strengthened by layer upon layer of bureaucratic insulation.

Corporate inertia and bulk, however, did not mean invulnerability. Immediately after the 1894 Pullman strike, University of California professor Thomas Bacon forecast more troubles on the California horizon "if the chains of corporate tyranny are not loosed from the chafed limbs of California." Bacon feared that the federal government might eventually be forced to "put down an armed rebellion of the people of California," an uprising of far greater magnitude than that exemplified by the Pullman strike.[7] That sort of conflagration did not come, although the strike itself served as proof enough that something was seriously amiss in late-nineteenth-century California—and that such troubles were intricately related to the place of the railroad in the state's political economy.

Following on the heels of the Populists and workers who rose up against the railroad corporation in the 1890s came California's Progressives. As George Mowry and others have demonstrated, these reformers also believed that the power and influence of the railroad corporation, especially the Southern Pacific, had grown to dangerous proportions. But just as surely as they spoke out against the railroad, this generation of political activists *needed* "the octopus." They too feared the specter of massive and violent conflict in their state and sought ways to exercise influence in the public arena. Through the founding and growth of the Lincoln-Roosevelt League, the Progressives discovered the sheer political potency of the railroad issue, especially when that issue was properly massaged. Their brand of railroad opposition permitted them to manufacture a compelling program, one that pledged allegiance neither to the Populist radicalism of the 1890s nor to the machine-tainted antics of their forebears in the Republican Party.

"It is funny how we have all found the octopus," William Allen White wrote of his generation of Progressive reformers.[8] After assailing Populists and other radicals for their political program in the 1890s, the Progressives found themselves last in the long line of political activists out to rearrange their society's relationship with the railroad—a continuity that White traced as far back as the 1870s.

Yet the Progressives' understanding of the "railroad problem" and their solutions to it differed widely from those of their elders. Although they may not have realized it themselves, their "octopus" was not the same as the one that nineteenth-century railroad opponents had fought. "Traffic-tamping"—the process by which railroad tracks and perpendicular ties nestle into the embrace of the railroad bed through time and use—had occurred at all levels of railroad reality: technological, cultural, corporate. The railroad was not going anywhere (especially not *away*), at least not through the efforts of the more-bark-than-bite Progressives. It seems that Octopus fighters in the armor of Progressivism could not even count on the opposition of their enemy! William F. Herrin, the great villain, supposedly welcomed the Progressives and, particularly, their ordering of the railroad rate system. "I think no railroad manager would agree to dispense with government regulation at the cost of returning to the old conditions," Herrin remarked in a candid observation.[9] Railroad regulation may or may not have been a "good thing" as far as railway officials were concerned.

But the brand of railroad opposition expressed by the state's Progressives was, given the potential alternatives, something that the railroad company could and did find palatable. In other words, by the early years of this century, the issue of railroad opposition in California had been again refashioned to suit particular political needs and agendas, both inside and outside the corporate railroad camp.

Notes

INTRODUCTION

1. James Bryce, *The American Commonwealth* (London and New York: Macmillan, 1889), 2:506.

2. James A. Ward discusses the nation's railroad craze and foreign observations of the same in *Railroads and the Character of America, 1820–1877* (Knoxville: University of Tennessee Press, 1986), especially chap. 1. See also Keith Bryant's introduction to *Encyclopedia of American Business History and Biography: Railroads in the Age of Regulation, 1900–1980*, ed. Keith L. Bryant, Jr. (New York: Bruccoli Clark Layman and Facts on File, 1988).

3. For an insightful discussion of the railroad's effect on American notions and understandings of time, see Michael O'Malley's *Keeping Watch: A History of American Time* (New York: Viking Press, 1990), chap. 2.

4. Ambrose Bierce, San Francisco journalist and on-again, off-again railroad foe, captured well this sentiment when he wrote of the peaceful country village destroyed by its inhabitants' "unwavering determination to introduce manufactures, railroads, and other metropolitan nonsense." See Dod Grile [Ambrose Bierce], *Nuggets and Dust* (London: Chatto and Windus, [1873]), p. 161.

5. The briefest glimpse at nineteenth-century accident reports reveals the myriad reasons why trains could run into problems: insufficient water for steam, hot bearings, open switches, derailments, passengers playing with air brakes, bad flanges, flat wheels, bad track, bad oil, spread rails, split switches, bad engines, side swipes, and countless others.

6. See Leonard Pitt, *The Decline of the Californios* (Berkeley: University of California Press, 1966), pp. 249, 286.

7. The police department in Oakland declared protectively that all incoming and outgoing trains would be searched to root out criminals, even though most of the city's crimes were committed by drunken locals.

See Lawrence Friedman and Robert Percival, *The Roots of Justice: Crime and Punishment in Alameda County, California, 1870–1910* (Chapel Hill: University of North Carolina Press, 1981), p. 104.

8. In other words, terrifying descriptions of railroad machinery (as in Frank Norris's famed novel *The Octopus*) were, for California, often metaphors for the corporation's impact rather than fearful suspicions of rail technology. Conversely, when Thoreau wrote much earlier of "that devilish Iron Horse" with the "ear-rending neigh," he was referring to the impact of the railroad's technological identity. See Leo Marx, *The Machine in the Garden: Technology and the New Pastoral Idea in America* (New York: Oxford University Press, 1964), p. 260. For more on Thoreau and the railroad, see Marx, pp. 249–65, and Robert D. Richardson, Jr., *Henry Thoreau: A Life of the Mind* (Berkeley: University of California Press, 1986), pp. 137–39, 227.

9. According to historian R. Hal Williams, in *The Democratic Party and California Politics, 1880–1896* (Stanford, Calif.: Stanford University Press, 1973), p. 206, opposition to the Central and Southern Pacific overshadowed all other California political issues in the Gilded Age.

10. Antagonistic newspapers, especially by the close of the century, were quick to point out that even the self-important bearing of the railroad magnates had "made the railroad a hated thing in California." See, for instance, the description of leading Southern Pacific officials in the San Francisco *Examiner*, April 7, 1895.

11. Well-known railroad critic Arthur McEwen, quoted in the San Bernardino *Daily Courier*, July 4, 1890. From a clipping in the George Kenyon Fitch Papers, Bancroft Library.

12. George J. Emerson to Collis P. Huntington, December 10, 1896, Henry E. Huntington Papers, Huntington Library. Emerson's letter raises another important point: California history suffers from too great a focus on the Big Four. We need more studies about the rank-and-file railroad workers and, perhaps especially, the middle management of the Southern Pacific, about which we know virtually nothing.

13. Hiram Johnson, for instance, wore out several automobiles in his 1910 gubernatorial campaign. There is a tradition predating Johnson of anti-railroad politicians refusing to ride trains (or at least particular trains). James H. Budd, who ran for governor on the Democratic ticket in 1894, was known as "Buckboard Jim" for his refusal to take Southern Pacific trains. See Royce D. Delmatier, Clarence F. McIntosh, and Earl G. Waters, eds., *The Rumble of California Politics, 1848–1970* (New York: Wiley, 1970), p. 167; Williams, *The Democratic Party and California Politics*, p. 199.

14. Instances of explicit "Luddite-like" anti-railroad behavior do not appear to have been prevalent in California. In the late nineteenth century, the "Gorras Blancas" nightriders of San Miguel County, New Mexico,

tore up tracks, burned railroad bridges, and cut ties in half. Whereas these incidents have been interpreted as actions springing from opposition to generic railroad *technology*, similar incidents in California tended to be directed at the Central or the Southern Pacific Railroad *corporations*.

15. The sheer variety (not to mention volume) of lawsuits against the Southern Pacific in the nineteenth century is amazing. See, for instance, the John D. Bicknell Papers at the Huntington Library. Bicknell was a Los Angeles attorney working with the Southern Pacific's legal office in Los Angeles.

16. John R. Stilgoe, in *Metropolitan Corridor: Railroads and the American Scene* (New Haven, Conn.: Yale University Press, 1983), p. xi, notes a similar problem: how individuals could reconcile aesthetic appreciation of railroad technological or architectural innovation with widespread and troubling railroad controversy and opposition.

17. As Williams (*The Democratic Party and California Politics*, p. 13) notes, Californians were quick to blame the railroad for a wide variety of the state's ills: "There the railways came to be regarded as a monolithic and malevolent force whose policies retarded economic development and whose power corrupted all levels of government. This conception stressed simplicity at the expense of accuracy and sometimes hindered a realistic approach to the state's railroad problem."

18. In an often-quoted passage, Bryce (*American Commonwealth*, 2:372) wrote: "What America is to Europe, what Western America is to Eastern, that California is to other Western States." And while he found the state "thoroughly American," Bryce used his analysis of California as a metaphor for much that he found detestable in the United States (2:506).

19. Hubert Howe Bancroft, *History of California* (San Francisco: The History Company, 1890), 7:627, n. 38.

20. Stuart Daggett, *Chapters on the History of the Southern Pacific* (New York, Ronald Press, 1922). See also Don L. Hofsommer, *The Southern Pacific, 1901–1985* (College Station: Texas A&M University Press, 1986).

CHAPTER ONE

1. Mark Twain to Thomas Bailey Aldrich, January 28, 1871, quoted in George R. Stewart, Jr., *Bret Harte, Argonaut and Exile* (Boston: Houghton Mifflin, 1931), p. 159. See also Albert Bigelow Paine, ed., *Mark Twain's Letters* (New York: Harper and Brothers, 1917), 1:184; Noah Brooks, "Bret Harte in California," *Century Magazine* 58 (July 1899): 447–51.

2. Stewart (*Bret Harte*, p. 160) writes that Harte looked forward to the arrival of "carloads of ready-made culture and progress."

3. Ralph Waldo Emerson, quoted in Leo Marx, "Impact of the Railroad on American Imagination as a Possible Comparison for the Space Impact," in *The Railroad and the Space Program: An Exploration in Historical Analogy*, ed. Bruce Mazlish (Cambridge, Mass.: MIT Press, 1965), p. 208. For an excellent compilation of American railroad art, see Susan Danly and Leo Marx, eds., *The Railroad in American Art* (Cambridge, Mass.: MIT Press, 1988).

4. Henry Fitch, *Pacific Railroad* (San Francisco: Frank Eastman, 1859), p. 14.

5. Ibid., p. 16.

6. The suggestion for sending expedition teams had come from Secretary of War Jefferson Davis. The five possible railroad routes (the Oregon Trail did not receive another reconnaissance) included a northern route, to terminate in Seattle; a route from Council Bluffs to San Francisco; a central route from the Arkansas River to San Francisco; a southerly route from Arkansas to Los Angeles; and a Deep South route from the Red River to San Diego. See John Hoyt Williams, *A Great and Shining Road: The Epic Story of the Transcontinental Railroad* (New York: Times Books, 1988), pp. 24–25. See also Anne F. Hyde, *An American Vision: Far Western Landscape and National Culture, 1820–1920* (New York: New York University Press, 1990), especially chap. 2.

7. See David M. Potter, *The Impending Crisis, 1848–1861* (New York: Harper and Row, 1976), especially chap. 7. An enthusiastic California senator, William Gwin, even suggested a transcontinental scheme that would fan out once it crossed the Rockies and terminate in four different cities.

8. Potter, *The Impending Crisis*, p. 146.

9. An informative discussion of the early stages of Central Pacific planning and construction can be found in Carl I. Wheat, "Sketch of the Life of Theodore D. Judah," *California Historical Society Quarterly* 4 (September 1925): 219–71.

10. For Booth's speech, see Lauren E. Crane, ed., *Newton Booth of California* (New York: Putnam's, 1894), p. 123. Congressional authorization originally granted the Central Pacific the opportunity to build as far east as the Missouri River or to the point of meeting the Union Pacific. At one point in the construction, Congress limited Central Pacific construction to 150 miles beyond California's borders, but this limitation was later removed. See E. G. Campbell, *The Reorganization of the American Railroad System, 1893–1900* (New York: Columbia University Press, 1938; reprint, New York: AMS Press, 1968), p. 252.

11. See, generally, Williams, *A Great and Shining Road*; Stuart Daggett, *Chapters on the History of the Southern Pacific* (New York: Ronald Press, 1922); and J. Valerie Fifer, *American Progress: The Growth of the*

Transport, Tourist, and Information Industries in the Nineteenth-Century West (Chester, Conn.: Globe Pequot Press, 1988).

12. Charles Wadsworth, *War, a Discipline: A Sermon Preached in Calvary Church, San Francisco, on Thanksgiving Day, November 24, 1864* (San Francisco: H. H. Bancroft, 1864).

13. I. E. Dwinnell, *The Higher Reaches of the Great Continental Railway: A Highway for Our God* (Sacramento: H. S. Crocker, 1869).

14. Charles Wadsworth, *A Call to Praise* (San Francisco: John H. Carmany, 1868).

15. Dwinnell, *Higher Reaches of the Great Continental Railway.*

16. See Williams, *A Great and Shining Road*, pp. 36–42.

17. See Campbell, *Reorganization of the American Railway System,* p. 299. For a full-length portrait of Collis Huntington, see David Lavender's *The Great Persuader* (New York: Doubleday, 1970).

18. Leland Stanford as described by Nicholas John Russel in 1891. See Terence Emmons, *Around California in 1891* (Stanford, Calif.: Stanford University Alumni Association, 1991), p. 8. The description is ironically fitting as well in that "Jupiter" was the name of the Central Pacific locomotive present at the driving of the final spike that connected the transcontinental railway in 1869.

19. Of the unwillingness on the part of Californians to support Central Pacific construction, Daggett (*Chapters on the History of the Southern Pacific,* p. 40) writes: "The reluctance of San Francisco to subscribe was not typical of the general attitude toward the Central Pacific in 1865. But it became more typical as the years went on." See also William Issel and Robert Cherny, *San Francisco, 1865–1932* (Berkeley: University of California Press, 1986), pp. 120–21.

20. Williams, *A Great and Shining Road*, p. 60.

21. As Williams (p. 63) writes, "With incredible openness, [Stanford] bludgeoned legislators into passing various helpful bills, including one that authorized San Francisco, Sacramento, and Placer counties to purchase specified amounts of Central Pacific stock, at par."

22. Collis P. Huntington to "Friend Crocker," October 3, 1867, *Letters from Collis P. Huntington to Mark Hopkins, Leland Stanford, Charles Crocker, E. B. Crocker, Charles F. Crocker, and D. D. Colton. From August 20, 1867, to August 5, 1869* (New York: privately printed, 1892). This volume, two companion volumes, and a collection of letters to Huntington from corporation officials provide detailed information regarding railroad construction, financing, politicking, and the relationship between various company executives. The three other volumes are *Letters from Collis P. Huntington to Mark Hopkins, Leland Stanford, Charles Crocker, and E. B. Crocker. From August 5, 1869, to March 26, 1873* (New York: privately printed, 1892); *Letters from Collis Huntington to Mark Hopkins, Leland*

Stanford, Charles Crocker, and D. D. Colton. From April 2, 1873, to March 31, 1876 (New York: privately printed, 1894); and *Letters from Mark Hopkins, Leland Stanford, Charles Crocker, Charles F. Crocker, and David D. Colton, to Collis P. Huntington. From August 27th, 1869, to December 30th, 1879* (New York: John C. Rankin, 1891). Hereafter cited as *Letters from Collis Huntington*, vols. 1–3, and *Letters from Mark Hopkins et al.*

The letter to "Friend Crocker" was sent to E. B. Crocker, the brother of Charles Crocker and an important legal adviser to the Big Four. Crocker later testified before Congress about his reasons for employing large numbers of Chinese laborers: "Wherever we put them we found them good, and they worked themselves into our favor to such an extent that if we found we were in a hurry for a job of work, it was better to put on Chinese at once." Quoted in T. K. Yen, "Chinese Workers and the First Transcontinental Railroad of the United States of America," Ph.D. diss., St. John's University, 1976, p. 34.

23. Collis P. Huntington to Charles Crocker, January 26, 1868, and July 1, 1868, *Letters from Collis Huntington*, vol. 1.

24. Crocker's reminiscence from Oscar Lewis, *The Big Four* (New York: Knopf, 1938), p. 73; quoted in Yen, "Chinese Workers," p. 38.

25. See frontispiece, "Map of Central California" [1860], in *Reports of the Board of Directors and Chief Engineer of the San Francisco and Marysville Railroad Company* (Marysville, Calif.: W. F. Hicks, 1860). A brief overview of early railroading in California can be found in John H. White, Jr., "The Railroad Reaches California: Men, Machines, and Cultural Migration," *California Historical Quarterly* 52 (Summer 1973): 131–44.

26. Frank Shay, "A Lifetime in California, 1860–1939," Frank Shay Papers, Department of Special Collections and Archives, Stanford University. See also *The Pacific Railroad: A Defense against Its Enemies . . . and Report of Mr. Montoya, Made to the Supervisors of the City and County of San Francisco* (San Francisco: n.p., 1864); Daggett, *Chapters on the History of the Southern Pacific*, pp. 42–43; Ward McAfee, *California's Railroad Era, 1850–1911* (San Marino, Calif.: Golden West Books, 1973), especially chap. 5.

27. "The influences that have been brought to bear by residents of Sacramento city, against the progress of your enterprize have been felt, though they have not been so virulent as to stay its onward course towards completion." *Reports of the Board of Directors*, p. 26.

28. Albertus Meyer, *Pro Memoria* ([Oakland, Calif.?] n.p., 1863). From Central Pacific Railroad Company Pamphlets, vol. 5, Huntington Library.

29. See the table of construction progress in Daggett, *Chapters on the*

History of the Southern Pacific, p. 83. See also *The Central Pacific of California* (New York: Hosford and Sons, 1867).

30. One of Huntington's additional motives in orchestrating such a campaign was to entice Union Pacific employees into working for the Central Pacific. As he wrote to Charles Crocker during the winter of 1868: "I am having some articles written for the papers here, showing the great demand for common and skilled labor in California, and as labor is very plenty here and the fare to California is so very cheap, I am disposed to think there will be a very large emigration to California this coming spring and summer." See Collis P. Huntington to Charles Crocker, January 13, 1868, and January 26, 1868, *Letters from Collis Huntington*, vol. 1.

31. Collis P. Huntington to Charles Crocker, March 28, 1868, *Letters from Collis Huntington*, vol. 1.

32. Collis P. Huntington to Mark Hopkins, April 14, 1868, *Letters from Collis Huntington*, vol. 1.

33. Richard J. Orsi, "Railroads in the History of California and the Far West: An Introduction," *California History* 70 (Spring 1991): 7.

34. Collis P. Huntington to Charles Crocker, November 26, 1867, *Letters from Collis Huntington*, vol. 1. Huntington was still trying three months later. "If you could get a law passed in the California Legislature fixing rates that could not be disturbed, it would be a good thing to do," he wrote to Crocker on February 25, 1868.

35. *Majority Report of the Committee on Corporations in Relation to Fares and Freights on Railroads* (Sacramento: D. W. Gelwicks, 1868), p. 5. See also *Report of the Assembly Committee on Railroads upon the Question of a Reduction in Railroad Freight and Fare Rates* (Sacramento: D. W. Gelwicks, 1870).

36. Charles Crocker typescript prepared for H. H. Bancroft (n.d.), in Leland Stanford Papers, Department of Special Collections and Archives, Stanford University; Collis P. Huntington to Leland Stanford, July 30, 1868, *Letters from Collis Huntington*, vol. 1.

37. Collis P. Huntington to Mark Hopkins, March 31, 1868, and Huntington to Charles Crocker, March 21, 1868, *Letters from Collis Huntington*, vol. 1. Two years later, Huntington opposed Democratic gubernatorial nominee H. H. Haight. "We must beat Haight some way," he wrote to Crocker. Presumably Huntington wished to poison Haight's campaign, since he suggested that "some of us ought to act with the Democratic party." Collis P. Huntington to Charles Crocker, February 3, 1871, *Letters from Collis Huntington*, vol. 2.

38. Collis P. Huntington to Charles Crocker, June 9, 1868, *Letters from Collis Huntington*, vol. 1.

39. See Henry George, Jr., *The Life of Henry George* (New York: Doubleday, 1911), p. 100. George told the story during an 1890 speech in San Francisco.

40. Henry George, "What the Railroad Will Bring Us," *Overland Monthly* 1 (October 1868): 297–306. See also Charles A. Barker, "Henry George and the California Background of *Progress and Poverty*," *California Historical Society Quarterly* 24 (June 1945): 97–115.

41. "She will be not merely the metropolis of the Western front of the United States, as New York is the metropolis of the Eastern front, but *the city*, the sole great city." George, "What the Railroad Will Bring Us," p. 300.

42. Ibid., pp. 300–302.

43. Ibid., p. 303.

44. B. P. Avery, "The Building of the Iron Road," *Overland Monthly* 2 (May 1869): 469–78.

45. See J. D. B. Stillman, "The Last Tie," *Overland Monthly* 3 (July 1869): 83. Western promoter George A. Crofutt quoted in Fifer, *American Progress*, pp. 149–50.

46. For a glimpse at local excitement and pride, see *Information concerning the Terminus of the Railroad System of the Pacific Coast* (Oakland, Calif.: Oakland Daily Transcript, 1871); and *The Railroad System of California: Oakland and Vicinity* (San Francisco: J. H. Carmany, 1871). Also see William Deverell, "Railroads and Other Metropolitan Nonsense," unpublished paper, 1988.

47. George Mooar, *God's Highways Exalted: A Discourse on the Completion of the Pacific Railroad* (Oakland, Calif.: [Oakland Daily Transcript,] 1869).

48. For a description of the state's (especially San Francisco's) post–Gold Rush economy, see Peter R. Decker, *Fortunes and Failures: White-Collar Mobility in Nineteenth-Century San Francisco* (Cambridge, Mass.: Harvard University Press, 1978), chap. 2.

49. Mooar, *God's Highways*.

50. J. Ross Browne, *Letter from J. Ross Browne* (San Francisco: Excelsior Press, 1870), p. 14.

51. N. J. Thompson to "Friend Croswell," March 30, 1870, Croswell Family Papers, Bancroft Library, University of California, Berkeley. For a brief discussion of the effect of the transcontinental railroad's arrival on Oakland, see Richard B. Rice, William A. Bullough, and Richard J. Orsi, *The Elusive Eden: A New History of California* (New York: Knopf, 1988), p. 259. See also chap. 4 of Shelton Stromquist's *A Generation of Boomers: The Pattern of Railroad Labor Conflict in Nineteenth-Century America* (Urbana: University of Illinois Press, 1987), for an excellent description of the nineteenth-century railroad town. Oakland does not perfectly match Stromquist's model, but many of the city's characteristics do make it a representative railroad town. Amidst all the commercial development, home building, and rising boosterism, however, was evidence of growing inequities. Riding through the Oakland hills in 1870, Henry George "re-

alized with the clarity of a revelation" that California society would forever be divided into unequal divisions of haves and have-nots as long as land monopoly existed. See John L. Thomas, *Alternative America: Henry George, Edward Bellamy, Henry Demarest Lloyd, and the Adversary Tradition* (Cambridge, Mass.: Belknap Press of Harvard University Press, 1983), pp. 49–52; and Kevin Starr, *Americans and the California Dream* (New York: Oxford University Press, 1973), p. 136. See also George, *Life of Henry George*, p. 210.

52. Jonathan Scott to "Mama," March 28, 1871, Jonathan Scott Papers, Bancroft Library.

53. Quoted in Bruce Mazlish, "Historical Analogy: The Railroad and the Space Program and Their Impact on Society," in Mazlish, *The Railroad and the Space Program*, p. 31. Leo Marx, in *The Machine in the Garden: Technology and the New Pastoral Idea in America* (New York: Oxford University Press, 1964), p. 17, notes that such reflections, usually with both a figurative and a literal meaning, were "literary commonplaces" of the antebellum era.

54. Marx, *The Machine in the Garden*, p. 213. In his book, and in his article in *The Railroad and the Space Program*, Marx discusses the railroad's intrusion into the American imagination.

55. It seems a cliché to suggest that a ride in a rocket or on the space shuttle would provide a similar experience today, but the comparison might be helpful. See Mazlish, *The Railroad and the Space Program*, especially Mazlish, "Historical Analogy," pp. 1–52; Thomas P. Hughes, "A Technological Frontier: The Railway," pp. 53–73; and Leo Marx, "The Impact of the Railroad on the American Imagination, as a Possible Comparison for the Space Impact," pp. 202–16.

56. Thomas Creevy (1829), quoted in Wolfgang Schivelbusch, *The Railway Journey: Trains and Travel in the 19th Century*, trans. Anselm Hollo (New York: Urizen Books, 1979), p. 131.

57. A number of writers have examined the railroad's shaping of time. See especially Schivelbusch, *The Railway Journey*, chap. 3: "Railroad Space and Railroad Time." See also the brief discussion in Stephen Kern, *The Culture of Time and Space* (Cambridge, Mass.: Harvard University Press, 1983); and Michael O'Malley, *Keeping Watch: A History of American Time* (New York: Viking Press, 1990).

58. The phrase is apparently de Tocqueville's; see Mazlish, "Historical Analogy," p. 33. See also Schivelbusch, *The Railway Journey*, chap. 3.

59. As one eastern visitor to Oakland noted in 1875, "Space has been almost annihilated between here and the East." See D. L. Emerson, *Oakland, Judged from an Eastern Standpoint* (Oakland, Calif.: Butler and Bowman, 1875), p. 22.

60. John R. Stilgoe, *Metropolitan Corridor: Railroads and the American Scene* (New Haven, Conn.: Yale University Press, 1983). Stilgoe's

emphasis is on the period after 1880; nonetheless, the "metropolitization" encouraged by the railroad did have earlier roots. See also Kenneth Jackson, *Crabgrass Frontier: The Suburbanization of the United States* (New York: Oxford University Press, 1985); Robert Fishman, *Bourgeois Utopias: The Rise and Fall of Suburbia* (New York: Basic Books, 1987); Sam Bass Warner, *Streetcar Suburbs: The Process of Growth in Boston, 1870–1900* (Cambridge, Mass.: Harvard University Press and MIT Press, 1962).

61. Stromquist, *Generation of Boomers*, p. 143.

62. Fishman, *Bourgeois Utopias*, p. 136. Fishman also notes: "The structure of the rail system in a late nineteenth century metropolis . . . came to resemble a diagram of the class structure." See also the appendix to Jackson, *Crabgrass Frontier*.

63. For a glorified description of the railroad's supposedly class-smashing tendencies, see Robert W. Fogel, *Railroads and American Economic Growth: Essays in Econometric History* (Baltimore: Johns Hopkins University Press, 1964), pp. 3–4. Fogel paraphrases an 1867 article from the *North American Review*.

64. Alfred D. Chandler, Jr., *The Visible Hand: The Managerial Revolution in American Business* (Cambridge, Mass.: Belknap Press of Harvard University Press, 1977), especially part 2: "The Revolution in Transportation and Communication." For a discussion of the railroad corporation's role in deepening the rift between management and labor, see Chandler and Stephen Salsbury, "The Railroads: Innovators in Modern Business Administration," in Mazlish, *The Railroad and the Space Program*, pp. 127–62.

65. Quoted in John Kasson, *Civilizing the Machine: Technology and Republican Values in America, 1776–1900* (New York: Grossman, 1976), pp. 114–15.

66. Collis Huntington to Charles Crocker, June 9, 1868, *Letters from Collis Huntington*, vol. 1.

67. Collis Huntington to Leland Stanford, January 4, 1870, *Letters from Collis Huntington*, vol. 2.

68. Collis Huntington to Leland Stanford, January 13, 1870, *Letters from Collis Huntington*, vol. 2. Huntington in particular wished to keep secret much of the Big Four's railroad consolidation. Commenting on a speech that Stanford had given, Huntington wrote that it was "unfortunate that he should so closely connect the C.P. with the S.P., as that is the only weapon our enemies have to fight us with in Congress." Collis Huntington to David D. Colton, May 28, 1875, *Letters from Collis Huntington*, vol. 3. See also Collis Huntington to Charles Crocker, April 28, 1868, *Letters from Collis Huntington*, vol. 1; and *Thirty-second Parallel Pacific Railroad: Remarks of C. P. Huntington . . . before the Committee on Pacific Railroads . . . January 31, 1878* (Washington, D.C.: Judd and Detweiler, 1878).

69. Each of these companies was likewise the result of earlier mergers. See *Official Statement of the Central Pacific Railroad Company, to the New York Stock Exchange* (n.p., n.d.) for a list and brief outline of these consolidations and those that preceded them. The pamphlet can be found in volume 5 of the Central Pacific Railroad Company Pamphlets in the Huntington Library. See also Edna M. Parker, "The Southern Pacific and Settlement in Southern California," *Pacific Historical Review* 6 (June 1937): 103–19. See also Norman E. Tutorow, "Stanford's Responses to Competition: Rhetoric versus Reality," *Southern California Quarterly* 52 (September 1970): 239.

70. Collis Huntington to Mark Hopkins, February 19 and March 23, 1874, *Letters from Collis P. Huntington*, vol. 3.

71. As early as 1869, both Republicans and Democrats pledged to end public subsidies in aid of private corporations. See Carl Brent Swisher, *Motivation and Political Technique in the California Constitutional Convention, 1878–79*, Political Science Monograph Series (Claremont, Calif.: Pomona College, 1930), p. 51; see also Daggett, *Chapters on the History of the Southern Pacific*, p. 44.

72. Collis Huntington to Charles Crocker, February 3, 1871, *Letters from Collis Huntington*, vol. 2. Huntington added, "Some of us ought to act with the Democratic party."

73. "I cannot help feeling a *little nervous* when I hear their [i.e., the railroad's] enemies professing to be the depositories of your confidence, and asserting that they *know* that you have made up your mind to veto the bills." Edward Tompkins to Henry H. Haight, March 26, 1870, Henry H. Haight Papers, Huntington Library.

74. Ibid.

75. Henry H. Haight to L. T. Carr, January 25, 1871, Haight Papers (Haight's use of "+" signs for "and" has been changed throughout).

76. Ibid. Haight added, "We are on the eve of a great struggle in 1872. Is it not manifest that on one side will be the manufacturing, railway and banking corporations contending for power and exclusive privileges and on the other side the people contending for equal rights and especially for the right of governing themselves."

77. Ibid. Haight also maintained that "protective tariffs and taxation for the benefit of private corporations are violations of natural right and not defensible either upon principle or policy."

78. Ibid.

79. In his book *The Transportation Frontier* (New York: Holt, Rinehart and Winston, 1964), p. 104, historian Oscar O. Winther writes of the rising tide of western discontent with railroad corporations during this period: "In general, all major segments of western society—merchants, farmers, and laborers—came to feel abused by the railroads. Through the press, from the pulpit, political, even academic rostrums, and in many

other ways these grievances were vehemently expressed. The railroad companies were accused of condoning dishonest practices; they were charged with capitalization and bonded indebtedness in excess of actual cost of construction. They were blamed for exacting excessive rates, practicing favoritisms and discriminations, and for operating as monopolies indifferent to public interests."

80. Royce D. Delmatier, Clarence F. McIntosh, and Earl G. Waters, eds., *The Rumble of California Politics, 1848–1970* (New York: Wiley, 1970), p. 60. See also Crane, *Newton Booth of California*; and David B. Griffiths, "Anti-monopoly Movements in California, 1873–1898," *Southern California Quarterly* 52 (June 1970): 93–121.

81. [Newton Booth,] *The Issue of the Day: Gov. Booth's Great Speech on the Railroad Question* (San Francisco: n.p., c. 1873), p. 4. The People's Independent Party was primarily a coalition group formed of disgruntled farmers and reform-minded anti-subsidy Republicans. See Griffiths, "Anti-Monopoly movements in California."

82. For instance, as Booth wrote to one detractor, "I say that railroads should not be political machines, and you accuse me of inciting a spirit which would tear up their tracks." [Newton Booth,] *Open Letter of Newton Booth to John B. Felton* (Sacramento: H. A. Weaver, 1873).

83. Booth, *Issue of the Day*.

84. Henry George, *Our Land and Land Policy* (1871), in *The Writings of Henry George* (New York: Doubleday, 1901), 9:21–22.

85. William Gouverneur Morris and H. C. Bennett, *An Essay on the Manufacturing Interests of California: The Causes That Impede and Those That Would Aid Their Development* (San Francisco, Cosmopolitan Printing, 1872), p. 36.

86. See Barker, "Henry George and the California Background," p. 107: "What concerned this region, and in particular the business mind of the region, was that the completed railroad, in 1869 and after, did not appreciably stimulate the growth of the population."

87. From Caspar T. Hopkins, *Common-Sense Applied to the Immigrant Question* (San Francisco: Turnbull and Smith, 1869), quoted in Barker, "Henry George and the California Background," p. 108.

88. Oakland *Daily News*, August 30, 1872. The paper also insisted that the San Francisco *Bulletin* and the Sacramento *Union* were "trying to convince the people that California's worst enemy is the Central Pacific Railroad Company."

89. Eustace Neale to [his mother], March 2, 1872, Eustace Neale Papers, Bancroft Library.

CHAPTER TWO

1. James J. Ayers, "Gold and Sunshine" (1896), typescript at the Henry E. Huntington Library, see especially pp. 225–27. Ayer's memoirs were

published as *Gold and Sunshine: Reminiscences of Early California* (Boston: Gorham Press, 1922).

Another visitor to Stanford's mansion observed that the interior "looked as if the old palaces of Europe had been ransacked of their art and other treasures." Quoted in Peter R. Decker, *Fortunes and Failures: White-Collar Mobility in Nineteenth-Century San Francisco* (Cambridge, Mass.: Harvard University Press, 1978), p. 218.

2. See James Bryce's description of the railroad monarchy in *The American Commonwealth*, 2 vols. (London and New York: Macmillan, 1889), 2:515.

3. The influx of railroad-borne eastern goods flooded California markets and brought about local economic stagnation. See Ira Cross, *History of the Labor Movement in California* (Berkeley: University of California Press, 1935), pp. 61–63.

4. John W. Reynolds to [his mother], May 27, 1875, John W. Reynolds Papers, Bancroft Library. Two years earlier, another visitor had observed that "San Diego is a pleasant place, but real estate is ten years ahead of Commerce. When they get a railroad and good water there will be business openings there." D. M. Berry to Thomas B. Elliott, September 19, 1873, Thomas Balch Elliott Papers, Huntington Library.

5. John W. Reynolds to [his mother], October 7, 1875, Reynolds Papers. Frank Shay, who later became personal secretary to Leland Stanford, remembered of the same period that "nearly everybody speculated, from the leader in business to his janitor; from the office man to the office boy; from mistress to maid and the cook." See "A Lifetime in California, 1860–1939," Frank Shay Papers, Department of Special Collections and Archives, Stanford University, p. 92.

6. As Decker (*Fortunes and Failures*, p. 160) writes: "by tying San Francisco to a national market and opening up the Mountain states to eastern merchants, [the railroad] had in effect weakened San Francisco's trading preeminence in the western territories; and worse, it forever destroyed San Francisco's geographic isolation and hence disrupted the West Coast trade network that San Francisco had so fortuitously monopolized for twenty years."

7. By 1868, wheat producers in California had a surplus crop greater than that of any other region in the Union. Yet one writer still wondered whether, with the extension of railroads into new markets, production could stay ahead of demand. See "Wheat in California," *Overland Monthly* 1 (November 1868): 452. Three months earlier, another writer advised immigrants that agricultural possibilities in the state had diminished, cautioning that "there is no room at present for any emigration of wheat-growers. Fruit men may be advised that the orchards of the State are in excess of the existing markets." "Farming Facts for California Immigrants," *Overland Monthly* 1 (August 1868): 182.

8. Anonymous state official, quoted in Henry George, *Our Land and*

Land Policy (1871), in *Writings of Henry George* (New York: Doubleday, 1901), 9:69, n. 1.

9. Ira Cross, *Financing an Empire: History of Banking in California* (Chicago: S. J. Clarke, 1927), 1:364–65. See also Michael Kazin, "Prelude to Kearneyism: The July Days in San Francisco, 1877," *New Labor Review* 3 (1980): 10.

10. D. M. Berry to Dr. Elliott, August 21, 1873, Elliott Papers.

11. The standard work on nineteenth-century anti-Chinese behavior in California is Alexander Saxton, *The Indispensable Enemy: Labor and the Anti-Chinese Movement in California* (Berkeley: University of California Press, 1971). See also the brief discussion in R. Hal Williams, *The Democratic Party and California Politics, 1880–1896* (Stanford, Calif.: Stanford University Press, 1973), pp. 7–14; and Ronald Takaki, *Strangers from a Different Shore: A History of Asian Americans* (New York: Penguin Books, 1989), chap. 3.

12. Mark Hopkins to Collis Huntington, November 8, 1873, *Letters from Mark Hopkins, Leland Stanford, Charles Crocker, Charles F. Crocker, and David D. Colton, to Collis P. Huntington. From August 27th, 1869, to December 30th, 1879* (New York: John C. Rankin, 1891). Hereafter cited as *Letters from Mark Hopkins et al.*

13. For a discussion of elite culture in San Francisco during this period, see chap. 9 ("A View toward the Nob") of Decker's *Fortunes and Failures.*

14. Decker (*Fortunes and Failures*, p. 260) has suggested that Yung was a Chinese immigrant. If so, rabid Sinophobe Denis Kearney's subsequent defense of him would have been extraordinarily ironic. However, census rolls list Yung as from Prussia. See United States Record Group 29, 1870 Population Schedules, City of San Francisco, Ward 6, p. 201.

15. Bryce, *The American Commonwealth*, 2:374.

16. Kazin, "Prelude to Kearneyism," p. 11.

17. Frank Roney, "History of Workingmen's Party of California" [p. 5], Frank Roney Papers, Bancroft Library.

18. Saxton (*The Indispensable Enemy*, p. 121) notes that Roney found work "almost immediately" after his 1875 arrival in San Francisco. Yet Roney's diary (Frank Roney Papers, Bancroft Library) makes clear that keeping such work was not nearly so simple.

19. Roney Diary, October/November 1875. Decker (*Fortunes and Failures*, p. 254) notes sensitively that such disillusionment was "the result of personal experiences which cannot easily be dismissed as an exaggerated sense of self-pity." The city plainly had no infrastructure capable of dealing with the plight of the poor.

20. Roney Diary, mid-January 1876. Cross (*Financing an Empire*, 1:370) likewise notes that during the winter of 1875–76 "an astounding amount of destitution prevailed among the poor of the state."

21. John Reynolds to [his mother], November 17, 1875, Reynolds Papers.

22. Saxton, *The Indispensable Enemy*, p. 106.

23. Cross, *Financing an Empire*, 1:365.

24. George W. Kelley to "Frank," July 8, 1877, George W. Kelley Papers, Bancroft Library.

25. Henry George, "The American Republic: Its Dangers and Possibilities," in *Writings of Henry George*, 9:156–66, 171.

26. For a contemporary view of the underside of the 1870s in San Francisco, see B. E. Lloyd, *Lights and Shades in San Francisco* (San Francisco: A. L. Bancroft, 1876). Much of the trouble was brought on by mining fluctuations, speculative excesses, concentration of capital (and resulting sharper definitions between classes), and a wildly unstable economy. See Cross, *Financing an Empire*, 1:363–69; Ayers, "Gold and Sunshine," p. 246.

27. William Tell Coleman manuscript (c. 1890), Hubert Howe Bancroft Collection, Bancroft Library.

28. The sarcastic "society savers" label comes from the pen of Henry George, Jr., in *The Life of Henry George* (New York: Doubleday, 1911), p. 291.

29. According to Saxton (*Indispensable Enemy*, pp. 154–55), "This hostility, composed of a rational economic argument mingled with and disguising an older complex of ideas and emotions, was constantly reinforced by the sense of deprivation and displacement which unified California's diverse labor force." See also Sucheng Chan, *This Bitter Soil: The Chinese in California Agriculture, 1860–1910* (Berkeley: University of California Press, 1986).

30. A striking example of such ostracism can be found in the literature surrounding the Workingman's Party movement. Advertisements for San Francisco commercial and business establishments made clear that white San Franciscans could and should patronize only those shops that employed white labor and had no connection with the Chinese. See J. C. Stedman and R. A. Leonard, *The Workingman's Party of California: An Epitome of Its Rise and Progress* (San Francisco: Bacon and Co., 1878).

31. Both the Republican and the Democratic Parties adopted anti-Chinese planks in their 1876 national platforms. See Saxton, *Indispensable Enemy*, pp. 105–8.

32. John L. Thomas, in *Alternative America: Henry George, Edward Bellamy, Henry Demarest Lloyd, and the Adversary Tradition* (Cambridge, Mass.: Belknap Press of Harvard University Press, 1983), p. 62, writes of George's Sinophobia: "If his view of the virtuous republic encompassed the rural cottage complete with garden and family hearth, then hell on earth was Chinatown with its fetid alleys and filthy tenements brimming with yellow devils." Some theorists on the left, recognizing Sinophobia as a misdirected attack against industrial capitalism, felt less disposed to attack the Chinese presence in the state. Some writers and thinkers on the right, basically apologists for the railroad builders, also

supported immigration. See Ira Cross, ed., *Frank Roney, Irish Rebel and California Labor Leader: An Autobiography* (Berkeley: University of California Press, 1931). On Henry George, see Charles Albro Barker, *Henry George* (New York: Oxford University Press, 1955), pp. 122–23. See also George, *Life of Henry George*, pp. 193–97.

33. The most notorious example of anti-Chinese violence in California's history occurred in 1871, when a Los Angeles mob lynched nineteen Chinese.

34. Perhaps the best-known case is the gubernatorial campaign of 1882, in which both Democratic candidate Stoneman and Republican candidate Estee stood on anti-railroad platforms. Stoneman, in part because of his reputation as an (if not the only) honest commissioner from the new railroad commission, won easily.

35. The historians who engineered much of the "Octopus" understanding of Southern Pacific hegemony in California life and politics too often mimicked Progressive politicians in excoriating the Southern Pacific. But those political actors belonged to an insurgent anti-railroad tradition and had a point to make: they were repudiating the corporation's control of the Republican Party and they were going to outflank the Democratic Party (not to mention the ever present but weak Socialists) in their antagonism to the railroad. Painting that railroad as all-powerful and insidious would make their crusade appear all the more glorious and heroic. (This notion of the railroad corporation's power will be discussed more fully in chapter 6.)

36. See Saxton, *Indispensable Enemy*, especially chap. 6. See also Neil Larry Shumsky, "Dissatisfaction, Mobility, and Expectation: San Francisco Workingmen in the 1870s," *Pacific Historian* 30 (Summer 1986): 21–28.

37. Cross, *Frank Roney, Irish Rebel and California Labor Leader*, pp. 268–69.

38. See Griffiths, "Anti-monopoly Movements in California"; and Gerald L. Prescott, "Farm Gentry vs. the Grangers: Conflict in Rural California," *California Historical Quarterly* 56 (Winter 1977/78): 328–45.

39. Neil Larry Shumsky, "Tar Flat and Nob Hill: A Social History of Industrial San Francisco during the 1870's," Ph.D. diss., University of California, Berkeley, 1972, p. 256.

40. Shumsky ("Tar Flat and Nob Hill," p. 255) writes that the WPC appealed to "men who had been dispossessed by industrialization and urbanization." However, the WPC constituency was not opposed to industrialization, at least not that exemplified by the presence of the railroad; the party sought the regulation of the principal bodies of industry and not, for the most part, their abolition.

41. Architectural historian Harold Kirker, in *California's Architectural Frontier* (San Marino, Calif.: Huntington Library, 1960), p. 73, writes of

the symbolism of the Nob Hill mansions: "The worker whose job was lost to a Chinaman discharged from railroad construction, the shopkeeper whose business was ruined by the sudden flood of eastern goods, the farmer whose community was isolated when it refused subsidy to Charles Crocker—all of these found appropriate hate symbols in the architecture of Nob Hill." Even Collis P. Huntington, with a mix of regret and pride, recognized that the Nob Hill homes represented perhaps an impolitic gesture. Writing at century's end, Huntington noted that the building of large homes in Sacramento "did us some harm and lost us some friends, though less than the later building of three great mansions in San Francisco, costing in the aggregate about five millions of dollars." Collis P. Huntington to James Speyer, December 6, 1899, Collis P. Huntington Papers (microfilm), Syracuse University, Series I, Reel 54.

42. From San Francisco *Chronicle*, November 4, 1877, and *Alta California*, November 4, 1877, quoted in Frank M. Fahey, "Denis Kearney: A Study in Demagoguery," Ph.D. diss., Stanford University, 1956, pp. 68–69. See also San Francisco *Evening Bulletin*, November 5, 1877, Cross, *History of the Labor Movement in California*, p. 100. Getting completely accurate transcriptions of Kearney's speeches (or anyone's, for that matter) from the newspapers of the day is highly unlikely. Kearney was alternately the darling and the devil of the San Francisco press, and the papers often chose which passages to quote and which to excise from his speeches. But by comparing the various newspapers' accounts, one can get an idea of how much creative editing has occurred. As Fahey notes (p. 46), "Speculation as to the motives of a man whose recorded sentiments were almost entirely public ones is especially hazardous."

43. Cross, *History of the Labor Movement*, p. 100; San Francisco *Evening Bulletin*, November 5, 1877.

44. San Francisco *Alta California*, November 1, 1877.

45. See San Francisco *Chronicle*, November 25, 1877.

46. Charles Crocker to Collis P. Huntington, January 22, 1878, *Letters from Mark Hopkins et al.*

47. Henry George, "The Kearney Agitation in California," *Popular Science Monthly*, August 17, 1880, pp. 433–53; quotes are from pp. 434, 436, 438.

48. Ibid., p. 451.

49. Such action was not unknown in California and other parts of the American West. For instance, the "Gorras Blancas" of late-nineteenth-century New Mexico rode through San Miguel County tearing up tracks, burning bridges, and cutting ties in half. For a description of the activities of the "white caps," see Sarah Deutsch, *No Separate Refuge: Culture, Class, and Gender on an Anglo-Hispanic Frontier in the American Southwest, 1880–1940* (New York: Oxford University Press, 1987), pp. 25–26. One California memoir suggests that Creed Haymond, who would later become

chief counsel for the Southern Pacific, promoted railroad sabotage in his early political career. See Jackson A. Graves, *California Memories, 1857–1930* (Los Angeles: Times-Mirror Press, 1930), p. 45.

50. See Carl Brent Swisher, *Motivation and Political Technique in the California Constitutional Convention, 1878–79*, Political Science Monograph Series (Claremont, Calif.: Pomona College, 1930), pp. 6–10. Swisher notes that popular support for a new constitution had been building since the mid-1850s.

51. See Leland Stanford to Collis P. Huntington, November 13 and December 5, 1878, *Letters from Mark Hopkins et al.*

52. San Francisco *Argonaut*, April 13, 1878, quoted in Fahey, "Denis Kearney," p. 195.

53. The breakdown of the remaining delegates: fifty-one WPC members, eleven Republicans, ten Democrats, and three Independents. From Swisher, *California Constitutional Convention*, p. 24.

54. Sacramento *Record Union*, June 17, 1878. Quoted in Fahey, "Denis Kearney," p. 222.

55. Ayers, "Gold and Sunshine," p. 221.

56. In retrospect, Ayers (p. 224) assigned the actions of the railroad executives to fallible human nature: "they could not resist the temptation to squeeze the orange they held in their grip to the last drop."

57. See Swisher, *California Constitutional Convention*.

58. Prescott, "Farm Gentry vs. the Grangers."

59. Quoted in Swisher, *California Constitutional Convention*, p. 36; see also Ezra S. Carr, *The Patrons of Husbandry on the Pacific Coast* (San Francisco: A. L. Bancroft, 1875).

60. Non-Partisan delegate William H. Barnes, quoted in *Debates and Proceedings of the Constitutional Convention of the State of California* (Sacramento: State Printing Office, 1880), 1:564. Hereafter cited as *Constitutional Debates*.

61. One historian argues that this agenda of reform actually made the WPC movement a far more conservative political entity than contemporaries understood. See Gordon Bakken, "California Constitutionalism: Politics, the Press, and the Death of Fundamental Law," *Pacific Historian* 30 (Winter 1986): 5–17. Henry George ("Kearney Agitation in California") made a similar argument regarding the political nature of Kearneyism.

62. *Constitutional Debates*, 1:567–69.

63. Ibid., 1:600.

64. Quoted in Kevin Starr, *Americans and the California Dream* (New York: Oxford University Press, 1973), p. 110.

65. *Constitutional Debates*, 1:567–69.

66. William H. L. Barnes, San Francisco attorney and Non-Partisan Party delegate to the 1878–79 constitutional convention, argued before other delegates that railroad opposition resulted from "the personal bear-

ing of some of the managers. . . . It is a question of personal popularity, rather than anything else." *Constitutional Debates*, 1:565.

67. One delegate to the constitutional convention, Henry Smith, a plumber and WPC member from San Francisco, declared that there were "three great propositions" that motivated the calling of the convention. "One was the railroad, another the land, and the other the water question." This denunciation of monopoly was notable not only for its clear-cut antagonism toward corporate authority but for its neglect of the Chinese issue. *Constitutional Debates*, 2:1143.

68. Ibid., 1:456.

69. Ibid., 1:640. White became the WPC candidate for governor in 1880. His son, Stephen Mallory White, was a Southern Pacific attorney before becoming a U.S. senator (and thorn in the Southern Pacific's side) in the 1890s.

70. [California Assembly,] *Majority Report of the Committee on Corporations in Relation to Fares and Freights on Railroads* (Sacramento: n.p., c. 1865), in Central Pacific Railroad Company Pamphlets, vol. 4, Huntington Library.

71. See [San Francisco Chamber of Commerce,] *Extracts from Report . . . Fares and Freights* (San Francisco: n.p., 1874), in Central Pacific Railroad Company Pamphlets, vol. 4, Huntington Library.

72. Oakland *Daily News*, January 5, 1874.

73. Nathaniel G. Wyatt of the WPC, lawyer from Monterey City, reading from the 1876 report of the Board of Commissioners of Transportation, in *Constitutional Debates*, 1:470–71.

74. Ibid.

75. My discussion here is drawn largely from Swisher, *California Constitutional Convention*, especially chap. 4: "Corralling Corporations."

76. Swisher (p. 54) argues that Estee's appointment was the result of the demand for railroad regulation: "Although the conservatives were in nominal control of the convention it seems probable that it was in response to a highly insistent popular demand for regulation that he was appointed to this strategic position."

77. Quoted in Swisher, *California Constitutional Convention*, p. 55.

78. *Constitutional Debates*, 1:473.

79. Ibid., 1:573.

80. Ibid., 1:454.

81. Ibid., 1:575.

82. Ibid., 1:565, 613, 614.

83. *The New Constitution: Look before You Leap* (n.p.: 1878); Workingmen's Party of California, *The Proposed Constitution Reviewed in an Address to the Reformers in California* (n.p.: [1879]), see especially pp. 35–36.

84. Ratification was defeated in WPC stronghold San Francisco. See

Dudley T. Moorhead, "Sectionalism and the California Constitution of 1879," *Pacific Historical Review* 12 (September 1943): 287–93.

85. Edward Fitzgerald Beale to Robert S. Baker, March 27, 1879, Robert S. Baker Papers, Huntington Library.

86. See Richard B. Rice, William A. Bullough, and Richard J. Orsi, *The Elusive Eden: A New History of California* (New York: Knopf, 1988), pp. 217–36. This chapter, "The Confrontation at Mussel Slough," was written by Richard J. Orsi. I am grateful to him for sharing many of his thoughts and findings with me. See also Wallace P. V. Smith, "The Development of the San Joaquin Valley, 1772–1882," Ph.D. diss., University of California, Berkeley, 1932. For insight into the position of the Settlers' Grand League, see *The Struggle of the Mussel Slough Settlers for Their Homes* (Visalia, Calif.: Delta Printing Establishment, 1880); and *An Appeal to the People* (Visalia, Calif.: Visalia Delta Book and Job, 1880).

87. The league published a "Warning to Land Grabbers" in local newspapers, arguing that no one could "peaceably occupy" any of the disputed lands until the case had been resolved. See, for instance, Fresno *Weekly Expositor*, May 29, 1878.

88. Minutes of the California Railroad Commission, 4 vols., California State Archives, Sacramento.

89. Ibid., October 23, 1880. Farmers occasionally insisted that they did not go before the commission because they feared economic reprisals from the railroad; this charge deserves more study.

90. Such difficulties were by no means limited to California. States throughout the country had already experimented with railroad commissions (as well as other regulatory bodies), only to discover that regulation invariably required levels of knowledge and expertise that only railroad corporations possessed. See, for instance, David P. Thelen, *The New Citizenship: Origins of Progressivism in Wisconsin, 1885–1900* (Columbia: University of Missouri Press, 1972).

91. *Wasp* [San Francisco], March 26, 1881.

92. Ibid., January 29, 1881.

93. See, for instance, *Wasp*, November 27, 1880: "One of the chief planks in the platform of a new party should be a demand for the regulation of freights and fares, or, better still, the acquisition by the national government of all our iron highways, which might then be run in the interest of the people, and not for the purpose of adding additional millions to the already replete purses of a dozen selfish millionaires."

94. *Wasp*, November 27, 1880.

95. Ibid., April 9, 1881.

96. Ibid., May 20, 1881.

97. Ibid., January 8, 1881.

98. Gerald Nash, "The California Railroad Commission, 1876–1911," *Southern California Quarterly* 44 (December 1962): 287–305.

99. See Saxton, *The Indispensable Enemy*, pp. 153–54. Beerstecher was subsequently shot in the chest by a disgruntled citizen in late 1880.

100. Williams, *The Democratic Party and California Politics*, p. 18.

101. Swisher, *California Constitutional Convention*, p. 50.

CHAPTER THREE

1. Rockwell D. Hunt, *California and Californians*, 5 vols. (Chicago: Lewis Publishing Co., 1926), 4:417.

2. See Stuart Daggett, *Chapters on the History of the Southern Pacific* (New York: Ronald Press, 1922), especially chaps. 9 and 12. Now and again through the 1870s, the Southern Pacific railroad magnates would be referred to as the "Big Five" if Colton were included.

3. See R. Hal Williams, *The Democratic Party and California Politics, 1880–1896* (Stanford, Calif.: Stanford University Press, 1973), pp. 32–39.

4. Atchison, Topeka & Santa Fe traffic manager Nicholson, quoted in the newsmagazine *The Earth* 4 (May 1904): 9.

5. Charles Dwight Willard to Harriet Edgar Willard, October 31, 1886, and Charles Dwight Willard to Sarah Willard Hiestand, December 16, 1886, Charles Dwight Willard Papers, Huntington Library. See also Glenn S. Dumke, *The Boom of the Eighties in Southern California* (San Marino, Calif.: Huntington Library, 1944), especially chap. 3.

6. United States Pacific Railway Commission, *Testimony Taken by the United States Pacific Railway Commission Approved March 3, 1887, Entitled "An Act Authorizing an Investigation of the Books, Accounts, and Methods of Railroads Which Have Received Aid from the United States, and for Other Purposes,"* 6 vols. (Washington, D.C.: U.S. Government Printing Office, 1887).

7. See Williams, *The Democratic Party and California Politics*, pp. 208–9. See also Richard Orsi, "*The Octopus* Reconsidered: The Southern Pacific and Agricultural Modernization in California, 1865–1915," *California Historical Quarterly* 54 (Fall 1975): 198. Orsi notes that the Southern Pacific was "profoundly affected by California's arrested development." The state—hampered by the periodic stops and starts of recession and depression—could not move smoothly from an economy heavily dependent on mining into one more reliant on agricultural diversification. This "arrested development" not only handicapped the railroad's ability to do business but also reawakened discontent, as the 1890s aptly demonstrate.

8. See William W. Ray, "Crusade or Civil War? The Pullman Strike in California," *California History* 58 (Spring 1979): 20–37, and "The Great Strike of 1894: The Pullman Boycott in California," Master's thesis, California State University, Hayward, 1972; Grace H. Stimson, *Rise of the*

Labor Movement in Los Angeles (Berkeley: University of California Press, 1955), pp. 161–71; Williams, *The Democratic Party and California Politics*, pp. 194–99; Thomas R. Bacon, "The Pullman Strike in California," *Yale Review* 3 (1895): 241–50. For a firsthand account by members of the California National Guard, see George Filmer et al., *The "City Guard": A History of Company "B," First Regiment Infantry, N.G.C. during the Sacramento Campaign, July 3 to 26, 1894* (San Francisco: Filmer-Rollins Electrotype Co., 1895). See also J. J. O'Connell, "The Great Strike of 1894," *United Service* 15, n.s. (1896): 310–13. For an analysis of labor disputes within the railroad industry, see Gerald G. Eggert, *Railroad Labor Disputes: The Beginnings of Federal Strike Policy* (Ann Arbor: University of Michigan Press, 1967), especially pp. 152–91.

9. See Nick Salvatore, *Eugene V. Debs: Citizen and Socialist* (Ithaca, N.Y.: Cornell University Press, 1982); and Stimson, *Rise of the Labor Movement*, p. 164.

10. See, for instance, the interview with an Oakland trainman in the San Francisco *Call*, June 26, 1894. While he did not think that the strike would have much effect in California, this trainman did admit that, should the strike come West, "we could expect nothing else than to find the full power of the railroad directed against us."

11. Williams (*The Democratic Party and California Politics*, p. 195) lists the number of California railroad employees affected by the strike as approximately 11,500. The *Tenth Annual Report of the Commission of Labor, 1894*, vol. 1 (Washington, D.C.: U.S. Government Printing Office, 1896), puts the number at over 14,000. Public perceptions notwithstanding, Southern Pacific employees had absorbed a severe cut in wages in the first and worst year of the depression of 1893. See E. G. Campbell, *The Reorganization of American Railways, 1893–1900* (New York: Columbia University Press, 1938; reprint, New York: AMS Press, 1968), p. 300.

12. Arthur McEwen in San Bernardino *Daily Courier*, July 4, 1890; from clipping in the George Kenyon Fitch Papers, Bancroft Library, University of California, Berkeley.

13. In the 1892 presidential election, for instance, the Populist candidate polled 9 percent of the California vote. In 1892, Cator published a tract called *Rescue the Republic: The Necessity and Advantages of National Ownership of Railroads* (San Francisco: Citizens' Alliance, 1892).

14. P. O. Chilstrom, *Prostituted Manhood* (San Francisco: n.p., 1893).

15. George S. Patton, in *Address to the Voters of the 6th Congressional District of California* (Los Angeles: Kinsell and Doan, 1896), p. 3, noted the similarity between the railroad antagonism of the Democrats and the Republicans. Yet, in his attempt to woo Populist voters, Patton championed government ownership of the Southern Pacific and "the bold and radical stand taken by the Democratic party."

16. William M. Cubery, *An Open Letter to C. P. Huntington* (San Francisco: n.p., [1891]).

17. In the spring of 1894, Jacob Coxey led an estimated thirty thousand people to Washington, D.C., to march in protest against massive unemployment. Georgina Jones, wife of Senator John P. Jones, wrote her husband about an encounter with Coxeyites in the San Joaquin Valley: "We had quite an exciting time on the train this morning just after reaching Tulare. It seems that over two hundred men were ready to board the train and take it South but warning was given in time [and] a posse of deputy sheriffs were sent ahead of us to clear the way [and] our train went through a long line of howling, dirty looking ruffians, armed with sticks and guns." Georgina Jones to John P. Jones, June 3, 1894, John P. Jones Papers, Huntington Library. My thanks to John Farquhar for allowing me to examine, cite, and publish from the Jones Papers. See also Carlos A. Schwantes, *Coxey's Army* (Lincoln: University of Nebraska Press, 1985).

18. See William Issel, "'Citizens outside the Government': Business and Urban Policy in San Francisco and Los Angeles, 1890–1932," *Pacific Historical Review* 57 (May 1988): 117–45.

19. For example, the Trans-Mississippi Congress of 1894, a gathering of delegates from western chambers of commerce (whose two Los Angeles delegates were both officials of a rival railroad), passed a resolution opposing the Southern Pacific in its attempts to obtain a federal appropriation for a deep-water harbor at Santa Monica.

20. Historian Robert Wiebe, in *The Search for Order* (New York: Hill and Wang, 1967), p. 53, sketches the "remarkable range" of railroad opposition in this period: "the farmer saw [the railroad] as the arrogant manipulator of his profit, the small-town entrepreneur as the destroyer of his dreams, the city businessman as the sinister ally of his competitors, the labor leader as a model of the callous, distant employer, and the principled gentleman as the source of unscrupulous wealth and political corruption."

21. Stimson, *Rise of the Labor Movement*, p. 164. Accurate statistics are difficult to come by, however, since membership was highly secretive. Southern Pacific blacklisting of known ARU members forced the movement underground.

22. Thomas Roberts, quoted in San Francisco *Examiner*, June 29, 1894, from American Railway Union Strike Scrapbooks (25 vols.), vol. 1, Henry Huntington Papers, Huntington Library. Hereafter cited as ARU Strike Scrapbooks.

23. Knox was the ARU leader in Sacramento. Quoted in San Francisco *Call*, July 1, 1894, ARU Strike Scrapbooks, vol. 3.

24. Jane Stanford to A. N. Towne, H. C. Nash, J. Agar, July 1, 1894, Jane Stanford Papers, Department of Special Collections and Archives, Stanford University.

25. Jane Stanford to Eugene Debbs [*sic*], July 1, 1894, Jane Stanford Papers.

26. Eugene V. Debs to "Mrs. Leland Stanford," July 2, 1894, Jane Stanford Papers.

27. Jane Stanford to Eugene Debbs [*sic*], July 2, 1894, Jane Stanford Papers.

28. Newspaper commentary on the strike invariably pointed out that violence was the one sure way to end any public sympathy. As one paper editorialized, support "will be lost if unlawful violence is employed to make the strike win or to avenge the loss of any points in the battle." Oakland *Enquirer*, July 2, 1894.

29. See San Francisco *Examiner*, June 30, 1894, ARU Strike Scrapbooks, vol. 2; see also the cartoon in the *Examiner*, July 3, 1894.

30. San Francisco *Call*, July 1, 1894, ARU Strike Scrapbooks, vol. 3.

31. San Francisco *Chronicle*, July 2, 1894, ARU Strike Scrapbooks, vol. 3.

32. San Francisco *Examiner*, June 29, and July 1, 1894, ARU Strike Scrapbooks, vol. 3. The *Examiner* also reported on bands of strikers that wanted to smash Pullman cars with axes.

33. Henry E. Huntington to Collis P. Huntington, July 2, 1894, Henry Huntington Papers, Huntington Library.

34. See William Friedricks, *Henry E. Huntington and the Creation of Southern California* (Columbus: Ohio State University Press, 1992), p. 43.

35. Collis P. Huntington to Henry E. Huntington, July 6, 1894, Henry Huntington Papers.

36. Ibid.

37. San Francisco *Call*, June 28, 1894, ARU Strike Scrapbooks, vol. 1.

38. Oakland *Railroad Men's Advocate*, June 28, 1894, quoted in San Francisco *Chronicle*, June 29, 1894, ARU Strike Scrapbooks, vol. 1. Stimson (*Rise of the Labor Movement*, pp. 166–67) writes that "hatred of the Southern Pacific monopoly went deep enough in California to make public reaction to the strike markedly different from that in other parts of the country; the employees were upheld even by farmers and others suffering financial loss." See also Jerry Cooper, *The Army and Civil Disorder* (Westport, Conn.: Greenwood Press, 1980), pp. 116–21.

39. In fact, initial complaints about the railroad company suggested that the corporate stubbornness of the Southern Pacific threatened to produce frightening alliances of the working class. An editorial in a San Francisco newspaper voiced this concern at the dawn of the strike, when it termed the railroad company's intransigence "contemptibly vindictive. . . . It is inciting to riot." San Francisco *Examiner*, June 28, 1894, ARU Strike Scrapbooks, vol. 1.

40. Quoted in San Francisco *Report*, June 29, 1894, ARU Strike Scrapbooks, vol. 1.

41. San Francisco *Call*, June 29, 1894, ARU Strike Scrapbooks, vol. 1.

42. San Francisco *Daily Report*, June 29, 1894, ARU Strike Scrapbooks, vol. 1.

43. William F. Herrin to John D. Bicknell, June 27, 1894, John D. Bicknell Papers, Huntington Library.

44. San Francisco *Call*, July 1, 1894, ARU Strike Scrapbooks, vol. 3.

45. The corporation's quick decision to seek aid from the federal government in this manner sparked the annoyance of numerous Californians. For instance, Charles E. Bowen, in a letter published in the July 2, 1894, edition of the San Francisco *Call* (ARU Strike Scrapbooks, vol. 3), asked, "Before the Federal Government calls upon its troops to assist in manning 'customary' trains arbitrarily designated by any corporation, would it not be a justice to the people to define in positive terms what constitutes a train of cars?"

46. Judge Erskine M. Ross, quoted in Eggert, *Railroad Labor Disputes*, p. 176.

47. Barry Baldwin, U.S. marshal, quoted in San Francisco *Examiner*, July 2, 1894, ARU Strike Scrapbooks, vol. 3. See also David Montgomery, "Strikes in Nineteenth-Century America," *Social Science History* 4 (February 1980): 85. Montgomery, among others, points out that a strike could be "a modern-day festival of the poor." Ironically, Baldwin himself was an anti-railroad activist, albeit of a different stripe than the Pullman strikers. He had been a founder and president of the Traffic Association of San Francisco, formed in part to lobby for an end to the Southern Pacific's northern California railroad monopoly.

48. In describing affairs in Sacramento, the U.S. marshal, Barry Baldwin, said that the crowd was "demonstrative and ugly," that the strikers held a better than four-to-one advantage over the militia, and that local police authorities "are in thorough sympathy with strikers." Baldwin to U.S. Attorney Garter, July 4, 1894, enclosed in U.S. Attorney Garter to Attorney General Olney, July 5, 1894, *Appendix to the Annual Report of the Attorney-General of the United States for the Year 1896* (Washington, D.C.: U.S. Government Printing Office, 1896), pp. 25–26.

49. Governor H. H. Markham agreed with Dimond. "The larger the force the surer of success," Markham telegraphed. Markham to Major-General W. H. Dimond, July 3, 1894, *Appendix to the Biennial Report of the Adjutant-General of the State of California, 1893–1894* (Sacramento: State Printing Office, 1894), p. 212.

50. Adjutant-General C. C. Allen instructed Dimond to postpone any acceptance of the G.A.R. veterans: "The old Vets have done their share." Allen to Dimond, July 3, 1894, *Appendix to the Biennial Report of the Adjutant-General*, p. 214.

51. Filmer, *City Guard*, p. 21.

52. "Among the persons gathered to see us take our departure were a large number of men endowed with socialistic tendencies, whose view of

the situation was so narrow that they viewed the calling out of the militia as an act of the Government's to abet the railroad company in oppressing its employees, and not as an act necessary to maintain the laws of the land which guarantee to all equal rights in the protection of their property." Filmer, *City Guard*, p. 21.

53. Guard commanders considered disarming the men of Company A but decided against it; General Dimond reported that disarming the men "would be disastrous on the morale of our troops, and would correspondingly encourage the strikers." *Appendix to the Biennial Report of the Adjutant-General*, p. 216.

54. Filmer, *City Guard*, p. 34.

55. Sheehan was manager of the Sacramento *Record-Union*, a decidedly pro–Southern Pacific newspaper run by William Mills from Southern Pacific headquarters in San Francisco. His pleading with the strikers, which apparently continued for nearly an hour, was later found to be in violation of military law.

56. The text of Baldwin's order reads: "I hereby order you to fire upon the crowds assembled in S.P. Co.'s depot, grounds, and on bridges, in order to clear the same of unlawful, riotous assemblages therein." *Appendix to the Biennial Report of the Adjutant-General*, p. 217.

57. Reported in San Francisco *Call*, July 5, 1894, ARU Strike Scrapbooks, vol. 6.

58. The events in Sacramento read remarkably like those described by Herbert Gutman in his essay "Trouble on the Railroads in 1873–1874: Prelude to the 1877 Crisis?" in *Work, Culture, and Society in Industrializing America* (New York: Knopf, 1976), pp. 295–320. As Gutman found in Ohio, New Jersey, and Pennsylvania, local support for railroad strikers often ran high. Similar ties of community, class, family, and ethnicity linked the Sacramento militia units with the strikers there.

59. See A. D. Cutler to General John H. Dickinson, July 19, 1894, in *Appendix to the Biennial Report of the Adjutant-General*, p. 230.

60. Thirty-two men of Sacramento Company G eventually faced court-martial for their actions at the depot on July 4. All pleaded not guilty to the charge of refusal to return to military position. Most were convicted, received dishonorable discharges, and were sent to military prisons for terms not exceeding one month.

61. "There was not a squad of men in Company B . . . who would not willingly, even gladly have charged the mob of strikers." Filmer, *City Guard*, p. 64.

62. "From that moment the strikers knew that the day was won. How that mob enjoyed our humiliation and the scene of a United States marshall pleading with them like a child." Filmer, *City Guard*, p. 36.

63. In its July 21, 1894, issue, San Francisco's satirical magazine the *Wasp* called the farce that "cruel war between the mosquitoes and the city militia."

64. Filmer, *City Guard*, p. 88.

65. Colonel Park Henshaw, quoted in General W. H. Dimond to H. H. Markham, July 6, 1894, *Appendix to the Biennial Report of the Adjutant-General*, p. 221.

66. San Francisco *Call*, July 3, 1894, ARU Strike Scrapbooks, vol. 4.

67. Oakland councilman, quoted in Oakland *Enquirer*, June 29, 1894. From the Scrapbooks of George C. Pardee, vol. 9, Department of Special Collections and Archives, Stanford University. Hereafter cited as Pardee Scrapbooks.

68. Quoted in Oakland *Enquirer*, July 7, 1894; clipping in Pardee Scrapbooks, vol. 9. For a stimulating discussion of the alliance between San Francisco labor and the Populists, see Alexander Saxton, "San Francisco Labor and the Populist and Progressive Insurgencies," *Pacific Historical Review* 34 (1965): 421–38. See also Shelton Stromquist, *A Generation of Boomers: The Pattern of Railroad Labor Conflict in Nineteenth-Century America* (Urbana: University of Illinois Press, 1987), especially chaps. 4–6.

69. The fact that the Southern Pacific trains ran directly in front of this woman's home may help explain some of her opposition to the railroad and her "grief" at its "death." See San Francisco *Call*, July 6, 1894, ARU Strike Scrapbooks, vol. 7.

70. Mrs. Roberts, quoted in San Francisco *Call*, July 5, 1894, ARU Strike Scrapbooks, vol. 6.

71. See San Francisco *Chronicle*, July 5, 1894, and San Francisco *Call*, July 5, 1894, ARU Strike Scrapbooks, vol. 6.

72. San Francisco *Examiner*, as quoted in the Oakland *Tribune*, June 29, 1894.

73. See Donald E. Walters, "Populism in California, 1889–1900," Ph.D. diss., University of California, Berkeley, 1952; John T. McGreevy, "Origins of California Populism," seminar paper, Stanford University, 1987.

74. In the spring of 1894, Pardee demanded that the Bay Area contingent of Coxey's rag-tag followers leave his city. Backed by an impressively outrageous show of force, which included a Gatling gun and large numbers of police officers, the mayor enforced his demand.

75. Oakland *Times*, July 18, 1894.

76. Ibid.

77. In one crossed-out passage, Olney called for the army: "Have had all the fighting I want, but if this generation of young men have not the manhood to put down mob violence and riot now so rampant, then let them call on the veterans of '61." Warren Olney to George C. Pardee, July 20, 1894, Olney Papers, Bancroft Library.

78. Ibid.

79. Oakland *Times*, July 25, 1894. See also the *Railroad Men's Advocate*, July 25, 1894, single issue in Pardee Scrapbooks, vol. 9.

80. In its July 5, 1894, issue, the San Francisco *Chronicle* suggested

that such calculated patriotism "won the southern capital entirely, for this is an out and out American city" (ARU Strike Scrapbooks, vol. 6). ARU members and supporters also wore the white ribbons that Debs promoted; this gesture prompted Harrison Gray Otis to encourage anti-strike Angelenos to wear red, white, and blue as a sign of their greater patriotism and love of law and order.

81. Denis to Olney, June 29, 1894, *Appendix to the Annual Report of the Attorney-General*, pp. 17–18.

82. John D. Bicknell to William F. Herrin, June 29, 1894, Bicknell Papers, Huntington Library.

83. Los Angeles *Times*, June 30, 1894.

84. Los Angeles *Times*, July 8, 1894. The paper printed letters from Los Angeles citizens unanimously supporting its position. "Who of us has not felt the oppressive exercise of power and privilege of our California railroads?" one reader asked. "But have we, who have watched their methods from the beginning, not seen vast improvements brought about by legal enactments?" Letter to the editor from "A Democrat from 'Way Back,'" Los Angeles *Times*, July 7, 1894. The truculent anti-union attitude of the *Times* brought the paper into difficulties with newsboys and advertisers and prompted a boycott by Pullman strikers. See Stimson, *Labor Movement in Los Angeles*, p. 168; Walters, "Populism in California," pp. 263–64; and *Overland Monthly* 28 (July 1896): 124–26.

85. *Appendix to the Annual Report of the Attorney-General*, pp. 22–23, quoted in Williams, *The Democratic Party and California Politics*, p. 197, n. 42.

86. Olney also authorized the use of troops because the U.S. marshal in southern California was incapacitated by sickness.

87. "Judge Gibson," from the San Francisco *Daily Report*, July 3, 1894; Roberts quoted in San Francisco *Bulletin*, July 3, 1894, ARU Strike Scrapbooks, vol. 4.

88. San Francisco *Chronicle*, July 3, 1894, ARU Strike Scrapbooks, vol. 4. Civil War veteran (and Southern Pacific attorney) John S. Mosby had no qualms about U.S. action against the strikers. In a telegram to officials in the Department of Justice, Mosby announced that northern California was "in a state of siege; mob in possession of railroad, blockading communications." Mosby declared that only U.S. regulars could end the "reign of terror" and "quell the insurrections." See John S. Mosby to Majors Conrad and Russell, July 6, 1894, *Appendix to the Annual Report of the Attorney-General*, p. 27.

89. San Francisco *Chronicle*, July 4, 1894, ARU Strike Scrapbooks, vol. 4.

90. U.S. Attorney Denis, quoted in San Francisco *Chronicle*, July 5, 1894, ARU Strike Scrapbooks, vol. 6.

91. Southern Pacific officials suspected Denis of addressing the ARU

and supporting the strike. It was rumored that he had declared that he would rather see Collis Huntington behind bars than the striking employees of the railroad. See John Bicknell to William F. Herrin, August 11, 1894, and William F. Herrin to John D. Bicknell, August 22, 1894, Bicknell Papers.

92. Denis wrote to Olney on July 8 that he had served injunctions on the Southern Pacific requiring the company to move mails and commerce, "which they can do, but are afraid of losing their own men after the strike is quelled." *Appendix to the Annual Report of the Attorney-General*, p. 29. See also John Bicknell to William F. Herrin, July 20, 1894, Bicknell Papers.

93. See San Francisco *Chronicle*, July 5, 1894, ARU Strike Scrapbooks, vol. 6.

94. U.S. Attorney Denis, quoted in San Francisco *Chronicle*, July 5, 1894, ARU Strike Scrapbooks, vol. 6, p. 6.

95. Pro-strike meetings in San Francisco were directed by leading Populists, and the party's local paper, *Voice of Labor*, became the leading ARU organ during the strike. Sacramento-area Farmers' Alliance members offered to support the strikers at the Southern Pacific depot with food and supplies, and farmers around the Sacramento area allegedly greased Southern Pacific rails to prevent train travel during the boycott. The San Francisco *Chronicle* published a rumor that the Farmers' Alliance had committed two hundred armed men to aid the strikers in Sacramento. See San Francisco *Report*, July 5, 1894, ARU Strike Scrapbooks, vol. 6; San Francisco *Chronicle*, July 7, 1894, ARU Strike Scrapbooks, vol. 7.

96. Filmer, *City Guard*, p. 63.

97. These papers clearly attempted to sensationalize the violence of the strike, in both the East and the West. For instance, *Post* headlines on July 3 read: "Deeds of Desperation" and "Violent Acts of the Strikers." On July 4, the headlines sensationalized the outbreak of shooting in Sacramento, without making it clear that the incident referred to was an accidental shooting of a Sacramento man by a guardsman; another headline, ostensibly about strikers disabling locomotives, read: "Train Wrecked." San Francisco *Post*, July 3 and 4, 1894, ARU Strike Scrapbooks, vols. 4 and 5.

98. See, for instance, the Los Angeles *Times*, July 9, 1894, for a survey of local clerical opinion regarding the strike. Wiebe (*The Search for Order*, chap. 4) describes the nation's paranoid preoccupation with the threat of revolution.

99. Oakland *Times*, July 2, 1894, ARU Strike Scrapbooks, vol. 4.

100. San Francisco *Call*, July 5, 1894, ARU Strike Scrapbooks, vol. 6.

101. James Lloyd La Fayette Warren to Edwin H. Frost, July 22, 1894, Huntington Library manuscript collection.

102. Collis P. Huntington to Gates, July 7, 1894, Collis P. Huntington

Papers (microfilm), Syracuse University, Series I, Reel 53. Huntington told Gates to forward this response to Michael De Young of the San Francisco *Chronicle*.

103. The same letter writer chastised local papers for coddling the strikers, arguing that "they did the same to the sandlotters [i.e., the supporters of Denis Kearney]." Oakland *Tribune*, July 2, 1894, ARU Strike Scrapbooks, vol. 4.

104. Walters, "Populism in California," pp. 269–70.

105. See, for instance, Bacon, "The Pullman Strike in California," p. 244. The success of the strike, especially the public's support for those whom he regarded as revolutionary radicals, completely dumbfounded the University of California professor: "It is difficult to understand how any man of sane mind could suppose that the management of railroad property throughout the country could be carried on according to the whims of Debs and his friends, without also expecting the annihilation of all law, the destruction of all government, and the coming in of complete anarchy."

106. San Francisco *Daily Report*, July 3, quoting from the Vacaville *Reporter*, ARU Strike Scrapbooks, vol. 4.

107. Of course the faint voices of California Socialists had been placing, or attempting to place, the struggle in more radical terms from the start. For a description of a Socialist meeting in San Francisco in July, see San Francisco *Call*, July 3, 1894, ARU Strike Scrapbooks, vol. 4. See also Walters, "Populism in California," p. 269.

108. Richard Slotkin, in *The Fatal Environment* (New York: Atheneum, 1985), p. 479, discusses a similar occurrence in the railroad strike of 1877, wherein the eastern press helped foster an awareness that the strikers and trade unionists were one and the same with the "dangerous classes." "Only by pointing up the differences between 'honest workmen' and the 'dangerous classes' [i.e., strikers] could they drive a wedge between the strikers and their middle-class sympathizers."

109. Henry Huntington, in a letter to Collis P. Huntington on July 18, 1894 (Henry Huntington Papers), called Williams "a dynamiter."

110. The author of an article in *The Nation* attempted to explain the perplexing fact of California's support for the strike by trotting out the myriad reasons people could dislike the monopolistic Southern Pacific: "Every complaint . . . that is made against a railroad there—quality of service, rates of fare, and freight charges—falls on this company." "The Situation in California," *The Nation*, July 12, 1894.

111. From San Francisco *Examiner*, July 1, 1894, quoted in Ray, "The Great Strike of 1894," p. 44.

112. Filmer, *City Guard*, pp. 111, 31.

113. Stephen Mallory White to Thomas L. Thompson, July 14, 1894, Stephen M. White Papers, Department of Special Collections and Archives, Stanford University.

114. Stephen M. White to J. Marion Brooks, July 13, 1894, White Papers. See also White to "The President," July 8, 1894, White Papers.

115. John P. Irish, "California and the Railroad," *Overland Monthly* 25 (June 1895): 675–81.

116. Denis and Call to Attorney General Olney, July 11, 1894, *Appendix to the Annual Report of the Attorney-General*, p. 33.

117. See Henry Huntington and A. N. Towne to Collis P. Huntington, July 17, 1894, Henry Huntington Papers.

118. Herrin to John Muir and John D. Bicknell, July 19, 1894, John D. Bicknell Papers, Huntington Library. See also Williams, *The Democratic Party and California Politics*, pp. 210–11.

119. Call to Olney, July 18, 1894, *Appendix to the Annual Report of the Attorney-General*, pp. 34–35. See also Denis to Olney, August 2, 1894, *Appendix to the Annual Report of the Attorney-General*, p. 35.

120. Henry E. Huntington to Collis P. Huntington, July 21, 1894, Henry E. Huntington Papers, Huntington Library. Although the allegation is difficult to prove, the rail corporation apparently used several effective methods to make sure that union members lost their jobs. One traditional practice seems to have been to use different company stationery for union members' files. Those with union credentials, or suspected union affiliation, would have official letters printed on corporation stationery with a headless crane watermark.

121. Collis P. Huntington to Henry Huntington, July 26, 1894, Henry Huntington Papers.

122. Collis P. Huntington to William H. Mills, August 2, 1894, Collis P. Huntington Papers (microfilm), Syracuse University, Series II, Reel 34.

123. William H. Mills to Collis P. Huntington, July 27, 1894, Collis Huntington Papers, Series I, Reel 53.

124. Charles F. Crocker to Collis P. Huntington, July 23, 1894, Collis Huntington Papers, Series I, Reel 53.

125. William H. Mills to Collis P. Huntington, July 27, 1894, Collis Huntington Papers, Series I, Reel 53.

126. "In the aggregate, the rural press controls public thought; but you cannot get immediate direction of a large number of papers in an emergency, and revolutions always begin in cities." William H. Mills to Collis P. Huntington, Collis Huntington Papers, Series I, Reel 53.

127. Mills to Huntington, August 15, 1894, and August 27, 1894, Collis Huntington Papers, Series I, Reel 53.

128. See Williams, *The Democratic Party and California Politics*, pp. 217–23.

129. The government had recently placed the Santa Fe in receivership; that fact allowed ostensibly pro-railroad advocates to look as if they were part of the anti-railroad bandwagon: they could speak of government control of at least one major transcontinental line.

130. William H. Mills to Collis P. Huntington, August 27, 1894, Collis Huntington Papers, Series I, Reel 53.

131. See, for instance, Henry Huntington to Collis P. Huntington, July 25, 1894; Henry Huntington Papers. Southern Pacific officials W. W. Stow and Henry Huntington had recently gone over a speech with Estee; Huntington reported to his uncle that Estee would claim that the funding bill was a Democratic issue, would support nationalization of "one line of road between the Pacific and the Atlantic," and would argue that men had the right to strike but not the right to forcibly keep others from working.

132. The prevailing assumption that the Southern Pacific worked only within the Republican Party, though for the most part true, ignores the fact that the corporation was perfectly willing to work with whatever group or party was in power at a particular moment. This stance is aptly expressed in a letter from Collis Huntington to Henry Huntington regarding political affairs in Nevada, especially the success of that state's Populist Party. Should the state be carried by the Populists, Huntington wrote, "of course we want to be on friendly terms with them, hoping that by working with them we can do more to prevent them from doing harm, than we could by opposing them." Collis Huntington to Henry Huntington, July 27, 1894, Henry Huntington Papers.

133. See Ray, "The Great Strike of 1894," pp. 4–5.

134. Saxton, "San Francisco Labor," p. 426. Sutro was attacked by Bay Area Socialists for being a capitalist in workingman's guise; the Socialists ran a different candidate for mayor. See Walters, "Populism in California," p. 283.

135. Ray, "The Great Strike of 1894," pp. 4–5.

136. "Since farmers and laborers could easily agree that the railroad was chief villain, this served for demonstration of the *identical enemies* text from the Omaha platform. The Populists organized mass meetings, raised money, and denounced the governor for calling out militia at the demand of the Southern Pacific." Saxton, "San Francisco Labor," p. 425.

137. R. B. Carpenter to Collis P. Huntington, February 21, 1895, Collis Huntington Papers, Series I, Reel 53.

138. "The Company has gained rather than lost in the recent uprising," William H. Mills wrote to Collis Huntington on July 27, 1894 (Collis Huntington Papers, Series I, Reel 53).

139. George Mowry, in *The California Progressives* (Berkeley: University of California Press, 1951), p. 20, inexplicably writes that anti-railroad efforts in the 1890s "were extremely scanty." Williams, however, (in *The Democratic Party and California Politics*, chap. 9) notes that anti-railroad reform efforts of the 1890s exhibited more intensity than even those of the 1870s. See also Eugene Debs to "My dear Frank" (typescript), May 15, 1895, Eugene V. Debs Letters, Hoover Institution on War, Revolution and Peace, Stanford University.

CHAPTER FOUR

1. See, for example, Boyle Workman, *The City That Grew* (Los Angeles: Southland Publishing Company, 1936); J. M. Guinn, *Historical and Biographical Record of Los Angeles* (Chicago: Chapman Publishing Co., 1901); A. Bert Bynon, *San Pedro: Its History* (Los Angeles: Boyle Heights Press, 1899); Charles Edward Russell, *Stories of the Great Railroads* (Chicago: Charles H. Kerr and Company, 1914), chap. 11. Each of these studies depicts the harbor fight as a struggle between "the people" and "the Octopus"; each celebrates the triumph of the former.

2. See Curtis Grassman, "The Los Angeles Free Harbor Controversy and the Creation of a Progressive Coalition," *Southern California Quarterly* 55 (Winter 1973): 445–68; Donald R. Culton, "Los Angeles' 'Citizen Fixit': Charles Dwight Willard, City Booster and Progressive Reformer," *California History* 57 (Summer 1978): 156–71. Many studies make use of Charles Dwight Willard's *The Free Harbor Contest at Los Angeles* (Los Angeles: Kingsley-Barnes and Neuner, 1899) as an important secondary source. While there is much detail in Willard's book, it should be remembered that Willard himself was intricately involved in the anti–Southern Pacific side of the struggle, serving as secretary of the Los Angeles Chamber of Commerce. His treatment of the harbor fight ought therefore to be addressed critically. As Willard's biographer notes, the free harbor contest "demonstrated well that when Willard spoke of 'the people' he usually referred to those having property interests to protect." See Donald Ray Culton, "Charles Dwight Willard: Los Angeles City Booster and Professional Reformer, 1888–1914," Ph.D. diss., University of Southern California, 1971, p. 104. Richard Barsness's brief article "Railroads and Los Angeles: The Quest for a Deep-Water Port," *Southern California Quarterly* 47 (December 1965): 379–94, avoids the "people vs. railroad" dichotomy of other studies. In *The Democratic Party and California Politics, 1880–1896* (Stanford, Calif.: Stanford University Press, 1973), R. Hal Williams gives the harbor fight only a few pages. Save for a few oblique references to San Pedro property owners, Williams writes of the controversy primarily as an instance of the people's triumph over the railroad. One of a few historians to take a different perspective is Frederic Jaher, in *The Urban Establishment* (Urbana: University of Illinois Press, 1982). Jaher writes briefly of the harbor issue in the context of conflict between established elites and newer arrivals (see especially pp. 622–23, 630–32).

3. For an analysis of the boom, see Glen Dumke, *The Boom of the Eighties in Southern California* (San Marino, Calif.: Huntington Library, 1944), especially chap. 5.

4. See, for instance, Charles Dwight Willard, *History of the Los Angeles Chamber of Commerce* (Los Angeles: Kingsley-Barnes and Neuner, 1899); and Jaher, *The Urban Establishment*.

5. On railroad passes, see Charles Dwight Willard to Samuel Willard, November 2, 1891, Charles Dwight Willard Papers, Huntington Library.

6. Minutes of the Los Angeles Chamber of Commerce, February 22, 1893, in the California Historical Society's Los Angeles research center. I would like to thank Anne Salsich and Janet Evander of the California Historical Society for allowing me to look at these records while the research center was in the midst of moving.

7. The Santa Fe had recently built a wharf at Redondo and was taking away freight and passengers from the S.P. operation in San Pedro. If the Southern Pacific was allowed into Santa Monica, Collis Huntington (or so he told John P. Jones, a U.S. senator who owned land in Santa Monica) intended to "run fierce opposition to Redondo [and] Every other place that may set itself up against Santa Monica." John P. Jones to Georgina Jones, October 8, 1891, John P. Jones Papers, Henry Huntington Library. I would like to thank John Farquhar for allowing me to examine the Jones Papers. Unless otherwise noted, citations are from this collection.

8. Huntington visited Santa Monica in May of 1890, probably to look at the area's suitability for both a beachfront railroad and a deep-water harbor. See Diary of Juan Bandini (trans. Margaret Mel), May 18 and 19, 1890, in the Stearns-Gaffey Papers at the Huntington Library; hereafter cited as Bandini Diary.

9. Collis P. Huntington to Abbot Robinson, October 24, 1891, in the Letterbooks of Collis P. Huntington, Henry E. Huntington Papers, Henry Huntington Library.

10. Some have regarded this transaction as evidence of an earlier partnership between Jones and the railroad. Yet Jones hardly saw it that way. When his wife warned him that selling land to the railroad on the Santa Monica beachfront would be the second mistake he had made with the Southern Pacific, the first being the sale of the Los Angeles & Independence Railroad, Jones replied, "If you only knew how my heart ached when I was obliged by stress of circumstance to part with the RR which together with matters connected with it was the pet project of my life. You would not call it a *mistake*." Georgina Jones to John P. Jones, August 29, 1891, and John P. Jones to Georgina Jones, September 5, 1891, Jones Papers. Collis Huntington, however, as he had written to business partner David Colton in 1877, only wanted the little railroad to ensure the senatorial good will of Jones at a time when the Southern Pacific needed help in Congress. See Collis Huntington to David Colton, April 20 and August 21, 1877, published in the San Francisco *Chronicle*, December 23, 1883, p. 11.

11. Of Huntington's impatient negotiations, Jones wrote: "He is so grasping [and] is in possession of so many unearned millions that he perhaps naturally concludes that everything else in sight naturally belongs to him." John P. Jones to Georgina Jones, August 24, 1891, Jones Papers.

12. Georgina Jones to John P. Jones, August 27 and October 8, 1891, Jones Papers.

13. John P. Jones to Georgina Jones, September 5, 1891, Jones Papers. Similarly, Jones wrote to his wife that he would rather the Southern Pacific "continue their business at San Pedro than to transfer it to Santa Monica if the only result is to be a coal depot at our place. We would be better off without it. . . . It would be a species of vandalism." John P. Jones to Georgina Jones, October 13, 1891, Jones Papers.

14. John P. Jones to Georgina Jones, August 29, 1891, and Georgina Jones to John P. Jones, October 8 and August 29, 1891, Jones Papers.

15. Georgina Jones to John P. Jones, October 15 and September 30, 1891, Jones Papers.

16. John P. Jones to Georgina Jones, August 29, 1891, Jones Papers.

17. "With the Southern Pacific actively working with us I believe the opposition of the Engineers would be quelled." That power, Jones felt, was what kept the engineers from ever favoring Santa Monica when the Southern Pacific concentrated its activities at San Pedro. John P. Jones to Georgina Jones, September 5, 1891, Jones Papers.

18. Ibid.

19. Regarding the final purchase of remaining land, see Henry Huntington to Collis Huntington, August 7, 1894, Henry Huntington Papers: "At last we have bought the land of Baker and Jones on the top of the grade at Santa Monica." The remaining fifty-five acres were purchased for $125 an acre.

20. Georgina Jones to John P. Jones, January 26, 1892, Jones Papers.

21. Senator Cornelius Cole, a friend of both Huntington and Jones, thought that this was the case. See Georgina Jones to John P. Jones, May 9, 1892, Jones Papers.

22. *Before the Honorable Board of Government Engineers, Col. Wm. P. Craighill, Presiding. In the Matter of the Location of a Deep-Water Harbor in San Pedro or Santa Monica Bays* [September 1892]. From Chamber of Commerce, Miscellaneous Pamphlets, Chamber of Commerce Archives, California Historical Society, Los Angeles, 1:1. Hereafter cited as *Location of a Deep-Water Harbor*.

23. Redondo was weakly represented as well; apparently the Santa Fe Railroad had a token interest in it.

24. *Location of a Deep-Water Harbor*, pp. 8–9.

25. Ibid., pp. 28–29. Jones had written to his wife that he was very anxious for the Santa Fe to be allowed to come into Santa Monica.

26. *Location of a Deep-Water Harbor*, p. 32. Crawley went on to argue, with some dubious arithmetic, that though the time difference between the two ports, for a steamer coming from San Francisco, was in the neighborhood of two hours, Santa Monica actually enjoyed a six- to ten-hour advantage over the rival port because of the unloading time.

27. See Los Angeles *Times*, for instance, August 27 and September 6, 1892.

28. *Location of a Deep-Water Harbor*, p. 40.

29. Ibid.

30. See Franklyn Hoyt, "The Los Angeles Terminal Railroad," *Historical Society of Southern California Quarterly* 36 (September 1954): 188–89. There can be little doubt that the backers of the railroad saw the potential for great growth in the San Gabriel Valley; since their railroad ran through that area, the outcome of the harbor controversy was of no small concern to that future. By 1895, the Terminal line ran six trains a day from Los Angeles, Long Beach, and San Pedro; twenty-six from Los Angeles to Pasadena; eight from Los Angeles to Glendale and Verdugo Park; six between Los Angeles and Altadena. See *Maxwell's Los Angeles City Directory, 1895* (Los Angeles: Directory Co., 1895).

31. Richard C. Kerens to Thomas E. Gibbon, September 3 and July 6, 1893, Thomas E. Gibbon Papers, Huntington Library. Kerens expected a million people in the San Gabriel Valley by century's end. The inability of Los Angeles to develop, or fully develop, local coal resources helped prompt the need for the Salt Lake connector. See Edward Leo Lyman, "From the City of Angels to the City of Saints: The Struggle to Build a Railroad from Los Angeles to Salt Lake City," *California History* 70 (Spring 1991): 76–93.

32. Kerens to Gibbon, July 6, 1893, Gibbon Papers.

33. Testimony of Judge R. B. Carpenter, *Location of a Deep-Water Harbor* [T. E. Gibbon personal copy of stenographic report], pp. 70–71.

34. Forman was likely not the most objective representative of Los Angeles opinion. Three years later, he would be elected to the board of directors of the Terminal Railway—an indication, one suspects, of earlier ties to that corporation. See *Poor's Manual of Railroads, 1896* (New York: American Banknote Company, 1896). Furthermore, in July of 1893, Richard Kerens had authorized T. E. Gibbon that he was "at liberty to let Mr. Forman and our friends know what is going on without using any names." Kerens to Gibbon, July 6, 1893, Gibbon Papers.

35. Gibbon had been to Washington the previous year (and Forman had been slated to accompany him). Over the course of the next several years, Gibbon would make the trip to Washington many times.

36. Richard Kerens and George Leighton, both of St. Louis and both top officials with the Terminal Railway, were also the only out-of-state members of the Los Angeles Chamber of Commerce.

37. Richard Kerens to Thomas E. Gibbon, September 20, July 29, and June 10, 1893, Gibbon Papers. Kerens wrote that junior senator White had been given a seat on the Commerce Committee "through the efforts of our friends in the Senate."

38. Kerens to Gibbon, January 12, 1894, Gibbon Papers.

39. Minutes of the Los Angeles Chamber of Commerce, February 10, 1893.

40. J. A. Muir to William H. Mills, January 27, 1896; attached to Henry E. Huntington to Collis P. Huntington, April 7, 1896, Henry Huntington Papers.

41. Mills to Huntington, September 8 and October 3, 1894, Collis P. Huntington Papers, Syracuse University (microfilm), Series I, Reel 53. My thanks to James Thorpe for pointing out these letters to me. In an editorial published in its July 1896 number, pp. 124–26, the *Overland Monthly* also hinted at Otis's ability to profit from a pro–San Pedro decision.

42. For a brief sketch of Otis and his relationship with the Southern Pacific, see Robert Gottlieb and Irene Wolt, *Thinking Big: The Story of the Los Angeles Times* (New York: Putnam's, 1972), especially pp. 53–64. Otis's influence over White is briefly alluded to in Jaher, *The Urban Establishment*, pp. 630–31. By early 1895, when he had become a valuable, if a bit quiet, supporter of San Pedro, White wondered why Otis persisted in "stupid attacks on me." See White to John Frances [should be Francis], January 24, 1895, Stephen M. White Papers, Department of Special Collections and Archives, Stanford University.

43. In July of 1891, Juan Bandini, Gaffey's father-in-law, noted in his diary that Gaffey wanted to buy land in the Santa Monica Canon because of planned Southern Pacific activity in the region. See Bandini Diary.

44. Bandini noted in October of 1891 that Gaffey was on his way to Mexico "on business for Gen[eral] McCook and another señor of the S. Fe." Bandini Diary, October 27, 1891.

45. See the notation of Margaret (Gaffey) Mel in Bandini Diary, May 13, 1896. See also Culton, "Charles Dwight Willard," p. 96.

46. See Thomas E. Gibbon, "The Telegram That Never Came," *California Outlook* 10 (March 4, 1911): 9–10. Culton ("Charles Dwight Willard," p. 95) writes that Willard, the chamber secretary, burned the telegram.

47. See Hoyt, "The Los Angeles Terminal Railroad." See also Barsness, "Railroads and Los Angeles"; and *Annual Report of the Los Angeles Terminal Railway Company to the Board of Railroad Commissioners* (Sacramento: State Printing Office, 1896).

48. T. B. Burnett letter [unaddressed; apparently sent to all or selected members of the Los Angeles Chamber of Commerce], April 4, 1894; in Benjamin D. Wilson Papers, George S. Patton addenda, Huntington Library.

49. Terminal Railway vice president Burnett thought that Houghton ought to be sent to Washington to represent the railroad's interests with or without the blessing of the chamber of commerce, an opinion that Richard Kerens was less certain of. Richard Kerens to Thomas E. Gibbon, March 13, 1894, with enclosed telegram, T. B. Burnett to Richard Kerens, March 12, 1894, Gibbon Papers. For an indication of the friendship be-

tween Houghton and Terminal officials, see Stephen B. Elkins to Sherman O. Houghton, April 2, 1897, and Richard Kerens to Benjamin Harrison, September 18, 1881, Sherman O. Houghton Papers, Huntington Library.

50. The Los Angeles Chamber of Commerce did not want to pay the way of its representatives to Washington. Members were asked to contribute to a fund if they wished. Nevertheless, Gibbon may have arranged for Patton's trip and expenses. In mid-May of 1894, he wrote to Patton informing him that his train travel to Washington had been arranged and that there was $250 at his disposal. See Gibbon to Patton, May 16, 1894, George S. Patton Papers, Huntington Library.

51. John P. Jones to Georgina Jones, June 22, 1894, Jones Papers; Collis P. Huntington to I. E. Gates, April 9, 1894, Collis Huntington Papers, Series I, Reel 53.

52. John P. Jones to Georgina Jones, June 26, 1894, Jones Papers.

53. See Stephen M. White to J. W. Reinhart, July 21, 1894, White Papers.

54. Reinhart to Kerens, July 8, 1894, Patton Papers. Henry Huntington noted the Santa Fe's "moral support" of the Terminal in a letter to Collis P. Huntington, December 30, 1895, Henry Huntington Papers. T. E. Gibbon had apparently also fostered ties with the Atchison, Topeka & Santa Fe. A letter to Gibbon from Richard Kerens on June 10, 1893 (Gibbon Papers), reveals that Gibbon was then attempting to become the Santa Fe's Los Angeles attorney. Stephen M. White once encouraged Gibbon in this regard. See Curtis Grassman, "Prologue to Progressivism: Senator Stephen M. White and the California Reform Impulse, 1875–1905," Ph.D. diss., University of California, Los Angeles, 1970, p. 289.

55. In the spring of 1894, Charles Dwight Willard of the chamber of commerce had written to his father that he and others were attempting to buy the *Herald* in order to consolidate "corporate and railway interests." See Charles Dwight Willard to Samuel Willard, May 25, 1894, Willard Papers. White was involved in the plans, as was—strangely enough—Otis. See Stephen M. White to Harrison Gray Otis, May 22, 1894, White Papers; see also White to Joseph Lynch, May 27, 1894, and White to Harrison Gray Otis, June 18, 1894. In May of 1895, White and Gibbon cosigned a loan guarantee of $5,000, loaned to the Herald Publishing Company by the First National Bank in Los Angeles. See guarantee (May 6, 1895) in the White Papers. George S. Patton's wife noted in a letter to her husband that the press had determined Patton's role in the *Herald* transfer. See Ruth Patton to George S. Patton, October 14, 1894, Patton Papers. The Los Angeles *Times* noted on October 5 and October 6 that White was involved in the venture. Named as stockholders of the new company were W. H. Workman (an original Terminal Railway stockholder, who became a member of the railroad's board of directors in early 1896)

and William Kerckhoff, a principal in the San Pedro lumber company Kerckhoff-Cuzner; also named as a director was John F. Francis, later president of the Free Harbor League. I would like to thank Midge Sherwood for bringing the *Times* articles to my attention.

56. Richard Kerens to Thomas E. Gibbon, April 23, 1894, Gibbon Papers. White had written Otis in July that "Gibbon is on his way home and is going to examine the situation pretty carefully. We will make a great effort to capture the paper." See Stephen M. White to Harrison Gray Otis, July 25, 1894, White Papers. William H. Mills noted the connections between the *Herald* and the Terminal as well as connections between the Terminal and the Atchison, Topeka & Santa Fe Railroad. In a letter to Collis Huntington, Mills referred to the Terminal as a "collateral branch of the A.T. & S.F." Mills to Huntington, September 8, 1894, Collis Huntington Papers, Series I, Reel 53.

57. In his diary entry of January 26, 1895, Juan Bandini noted that he "saw in the paper that the people of Santa Monica have a great antipathy to the Los Angeles Herald and Gaffey."

58. Richard Kerens to Thomas E. Gibbon, November 30, 1894, Gibbon Papers. At the congress of the following year, the chamber delegates were Gibbon, S. O. Houghton, and Charles Forman (elected to the board of directors of the Terminal in 1896).

59. One of White's speeches, in El Monte, California, was geared entirely to the harbor issue. The title page of the printed remarks asks, "Do You Want a Free Harbor for the People, at San Pedro?" If so, voters were encouraged to vote for Patton. For a copy of the undated speech, see the Scrapbooks of George S. Patton in the Huntington Library (cataloged).

60. The letter was signed by several Los Angeles businessmen. Willard did not sign the circular, but noted in sending a copy to his father that "I wrote it" and "I do most of the writing in this fight." See Charles D. Willard to Samuel Willard, February 17, 1895, Willard Papers.

61. Richard Kerens to Thomas E. Gibbon, February 11, 1895, Gibbon Papers. Kerens apparently believed that Stephen B. Elkins, now U.S. senator from West Virginia, might counterbalance the effect of any pro–Santa Monica mischief on White's part. In a handwritten addendum to this letter, Kerens added: "Mr. Elkins cannot be Hoodwinked Oh No."

62. As an indication of the increasing tilt in favor of San Pedro within the chamber, Roy and Robert F. Jones, son and nephew of Senator John P. Jones and both strong Santa Monica supporters, resigned from the organization in May of 1895.

63. See, for instance, Los Angeles *Times*, February 18, 1896.

64. A year later, Patterson would be elected to the board of directors of the Terminal Railway. See *Poor's Manual of Railroads, 1897* (New York: American Banknote Company, 1897).

65. See Henry E. Huntington to Collis P. Huntington, December 30 and 31, 1895, and Collis P. Huntington to Henry E. Huntington, January 19, 1896, Henry Huntington Papers.

66. Richard Kerens to Thomas Gibbon, February 11, 1895, and December 18, 1893, Gibbon Papers.

67. Collis P. Huntington to Matthew S. Quay, June 23, 1894, Jones Papers.

68. It would "be best for the Terminal Company's interest" for the supporters of San Pedro to back an inner harbor appropriation; following that, pressure could be exerted to improve the outer harbor. See Richard Kerens to Thomas E. Gibbon, November 30, 1894, Gibbon Papers.

69. See James McLachlan to Harrison Gray Otis, December 31, 1895, H. H. Markham Papers, Huntington Library. McLachlan wrote to one constituent that "the friends of San Pedro at the outset tied my hands." See McLachlan to Horatio N. Rust, May 19, 1896, Horatio Nelson Rust Papers, Huntington Library.

70. Los Angeles *Times*, March 30, 1896.

71. The double-appropriation request apparently came from Collis Huntington at a closed-door meeting with the committee; see Grassman, "Los Angeles Free Harbor Controversy."

72. Los Angeles *Times*, April 4 and 5, 1896.

73. A small $50,000 appropriation for the inner harbor was maintained in the bill, but the more than $300,000 originally proposed was eliminated.

74. McLachlan to Harrison Gray Otis, April 8, 1896, Markham Papers.

75. Los Angeles *Times*, April 6, 1896.

76. Stephen M. White to Harrison Gray Otis, December 6, 1895, Los Angeles *Times* History Center archives; Otis to White, April 5, 1896, Stephen M. White Scrapbooks, Seaver Center, Los Angeles County Museum of Natural History. Hereafter cited as White Scrapbooks.

77. Georgina Jones to John P. Jones, April 5, 1896, Jones Papers.

78. Undated clipping from Santa Monica *Daily Outlook*, Cornelius Cole Papers, Department of Special Collections, University of California, Los Angeles. It seems likely that Cole himself wrote this editorial.

79. Free Harbor League to James McLachlan, April 30, 1896, White Scrapbooks.

80. For a discussion of Otis's early anti-unionism, see Grace H. Stimson, *Rise of the Labor Movement in Los Angeles* (Berkeley: University of California Press, 1955), pp. 35–37.

81. See Los Angeles *Times*, May 3 and April 7, 1896.

82. Patterson, by the following year, was listed as a member of the board of directors of the Terminal Railway.

83. S. Hubbell et al. to Stephen M. White, April 9, 1896, White Scrapbooks.

84. Los Angeles *Evening Express*, April 19, 1896; H. Z. Osborne to Stephen M. White, April 9, 1896, White Scrapbooks.

85. Henry E. Huntington to Collis P. Huntington, April 9, 1896, Henry Huntington Papers.

86. G. Montgomery to Stephen M. White, April 24, 1896, White Scrapbooks. Anonymous constituent to White; see *Speech of Hon. Stephen M. White of California in the Senate of the United States, May 8, 9, and 12, 1896* (Washington, D.C.: n.p., 1896), p. 18.

87. Free Harbor League to George Perkins and Stephen M. White, April 8, 1896; George S. Patton to White, April 24, 1896. Both from White Scrapbooks.

88. Stephen M. White to John T. Gaffey, April 14, 1896, Stearns-Gaffey Papers. Earlier, in a letter to another constituent, White had whined about his difficult position. Yes, he had written, he would cover himself in personal glory if he could quickly resolve the harbor question; "So would I attract a great deal of public attention to my individual prowess if I could take the San Bernardino Mountain on my back and transport it to the seashore." White to William Burke, January 23, 1895, White Papers.

89. John D. Bicknell to Stephen M. White, April 15, 1896, White Scrapbooks; White to Bicknell, April 16, 1896, John D. Bicknell Papers, Huntington Library.

90. Robert F. Jones to Walter J. Trask, April 25, 1896, Bicknell Papers.

91. White wrote Gaffey that Jones had probably influenced Gorman's vote; see White to Gaffey, May 4, 1896, Stearns-Gaffey Papers. Elkins's reasons for voting against San Pedro remain a mystery; yet, as early as February of 1895, Elkins had asked White if perhaps Kerens of the Terminal and Huntington of the Southern Pacific could come to some sort of compromise on the harbor issue. See Stephen M. White to Thomas E. Gibbon, February 11, 1895, White Papers.

92. Collis P. Huntington to C. F. Crocker, April 28, 1896, Henry Huntington Papers.

93. Georgina Jones to John P. Jones, May 13, 1896, Jones Papers.

94. Cornelius Cole wrote that White was "much embarrassed" by his stance in favor of San Pedro, but since he had proclaimed himself so on the stump in California, he felt bound to that view. See Cornelius Cole to Olive Cole, April 22, 1896, Cole Papers.

95. *Speech of Hon. Stephen M. White*, p. 20.

96. Ibid., p. 53.

97. See Cornelius Cole to Olive Cole, April 26 and May 7, 1896, Cole Papers.

98. Henry E. Huntington to Collis P. Huntington, May 13, 1896, Henry Huntington Papers.

99. See E. F. Ripley to Henry E. Huntington, May 13, 1896; see also

Collis P. Huntington to Henry E. Huntington, June 3, 5, and 17, 1896, Henry Huntington Papers.

100. Collis P. Huntington to W. H. Mills, June 24, 1896, Henry Huntington Papers. Patton's stand-pat stance on San Pedro, among other political beliefs, prompted J. A. Muir of the Southern Pacific to refer to him as "one of the worst demagogues that has ever been developed in southern California." See J. A. Muir to Collis P. Huntington, May 5, 1896, attached to J. A. Muir to Henry E. Huntington, May 5, 1896, Henry Huntington Papers.

101. Los Angeles *Times*, December 16, 1896.

102. See *Deep-Water Harbor in Southern California; Port Los Angeles vs. San Pedro; Full Report of Oral Testimony at Public Hearings in Los Angeles; December 1896* (Los Angeles: Evening Express Co., 1896).

103. William Hood to Collis P. Huntington, January 25, 1897, Henry Huntington Papers.

104. *Greater Los Angeles*, December 26, 1896. In a subsequent letter to Senator Jones, Lynch referred to "an artificially created sentiment" in favor of San Pedro. Joseph D. Lynch to John P. Jones, May 28, 1897, Jones Papers.

105. *Greater Los Angeles*, March 13, 1897; Thomas Gibbon to Stephen M. White, March 12, 1897, White Papers.

106. De Witt C. Jackson to John T. Gaffey, October 3, 1897, Stearns-Gaffey Papers. At a mass celebration in 1897 marking the San Pedro victory, one prominent member of the Free Harbor League joked that San Pedro ought to be renamed "Gaffey." From an undated news clipping in the Cole Papers.

107. Some of the best scholarship that reinterprets the place of the railroad in the lives of Californians includes Williams, *The Democratic Party and California Politics*, especially "The Railroad in California Politics"; W. H. Hutchinson, "Southern Pacific: Myth and Reality," *California Historical Society Quarterly* 48 (December 1969): 325–34; Richard Orsi, "*The Octopus* Reconsidered: The Southern Pacific and Agricultural Modernization in California, 1865–1915," *California Historical Quarterly* 54 (Fall 1975): 197–220.

108. See, in particular, Grassman, "The Los Angeles Free Harbor Controversy"; and Culton, "Los Angeles' 'Citizen Fixit.'"

109. Robert Fogelson, *The Fragmented Metropolis: Los Angeles, 1850–1930* (Cambridge, Mass.: Harvard University Press, 1967), p. 113. George S. Patton perhaps unwittingly described this agenda, and its sequence, by writing that he favored San Pedro "for every reason personal and political as well as for the general good." George S. Patton to Stephen M. White, June 4, 1897, White Papers.

110. Stephen M. White to Harrison Gray Otis, January 28, 1895, White Papers; White to Otis, December 23, 1896, Los Angeles *Times*

History Center Archives. Much of the harbor fight correspondence from many of the principals involved on the San Pedro side of the struggle is missing from their papers. For instance, the White Papers at Stanford do not contain White's 1894–96 replies to San Pedro supporters Daniel Freeman and Charles Forman and the bulk of his 1895–96 correspondence to Thomas Gibbon, John Gaffey, and Harrison Gray Otis.

111. In his history of the harbor fight, Charles Dwight Willard (*Free Harbor Contest*, p. 12) took pains to correct the notion of easterners that "the residents of this State entertain a violent, unreasoning prejudice against the Southern Pacific railroad, and that populistic ideas are generally much in vogue among us." That was not true, Willard claimed, but the harbor fight tale indicates that if there was such a groundswell (or perception of one), Willard and his allies could be counted on to massage it politically.

112. See, for instance, Grassman, "The Los Angeles Free Harbor Controversy" and "Prologue to Progressivism," p. 288.

CHAPTER FIVE

1. The use of the turn of the century as a boundary between "the old-style press" and the "new" is admittedly quite arbitrary. For a stimulating discussion of specific newspapers and their not-too-subtle involvement in twentieth-century politics, see David Halberstam, *The Powers That Be* (New York: Knopf, 1979).

2. Thomas C. Leonard, *The Power of the Press* (New York: Oxford University Press, 1986), p. 133.

3. William H. Mills to Collis P. Huntington, March 29, 1896, Collis P. Huntington Papers (microfilm), Syracuse University, Series I, Reel 53.

4. Fremont Older, *My Own Story* (San Francisco: Call Publishing Company, 1919), p. 21.

5. Thomas M. Storke, *California Editor* (Los Angeles: Westernlore Press, 1958), p. 157. Storke described the political power of the Southern Pacific as "an absolute dictatorship for nearly forty years, from the lowest to the highest political levels."

6. See Anne F. Hyde, *An American Vision: Far Western Landscape and National Culture, 1820–1920* (New York: New York University Press, 1990), especially chap. 2.

7. On pro-railroad propaganda, see Hyde, *An American Vision*, and Edna M. Parker, "The Southern Pacific and Settlement in Southern California," *Pacific Historical Review* 6 (June 1937): 103–19; *Sacramento Union*, February 21, 1868, from a clipping in the Leland Stanford Papers, Department of Special Collections and Archives, Stanford University.

8. Mark Hopkins to Collis P. Huntington, February 15, 1873, *Letters from Mark Hopkins, Leland Stanford, Charles Crocker, Charles F. Crocker,*

and David D. Colton, to Collis P. Huntington. From August 27th, 1869, to December 30th, 1879 (New York: John C. Rankin, 1891); hereafter cited as *Letters from Mark Hopkins et al.* See also the typescript statement of Charles Crocker (n.d.) in Leland Stanford Papers.

9. Collis P. Huntington to Charles Crocker, March 18, February 25, and May 13, 1868, in *Letters from Collis P. Huntington to Mark Hopkins, Leland Stanford, Charles Crocker, E. B. Crocker, Charles F. Crocker, and D. D. Colton. From August 20, 1867, to August 5, 1869* (New York: privately printed, 1892). Hereafter cited as *Letters from Collis Huntington.*

10. "I shall go to work to-day to get the New York papers to say good-natured things about this Government aiding a Southern Pacific Road." Collis P. Huntington to Charles Crocker, April 25, 1868, *Letters from Collis Huntington.*

11. "I won't say we own the Record, but we have such an interest in its welfare, success and influence that we can't afford to give any of its competitors any monopoly advantage." Mark Hopkins to Collis P. Huntington, February 17, 1873, *Letters from Mark Hopkins et al.*

12. Collis P. Huntington to Charles Crocker, April 17, 1868, *Letters from Collis Huntington.*

13. See, for instance, Fremont Older, *Growing Up* (San Francisco: Call-Bulletin, 1931), p. 69.

14. Oakland *Daily News*, November 15, 1869.

15. The crash dominated local news stories for weeks, and thousands of people came from surrounding towns to gape at the wreckage. Blame for the disaster eventually fell to an illiterate switchman and foggy weather. The rival paper was the Vallejo *Chronicle*; see Oakland *Daily News*, November 20, 1869.

16. Collis P. Huntington to Mark Hopkins, July 14, 1869, *Letters from Collis Huntington.*

17. Mark Hopkins to Collis P. Huntington, January 29, 1873, *Letters from Mark Hopkins et al.*

18. George Fitch to James H. Simonton, December 8, 1875, George Fitch Papers, Bancroft Library.

19. Storke, *California Editor*, pp. 169–70. See also Older, *My Own Story*, pp. 21–22. When the last spike ceremony took place in May of 1869, Leland Stanford forwarded free passes to journalist Fitch. Fitch declined to accept the passes, pointing out to Stanford that to do so would violate the policy of his newspaper. George Fitch to Leland Stanford, June 16, 1869, Fitch Papers. See also Frank C. Jordan, "Fifty Years in Politics in California" (manuscript), Frank C. Jordan Papers, Bancroft Library, p. 15. A recent book looks briefly at the issue of railroad passes in the Gilded Age. See Mark W. Summers, *The Plundering Generation* (New York: Oxford University Press, 1987), especially pp. 101–3.

20. Charles Crocker to Charles Maclay, January 24, 1877, Charles Maclay Papers, Huntington Library.

21. *Wasp*, April 9, 1881.

22. E. C. MacFarlane to Ambrose Bierce, August [26?] 1884, Ambrose Bierce Papers, Department of Special Collections and Archives, Stanford University.

23. E. C. MacFarlane to Ambrose Bierce, September 20, 1884, Bierce Papers, Stanford.

24. See, for instance, the Los Angeles *Times* discussion of Stanford's political clumsiness, January 16 and 17, 1891. For a brief discussion of the rivalry and resulting feud between Stanford and Huntington, see Stuart Daggett, *Chapters on the History of the Southern Pacific* (New York: Ronald Press, 1922), pp. 217–21.

25. Collis P. Huntington to Henry E. Huntington, April 30, 1896, and Collis P. Huntington to John A. Muir, May 12, 1896, Henry E. Huntington Papers, Huntington Library. Huntington's convoluted statements on S.P. political meddling are legion in his correspondence. "We sometimes have to use money to bring influence to bear to prevent great wrongs from being done to corporate interests, but in all my business with Legislative bodies I have never allowed my money to be used wrongfully," he wrote in 1891. Collis P. Huntington to Ed[ward] Curtis, August 10, 1891, Collis P. Huntington Letterbooks, Henry Huntington Papers.

26. Collis P. Huntington to William H. Mills, August 19, 1891, Collis Huntington Letterbooks, Henry Huntington Papers.

27. Henry E. Huntington to Collis P. Huntington, November 14, 1894, Henry Huntington Papers. By mid-decade, Collis Huntington opposed such a policy. In a letter to Southern Pacific propagandist William H. Mills, Huntington wrote that "one great trouble in California has been that our people have sometimes advised our candidates to go up on the stump and abuse us, thinking they could get a few more votes by so doing." Collis P. Huntington to William H. Mills, April 16, 1896, Henry Huntington Papers.

28. Henry Huntington to Thomas H. Hubbard, April 10, 1896, Henry Huntington Papers.

29. Collis P. Huntington to William H. Mills, July 3, 1890, Collis Huntington Letterbooks, Henry Huntington Papers. Mrs. Stanford continued to support Pixley after her husband's death. In January of 1894, Pixley wrote to Jane Stanford, thanking her for sending him an annual railroad pass. See Frank Pixley to Jane Stanford, Jane Stanford Papers, Department of Special Collections and Archives, Stanford University.

30. Collis P. Huntington to A. N. Towne, September 2, 1891, Collis Huntington Letterbooks, Henry Huntington Papers.

31. Bassett had once been secretary to Leland Stanford; his articles,

written as letters to Huntington, appeared mostly in the San Francisco *Daily Report* and doubtless furthered the estrangement of Stanford and Huntington. Of his attacks, Daggett (*Chapters on the History of the Southern Pacific*, p. 214) writes: "The sustained vivacity and pungency of this polemic, and the systematic virulence with which Bassett reviewed and criticized the Huntington policies, make the series a noteworthy journalistic achievement."

32. Southern Pacific Law Department [William F. Herrin] to San Francisco *Examiner* [T. T. Williams], September 27, 1894, Henry Huntington Papers.

33. Cartoonists often drew Huntington with a hat that looked like a skullcap. The style was apparently fashionable for the WASP elite, but *Examiner* and Los Angeles *Times* cartoonists made the hat look distinctly like a yarmulke. By century's end, the notoriety of such cartoons prompted an "Anti-Cartoon" bill to be proposed in the legislature, forbidding the publication of any cartoon without the subject's permission! See San Francisco *Call*, February 2, 1899.

34. From a letter McEwen wrote to the editor of the San Bernardino *Daily Courier*, July 4, 1890; clipping found in Fitch Papers. McEwen's editorial writings can be found in the pages of the San Francisco *Examiner* in the mid-1890s as well as in the short-lived *Arthur McEwen's Letter*.

35. "There is only one thing about all this matter, regarding which you can be certain, and that is that I am under no obligations of any kind to any corporation, or to anybody in the world; save to friends who are a part of the unfavored classes," White wrote to T. Carl Spelling on November 22, 1892. A copy of this letter was enclosed in Stephen M. White to Loring Pickering, November 22, 1892, Fitch Papers.

36. San Francisco *Examiner*, April 7, 1895, from a clipping in the Henry Huntington Papers; San Francisco *Examiner*, January 12, 1897, Henry Huntington Scrapbooks, Henry Huntington Papers. Hereafter cited as Huntington Scrapbooks. R. Hal Williams reviews the funding bill battle in *The Democratic Party and California Politics, 1880–1896* (Stanford, Calif.: Stanford University Press, 1973), pp. 216–23.

37. In April of 1896, Bierce's editor wrote asking whether Senator Stephen B. Elkins, known to be involved with the Terminal Railway, might be enlisted on the side of those opposed to the funding bill. See Ed[ward] H. Hamilton to Ambrose Bierce, April 5, 1896, Bierce Papers, Stanford.

38. George E. Miles to Henry E. Huntington, May 14, 1896, Henry Huntington Papers.

39. Richard C. Kerens to Thomas E. Gibbon, July 1, 1893, January 12 and April 23, 1894, Thomas E. Gibbon Papers, Huntington Library.

40. San Francisco *Examiner*, January 20, 1897, from clipping in Huntington Scrapbooks. See also Cora B. Older, *William Randolph Hearst, American* (New York: D. Appleton-Century, 1936), pp. 98–99.

41. San Francisco *Examiner*, January 6, 1897, Huntington Scrapbooks.

42. In February of 1897, seven hundred motormen and gripmen in San Francisco met and passed a resolution against the *Examiner*; one worker argued that the paper "is not a friend of the railroad men of San Francisco; that it is not the friend of labor for all its pratings." San Francisco *Call*, February 20, 1897, Huntington Scrapbooks.

43. San Francisco *Call*, January 17, 1897, Huntington Scrapbooks.

44. San Francisco *Examiner*, February 2, 1896, Huntington Scrapbooks. Another headline declared that "Huntington's Peculiar Method of Exercising Economy Endangers the Lives of Hundreds of People." San Francisco *Examiner*, April 2, 1897, Huntington Scrapbooks.

45. William H. Mills to Collis P. Huntington, September 22, 1894, Collis Huntington Papers, Series I, Reel 53; Mills to Huntington, May 13, 1895, Series I, Reel 53; Mills to Huntington, November 5, 1896, Series I, Reel 54.

46. Mills to Huntington, October 23, 1897, Collis Huntington Papers, Series I, Reel 54.

47. For a discussion of California Populism's disintegration, see chap. 8 of Donald E. Walters, "Populism in California, 1889–1900," Ph.D. diss., University of California, Berkeley, 1952.

48. William H. Mills to Collis P. Huntington, November 9, 1898, Collis Huntington Papers, Series I, Reel 54.

49. Collis P. Huntington to James Speyer, December 6, 1899, Collis Huntington Papers, Series I, Reel 54.

50. According to Storke (*California Editor*, p. 181), Johnson received the endorsement of 142 papers in the state.

51. See Irving McKee, "Notable Memorials to Mussel Slough," *Pacific Historical Review* 17 (February 1948): 19–27.

52. William C. Morrow, *Blood-Money* (San Francisco: F. J. Walker, 1882); C. C. Post, *Driven from Sea to Sea; or, Just a Campin'* (Chicago: J. E. Downey, 1884); C. Loyal [pseud.], *The Squatter and the Don* (San Francisco: n.p., 1885).

53. *The Monarch Philanthropist* (San Francisco: Cubery and Co., 1892). The manuscript for the book was said to have been found near the San Francisco docks. The book was dedicated to "the Farmers' Alliance, Labor Organizations, and All Who Are True Defenders of Free Institutions." "Lanford's" dastardly traits are references, respectively, to the Central Pacific's federal grants and local construction subsidies, refunding of the corporate debt, and Stanford's extensive northern California vineyards.

54. Frank Norris to Harry Wright, April 5, 1899, copy in Franklin Walker Papers, Bancroft Library. See also Franklin Walker, *Frank Norris: A Biography* (New York: Russel and Russel, 1963), pp. 243–44; originally published 1932.

55. Frank Norris to Harry Wright, April 5, 1899, Walker Papers.

56. Distinguished California historian Richard J. Orsi, in "Railroads in the History of California and the Far West: An Introduction" (*California History* 70 [Spring 1991]: 2–11), notes the troubling tendency to use fiction as history: "Even works of anti-railroad fiction, such as Norris's superficial and distorted tale of the abuses of the Southern Pacific, have been cited as historical fact" (p. 9).

57. See William B. Dillingham's fine overview of Norris criticism, "Frank Norris," in *Fifteen American Authors before 1900*, ed. Earl N. Harbert and Robert A. Rees (Madison: University of Wisconsin Press, 1984), pp. 402–34. See also the useful compendium by Jesse S. Crisler and Joseph R. McElrath, Jr., *Frank Norris: A Reference Guide* (Boston: G. K. Hall, 1974).

58. Upton Sinclair himself acknowledged that Norris had made him aware of the power of trusts in American life. See "The California Octopus," in *Mammonart: An Essay in Economic Interpretation* (Pasadena, Calif.: privately printed, 1925), pp. 349–52.

59. Edward Staniford, *The Pattern of California History* (San Francisco: Canfield Press, 1975), p. 353.

60. Andrew Rolle, *California: A History*, 2nd ed. (New York: Crowell, 1969), p. 554; see also pp. 432–33. A recent textbook, which argues convincingly that Norris misunderstood the events at Mussel Slough, claims that the novel nonetheless "intensified public outrage against the Southern Pacific and helped pave the way for the progressives to capture the state government in 1910 and institute stricter controls on corporations." Richard B. Rice, William A. Bullough, and Richard J. Orsi, *The Elusive Eden: A New History of California* (New York: Knopf, 1988), p. 236.

61. Reformers (and the same is true for many historians) "described what they wanted to see in *The Octopus*: a Thomas Nast cartoon in prose." Joseph R. McElrath, Jr., "Frank Norris's *The Octopus*: The Christian Ethic as Pragmatic Response," in Don Graham, ed., *Critical Essays on Frank Norris* (Boston: G. K. Hall, 1980), p. 142.

62. Norris's biographer (Walker, *Frank Norris*, p. 257) writes that the novel "was not written to reveal the injustice of the railroads or to attack the control of the trusts."

63. Frank Norris to George Henry Sargent, June 9, 1901, transcription in Walker Papers. For a discussion of Norris's attitudes toward naturalism, realism, and reform, see Walker, *Frank Norris*, especially chap. 4.

64. Frank Norris, *The Octopus: A Story of California*, in *Frank Norris: Novels and Essays*, ed. Donald Pizer (New York: Library of America, 1986), p. 586. All textual citations are from this edition of Norris's collected works.

65. In his essay "The True Reward of the Novelist" (*Novels and Essays*, p. 1151), Norris wrote: "To make money is not the province of the

novelist. If he be the right sort he has other responsibilities, heavy ones. . . . When the last page is written . . . he will be able to say . . . 'By God, I told them the truth. They liked it or they didn't like it. What had that to do with me? I told them the truth; I knew it for the truth then, and I know it for the truth now.'"

66. Scholars have long been impressed with Norris's research abilities and have incorrectly equated those efforts with both exhaustiveness and truthfulness. For instance, Robert Donald Lundy ("The Making of *Mc-Teague* and *The Octopus*," Ph.D. diss., University of California, Berkeley, 1956, pp. 260–61) writes that "Norris plunged into the task of collecting information not only about the Mussel Slough incident, but also about every facet of the almost half-a-century struggle between the Southern Pacific and Californians. Though at first one may find something ludicrous, almost pathetic, about his voracious, indiscriminate collecting of facts, one is quickly moved to respect the skill with which Norris moved among the data. . . . His picture [of the conflict] is thorough and, if not always accurate, true."

67. Frank Norris to Ernest Peixotto, May 7, 1899, quoted in Walker, *Frank Norris*, p. 245.

68. Unable to satisfy the mathematics requirement, Norris never got his degree. He subsequently studied for a year at Harvard as well.

69. *McTeague* chronicles the brutal life of a San Francisco dentist who murders his wife. Norris based the tale on an actual murder in 1890s San Francisco. See Lundy, "The Making of *McTeague* and *The Octopus*"; see also Donald Pizer, *The Novels of Frank Norris* (Bloomington: Indiana University Press, 1966), pp. 52–63.

70. Frank Norris to John P. Irish [spring 1899?], Frank Norris Papers, Bancroft Library.

71. John P. Irish, "California and the Railroad," *Overland Monthly* 25 (June 1895): 675–81.

72. Ibid., pp. 680–81. Irish's point of view, deterministic in its explanation of corporate political activity, sounds very much like the thoughts of Shelgrim, the novel's Collis Huntington character.

73. Norris to Isaac Marcosson, September 13, 1900, Walker Papers. I tried and failed to find reference to these letters or meetings in the relevant literature.

74. These rituals included the rabbit drive and great feasts, for instance. See chap. 5 of David Wyatt's *The Fall into Eden: Landscape and Imagination in California* (Cambridge: Cambridge University Press, 1986).

75. Critics have argued that Norris's meeting with Huntington softened his approach to the railroad corporation and may have prompted the philosophical shift at the novel's end. See Oscar Cargill, "Afterword," *The Octopus* (New York: New American Library, 1964), pp. 459–69. Cargill writes that "Norris' visit to the 'ogre' of the Southern Pacific changed

utterly the emphasis of his novel." I can find no record of the meeting in Huntington's papers.

76. Collis P. Huntington to James Speyer, December 6, 1899, Collis Huntington Papers, Series I, Reel 54.

77. Norris to Isaac Marcosson, September 13, 1900, Walker Papers. See also Isaac Marcosson, *Adventures in Interviewing* (New York: John Lane, 1920), pp. 233–39.

78. Wallace Rice, "Norris's *The Octopus*," in Graham, *Critical Essays*, p. 26. Rice went on to say that "a book with a self-defeated purpose can hardly be called a book at all."

79. The most current collection of such revisionism appears in the Spring 1991 issue of *California History*.

80. For instance, Lundy ("The Making of *McTeague* and *The Octopus*," p. 217) noted that the Southern Pacific was "for its owners a paradise, for Californians, a hell."

81. Norris, *The Octopus*, pp. 1096–97.

82. More credible models for these fictional characters would be Norris's own friends or Norris himself (as the character Presley). Other characters were doubtlessly modeled after figures in the San Francisco art and literature scene of the 1890s. See Don Graham, *The Fiction of Frank Norris: The Aesthetic Context* (Columbia: University of Missouri Press, 1978), especially "The Aesthetic Nineties and the Huge Conglomerate West of *The Octopus*."

83. Graham, *The Fiction of Frank Norris*, p. 67. See also Pizer, *The Novels of Frank Norris*, p. 196. Wyatt (*The Fall into Eden*, p. 97) notes that "Norris did not much trouble himself about accuracy of geographic and historical detail. He superimposed two California places to create a nowhere land in which his characters could play out a fable about survival in time."

84. Norris had lived in the Bay Area at the start of Adolph Sutro's "destroy the Octopus" 1894 San Francisco mayoral campaign.

85. See Richard J. Orsi, "The Confrontation at Mussel Slough," in Rice, Bullough, and Orsi, *The Elusive Eden*, pp. 217–36. Because of the textbook format of the book, this revisionist interpretation of the Mussel Slough controversy is unfortunately written without full scholarly apparatus. Professor Orsi will soon publish an account of the affair complete with source citations. He is one of a very few historians who have done extensive research in the corporate archives of the Southern Pacific. I am grateful to him for sharing many of his ideas and findings with me.

86. McElrath ("Frank Norris's *The Octopus*," pp. 138–52) points out that the ranchers in the novel are hopelessly outwitted by the wiles and strength of the railroad corporation. He argues that Norris is in effect making fun of their ineptitude and inability to compete within the "new order." While I am persuaded by McElrath's judgment that the ranchers

hardly represented "Good" in the battle versus "Evil," I do think that the railroad receives the ultimate blame for the ranchers' downfall.

87. The railroad-sexual theme is one that Norris had used before, particularly in *McTeague*. In one memorable passage in that novel, McTeague is with Trina alongside the railroad tracks in Oakland. As they embrace and kiss, they are suddenly startled by the rush of the overland train—"A roar and a jarring of the earth suddenly grew near and passed them in a reek of steam and hot air." It is clear that they are as surprised by their own sexuality, symbolized by the speeding locomotive. Trina and the train, then, are even more than anagrams of one another.

88. Wyatt (*The Fall into Eden*, chap. 5) suggests that even the railroad's "linearity" threatens the stature of the novel's characters. Wyatt argues persuasively that the novel chronicles both the literal and the figurative fall of the characters—down to corruption, down to the railroad's level, down to destruction and death.

89. Norris, *The Octopus*, pp. 836–37.

90. Ibid., p. 719.

91. Ibid., p. 835. It is precisely this sort of intrusion, represented and made possible by the railroad, that John Stilgoe discusses in *Metropolitan Corridor: Railroads and the American Scene* (New Haven, Conn.: Yale University Press, 1983).

92. Wyatt (*The Fall into Eden*, pp. 108–17) notes the significance of lines, intersections, and "tracks of terror" as well as the fact that, on the opening map, the sole "strong straight line is dictated by the bed of the railroad."

93. Norris, *The Octopus*, p. 662.

94. Ibid., p. 814.

95. Ibid., p. 813.

96. Dyke's story is patterned after the exploits of outlaw bandits Chris Evans and the Sontag brothers, who robbed Southern Pacific trains in the Central Valley in the 1890s. Norris would have read about these men in his newspaper research in San Francisco.

97. Norris, *The Octopus*, p. 859.

98. Ibid., p. 586.

99. Ibid., p. 861. In overhearing the conversation between red-surrounded Caraher and Dyke, "Presley forgot his black lead."

100. Ibid., p. 1004.

CHAPTER SIX

1. Several major studies of California Progressivism open with statements or analyses of the Southern Pacific Railroad's power at the dawn of the Progressive era. See George Mowry, *The California Progressives* (Berkeley: University of California Press, 1951); Spencer Olin, *Califor-*

nia's Prodigal Sons: Hiram Johnson and the Progressives, 1911–1917 (Berkeley: University of California Press, 1968); and Franklin Hichborn, *California Politics, 1891–1939*, 5 vols. (Los Angeles: Haynes Foundation, n.d.). See also John R. Haynes, "The Birth of Democracy in California," unpublished paper, copy in Alice Rose Collection, Department of Special Collections and Archives, Stanford University; Alice Rose, "Rise of California Insurgency: Origins of the League of Lincoln-Roosevelt Republican Clubs, 1900–1907," Ph.D. diss., Stanford University, 1942; Kevin Starr, *Inventing the Dream: California through the Progressive Era* (New York: Oxford University Press, 1985), pp. 235–82; Scott L. Bottles, *Los Angeles and the Automobile: The Making of the Modern City* (Berkeley: University of California Press, 1987); Richard Gruner, "The Politics of Individualism: Hiram Johnson and the California Progressives—1910 and 1914," senior thesis, California Institute of Technology, 1975.

2. "The psychological time for it had come," Rowell wrote to Wilfred B. Taylor, May 16, 1928, copy in Alice Rose Collection.

3. Ibid. Rowell's uncle (and political mentor) had expressed a similar conviction in 1905. Anti–Southern Pacific actions within the party would either "bring reforms within the party organization or . . . create a spirit of political revolution which will dethrone the bosses, even if it costs party defeat." Dr. Chester Rowell to Thomas R. Bard, February 4, 1905, Thomas R. Bard Papers, Huntington Library.

4. I agree with the comment of Michael P. Rogin and John L. Shover in their book *Political Change in California: Critical Elections and Social Movements, 1890–1966* (Westport, Conn.: Greenwood Press, 1970), p. 65: "California progressivism was greater than Hiram Johnson, but there can be little doubt that the forceful governor and senator was the prime representative of the movement in the state."

5. From 1898 onward, the Democratic Party ran at least one anti-railroad candidate in every gubernatorial election. Although California historians have largely excluded Democrats from the Progressive fold, they generally view Democrat Theodore Bell, gubernatorial candidate against Hiram Johnson in 1910, as a Progressive politician. In fact, distinguishing between the campaign stances of either candidate is extremely difficult. Bell had also run for governor in 1906, on a platform opposing William Randolph Hearst and William F. Herrin. See Curtis E. Grassman, "Prologue to California Reform: The Democratic Impulse, 1886–1898," *Pacific Historical Review* 42 (November 1973): 518–36. For a statement of the turn-of-the-century Democratic attitude toward the railroad, see the party pamphlet *The Railroad Is an Issue in Politics* (San Francisco: Star Press, 1898). For a recent synthesis examining the Democratic Party in the Progressive era, see David Sarasohn, *The Party of Reform: Democrats in the Progressive Era* (Jackson: University Press of Mississippi, 1989).

6. "Progressivism, in short, was to a very considerable extent led by men who suffered from the events of their time not through a shrinkage in their means but through the changed pattern in the distribution of deference and power." Richard Hofstadter, *The Age of Reform* (New York: Vintage, 1955), p. 135. See Mowry, *The California Progressives* and "The California Progressive and His Rationale: A Study in Middle Class Politics," *Mississippi Valley Historical Review* 36 (September 1949): 239–50.

7. Daniel T. Rodgers ("In Search of Progressivism," *Reviews in American History* 10 [December 1982]: 114) has argued that the conception of Progressivism as "a coherent reform movement" is a "mistaken assumption." Rather, Rodgers suggests, the era was marked by "shifting, ideologically fluid, issue-focused coalitions, all competing for the reshaping of American society." The shapelessness of Progressivism is also partly the result of definition problems. As Olin (*California's Prodigal Sons*, p. 179) has noted, with particular regard to California, "the term 'Progressive' may correctly be applied to a number of notions, ranging from a belief in efficient government by honest businessmen to a desire for radical alterations in the economic and social system."

8. Rogin and Shover, *Political Change in California*, p. 64.

9. Rogin and Shover, *Political Change in California*, especially chap. 2, "Progressivism and the California Electorate." See also John L. Shover, "The Progressives and the Working Class Vote in California," in *Voters, Parties, and Elections: Quantitative Essays in the History of American Popular Voting Behavior*, ed. Joel H. Silbey and Samuel T. McSeveney (Lexington, Mass.: Xerox College Publishing, 1972), pp. 260–73. Rogin and Shover are challenged in Gruner, "The Politics of Individualism."

10. See W. H. Hutchinson, "Prologue to Reform: The California Antirailroad Republicans, 1899–1905." *Southern California Quarterly* 44 (September 1962): 175–218.

11. See Commonwealth Club of California, *Transactions* 4 (March 1909). In early 1907, the City Club of Los Angeles was formed for much the same purpose as the Commonwealth Club. See Albert H. Clodius, "The Quest for Good Government in Los Angeles, 1890–1910," Ph.D. diss., Claremont Graduate School, 1953, pp. 401–2; Marshall Stimson, *Fun, Fights, and Fiestas in Old Los Angeles* (Los Angeles: privately printed, 1966), p. 168. See also Franklin Hichborn, *Story of the California Legislature of 1909* (San Francisco: James H. Barry Co., 1909), for a discussion of the Commonwealth Club's involvement in state legislation.

12. Franklin K. Lane to Edward B. Whitney, November 13, 1905, in *The Letters of Franklin K. Lane*, ed. Anne W. Lane and Louise H. Wall (Boston: Houghton Mifflin, 1922), pp. 51–52.

13. Ibid. Lane had at one point been on the staff of *Arthur McEwen's Letter*, a radical anti–Southern Pacific, anti-corporate newsletter in San Francisco.

14. Franklin K. Lane to William E. Smythe, December 15, 1905, *Letters of Franklin K. Lane*, p. 55. Lane's fellow members of the Interstate Commerce Commission apparently thought otherwise; Lane wrote that they perceived him as "a sort of a cross between "Dennis [*sic*] Kearney and Eugene Debs."

15. In the "Octopus" view of California history, William F. Herrin is generally cast as the great and all-powerful villain or as Collis P. Huntington's dastardly lieutenant: "From the village constable to the governor of the state, from the justice of the peace to the justice on the supreme bench, the final selection of the people's officials lay with Mr. Herrin or his subordinates in the railroad machine." John R. Haynes, "The Birth of Democracy in California," n.d., copy in Alice Rose Collection. That Herrin was powerful there can be little doubt. But that his role has been overestimated seems also incontrovertible. Few figures in California political history are more deserving of scholarly research than William F. Herrin. See also the reminiscences of Philip Bancroft in "Politics, Farming, and the Progressive Party in California," oral history conducted by University of California Regional Cultural History Project (interviewer: Willa Klug Baum), 1962, pp. 48, 95.

16. See Walton Bean, *Boss Ruef's San Francisco* (Berkeley: University of California Press, 1952).

17. See Fremont Older, *My Own Story* (San Francisco: Call Publishing Company, 1919).

18. The antagonism was apparently mutual. In a speech (quoted in Starr, *Inventing the Dream*, p. 264), Grove Johnson referred to his two sons—one, a political opponent; the other, a hopeless alcoholic—as "Hiram, full of egotism" and "Albert, full of booze."

19. Henry Huntington to Collis P. Huntington, May 6 and June 2, 1896, Henry E. Huntington Papers, Huntington Library. See also Irving McKee, "The Background and Early Career of Hiram Warren Johnson, 1866–1910," *Pacific Historical Review* 19 (February 1950): 17–30.

20. My discussion on Los Angeles reform efforts is drawn largely from Clodius, "The Quest for Good Government in Los Angeles"; and Thomas J. Sitton, *John Randolph Haynes, California Progressive* (Stanford, Calif.: Stanford University Press, 1992), especially chap. 8. See also Mowry, *The California Progressives*, pp. 38–48; Hichborn, *California Politics*; Stimson, *Fun, Fights, and Fiestas in Old Los Angeles*. Fred W. Viehe, in "The First Recall: Los Angeles Urban Reform or Machine Politics" (*Southern California Quarterly* 70 [Spring 1988]: 1–28), has argued that the Southern Pacific worked hand in hand with urban reformers in Los Angeles, an argument I do not find convincing given the evidence cited in Viehe's work. See also Viehe, "The Los Angeles Progressives: The Influence of the Southern Pacific Machine on Urban Reform, 1872–1913," Ph.D. diss., University of California, Santa Barbara, 1983. Leaders behind the Non-

Partisan group included E. A. Dickson, a journalist for the Los Angeles *Express,* and attorneys Meyer Lissner, Russ Avery, and Marshall Stimson.

21. The Non-Partisan group did far better in the 1906 elections than the Los Angeles Public Ownership Party, a group pushing for municipal ownership of public utilities. See Clodius, "Quest for Good Government in Los Angeles," pp. 123–30.

22. Lissner quoted in Ida Tarbell interview notes with Meyer Lissner, April 29, 1911 (copy), Alice Rose Collection. See also Thomas Sitton, "Urban Politics and Reform in New Deal Los Angeles: The Recall of Mayor Frank L. Shaw," Ph.D. diss., University of California, Riverside, 1983, pp. 12–17.

23. Meyer Lissner to E. A. Dickson, February 16, 1907, Meyer Lissner Papers, Department of Special Collections and Archives, Stanford University.

24. Rowell had been a supporter of the Mussel Slough settlers, in neighboring Tulare County, in their land dispute with the Southern Pacific. His nephew, in a letter to muckraking journalist Ida Tarbell, wrote that Rowell "was fighting the California end of the machine in the California legislature, way back from 1879 on." See Chester H. Rowell to Ida Tarbell, May 11, 1911 (copy), Alice Rose Collection.

25. See Miles C. Everett, "Chester Harvey Rowell, Pragmatic Humanist and California Progressive," Ph.D. diss., University of California, Berkeley, 1966.

26. As we saw in chapter 3, Pardee's anti-railroad credentials were at best dubious. As Oakland's mayor in 1894, he earned the lasting enmity of striking railroad and other workers by his hyperbolic statements and actions concerning a perceived threat of revolution. Following the strike, Pardee unwisely attempted to act as intermediary between the company and the workers, a paternalistic gesture held in contempt by Oakland's railroad workers. Mowry (*California Progressives,* p. 16) writes that Pardee was actually the railroad's choice in the 1902 governor's race and that Southern Pacific officials designed the Republican platform of that year. On the other hand, Pardee's autobiographical sketch (a copy is in the Alice Rose Collection), as well as Pardee's comments in a 1938 interview with Alice Rose (Alice Rose Collection), paints a portrait of an anti-railroad proto-Progressive champion: "During his term as Governor, the Southern Pacific did not attempt to put through the Legislature any particularly unpopular measures. It knew the Governor too well to attempt it." For a discussion of Pardee's actions during the Pullman strike, see Oakland *Times,* July 20, 1894.

27. Davis quoted in Los Angeles *Examiner,* February 13, 1908. In a letter to Arthur McEwen, written in the summer of 1895, Davis urged McEwen to postpone the folding of *Arthur McEwen's Newsletter,* a radical anti-corporate San Francisco paper. The proposed competing railroad through the Central Valley was cause for optimism, Davis wrote. "Isn't it the fact

that California is on the eve of freedom?" "Are we going to slide back this time as after other revolts before?" To McEwen, who had only a year before described the Pullman strike as the penultimate Labor versus Capital struggle, the battle doubtless was more complex. See W. R. Davis Scrapbooks (1895–96 vol.), W. R. Davis Papers, Bancroft Library.

28. In an interview with Alice Rose in 1939, W. C. Jerome emphasized the role played by Bryan in inspiring the Progressives. See Alice Rose interview notes, W. C. Jerome, July 18, 1939, Alice Rose Collection.

29. For example, the Non-Partisan Committee in Los Angeles (quickly known as "Teddy's Terrors") used Roosevelt's statements as an opening to its "Declaration of Principles." Edgar A. Luce claimed to have started a "Roosevelt Republican Club" in San Diego in 1906; the club was dedicated to the defeat of the railroad political machine in San Diego and the state. See Edgar A. Luce to George Mowry, February 7, 1953, Edgar A. Luce Papers, Bancroft Library.

30. Faced with formidable opposition from Harrison Gray Otis and the Los Angeles *Times*, reform leaders at work on forming a Progressive wing of the Republican Party thought of asking for Roosevelt's help. "The thought has occurred to me that if we wanted to get the Times in line, there is only one way to do it," Meyer Lissner wrote to E. A. Dickson, "and that is through the President. . . . If the President could be convinced that the Lincoln-Roosevelt movement was the proper thing in California and that the Times was hurting Roosevelt's cause here by lining up with the wolves in sheep's clothing, I believe that he would write a letter to Gen. Otis suggesting to him what he thought the proper thing to do." Meyer Lissner to E. A. Dickson, October 23, 1907, Lissner Papers. Roosevelt quoted in John Milton Cooper, *The Warrior and the Priest: Woodrow Wilson and Theodore Roosevelt* (Cambridge, Mass.: Belknap Press of Harvard University Press, 1983), p. 137.

31. Meyer Lissner to E. A. Dickson, February 16, 1907, Lissner Papers.

32. Meyer Lissner to Harris Weinstock, April 25, 1907, Lissner Papers.

33. Ibid.

34. Transcription of A. J. Pillsbury diary, June 5, 1907, in Alice Rose Collection. Stimson to Los Angeles Historical Society, December 23, 1937 (copy), Alice Rose Collection. See also Robert Waring to George Mowry, November 14, 1949, Robert Waring Papers, Bancroft Library. In *Ministers of Reform* (Urbana: University of Illinois Press, 1984), pp. 5–6, Robert Crunden has written of the Progressives' great regard for Lincoln.

35. Steffens was an important figure in the early days of the Progressive movement in the state. He enjoyed a considerable reputation, especially in southern California, and expressed a real interest in helping to lay the groundwork for California reform. Steffens was close to Heney and encouraged Heney in his reform efforts. See, for instance, Lincoln

Steffens to Francis Heney, June 1, 1908, Francis Heney Papers, Bancroft Library.

36. See the minutes of the meeting in the Waring Papers.

37. Lissner to Ed Roberts, October 9, 1907, Lissner Papers; Chester Rowell to Friend Richardson, November 14, 1907, Chester Rowell Papers, Bancroft Library.

38. Meyer Lissner to editor, Riverside *Press*, October 30, 1907, Lissner Papers.

39. Thomas R. Bard to Lee C. Gates, August 26, 1907, Bard Papers, Huntington Library; Lee C. Gates to Thomas R. Bard (copy), September 1, 1907, Alice Rose Collection.

40. Chester Rowell to S. C. Smith, December 17, 1907, Rowell Papers; Rowell to [unknown], n.d., fragment (copy) in Alice Rose Collection.

41. Thomas R. Bard to J. R. Gabbert, April 2, 1908, Bard Papers.

42. Bancroft, "Politics, Farming, and the Progressive Party in California" (oral history), p. 90. Bancroft explicitly repudiated socialism, saying that "we weren't for tearing down our whole economic system or turning it into a socialistic drive or anything of that kind."

43. Robert Waring to George P. Hammond, March 23, 1964, Waring Papers.

44. Chester Rowell to C. N. Whitaker, January 23, 1909, Rowell Papers.

45. Chester Rowell to Hiram Johnson, January 26, 1910, Rowell Papers.

46. See Bancroft, "Politics, Farming, and the Progressive Party in California" (oral history), pp. 80–81.

47. "You . . . typify opposition to both the organization [and] the R. R. Co.," a friend wrote to Johnson. A. A. DeLigne to Hiram Johnson, February 22, 1910, Hiram Johnson Papers, Bancroft Library.

48. Chester Rowell to Meyer Lissner, January 31, 1910, Rowell Papers.

49. See Chester Rowell to Francis J. Heney, February 2, 1910, and Chester Rowell to C. C. Young, February 2, 1910, Rowell Papers.

50. A. M. Drew to Hiram Johnson, February 8, 1910, Johnson Papers.

51. It is unlikely that Rowell could have remembered Johnson's poignant response thirty years after the event, but he did provide interviewer Alice Rose with the dialogue that supposedly took place between the two men. In reply to Rowell's confession that the conflict did cause him pain, Johnson said that Rowell could not feel "half as painfully as I do. I grew up thinking my father was the greatest man in the world. The fist fights I had on the schoolgrounds as a boy were about things which the other boys said that I afterwards had to realize were true. If I go into this fight, I can take everything else standing up and fight back. I'll have to take that lying down; and I don't want to face it." Alice Rose interview of Chester H. Rowell, November 11, 1939, transcription in Alice Rose Collection.

52. Hiram Johnson to Anna C. Weeks, February 26, 1910, Johnson

Papers. Also that month, Heney took credit for Johnson's agreeing to run ("I am responsible for Hiram Johnson agreeing to run"). See Heney to James D. Phelan, February 22, 1910, James D. Phelan Papers, Bancroft Library.

53. George B. Anderson to Hiram Johnson, February 20, 1910, Johnson Papers.

54. A. A. DeLigne to Hiram Johnson, February 22, 1910, and D. M. Duffy to E. T. Earl, February 26, 1910, Johnson Papers.

55. Hiram Johnson to "Mabel" (Mrs. Bruce Dray), February 26, 1910, and Johnson to C. K. McClatchy, February 26, 1910, Johnson Papers. Ironically, Johnson may have gained some political support because of his father. A newspaperman in Lodi, California, wrote him that he would support Johnson in part because he admired Johnson's father. "It is for consideration along those lines, rather than on account of any ideas of Reform or Anti-Railroad Sentiment. In fact, the people of the country districts are friendly to the Railroads and not particularly strong on Reform." S. B. Axtell to Hiram Johnson, March 11, 1910, Johnson Papers.

56. Willard quoted in Donald Ray Culton, "Charles Dwight Willard: Los Angeles City Booster and Professional Reformer, 1888–1914," Ph.D. diss., University of Southern California, 1971, p. 286.

57. Hiram Johnson to Meyer Lissner, March 1 and March 24, 1910, Johnson Papers.

58. William R. Davis to Hiram Johnson, March 22, 1910, Johnson Papers.

59. Hiram Johnson to James H. Hayes (and others), March 2, 1910, Johnson Papers.

60. Lincoln Steffens to Francis Heney, December 13, 1910, Heney Papers.

61. Johnson quoted in Richard C. Lower, "Hiram Johnson and the Progressive Denouement, 1910–1920," Ph.D. diss., University of California, Los Angeles, 1969, p. 36. Johnson invariably steered interviews back to the subject of the Southern Pacific's political might. For instance, after an interview with a reporter for the San Francisco *Daily News*, in which he gave vague replies to questions on Asiatic exclusion (which Johnson favored) and employers' liability laws, Johnson asked that the paper's editor publish an addendum. The addition praised the efforts of reformers in other states for making "the same fight we are making in California, a fight against the interests and the system and for true democracy. We are striving for the same things that Theodore Roosevelt demanded. . . . Our state has been appropriated by the Southern Pacific Railroad Company and its government has long been considered a mere asset of that corporation." Not only did the *Daily News* publish the addendum, but the Lincoln-Roosevelt League then peddled the interview to other friendly papers. See Hiram Johnson to "Mr. Brown," March 30 and April 22, 1910,

Johnson Papers. Mowry (*The California Progressives*, p. 135) relates a story in which Johnson confessed to his political advisers that he did not understand what the initiative, referendum, and recall entailed.

62. Hiram Johnson to C. L. Ortman, March 28, 1910, Johnson Papers. "I have just returned from the South," Johnson wrote to Leland S. Foulkes on March 25, "and am absolutely certain of a majority south of the Tehachapi" (Johnson Papers). At the time George Mowry did his research for *The California Progressives*, the Johnson Papers had not been opened for study. Consequently, Mowry did not see this optimistic side to Johnson and instead cast him as pessimistic about his chances in the campaign (see p. 135).

63. See Johnson to A. A. DeLigne, March 1, 1910, Johnson Papers. As Lincoln-Roosevelt League member William Carr remembered years later about the importance of the primary: "You must remember that in those days, and for some years afterwards, the Republican nomination was equivalent to election in this state, just the way a Democratic nomination is equivalent to election in the South." See "The Memoirs of William Jarvis Carr," Oral History Project, University of California, Los Angeles, 1959, p. 45.

64. A partial description of Johnson's spring and summer itinerary indicates the whirlwind nature of the campaign. Through mid-March, Johnson campaigned in Los Angeles and elsewhere in southern California. From there he went to northern California, through Yolo, Glenn, and Colusa counties. Two weeks were spent traversing the San Joaquin Valley in May; then the entourage worked back through southern California, including stops in Riverside and Long Beach. In late June, Johnson was back in northern California, out on the hustings in Sausalito, the South Bay region, and then up through the Gold Country. July campaigning brought him to the California coast, and in late July he returned to Los Angeles.

65. "Necessary Johnson do Humboldt thoroughly," a league supporter, W. R. Ellis, informed a Johnson adviser in May. Rural Humboldt County was isolated and economically dependent on logging operations. Johnson could not devote much time to daytime speeches, Ellis wrote, because it would interfere with the shifts of the workers. But the men favored Johnson's aggressive style, and the environment made the area conducive to great night meetings. W. R. Ellis to Charles Detrick, May 24, 1910, Johnson Papers.

66. Anti-Johnson leaflet, Johnson Papers; letter from American Railroad Employes and Investors' Association to "Fellow Railroad Employee," May 27, 1910, copy in Johnson Papers. Of course, these materials could have been made up at the Southern Pacific's suggestion.

67. Fresno *Herald*, April 13, 1910, clipping in Johnson Papers. Some of the *Herald*'s opposition to Johnson must be ascribed to the fact that

238 / Notes to Pages 167–70

Chester Rowell ran the opposing *Republican*. The *Herald* editorialized that Rowell was a political boss in his own right, presiding over the "rowell republican league."

68. Selma *Irrigator*, May 14, 1910, clipping in Johnson Papers.

69. Anderson quoted in Fresno *Herald*, July 16, 1910, clipping in Johnson Papers. Johnson quoted in Oakland *Saturday Press*, October 29, 1910, clipping in Johnson Papers.

70. Hiram Johnson to Al McCabe, May 29, 1910, Johnson Papers.

71. Hiram Johnson speech, June 3, 1910, Blanchard Hall, Los Angeles, copy in Johnson Papers.

72. Ibid. In a probable reference to Frank Norris's best-selling 1901 work, *The Octopus*, Johnson added that the history of the Southern Pacific's actions in the state was more "interesting and more eloquent . . . than any novel I have ever read."

73. Regression analysis of the 1910 primary vote indicates that both Johnson and Phillip Stanton did well with voters who had voted the Prohibitionist ticket in 1906 (better, in fact, than Simeon Meads, Prohibitionist candidate in 1910). Although the overall Prohibitionist vote was small, it was of some influence in the primary's outcome. See William Deverell, "Building an Octopus: Railroads and Society in the Late Nineteenth-Century Far West," Ph.D. diss., Princeton University, 1989, Appendix.

74. See Johnson Papers, Box 12.

75. Quoted in Mowry, *The California Progressives*, p. 130. Bell's statement was a reiteration of the state Democratic platform adopted in the fall of 1910.

76. As Rogin and Shover (*Political Change in California*, p. 44) have pointed out, "party allegiance was invariably the most important single predictor of a candidate's support in a general election." No matter the rhetoric and anti-railroad specificity: Johnson was a Republican in a Republican state. Victory in the primary virtually assured him the governor's chair. Despite what some scholars have argued regarding crossover voting in the Progressive era, it appears that Californians who had voted Democratic in 1906 did the same in 1910. See Sarasohn, *The Party of Reform*, pp. 81–82; and Michael Rogin, "Progressivism and the California Electorate," in Rogin and Shover, *Political Change in California*, chap. 2.

77. Mowry (*The California Progressives*, p. 130) argues that Bell would have won the 1906 gubernatorial election if not for the Independence League, a political plaything of William Randolph Hearst.

78. "Memoirs of Carr" (oral history project), p. 45.

79. See Clodius, "The Quest for Good Government," pp. 123–25.

80. Franklin Hichborn, *Story of the California Legislature of 1911* (San Francisco: James H. Barry Co., 1911). As Clodius ("The Quest for Good Government," pp. 482–83) notes, "The political reformers empha-

sized honesty and efficiency in government, and accepted with less criticism than the social reformers the competitive and individualistic aspects of capitalistic economy."

81. As Chester Rowell remembered, Johnson "never seemed to realize throughout most of the campaign that if he were elected, he would actually have to outline and defend a long list of reform measures." See Mowry, *The California Progressives*, p. 135.

82. Franklin K. Lane to Charles K. McClatchy, March 20, 1909, in Lane and Wall, *Letters of Franklin K. Lane*, p. 70. Lane wrote that he had been encouraged by California Republicans to switch parties and lead the Lincoln-Roosevelt League.

83. Transcription of A. J. Pillsbury diary, July 5, 1908, in Alice Rose Collection. Letters to Johnson (in Johnson Papers) during the campaign from Californians across the state attest to the same sort of feeling: that the Octopus ruled the state and that in Johnson lay the only hope for political redemption.

84. William F. Herrin of the Southern Pacific, speaking before the California Bar Association, even welcomed regulation, or so he said: "I think no railroad manager would agree to dispense with government regulation at the cost of returning to the old conditions." See Olin, *California's Prodigal Sons*, p. 171. It must be remembered, too, that the railroad commission was hardly innovative; the Grange–Workingman's Party of California coalition had created the regulatory body at the constitutional convention of 1878–79. The Progressives, to their credit, did provide the commission with enough teeth to be able to set transportation and freight rates and determine railroad property and capital values.

85. According to Olin (*California's Prodigal Sons*, p. 175), "California progressives did not think in terms of organized groups such as 'business' and 'labor' battling for political favors and recognition. Their principal desire was to achieve a balance among the many powerful interests without arousing feelings of class consciousness, and to advance the whole of society in which the conduct of individuals would be governed by such moral qualities as honesty, frugality, and high character. It would therefore have been inconsistent with their vision of society for progressives to have made special appeals to organized labor."

86. Olin, *California's Prodigal Sons*, p. 41.

87. Herrin quoted in Hichborn, *California Politics*, p. 146.

EPILOGUE

1. Thoreau quoted in Leo Marx, *The Machine in the Garden: Technology and the New Pastoral Idea in America* (New York: Oxford University Press, 1964), p. 260.

2. In *The Democratic Party and California Politics, 1880–1896* (Stan-

ford, Calif.: Stanford University Press, 1973), n. 3, pp. 206–7, historian R. Hal Williams correctly notes that, despite the assumption of the railroad's virtual chokehold on the state's political arena ("what people believed sometimes counted more than reality"), there were politicians throughout the nineteenth century who made successful careers as public opponents of the excesses of corporate power.

3. C. Loyal [pseud.], *The Squatter and the Don; A Novel Descriptive of Contemporary Occurrences in California* (San Francisco: Samuel Carson and Co., 1885), p. 421.

4. G. R. Blanchard, "Politico-Railway Problems and Theorists," *National Quarterly Review* 80 (April 1880): 35–72.

5. "It may be thought that some of the phenomena I have described belong to an era of colonization, and that when the West has been filled up, and all the arterial railways made, when, in fact, the United States have become even as England or France, the power of railroads and their presidents will decline." James Bryce, *The American Commonwealth* (London and New York: Macmillan, 1889), 2:516.

6. See, for instance, Williams's chapter "The Railroad in California Politics" in *The Democratic Party and California Politics*; W. H. Hutchinson, "Southern Pacific: Myth and Reality," *California Historical Society Quarterly* 48 (December 1969): 325–34; Gerald D. Nash, "The California Railroad Commission, 1876–1911," *Southern California Quarterly* 44 (December 1962): 287–305; Richard J. Orsi, "*The Octopus* Reconsidered: The Southern Pacific and Agricultural Modernization in California, 1865–1915," *California Historical Quarterly* 54 (Fall 1975): 197–220.

7. Thomas Bacon, "The Railroad Strike in California," *Yale Review* 3 (November 1894): 250.

8. See Daniel T. Rodgers, "In Search of Progressivism," *Reviews in American History* 10 (December 1982): 119.

9. William F. Herrin, "Government Regulation of Railways," *California Law Review* 2 (January 1914): 88–89.

Bibliography

MANUSCRIPTS AND SCRAPBOOKS

American Railway Union Strike Scrapbooks, Henry Huntington Papers, Huntington Library, San Marino, Calif.

Robert S. Baker Papers, Huntington Library.

Hubert Howe Bancroft Collection, Bancroft Library, University of California, Berkeley.

Thomas R. Bard Papers, Huntington Library.

Samuel L. M. Barlow Papers, Huntington Library.

John D. Bicknell Papers, Huntington Library.

Ambrose Bierce Papers, Bancroft Library.

Ambrose Bierce Papers, Department of Special Collections and Archives, Stanford University.

Ambrose Bierce Papers, Huntington Library.

Thomas Vincent Cator Papers, Department of Special Collections and Archives, Stanford University.

Central Pacific Railroad Company Pamphlets, Huntington Library.

Cornelius Cole Papers, Department of Special Collections, University of California, Los Angeles.

Croswell Family Papers, Bancroft Library.

W. R. Davis Papers, Bancroft Library.

Eugene V. Debs Letters, Hoover Institution on War, Revolution and Peace, Stanford University.

Stephen B. Elkins Papers, Department of Special Collections, West Virginia University.

Thomas Balch Elliott Papers, Huntington Library.

George Kenyon Fitch Papers, Bancroft Library.

Thomas E. Gibbon Papers, Huntington Library.

Thomas E. Gibbon Papers, Private Collection.

Jackson A. Graves Papers, Huntington Library.

Henry H. Haight Papers, Huntington Library.

Francis J. Heney Papers, Bancroft Library.

Sherman O. Houghton Papers, Huntington Library.

Collis P. Huntington Papers (microfilm), Syracuse University.

Henry E. Huntington Papers, Huntington Library.

Hiram Johnson Papers, Bancroft Library.

Herbert C. Jones Papers, Department of Special Collections and Archives, Stanford University.

John P. Jones Papers, Department of Special Collections, University of California, Los Angeles.

John P. Jones Papers, Huntington Library.

David Starr Jordan Papers, Department of Special Collections and Archives, Stanford University.

Frank C. Jordan Papers, Bancroft Library.

George W. Kelley Papers, Bancroft Library.

Meyer Lissner Papers, Department of Special Collections and Archives, Stanford University.

Edgar A. Luce Papers, Bancroft Library.

Charles Maclay Papers, Huntington Library.

Jerome Madden Papers, Bancroft Library.

H. H. Markham Papers, Huntington Library.

Minutes of the California Railroad Commission, 4 vols., California State Archives, Sacramento.

Minutes of the Los Angeles Chamber of Commerce, California Historical Society, Los Angeles.

Eustace Neale Papers, Bancroft Library.

Frank Norris Papers, Bancroft Library.

Warren Olney Papers, Bancroft Library.

George C. Pardee Papers, Bancroft Library.

George C. Pardee Scrapbooks, Department of Special Collections and Archives, Stanford University.

George S. Patton Papers, Huntington Library.

James D. Phelan Papers, Bancroft Library.

John W. Reynolds Papers, Bancroft Library.

Frank Roney Papers, Bancroft Library.

Alice Rose Collection, Department of Special Collections and Archives, Stanford University.

Chester Rowell Papers, Bancroft Library.

Horatio Nelson Rust Papers, Huntington Library.

Jonathan Scott Papers, Bancroft Library.

Frank Shay Papers, Department of Special Collections and Archives, Stanford University.

James DeBarth Shorb Papers, Huntington Library.

William Andrew Spalding Papers, Huntington Library.

Jane Stanford Papers, Department of Special Collections and Archives, Stanford University.

Leland Stanford Papers, Department of Special Collections and Archives, Stanford University.

Stearns-Gaffey Papers, Huntington Library.

Franklin Walker Papers, Bancroft Library.

Robert Waring Papers, Bancroft Library.
Harris Weinstock Scrapbooks, Bancroft Library.
Stephen M. White Papers, Department of Special Collections and Archives, Stanford University.
Stephen M. White Scrapbooks, Seaver Center, Los Angeles County Museum of Natural History.
Charles Dwight Willard Papers, Huntington Library.
Benjamin D. Wilson Papers, Huntington Library.
John D. Works Papers, Department of Special Collections and Archives, Stanford University.

BOOKS, PAMPHLETS, BROADSIDES, REPORTS

Annual Report of the Los Angeles Terminal Railway Company to the Board of Railroad Commissioners. Sacramento: State Printing Office, 1896.
An Appeal to the People. Visalia, Calif.: Visalia Delta Book and Job, 1880.
Appendix to the Annual Report of the Attorney-General of the United States for the Year 1896. Washington, D.C.: U.S. Government Printing Office, 1896.
Appendix to the Biennial Report of the Adjutant-General of the State of California, 1893–1894. Sacramento: State Printing Office, 1894.
Ayers, James J. *Gold and Sunshine: Reminiscences of Early California.* Boston: Gorham Press, 1922.
Bancroft, Hubert Howe. *History of California.* 7 vols. San Francisco: The History Company, 1890.
Barker, Charles Albro. *Henry George.* New York: Oxford University Press, 1955.
Bean, Walton. *Boss Ruef's San Francisco.* Berkeley: University of California Press, 1952.
Blackford, Mansel. *The Politics of Business in California, 1890–1920.* Columbus: Ohio State University Press, 1977.
[Booth, Newton.] *The Issue of the Day: Gov. Booth's Great Speech on the Railroad Question.* San Francisco: n.p., c. 1873.
[———.] *Open Letter of Newton Booth to John B. Felton.* Sacramento: H. A. Weaver, 1873.
[Booth, Newton, and M. M. Estee.] *"The Principles of the Republican Party Are Not for a Day but for All Time": Speeches of Hon. Newton Booth, U.S. Senator, and Hon. M. M. Estee, at Platt's Hall, Thursday Evening, July 31, 1879.* N.p.: n.d.
Bottles, Scott L. *Los Angeles and the Automobile: The Making of the Modern City.* Berkeley: University of California Press, 1987.
Browne, J. Ross. *Letter from J. Ross Browne.* San Francisco: Excelsior Press, 1870.
Bryant, Keith L., Jr., ed. *Encyclopedia of American Business History and Biography: Railroads in the Age of Regulation, 1900–1980.* New York: Bruccoli Clark Layman and Facts on File, 1988.
Bryce, James. *The American Commonwealth.* 2 vols. London and New York: Macmillan, 1889.
Bynon, A. Bert. *San Pedro: Its History.* Los Angeles: Boyle Heights Press, 1899.
Campbell, E. G. *The Reorganization of the American Railroad System, 1893–*

1900. New York: Columbia University Press, 1938; reprint, New York: AMS Press, 1968.

Carr, Ezra S. *The Patrons of Husbandry on the Pacific Coast*. San Francisco: A. L. Bancroft, 1875.

Cator, Thomas Vincent. *Rescue the Republic: The Necessity and Advantages of National Ownership of Railroads*. San Francisco: Citizens' Alliance, 1892.

Chan, Sucheng. *This Bitter Soil: The Chinese in California Agriculture, 1860–1910*. Berkeley: University of California Press, 1986.

Chandler, Alfred D., Jr. *The Railroads: The Nation's First Big Business*. New York: Harcourt, Brace, 1965.

———. *The Visible Hand: The Managerial Revolution in American Business*. Cambridge, Mass.: Belknap Press of Harvard University Press, 1977.

Chilstrom, P. O. *Prostituted Manhood*. San Francisco: n.p., 1893.

Cleland, Robert G. *California in Our Time: 1900–1940*. New York: Knopf, 1947.

Cochran, Thomas C. *Railroad Leaders, 1845–1900: The Business Mind in Action*. Cambridge, Mass.: Harvard University Press, 1953.

Cole, Cornelius. *Memoirs of Cornelius Cole*. New York: McLoughlin Brothers, 1908.

Cooper, Jerry. *The Army and Civil Disorder*. Westport, Conn.: Greenwood Press, 1980.

Cooper, John Milton. *The Warrior and the Priest: Woodrow Wilson and Theodore Roosevelt*. Cambridge, Mass.: Belknap Press of Harvard University Press, 1983.

Cornford, Daniel A. *Workers and Dissent in the Redwood Empire*. Philadelphia: Temple University Press, 1987.

Crane, Lauren E., ed. *Newton Booth of California: His Speeches and Addresses*. New York: Putnam's, 1894.

Crisler, Jesse S., and Joseph R. McElrath, Jr. *Frank Norris: A Reference Guide*. Boston: G. K. Hall, 1974.

Cross, Ira. *Financing an Empire: History of Banking in California*. 4 vols. Chicago: S. J. Clarke, 1927.

———. *A History of the Labor Movement in California*. Berkeley: University of California Press, 1935.

———, ed. *Frank Roney, Irish Rebel and California Labor Leader: An Autobiography*. Berkeley: University of California Press, 1931.

Crunden, Robert. *Ministers of Reform*. Urbana: University of Illinois Press, 1984.

Cubery, William M. *An Open Letter to C. P. Huntington*. San Francisco: n.p., [1891].

Daggett, Stuart. *Chapters on the History of the Southern Pacific*. New York: Ronald Press, 1922.

Daniel, Cletus A. *Bitter Harvest: A History of California Farmworkers, 1870–1941*. Ithaca, N.Y.: Cornell University Press, 1981.

Danly, Susan, and Leo Marx, eds. *The Railroad in American Art*. Cambridge, Mass.: MIT Press, 1988.

Davie, John L. *My Own Story*. Oakland, Calif.: Post-Enquirer Publishing Co., 1931.

Davis, Mike. *City of Quartz*. London: Verso Press, 1990.

Debates and Proceedings of the Constitutional Convention of the State of California. 3 vols. Sacramento: State Printing Office, 1880.

Decker, Peter R. *Fortunes and Failures: White-Collar Mobility in Nineteenth-Century San Francisco.* Cambridge, Mass.: Harvard University Press, 1978.

Deep-Water Harbor in Southern California; Port Los Angeles vs. San Pedro; Full Report of Oral Testimony at Public Hearings in Los Angeles; December 1896. Los Angeles: Evening Express Co., 1896.

Delmatier, Royce D., Clarence F. McIntosh, and Earl G. Waters, eds. *The Rumble of California Politics, 1848–1970.* New York: Wiley, 1970.

Deutsch, Sarah. *No Separate Refuge: Culture, Class, and Gender on an Anglo-Hispanic Frontier in the American Southwest, 1880–1940.* New York: Oxford University Press, 1987.

Doyle, John T. *Railroad Policy of California.* San Francisco: Women's Co-operative Union, 1873.

Dumke, Glenn S. *The Boom of the Eighties in Southern California.* San Marino, Calif.: Huntington Library, 1944.

Dwinnell, I. E. *The Higher Reaches of the Great Continental Railway: A Highway for Our God.* Sacramento: H. S. Crocker, 1869.

Eggert, Gerald G. *Railroad Labor Disputes: The Beginnings of Federal Strike Policy.* Ann Arbor: University of Michigan Press, 1967.

Emerson, D. L. *Oakland, Judged from an Eastern Standpoint.* Oakland, Calif.: Butler and Bowman, 1875.

Emmons, Terence. *Around California in 1891.* Stanford, Calif.: Stanford University Alumni Association, 1991.

Fifer, J. Valerie. *American Progress: The Growth of the Transport, Tourist, and Information Industries in the Nineteenth-Century West.* Chester, Conn.: Globe Pequot Press, 1988.

Filmer, George, et al. *The "City Guard": A History of Company "B," First Regiment Infantry, N.G.C. during the Sacramento Campaign, July 3 to 26, 1894.* San Francisco: Filmer-Rollins Electrotype Co., 1895.

Fishlow, Albert. *American Railroads and the Transformation of the Ante-bellum Economy.* Cambridge, Mass.: Harvard University Press, 1965.

Fishman, Robert. *Bourgeois Utopias: The Rise and Fall of Suburbia.* New York: Basic Books, 1987.

Fitch, Henry. *Pacific Railroad.* San Francisco: Frank Eastman, 1859.

Fogel, Robert W. *Railroads and American Economic Growth: Essays in Econometric History.* Baltimore: Johns Hopkins University Press, 1964.

Fogelson, Robert. *The Fragmented Metropolis: Los Angeles, 1850–1930.* Cambridge, Mass.: Harvard University Press, 1967.

Frey, Robert L., ed. *Encyclopedia of American Business History and Biography: Railroads in the Nineteenth Century.* New York: Bruccoli Clark Layman and Facts on File, 1988.

Friedman, Lawrence, and Robert Percival. *The Roots of Justice: Crime and Punishment in Alameda County, California, 1870–1910.* Chapel Hill: University of North Carolina Press, 1981.

Friedricks, William. *Henry E. Huntington and the Creation of Southern California.* Columbus: Ohio State University Press, 1992.

George, Henry. *Writings of Henry George*. Vol. 9. New York: Doubleday, 1901.

George, Henry, Jr. *The Life of Henry George*. New York: Doubleday, 1911.

Gottlieb, Robert, and Irene Wolt. *Thinking Big: The Story of the Los Angeles Times, Its Publishers and Their Influence on Southern California*. New York: Putnam's, 1972.

Graham, Don. *The Fiction of Frank Norris: The Aesthetic Context*. Columbia: University of Missouri Press, 1978.

————, ed. *Critical Essays on Frank Norris*. Boston: G. K. Hall, 1980.

Graves, Jackson A. *California Memories, 1857–1930*. Los Angeles: Times-Mirror Press, 1930.

Grile, Dod [Ambrose Bierce]. *Nuggets and Dust*. London: Chatto and Windus, [1873].

Grodinsky, Julius. *Transcontinental Railway Strategy, 1869–1893: A Study of Businessmen*. Philadelphia: University of Pennsylvania Press, 1962.

Guinn, J. M. *Historical and Biographical Record of Los Angeles*. Chicago: Chapman, 1901.

Gutman, Herbert. *Work, Culture, and Society in Industrializing America*. New York: Knopf, 1976.

Halberstam, David. *The Powers That Be*. New York: Knopf, 1979.

Haney, Lewis Henry. *A Congressional History of Railways in the United States, 1850–1887*. Madison: n.p., 1910.

Harbert, Earl N., and Robert A. Rees, eds. *Fifteen American Authors before 1900*. Madison: University of Wisconsin Press, 1984.

Hays, Samuel P. *The Response to Industrialism, 1885–1914*. Chicago: University of Chicago Press, 1957.

Hichborn, Franklin. *California Politics, 1891–1939*. 5 vols. Los Angeles: Haynes Foundation, n.d.

————. *Story of the California Legislature of 1909*. San Francisco: James H. Barry Co., 1909.

————. *Story of the California Legislature of 1911*. San Francisco: James H. Barry Co., 1911.

————. *"The System" as Uncovered by the San Francisco Graft Prosecution*. San Francisco: James H. Barry Co., 1915.

Hine, Robert V. *California's Utopian Colonies*. San Marino, Calif.: Huntington Library, 1953.

Hittell, John S. *The Commerce and Industries of the Pacific Coast of North America*. 2nd ed. San Francisco: A. L. Bancroft, 1882.

Hofsommer, Don L. *The Southern Pacific, 1901–1985*. College Station: Texas A&M University Press, 1986.

Hofstadter, Richard. *The Age of Reform*. New York: Vintage, 1955.

Hopkins, Caspar T. *Common-Sense Applied to the Immigrant Question*. San Francisco: Turnbull and Smith, 1869.

Hopkins, Mark, et al. *Letters from Mark Hopkins, Leland Stanford, Charles Crocker, Charles F. Crocker, and David D. Colton, to Collis P. Huntington. From August 27th, 1869, to December 30th, 1879*. New York: John C. Rankin, 1891.

Hunt, Rockwell D. *California and Californians*. 5 vols. Chicago: Lewis Publishing Co., 1926.

Huntington, Collis P. *Letters from Collis P. Huntington to Mark Hopkins, Leland*

Stanford, Charles Crocker, E. B. Crocker, Charles F. Crocker, and D. D. Colton. From August 20, 1867, to August 5, 1869. New York: privately printed, 1892.

——. *Letters from Collis P. Huntington to Mark Hopkins, Leland Stanford, Charles Crocker, and E. B. Crocker. From August 5, 1869, to March 26, 1873.* New York: privately printed, 1892.

——. *Letters from Collis Huntington to Mark Hopkins, Leland Stanford, Charles Crocker, and D. D. Colton. From April 2, 1873, to March 31, 1876.* New York: privately printed, 1894.

Hutchinson, W. M. *Oil, Land, and Politics: The California Career of Thomas Robert Bard.* 2 vols. Norman: University of Oklahoma Press, 1965.

Hyde, Anne F. *An American Vision: Far Western Landscape and National Culture, 1820–1920.* New York: New York University Press, 1990.

Information concerning the Terminus of the Railroad System of the Pacific Coast. Oakland, Calif.: Oakland Daily Transcript, 1871.

Issel, William, and Robert Cherny. *San Francisco, 1865–1932.* Berkeley: University of California Press, 1986.

Jackson, Kenneth. *Crabgrass Frontier: The Suburbanization of the United States.* New York: Oxford University Press, 1985.

Jaher, Frederic. *The Urban Establishment.* Urbana: University of Illinois Press, 1982.

Johnson, David. *Founding the Far West: California, Oregon, and Nevada, 1840–1890.* Berkeley: University of California Press, 1992.

Johnson, Kenneth M. *Stephen Mallory White.* Los Angeles: Dawson's Book Shop, 1980.

Kaplan, Justin. *Lincoln Steffens.* New York: Simon and Schuster, 1974.

Kasson, John. *Civilizing the Machine: Technology and Republican Values in America, 1776–1900.* New York: Grossman, 1976.

[Kearney, Denis.] *Speeches of Dennis Kearney, Labor Champion.* New York: Jesse Haney, 1878.

Kellett, John R. *Railways and Victorian Cities.* London: Routledge and Kegan Paul, 1979.

Kern, Stephen. *The Culture of Time and Space.* Cambridge, Mass.: Harvard University Press, 1983.

Kirker, Harold. *California's Architectural Frontier.* San Marino, Calif.: Huntington Library, 1960.

Knoles, George H., ed. *Essays and Assays: California History Reappraised.* San Francisco: California Historical Society, 1973.

Kolko, Gabriel. *Railroads and Regulation, 1877–1916.* Princeton, N.J.: Princeton University Press, 1965.

Lane, Anne W., and Louise H. Wall, eds. *The Letters of Franklin K. Lane.* Boston: Houghton Mifflin, 1922.

Lavender, David. *The Great Persuader.* New York: Doubleday, 1970.

Leonard, Thomas C. *The Power of the Press.* New York: Oxford University Press, 1986.

Lewis, Oscar. *The Big Four.* New York: Knopf, 1938.

Licht, Walter. *Working for the Railroad: The Organization of Work in the Nineteenth Century.* Princeton, N.J.: Princeton University Press, 1983.

Lindsey, Almont. *The Pullman Strike.* Chicago: University of Chicago Press, 1942.

Lloyd, B. E. *Lights and Shades in San Francisco*. San Francisco: A. L. Bancroft, 1876.

Loyal, C. [pseud.]. *The Squatter and the Don; A Novel Descriptive of Contemporary Occurrences in California*. San Francisco: Samuel Carson and Co., 1885.

McAfee, Ward. *California's Railroad Era, 1850–1911*. San Marino, Calif.: Golden West Books, 1973.

McClatchy, Eleanor, and Roy V. Bailey, eds. *Private Thinks by C. K. and Other Writings of Charles K. McClatchy*. New York: Scribner's, 1936.

McGowan, Joseph A. *History of the Sacramento Valley*. 3 vols. New York: Lewis Historical Publishing, 1961.

Majority Report of the Committee on Corporations in Relation to Fares and Freights on Railroads. Sacramento: D. W. Gelwicks, 1868.

Marcosson, Isaac. *Adventures in Interviewing*. New York: John Lane, 1920.

Marx, Leo. *The Machine in the Garden: Technology and the New Pastoral Idea in America*. New York: Oxford University Press, 1964.

Maxwell's Los Angeles City Directory, 1985. Los Angeles: Directory Co., 1895.

Mazlish, Bruce, ed. *The Railroad and the Space Program: An Exploration in Historical Analogy*. Cambridge, Mass.: MIT Press, 1965.

Meyer, Albertus. *Pro Memoria*. [Oakland, Calif.?] n.p., c. 1863. From Central Pacific Railroad Pamphlets, vol. 5, Huntington Library.

The Monarch Philanthropist. San Francisco: Cubery and Co., 1892.

Mooar, George. *God's Highways Exalted: A Discourse on the Completion of the Pacific Railroad*. Oakland, Calif.: [Oakland Daily Transcript,] 1869.

Morris, William Gouverneur, and H. C. Bennett. *An Essay on the Manufacturing Interests of California: The Causes That Impede and Those That Would Aid Their Development*. San Francisco: Cosmopolitan Printing, 1872.

Morrow, William C. *Blood-Money*. San Francisco: F. J. Walker, 1882.

Mowry, George. *The California Progressives*. Berkeley: University of California Press, 1951.

Nash, Gerald. *State Government and Economic Development: A History of Administrative Policies in California, 1849–1933*. Berkeley: University of California Press, 1964.

The New Constitution: Look before You Leap. N.p.: 1878.

Norris, Frank. *The Octopus: A Story of California*. In *Frank Norris: Novels and Essays*, ed. Donald Pizer, pp. 573–1098. New York: Library of America, 1986. (*The Octopus* originally published 1901.)

Older, Cora B. *William Randolph Hearst, American*. New York: D. Appleton–Century, 1936.

Older, Fremont. *Growing Up*. San Francisco: Call-Bulletin, 1931.

———. *My Own Story*. San Francisco: Call Publishing Company, 1919.

Olin, Spencer. *California's Prodigal Sons: Hiram Johnson and the Progressives, 1911–1917*. Berkeley: University of California Press, 1968.

O'Malley, Michael. *Keeping Watch: A History of American Time*. New York: Viking Press, 1990.

The Pacific Railroad: A Defense against Its Enemies . . . and Report of Mr. Montoya, Made to the Supervisors of the City and County of San Francisco. San Francisco: n.p., 1864.

Paine, Albert Bigelow, ed. *Mark Twain's Letters*. Vol. 1. New York: Harper and Brothers, 1917.

Patton, George S. *Address to the Voters of the 6th Congressional District of California*. Los Angeles: Kinsell and Doan, 1896.

Pitt, Leonard. *The Decline of the Californios*. Berkeley: University of California Press, 1966.

Pizer, Donald. *The Novels of Frank Norris*. Bloomington: Indiana University Press, 1966.

Pomeroy, Earl. *In Search of the Golden West: The Tourist in Western America*. New York: Knopf, 1957.

Poor's Manual of Railroads, 1896. New York: American Banknote Company, 1896.

The Proposed Constitution Reviewed in an Address to the Reformers in California. N.p.: [1879].

The Railroad Is an Issue in Politics. San Francisco: Star Press, 1898.

The Railroad System of California: Oakland and Vicinity. San Francisco: J. H. Carmany, 1871.

Report of the Assembly Committee on Railroads upon the Question of a Reduction in Railroad Freight and Fare Rates. Sacramento: D. W. Gelwicks, 1870.

Reports of the Board of Directors and Chief Engineer of the San Francisco and Marysville Railroad Company. Marysville, Calif.: W. F. Hicks, 1860.

Reps, John. *Cities of the American West: A History of Frontier Urban Planning*. Princeton, N.J.: Princeton University Press, 1979.

Rice, Richard B., William A. Bullough, and Richard J. Orsi. *The Elusive Eden: A New History of California*. New York: Knopf, 1988.

Richardson, Robert D., Jr. *Henry Thoreau: A Life of the Mind*. Berkeley: University of California Press, 1986.

Rogin, Michael P., and John L. Shover. *Political Change in California: Critical Elections and Social Movements, 1890–1966*. Westport, Conn.: Greenwood Press, 1970.

Rolle, Andrew. *California: A History*. 2nd ed. New York: Crowell, 1969.

Russell, Charles Edward. *Stories of the Great Railroads*. Chicago: Charles H. Kerr, 1914.

Salvatore, Nick. *Eugene V. Debs: Citizen and Socialist*. Ithaca, N.Y.: Cornell University Press, 1982.

Sarasohn, David. *The Party of Reform: Democrats in the Progressive Era*. Jackson: University Press of Mississippi, 1989.

Saxton, Alexander. *The Indispensable Enemy: Labor and the Anti-Chinese Movement in California*. Berkeley: University of California Press, 1971.

Schivelbusch, Wolfgang. *The Railway Journey: Trains and Travel in the 19th Century*. Trans. Anselm Hollo. New York: Urizen Books, 1979.

Schwantes, Carlos A. *Coxey's Army*. Lincoln: University of Nebraska Press, 1985.

Silbey, Joel H., and Samuel T. McSeveney, eds. *Voters, Parties, and Elections: Quantitative Essays in the History of American Popular Voting Behavior*. Lexington, Mass.: Xerox College Publishing, 1972.

Sinclair, Upton. *Mammonart: An Essay in Economic Interpretation*. Pasadena, Calif.: privately printed, 1925.

Sitton, Thomas J. *John Randolph Haynes, California Progressive*. Stanford, Calif.: Stanford University Press, 1992.

Slotkin, Richard. *The Fatal Environment*. New York: Atheneum, 1985.

Smith, Henry Nash. *Virgin Land: The American West as Symbol and Myth*. Cambridge, Mass.: Harvard University Press, 1950.

Staniford, Edward. *The Pattern of California History*. San Francisco: Canfield Press, 1975.

Starr, Kevin. *Americans and the California Dream*. New York: Oxford University Press, 1973.

———. *Inventing the Dream: California through the Progressive Era*. New York: Oxford University Press, 1985.

Stedman, J. C., and R. A. Leonard. *The Workingman's Party of California: An Epitome of Its Rise and Progress*. San Francisco: Bacon and Co., 1878.

Steffens, Lincoln. *The Autobiography of Lincoln Steffens*. New York: Harcourt, Brace, 1931.

Stewart, George R., Jr. *Bret Harte, Argonaut and Exile*. Boston: Houghton Mifflin, 1931.

Stilgoe, John R. *Metropolitan Corridor: Railroads and the American Scene*. New Haven, Conn.: Yale University Press, 1983.

Stimson, Grace H. *Rise of the Labor Movement in Los Angeles*. Berkeley: University of California Press, 1955.

Stimson, Marshall. *Fun, Fights, and Fiestas in Old Los Angeles*. Los Angeles: privately printed, 1966.

Storke, Thomas M. *California Editor*. Los Angeles: Westernlore Press, 1958.

Stover, John. *The Life and Decline of the American Railroad*. New York: Oxford University Press, 1970.

Stromquist, Shelton. *A Generation of Boomers: The Pattern of Railroad Labor Conflict in Nineteenth-Century America*. Urbana: University of Illinois Press, 1987.

The Struggle of the Mussel Slough Settlers for Their Homes! Visalia, Calif.: Delta Printing Establishment, 1880.

Summers, Mark W. *The Plundering Generation*. New York: Oxford University Press, 1987.

Swisher, Carl Brent. *Motivation and Political Technique in the California Constitutional Convention, 1878–79*. Political Science Monograph Series. Claremont, Calif.: Pomona College, 1930.

Takaki, Ronald. *Strangers from a Different Shore: A History of Asian Americans*. New York: Penguin Books, 1989.

Tenth Annual Report of the Commission of Labor, 1894. Vol. 1. Washington, D.C.: U.S. Government Printing Office, 1896.

Thelen, David P. *The New Citizenship: Origins of Progressivism in Wisconsin, 1885–1900*. Columbia: University of Missouri Press, 1972.

Thirty-second Parallel Pacific Railroad: Remarks of C. P. Huntington . . . before the Committee on the Pacific Railroads . . . January 31, 1878. Washington, D.C.: Judd and Detweiler, 1878.

Thomas, John L. *Alternative America: Henry George, Edward Bellamy, Henry Demarest Lloyd, and the Adversary Tradition*. Cambridge, Mass.: Belknap Press of Harvard University Press, 1983.

Tierney, Kevin. *Darrow: A Biography*. New York: Crowell, 1979.

Trenner, Richard, ed. *E. L. Doctorow: Essays and Conversations.* Princeton, N.J.: Ontario Review Press, 1983.

Wadsworth, Charles. *War, a Discipline: A Sermon Preached in Calvary Church, San Francisco, on Thanksgiving Day, November 24, 1864.* San Francisco: H. H. Bancroft, 1864.

Walker, Franklin. *Frank Norris: A Biography.* New York: Russel and Russel, 1963. (Originally published 1932.)

Ward, James A. *Railroads and the Character of America, 1820–1877.* Knoxville: University of Tennessee Press, 1986.

Warner, Sam Bass. *Streetcar Suburbs: The Process of Growth in Boston, 1870– 1900.* Cambridge, Mass.: Harvard University Press and MIT Press, 1962.

Weinstein, James. *The Corporate Ideal in the Liberal State: 1900–1918.* Boston: Beacon Press, 1968.

White, Richard. *"It's Your Misfortune and None of My Own": A New History of the American West.* Norman: University of Oklahoma Press, 1991.

Wiebe, Robert. *Businessmen and Reform: A Study of the Progressive Movement.* Chicago: Quadrangle, 1968. (Originally published 1962.)

———. *The Search for Order.* New York: Hill and Wang, 1967.

Willard, Charles Dwight. *The Free Harbor Contest at Los Angeles.* Los Angeles: Kingsley-Barnes and Neuner, 1899.

———. *History of the Los Angeles Chamber of Commerce.* Los Angeles: Kingsley-Barnes and Neuner, 1899.

Williams, John Hoyt. *A Great and Shining Road: The Epic Story of the Transcontinental Railroad.* New York: Times Books, 1988.

Williams, R. Hal. *The Democratic Party and California Politics, 1880–1896.* Stanford, Calif.: Stanford University Press, 1973.

Winther, Oscar O. *The Transportation Frontier.* New York: Holt, Rinehart and Winston, 1964.

Workman, Boyle. *The City That Grew.* Los Angeles: Southland Publishing Company, 1936.

Wyatt, David. *The Fall into Eden: Landscape and Imagination in California.* Cambridge: Cambridge University Press, 1986.

ARTICLES

Avery, B. P. "The Building of the Iron Road." *Overland Monthly* 2 (May 1869): 469–78.

Bacon, Thomas R. "The Pullman Strike in California." *Yale Review* 3 (1895): 241– 50.

Bakken, Gordon. "California Constitutionalism: Politics, the Press and the Death of Fundamental Law." *Pacific Historian* 30 (Winter 1986): 5–17.

Barker, Charles A. "Henry George and the California Background of *Progress and Poverty.*" *California Historical Society Quarterly* 24 (June 1945): 97–115.

Barsness, Richard. "Railroads and Los Angeles: The Quest for a Deep-Water Port." *Southern California Quarterly* 47 (December 1965): 379–94.

Bean, Walton. "Ideas of Reform in California." *California Historical Quarterly* 51 (Fall 1972): 213–26.

Blackford, Mansel G. "Businessmen and the Regulation of Railroads and Public Utilities in California during the Progressive Era." *Business History Review* 44 (Autumn 1970): 307–19.

Blanchard, G. R. "Politico-Railway Problems and Theorists." *National Quarterly Review* 80 (April 1880): 35–72.

Brooks, Noah. "Bret Harte in California." *Century Magazine* 58 (July 1899): 447–51.

Cooper, Jerry M. "The Army as Strikebreaker—The Railroad Strikes of 1877 and 1894." *Labor History* 18 (Spring 1977): 179–94.

Culton, Donald R. "Los Angeles' 'Citizen Fixit': Charles Dwight Willard, City Booster and Progressive Reformer." *California History* 57 (Summer 1978): 158–71.

Deverell, William F. "The Los Angeles 'Free Harbor Fight.'" *California History* 70 (Spring 1991): 12–29.

———. "Railroads and Other Metropolitan Nonsense." Unpublished paper, 1988.

"Farming Facts for California Immigrants." *Overland Monthly* 1 (August 1868): 182.

George, Henry. "The Kearney Agitation in California." *Popular Science Monthly* 17 (August 17, 1880): 433–53.

———. "What the Railroad Will Bring Us." *Overland Monthly* 1 (October 1868): 297–306.

Grassman, Curtis. "The Los Angeles Free Harbor Controversy and the Creation of a Progressive Coalition." *Southern California Quarterly* 55 (Winter 1973): 445–68.

———. "Prologue to California Reform: The Democratic Impulse, 1886–1898." *Pacific Historical Review* 42 (November 1973): 518–36.

Griffiths, David B. "Anti-monopoly Movements in California, 1873–1898." *Southern California Quarterly* 52 (June 1970): 93–121.

Gutman, Herbert. "Trouble on the Railroads, 1873–74: Prelude to the 1877 Crisis?" *Labor History* 2 (Spring 1961): 215–35.

———. "Workers Search for Power: Labor in the Gilded Age." In *The Gilded Age: A Reappraisal*, ed. H. Wayne Morgan, pp. 38–68. Syracuse, N.Y.: Syracuse University Press, 1963.

Hoyt, Franklin. "The Los Angeles Terminal Railroad." *Historical Society of Southern California Quarterly* 36 (September 1954): 185–91.

Hutchinson, W. H. "Prologue to Reform: The California Anti-railroad Republicans, 1899–1905." *Southern California Quarterly* 44 (September 1962): 175–218.

———. "Southern Pacific: Myth and Reality." *California Historical Society Quarterly* 48 (December 1969): 325–34.

Irish, John P. "California and the Railroad." *Overland Monthly* 25 (June 1895): 675–81.

Issel, William. "'Citizens outside the Government': Business and Urban Policy in San Francisco and Los Angeles, 1890–1932." *Pacific Historical Review* 57 (May 1988): 117–45.

Kauer, Ralph. "The Workingmen's Party of California." *Pacific Historical Review* 13 (September 1944): 278–91.

Kazin, Michael. "The Great Exception Revisited: Organized Labor and Politics in

San Francisco and Los Angeles, 1870–1940." *Pacific Historical Review* 55 (August 1986): 371–402.

———. "Prelude to Kearneyism: The July Days in San Francisco, 1877." *New Labor Review* 3 (1980): 5–47.

Krenkel, John H. "The Port of Los Angeles as a Municipal Enterprise." *Pacific Historical Review* 16 (August 1947): 285–97.

Lyman, Edward Leo. "From the City of Angels to the City of Saints: The Struggle to Build a Railroad from Los Angeles to Salt Lake City." *California History* 70 (Spring 1991): 76–93.

McAfee, Ward. "Constitutional History of Railroad Rate Regulation in California, 1879–1911." *Pacific Historical Review* 37 (August 1968): 265–79.

———. "Local Interests and Railroad Regulation in California during the Granger Decade." *Pacific Historical Review* 37 (February 1968): 51–66.

McClain, Charles J. "From the Huntington Papers: The Huntington-Conkling Connection." *Pacific Historian* 29 (Winter 1985): 31–46.

McCormick, Richard L. "The Discovery That Business Corrupts Politics: A Reappraisal of the Origins of Progressivism." *American Historical Review* 86 (April 1981): 247–74.

McGreevy, John T. "Origins of California Populism." Seminar paper, Stanford University, 1987.

McKee, Irving. "The Background and Early Career of Hiram Warren Johnson, 1866–1910." *Pacific Historical Review* 19 (February 1950): 17–30.

———. "Notable Memorials to Mussel Slough." *Pacific Historical Review* 17 (February 1948): 19–27.

Martin, Albro. "The Troubled Subject of Railroad Regulation in the Gilded Age—A Reappraisal." *Journal of American History* 61 (September 1974): 339–71.

Montgomery, David. "Strikes in Nineteenth-Century America." *Social Science History* 4 (February 1980): 81–100.

Moorhead, Dudley T. "Sectionalism and the California Constitution of 1879." *Pacific Historical Review* 12 (September 1943): 287–93.

Mowry, George. "The California Progressive and His Rationale: A Study in Middle Class Politics." *Mississippi Valley Historical Review* 36 (September 1949): 239–50.

Nash, Gerald. "The California Railroad Commission, 1876–1911." *Southern California Quarterly* 44 (December 1962): 287–305.

———. "Stages of California's Economic Growth, 1870–1970: An Interpretation." *California Historical Quarterly* 51 (Winter 1972): 315–30.

O'Connell, J. J. "The Great Strike of 1894." *United Service* 15, n.s. (1896): 310–13.

Orsi, Richard. "*The Octopus* Reconsidered: The Southern Pacific and Agricultural Modernization in California, 1865–1915." *California Historical Quarterly* 54 (Fall 1975): 197–220.

———. "Railroads in the History of California and the Far West: An Introduction." *California History* 70 (Spring 1991): 2–11.

———. "'Wilderness Saint' and 'Robber Baron': The Anomalous Partnership of John Muir and the Southern Pacific Company for Preservation of Yosemite National Park." *Pacific Historian* 29 (Summer/Fall 1985): 136–56.

Parker, Edna M. "The Southern Pacific and Settlement in Southern California." *Pacific Historical Review* 6 (June 1937): 103–19.

Paxson, Frederick Logan. "The Pacific Railroads and the Disappearance of the Frontier in America." In *American Historical Association Annual Report, 1907.* 2 vols. Washington, D.C.: U.S. Government Printing Office, 1908. Vol. 1, pp. 107–18.

Posner, Russell M. "The Lord and the Drayman: James Bryce vs. Denis Kearney." *California Historical Quarterly* 50 (September 1971): 277–84.

Prescott, Gerald L. "Farm Gentry vs. the Grangers: Conflict in Rural California." *California Historical Quarterly* 56 (Winter 1977/78): 328–45.

Ray, William W. "Crusade or Civil War? The Pullman Strike in California." *California History* 58 (Spring 1979): 20–37.

Rodgers, Daniel T. "In Search of Progressivism." *Reviews in American History* 10 (December 1982): 113–32.

Saxton, Alexander. "San Francisco Labor and the Populist and Progressive Insurgencies." *Pacific Historical Review* 34 (1965): 421–38.

Schiesl, Martin J. "Progressive Reform in Los Angeles under Mayor Alexander, 1909–1913." *California Historical Quarterly* 54 (Spring 1975): 37–56.

Shaw, John. "Railroads, Irrigation, and Economic Growth in the San Joaquin Valley of California." *Explorations in Economic History* 10 (Winter 1973): 211–27.

Shumsky, Neil Larry. "Dissatisfaction, Mobility, and Expectation: San Francisco Workingmen in the 1870s." *Pacific Historian* 30 (Summer 1986): 21–28.

"The Situation in California." *The Nation*, July 12, 1894, p. 23.

Stillman, J. D. B. "The Last Tie." *Overland Monthly* 3 (July 1869): 77–84.

Taggart, Harold F. "Thomas Vincent Cator, Populist Leader." *California Historical Society Quarterly* 27 (December 1948): 311–18, and 28 (March 1949): 47–55.

Tutorow, Norman E. "Stanford's Responses to Competition: Rhetoric versus Reality." *Southern California Quarterly* 52 (September 1970): 231–47.

Viehe, Fred W. "The First Recall: Los Angeles Urban Reform or Machine Politics." *Southern California Quarterly* 70 (Spring 1988): 1–28.

Walker, Don D. "The Western Naturalism of Frank Norris." *Western American Literature* 2 (Spring 1967): 14–29.

Walker, Philip. "*The Octopus* and Zola: A New Look." *Symposium* 21 (Summer 1967): 155–65.

Wheat, Carl I. "Sketch of the Life of Theodore D. Judah." *California Historical Society Quarterly* 4 (September 1925): 219–71.

"Wheat in California." *Overland Monthly* 1 (November 1868): 452.

White, John H., Jr. "The Railroad Reaches California: Men, Machines, and Cultural Migration." *California Historical Quarterly* 52 (Summer 1973): 131–44.

DISSERTATIONS AND THESES

Beach, Frank. "The Transformation of California, 1900–1920: The Effects of the Westward Movement on California's Growth and Development in the Progressive Period." Ph.D. diss., University of California, Berkeley, 1963.

Clodius, Albert H. "The Quest for Good Government in Los Angeles, 1890–1910." Ph.D. diss., Claremont Graduate School, 1953.

Culton, Donald Ray. "Charles Dwight Willard: Los Angeles City Booster and

Professional Reformer, 1888–1914." Ph.D. diss., University of Southern California, 1971.

Deverell, William. "Building an Octopus: Railroads and Society in the Late Nineteenth-Century Far West." Ph.D. diss., Princeton University, 1989.

Everett, Miles C. "Chester Harvey Rowell, Pragmatic Humanist and California Progressive." Ph.D. diss., University of California, Berkeley, 1966.

Fahey, Frank M. "Denis Kearney: A Study in Demagoguery." Ph.D. diss., Stanford University, 1956.

Grassman, Curtis. "Prologue to Progressivism: Senator Stephen M. White and the California Reform Impulse, 1875–1905." Ph.D. diss., University of California, Los Angeles, 1970.

Gruner, Richard. "The Politics of Individualism: Hiram Johnson and the California Progressives—1910 and 1914." Senior thesis, California Institute of Technology, 1975.

Hyde, Anne F. "An American Vision: Far Western Landscape and the Formation of a National Culture, 1820–1920." Ph.D. diss., University of California, Berkeley, 1988.

Lawrence, John A. "Behind the Palaces: The Working Class and the Labor Movement in San Francisco, 1877–1901." Ph.D. diss., University of California, Berkeley, 1979.

Lower, Richard C. "Hiram Johnson and the Progressive Denouement, 1910–1920." Ph.D. diss., University of California, Berkeley, 1969.

Lundy, Robert Donald. "The Making of *McTeague* and *The Octopus.*" Ph.D. diss., University of California, Berkeley, 1956.

MacRae, Allan A. "The Rise of the Progressive Movement in the State of California." Master's thesis, Occidental College, 1923.

Ray, William W. "The Great Strike of 1894: The Pullman Boycott in California." Master's thesis, California State University, Hayward, 1972.

Rose, Alice. "Rise of California Insurgency: Origins of the League of Lincoln-Roosevelt Republican Clubs, 1900–1907." Ph.D. diss., Stanford University, 1942.

Shapiro, Herbert. "Lincoln Steffens: The Evolution of an American Radical." Ph.D. diss., University of Rochester, 1964.

Sharp, Sarah L. "Social Criticism in California during the Gilded Age." Ph.D. diss., University of California, San Diego, 1979.

Shumsky, Neil Larry. "Tar Flat and Nob Hill: A Social History of Industrial San Francisco during the 1870's." Ph.D. diss., University of California, Berkeley, 1972.

Sitton, Thomas. "Urban Politics and Reform in New Deal Los Angeles: The Recall of Mayor Frank L. Shaw." Ph.D. diss., University of California, Riverside, 1983.

Smith, Richard H. "Towns along the Tracks: Railroad Strategy and Town Promotion in San Joaquin Valley, California." Ph.D. diss., University of California, Los Angeles, 1976.

Smith, Wallace P. V. "The Development of the San Joaquin Valley, 1772–1882." Ph.D. diss., University of California, Berkeley, 1932.

Staniford, Edward. "Governor in the Middle: George Pardee, 1903–1907." Ph.D. diss., University of California, Berkeley, 1953.

Viehe, Frederick William, III. "The Los Angeles Progressives: The Influence of the Southern Pacific Machine on Urban Reform, 1872–1913." Ph.D. diss., University of California, Santa Barbara, 1983.

Walters, Donald E. "Populism in California, 1889–1900." Ph.D. diss., University of California, Berkeley, 1952.

Yen, Tzu-Kuei. "Chinese Workers and the First Transcontinental Railroad of the United States of America." Ph.D. diss., St. John's University, 1976.

NEWSPAPERS AND PERIODICALS

Arthur McEwen's Letter
The Citizen [Oakland]
Commonwealth Club of California, *Transactions* [San Francisco]
The Earth [Chicago]
Fresno *Weekly Expositor*
Los Angeles *Evening Express*
Los Angeles *Times*
Oakland *Daily News*
Oakland *Enquirer*
Oakland *Railroad Men's Advocate*
Oakland *Times*
Oakland *Tribune*
Pacific Outlook [San Francisco]
Sacramento *Record*
Sacramento *Record-Union*
Sacramento *Times*
Sacramento *Union*
San Bernardino *Daily Courier*
San Francisco *Alta California*
San Francisco *Argonaut*
San Francisco *Bulletin*
San Francisco *Call*
San Francisco *Chronicle*
San Francisco *Daily Report*
San Francisco *Evening Bulletin*
San Francisco *Examiner*
San Francisco *Post*
San Francisco *Report*
San Francisco *Weekly Star*
Wasp [San Francisco]

ORAL HISTORY

Bancroft, Philip. "Philip Bancroft: Politics, Farming, and the Progressive Party in California." Interviewed by Willa Klug Baum, University of California, Berkeley, 1962.

Carr, William Jarvis. "The Memoirs of William Jarvis Carr." Oral History Project, University of California, Los Angeles, 1959.

Thelen, Max. "Max Thelen: California Progressive, Railroad Commissioner, and Attorney." Interviewed by Willa K. Baum, University of California, Berkeley, 1962.

Index

Compositor: Terry Robinson & Co.
Printer: Berryville
Binder: Berryville
Text: 10/13 Aldus
Display: Aldus